NEVER A GENTLEMEN'S GAME

NEVER A GENTLEMEN'S GAME

MALCOLM KNOX

hardie grant books
MELBOURNE · LONDON

Published in 2012 by Hardie Grant Books

Hardie Grant Books (Australia)
Ground Floor, Building 1
658 Church Street
Richmond, Victoria 3121
www.hardiegrant.com.au

Hardie Grant Books (UK)
Dudley House, North Suite
34–35 Southampton Street
London WC2E 7HF
www.hardiegrant.co.uk

Cataloguing-in-Publication data is available from the National Library of Australia.

Never a Gentlemen's Game
ISBN: 978 1 7427 0193 6

Cover and text design by Nada Backovic
Typeset in Centaur MT Regular by Kirby Jones
Printed in Australia by Griffin Press

CONTENTS

W.G. 'The Champion' Grace

INTRODUCTION

After the publication in 2010 of *The Captains*, an interviewer asked me to delve 'right back into cricket history' and talk about some of the early characters of the game. With relish, I began to talk about Dave Gregory and Billy Murdoch, Australia's first two Test captains. Quickly I was interrupted: by 'cricket history' my questioner meant the Chappell years, or, if I wanted to go prehistoric, maybe Richie Benaud?

This obscuring largeness of the present is not unusual. Most cricket appetites are fully satisfied by what can be consumed right now. History is one's own memory, whether that reaches back to the time of Steve Waugh, Allan Border, Lillee and Marsh, or perhaps Lawry and Simpson.

Even for the devoted cricket fan, history might reach back to Don Bradman and Bodyline, but not much further. As a cricket-mad child, I had skated over the Jurassic — that is, pre-photographic — age of cricket without curiosity. The nineteenth century featured a handful of eccentrics — W.G. Grace, the 'Demon' Spofforth, the expansive Victor Trumper of George Beldam's 1902 photograph — and there was the punch-up between Clem Hill and one of the selectors. But for the most part, the early days were sepia-tinted times, recorded by sepia-tinted men.

The present day also provided enough controversy, seemingly unprecedented: match-fixing and gambling, throwing, gamesmanship pushed to the brink of cheating, national teams being broken apart by Realpolitik, and, as a steady undertow, the wrenching inequalities of cricket's income and the vicious power of money to bend or break any principle.

When, while writing *The Captains*, I went back to the early days of Test cricket, I expected a tranquil backwater. Those sepia-tinted pioneers were playing for pure competition and camaraderie, lower stakes than now. Even the controversies must have been sporting matters, fought under Queensberry Rules and settled over a glass of port. I thought I was returning to the world described by Lord Harris, the first baron of international cricket: 'It is natural that a people so devoted to sport and pastimes as the British should have brought sporting expressions into their phraseology, but that one pastime should be picked out by common consent as descriptive of all that is straight, fair, and honourable is a very extraordinary, indeed I think I might claim an unrivalled, distinction.'

Of course, Lord Harris and I couldn't have been more mistaken. Cricket between the 1870s and 1914 was riven by match-fixing and gambling, throwing, gamesmanship pushed to the brink of cheating, national teams being broken apart by politics, and, as a steady undertow, the wrenching inequalities of cricket's income and the vicious power of money to bend or break any principle. In fact, today's controversies have been on a repeat-cycle, except perhaps for a moment, half-illusory, nostalgia-fuelled and by no means limited to cricket, where the belle-epoque spirit of Edwardian times really did pervade the game. This idea of cricket was put forward by the most literate of the Edwardians, Charles Burgess Fry:

'Anything that puts many very different kinds of people on a common ground must promote sympathy and kindly feelings ... The

game is full of fresh air and sunshine, internal as well as external ...
One gets from cricket a dim glimpse of the youth of the world.'

That was of course Fry's *idea*, just as the 'straight, fair and honourable'
was for Harris, a glow nursed late at night rather than a reality witnessed
on a cricket pitch. Harris was extolling 'the honour of cricket' from old
age in the 1920s; he must have forgotten his involvement in a serious
cricket riot and his subsequent role in boycotting uncouth Australians
from playing at Lord's. He must have forgotten his campaign to root
out an epidemic of throwing. He must have forgotten his ruling that a
dark-skinned man born in India could not play for England.

The truth is that Anglo-Australian cricket up to 1914 was cricket
in the raw. The disputes that subsequently became swallowed up
in euphemism — first of sportsmanship and social prestige, then of
corporate weasel-speech — were, in those early years, played out directly.
When one cricketer had a problem with another, he did not background
his media mates or manoeuvre with agents and sponsors. He punched
him in the nose. When the Australian captain had a problem with his
counterpart, he did not write a match report or tell a press conference
it was 'disappointing'. He rushed out and confronted the man, in front
of tens of thousands of spectators vociferously taking sides. When
bookmakers wanted to corrupt players, they actually used brown paper
bags. There was a refreshing absence of the codes of obfuscation we are
forced to interpret today. Things were upfront and honest. Violence was
physical, not metaphorical.

The controversies we see today have been played out before. By
examining history, we can see where our current disputes are headed and
how, perhaps, they may be settled. History provides not just data, but
current strategy.

The other prejudice about the sepia days is against the cricketers
themselves: let's face it, they can't have been very good, can they? We've all
seen pictures of a Grace or Murdoch with their quirky stances, Trumper
with his slatted pads (and his Test average of 39), Spofforth and his old-

man action (never mind that the Demon was 50 when photographed, 23 when he first tore England apart). Really, such judgements are instinctive but also plain dumb — cricketers can only be assessed by the standards of their age, otherwise you end up arguing such nonsense as Mitchell Johnson would be harder to face than Charlie Turner and Michael Clarke hits harder than Clem Hill. If we put aside the rank stupidity of infatuation with the present, and look a little more closely at the distant past, taking into account the customs of photography — just as every person frowned in the first photos, cricketers were *told* to take up those stiff postures — there is a glimpse, now and then, of how skilled the early players actually were.

My epiphany came from a photograph of W.G. Grace in the nets, taken by Beldam late in the Champion's career. He is playing a forcing on-drive, which he has hit on the up, and if not for the net the ball would be zinging between mid-wicket and mid-on. It is a fiendishly difficult shot to play well, requiring a high elbow and perfect timing and balance. Grace in that photo is anything but the odd-looking poseur with the upturned toe and idiosyncratic grip in staged portraits. In action, his every moving part is in perfect place. A master stylist of our time, a V.V.S. Laxman or a Ricky Ponting, would have feet, wrists, bat and weight in the same position as Grace's. What tops it off is the ball's location. It is flying downwards into that probable gap. You see that, one, Grace has timed it superbly, and two, for him to play the shot he has played, with his hands and bat and body in the position they are, the bowler must have been a reasonable pace. No dodgy round-arm trundler here: you sense that when veterans of the Golden Age said C.J. Kortright, Arthur Mold and Ernie Jones were as fast as Larwood — who we know, thanks to moving pictures, was as fast as anyone since — they were not exaggerating.

Cricket was never a gentlemen's game. It was a brutally competitive affair played with desperation for the highest stakes. The rudest illusion of the current day is that there is 'more at stake' than there used to be. The following pages should lay that to rest.

When Test cricket began, old-timers were amazed at how far the game had already come. In the early nineteenth century, cricket in England and Australia was mainly a conveyance for gambling. The leading cricket historian of those days, Reverend James Pycroft, talked about 'bought' men influencing results, 'proof positive that cricketers did take money to play badly at the latter end of the eighteenth century. Alfred Mynn was once accused of not doing his best; and I, even at a much later date, have actually heard it discussed whether a player had been got at: his play had been so erratic that suspicions were aroused.'

Matches, Pycroft said, 'were bought, and matches were sold, and gentlemen who meant honestly lost large sums of money, till the rogues beat themselves at last. They overdid it; they spoilt their own trade … Well, surely there was robbery enough; and not a few of the great players earned money to their own disgrace.'

Globalisation was invented by the British empire, and cricket corruption spread to Australia along with the game's supposedly high ethics. In 1873–74, an Australian newspaper commented that 'there is no doubt that the fundamental cause of our defeat was that the fine old manly English game of cricket (what a mockery to be sure) has — for this once, let us hope — transmogrified itself into a gigantic gambling transaction'. A year later, Alfred Park, a prominent New South Wales cricket figure, was revealed to have sent messages to Joseph Coates, the New South Wales captain, asking him to go easy on the Victorians in a match at the Albert Ground. Park had bet heavily against the home side winning by an innings. He did his dough: Victoria, needing 35 to make New South Wales bat again, were dismissed for 34. The New South Wales Cricket Association committee which investigated the incident exonerated Park in what was widely perceived as a whitewash, excusing his malfeasance because of his 'state of great excitement' about the game.

Gambling wasn't the only questionable activity attached to early cricket. In 1775, William Waterfall was charged at Derby Assizes with killing George Twigg during a cricket match on Bakewell Common in the Derbyshire Dales. The Dartford–Surrey match of 1765 had to be postponed after 'several people were dangerously wounded and bruised'. The venue, the Artillery Ground at Finsbury in London, was such a regular trouble spot that the proprietor took to patrolling the perimeter of the playing area with a 'smacking whip'. It wasn't only the spectators who needed physical restraint. Non-strikers were allowed to block bowlers from catching a ball, fielders could baulk batsmen, catches could be made in shirts and hats. 'It is not surprising,' concludes W.G. Grace's biographer Simon Rae, 'that things regularly got completely out of hand.'

By the time Test cricket arrived, the game was passing through what Harris called its 'cleansing fires'. By the First World War, it had 'passed through them and emerged refined, the scum and the dross scraped and cleared away; and as chicanery and fraud have been eliminated, so also I hope that mean tricks have been steadily and effectively discouraged'.

The period of 'cleansing fires' is the subject of this book. By historical coincidence this was also the period when teams representing the yet-unborn 'nation' of Australia started touring England, giving the English game's pillars of amateur control over a professional workforce a shake-up that no Englishman had foreseen or knew how to deal with.

In his book about English captains, the wonderful writer Alan Gibson asks, apropos an anecdote about Sammy Woods, 'I know this is an old story, but what is the purpose of books such as this if we are not allowed to recall old stories?'

Many of the stories in this book have been told before. But then they stopped being told. Talking of 'Fred Tate's Test' in 1902, one of the greatest matches of all time, Gibson remarks, 'Well, as everyone seems to know to this day, Tate was the last man out in the last innings, and dropped a crucial catch.'

He wrote those words not even 30 years ago. Can you still say 'as everyone seems to know to this day'? I would wager that, far from everyone, almost *no one* knows about Fred Tate.

There were games played between Australia and England in the nineteenth century that were so epoch-making that writers commonly reported that they 'will be talked about for as long as cricket is played'. Tom Horan said, as the Australian team were mobbed in the streets after leaving English cricket in ashes at the Oval in September 1882, they would be 'famous for all time'.

Such forecasts have proven sadly over-optimistic. Celebrity has an element of seeing-is-believing. Who now believes in what happened before television, let alone before photography? Those early Australian teams should be famous for all time, but 'all time', in the churn of fame, goes in a blink.

The past needs not just its chroniclers but its champions. I hope, in the hope that the former have done their job but there is always a call for the latter, to be a bit of both. In some cases I have been able to find new material, or material that has been forgotten, which adds a new embroidery to the old stories. But these minor variations are for the scholars who already know the basic themes. I suspect that for the wider cricket community, the story of the international game before 1914 is not only forgotten but was never known. For that reason alone, it is worth telling.

'THERE'D BE PLENTY OF MONEY IN IT'

Julian Thomas, journalist and social identity, was a man with a past and something of a future. In Melbourne in 1877, he was known as a smooth-talker who already had the ear of everyone important in town, even though he had only landed two years earlier. He was assumed, as a well-tailored Englishman, to be a gentleman of rank.

His real pedigree was much more interesting. Born as John Stanley James to a factory-owning family of lawyers in Staffordshire, he had fallen out with his father, worked on the Welsh railways before turning to journalism, been imprisoned as a spy in Paris, changed his name and run away to America, married a Virginia planter's widow for a brief time before emigrating to Australia 'sick in body and mind, and broken in fortune', and finally reinvented himself as a boulevardier of the Yarra.

A typical émigré, in other words.

Thomas had a taste for the double life. By night, as it were, he dwelt among the lowly. A George Orwell of his time, he consorted with beggars, prisoners, prostitutes, penniless immigrants and lunatic asylum inmates, documenting their plight under the pseudonym 'The Vagabond'.

By day – and here Thomas enters the story of cricket – he was enjoying such a sudden rise in society that we can only wonder at the silvery persuasions of his tongue. Nobody yet knew that the well-connected Julian Thomas was The Vagabond, even less the disowned John Stanley James.

In March 1877, Thomas became friendly with James Lillywhite, the professional cricketer-entrepreneur who was leading an 'All-England' team on a tour through Australia and New Zealand. They were not representative of the best English cricketers, but arrogated the right to call themselves 'All-England', a travelling circus in the tradition of William Clark's All-England Elevens, working-class men who plied their trade so attractively they could footle around the countryside for profit. When Thomas got to know Lillywhite, 'All-England' were playing two matches against a combined New South Wales–Victorian Eleven, brazenly called 'United Australia', at the Melbourne Cricket Ground. These would later be designated the first two 'Test matches', but they were really speculative shows put on for profit. The tour was of course expensive for Lillywhite – though less so than if he had brought any so-called 'amateurs', who cost a great deal more. But then, no amateur would have played under a working man like Lillywhite.

Thomas and Lillywhite were talking about the excitement surrounding the matches, thousands having poured into the Melbourne Cricket Ground's reversible grandstand to see the Sydney crack Charles Bannerman score 165 runs before having his finger broken by Yorkshire's George 'Happy Jack' Ulyett. Thomas asked Lillywhite if the same kind of interest could be generated by an Australian team visiting England.

Such a visit had never been contemplated. Nine years earlier, Charles Lawrence had taken an Aboriginal cricket team to England, more as an entertainment package of Aboriginality than a serious cricket tour, though the group did have some serious cricket talents, not least the stylish batsman Johnny Mullagh. But Thomas wasn't talking about an ethnological venture; he meant a true sporting one, taking on the English counties and clubs, the Players, the Gentlemen, possibly even a representative England, on equal terms.

Lillywhite's full response is not known. But one sentence floated across what we can imagine was a smoky, noisy room to catch the ear of the Melbourne all-rounder and cricket impresario John Conway.

'There'd be plenty of money in it,' Conway overheard Lillywhite reply to Thomas.

Conway moved in and probed Lillywhite. Before the Englishman left Melbourne, he had agreed to do some exploratory work at home, to see if the major teams would consider hosting an Australian Eleven – the best cricketers in the colonies, if such an idea could be taken seriously.

Conway and Lillywhite agreed to stay in touch, and soon Lillywhite was reporting interest, and possibly good money, in such a tour. If Conway liked, Lillywhite could organise a fixture list. Conway did indeed like the idea, and contacted David Gregory, the Sydney audit officer whose teammates had voted him captain of 'United Australia' in their Melbourne matches. Conway's proposal, on the Lillywhite model, was that the players would, rather than seeking investors or official sanction from the Victorian or New South Wales cricket associations, contribute £50 each to a joint-stock company. That money – some £600 in total – could float them initially, and they could raise further funds by playing matches in Australia and New Zealand, possibly North America too, on their way to England.

As selector and manager, Conway would take 7.5 per cent of their gross proceeds, plus whatever profits accrued from his shareholding. The players would net whatever surplus, or pay whatever deficit, that came from the venture.

Julian Thomas, by now, had been unmasked as The Vagabond. Like a superhero whose powers depended on his mask, he went into professional and personal decline. By late 1877 he was reporting on thieves in Sydney and Chinese gold diggers before sending shocking reports from colonialism's rough edges in New Caledonia, the New Hebrides and New Guinea. He died as a real vagabond in Fitzroy in 1896. But by starting the conversation that Conway overheard, Thomas had made his small contribution to the greatest mercantile-sporting adventure Australia has known.

THE ELEVEN

The idea of Australians competing with England at cricket was a daring novelty. Lillywhite's tour was the fourth by an English team, and in most games the touring Eleven was confronted by claustrophobic fields and snaking batting orders of fifteen, eighteen or twenty-two colonials. Even with such numbers, these hordes were seldom good enough to beat eleven Englishmen.

Cricket in Australia, though, was on a steep curve of improvement. The sports explosion, which percolated from the upper classes in England in the Victorian age, arrived in Australia ready-democratised. Men of all kinds mixed in the cricket clubs of Sydney and Melbourne. Better-organised club matches, the enclosure of grounds permitting the taking of gate money, the coalescence of accepted rules, and tuition from a professional player-coach, most notably English imports such as Charles Lawrence and the 'Surrey Pet' Billy Caffyn, but also homegrown stars such as Melbourne's Tom Wills, made a more appealing spectacle. Lawrence, Caffyn and Sam Cosstick had stayed on from English tours to coach in Australia while others such as Billy Greaves and George

Marshall were hired direct from England. Public interest and newspaper coverage followed, and by the 1860s the big club and intercolonial matches were feeding a growing appetite for the sporting event.

Australians' attitude to the English teams led by H.H. Stephenson (1861–62), George Parr (1863–64) and W.G. Grace (1873–74) was that of students to masters. The press said the English were touring to demonstrate 'perfection', and exhorted Australians to learn the lessons that came with certain defeat. There were other lessons, too.

Grace taught Australian cricketers not only batsmanship but the sharp practice of gamesmanship and shamateurism. 'Square Leg', a columnist in the *Sydney Mail*, recorded that 'the example of the champion cricketer of the world, in starting disputes in the field, has not been without its ill-effect here'. No sooner had the Champion pulled one of his notorious tricks than it would be copied on the club ovals of Sydney, Adelaide and Melbourne.

It was in turning his talent into money that Grace left his deepest mark. The Champion had demanded £1500 for his tour, enough to virtually sink its hopes of surplus, and used it as a paid honeymoon for himself and his wife Agnes. His worst of many crimes was to extort payment for an 'exclusive' South Australian game from the ambitious folk of the Yorke Peninsula. To the locals' surprise and dismay, nobody from Adelaide came to the match, which decimated their expected gate receipts. Why hadn't the Adelaide folk come to Grace's only appearance in South Australia? Their questions were answered when Grace left, literally half-way through dinner, to play in Adelaide, double-crossing his hosts and scooping the pool. Simon Rae, whose 1998 biography of Grace is sympathetic to the Doctor, said: 'With the exception of Douglas Jardine, he is the most unpopular England captain ever to tour down under. Never was he subject to such close scrutiny, and never – as he questioned umpires' decisions, appealed for catches that he knew were not out, threatened to come to blows with officials, and ran a piratical course through his contractual agreements – was his character shown up in such a bad light.'

Gambling on cricket was another part of the colonies' inheritance.

In the early nineteenth century, as historian David Kynaston puts it, 'the underlying purpose' of cricket was as 'a vehicle for betting'. John Conway had played in Grace's match against Victoria, which many thought was rigged. *Bell's Life* reported that 'the gentlemen of the grandest nation on the earth have sold themselves for lucre, and given away a match they could have won as easily as it has been lost ... Mr Grace and his coadjutors have been wilfully and dishonourably dishonest.' There were rumours that the Englishmen had cautioned friends against backing them; they were known as 'the bookmakers' team'. Playing a Combined Fifteen in Sydney, Grace led a walk-off when Sam Cosstick didn't accept the umpire's decision to give him out hit wicket. England won, but the *Sydney Mail* said: 'those who have strenuously opposed any attempt to introduce the betting element into cricket had a specimen on Saturday of how a game may be marred when the players are pecuniarily interested in the result.' 'Square Leg' wrote that 'the leading bookmaker of Melbourne has an interest in the project' and it was an 'accepted fact that [Grace] had wagers on the result ... The play of Grace and his team is looked upon with the utmost distrust, and even when they score an easy victory the public think they have all the more reason for saying that previous performances, where they were less fortunate, were not fair and above board.'

But suspicions about fixes did not stop colonial cricketers from believing they could compete, on level terms, with the best English players. Off the field, Australian confidence was flowing. Gold, wool and other agricultural exports gave the colonies new economic muscle. English capital flowed to and increasingly depended on Australian business. It wasn't long before this seeped into cricket. At the conclusion of his tour, Grace said, 'If you ever come to England, and your bowlers are as good there as they are here, you will make a name for yourselves.' When Victoria beat Grace's tourists, *Bell's Life* speculated: 'The effect will be to make cricket between England and Australia now and henceforth really interesting ... We may eventually see an Australian eleven ... doing battle at Lord's.'

This was, by 1877, Conway's dream: to take a representative team 'home'. As Conway and Gregory recruited the leading colonial cricketers through the winter of 1877, they agreed that Gregory might be the better figurehead. Conway had some lingering bad blood with Grace from the 1873–74 tour, which might pose a problem in England. Together they charmed the young players with two unheard-of ideas. One was entrepreneurial capitalism. The idea of twelve middle-class Australians investing in their own sporting circus, taking it around the world for profit, surviving on their entertainment value, was intoxicating. The second idea was that such a group could represent a 'nation' which, of course, did not exist. The tension between these two ideas – a nationally representative symbol in private, profit-oriented hands – would, over the next 35 years, be a constant pull at the seams of Australian cricket.

Gregory and Conway convinced their dream team to take the risk. The nucleus of the eleven that had played Lillywhite's professionals signed up: Charlie Bannerman, Melbourne's champion Tommy Horan, the wicketkeeper Jack Blackham, the bowlers Harry Boyle, Tom Garrett and Tom Kendall. Also in was Frank Allan, the 'bowler of the century' who hadn't played in the Melbourne 'Tests' owing to his commitments at the Warrnambool Show. On 19 April 1877 Conway invited John Arthur and George Bailey of Tasmania; the more colonially diverse, the better for 'the economical working of the team', meaning better able to pass themselves off as 'Australia'. Alas, Arthur died two days after receiving his invitation, but Bailey accepted.

Two key signatories were young mates from inner Sydney. Before he had played for Balmain against neighbouring Glebe, Billy Murdoch, a law student whose family had moved from Tasmania, couldn't sleep, as he would be facing the terrifying bank clerk Frederick Robert Spofforth. Murdoch said he had a 'very peculiar action' that made him 'difficult to watch'. Garrett called it 'extravagant'. In England, Home Gordon said Spofforth was 'like a human octopus'; Sammy Woods said he was 'all arms, legs and nose'.

However hard he is to describe, Spofforth soon made his name in club cricket. When he moved to Balmain, he and Murdoch became such friends that Spofforth famously refused to play in the first 'United Australia' team because Murdoch was not picked as wicketkeeper. Gregory, faithful to Blackham's skills and wanting not to be seen as favouring his New South Wales men, stood by the Victorian. Spofforth was dragged into the second match, where Blackham won his approval with a lightning stumping off his bowling, standing fearlessly up to the wickets.

Reporting on that match, the *Argus* depicted Spofforth's action:

'He took a run of 10 or 12 yards, and amidst a somewhat bewildering movement of legs and arms, hurled the ball forwards with the velocity and recklessness as to the consequences enough to make all timid people tremble for the safety of the batsman, the wicketkeeper and even the longstop.'

Beyond his physical gifts, Spofforth was the prototype of the thinking fast bowler who analysed batsmen's weaknesses and intimidated them with his brain power as much as his ability with the ball. Where he trod, Ray Lindwall, Graham McKenzie, Dennis Lillee and Glenn McGrath followed. He lay awake at nights scheming about how to remove specific batsmen. He was the first Australian scientist of bowling, even consulting university professors on the subject of aerodynamics and grip. After studying baseball, he developed four ways to move the ball: to the leg, to the off, upwards (with 'backswing') and downwards (with topspin).

As for his speed, that is something we can't know, but Spofforth's biographer Richard Cashman has correctly written that 'Pace is a relative concept: a bowler who is much faster than the others of his generation will appear fast.' The number of wickets Spofforth took bowled or lbw suggest that whatever his pace was, he was too slick for the batsmen of his day.

His personality got as many wickets as his speed and cut. Fifty-five years later, the Reverend Richard Llewellyn Hodgson, as 'Country Vicar', recalled: '[H]e had rather the type of countenance which one associates with the Spirit of Evil in *Faust*. A long face, somewhat sardonic; piercing eyes; a hooked nose; and his hair, parted in the middle, giving the impression of horns. He was also immensely tall – lean, sinewy and loose-limbed – with long, thin arms; he would have looked the part of the stage-demon.'

A player who had faced Spofforth told Neville Cardus exactly what it was like: 'His look went through me like a red-hot poker. But I walks on past him along t' wicket to t' batting end. And half-way down something made me turn round and look at him over my shoulder. And there he was, still fixin' me with his eye.'

Spofforth would be the central figure of the tour, and the avatar of a singularly Australian idea of cricket: that the big star of the game can as easily be a bowler as a batsman. In England (and later in the subcontinent, when cricket spread there), bowlers were the patsies of the game, whose purpose was to serve the ball up for the batsmen to provide the thrills. Spofforth – and through him, an animating spirit of Australian cricket – would challenge the idea that the stage belonged to batsmen.

His mate Murdoch was still a work in progress as a right-handed opening batsman, but the pair were intelligent, fun-loving goers prepared to take a risk. Upon graduation, Murdoch became a solicitor in partnership with his elder brother Gilbert. Spofforth had to ask for 12 months' leave without pay from the Bank of New South Wales' Balmain branch. His father Edward didn't want him to. His boss, Shepherd Smith, warned him against the risk. But Spofforth went and Edward, 'secretly admiring his independence, gave way'.

Through the winter of 1877, the ranks were winnowed: younger men came in for older. Sydney's Nat Thomson and Ned Gregory (Dave's brother) were replaced. The cricketing adventure to end all adventures was seen off from Sydney by about a hundred well-wishers on 3 November 1877. Gregory was the only man older than 30; their average age was 23. They travelled to Brisbane and beat a local Eighteen, a Toowoomba Twenty-Two, and then a NSW Fifteen before a tiny crowd in Sydney. They took their entertainment to Maitland, Newcastle and Adelaide, tied with a strong NSW-Victoria Fifteen in Melbourne, beat a Bendigo team, then swung for seven matches through New Zealand, losing only to a Canterbury Fifteen.

In New Zealand, Tom Kendall's drinking violated what would become an iron Australian rule of 'drink all you like but turn up fit to play'; he was dropped for Charles Bannerman's younger brother Alick, who came onto the tour as a 'professional cricketer' playing for a set fee, not a share of profits, although he had a job in the Sydney Government Printing Office and was not a professional in the English sense. Already the Australians were blurring the class definitions of cricket.

On their return to Sydney there was great anticipation for a rematch against a Combined Fifteen. But a rift had opened between the touring Eleven — moneymaking celebrities already — and those left behind. Four Combined Fifteen players refused to accept Conway's terms. Others, reported the *Argus*, 'took umbrage and would not play on account of derogatory reflections which some members of the Eleven had injudiciously cast upon them'. The Eleven were even known to be injudicious towards their own; during a storm off the New Zealand coast, Charles Bannerman, a strong swimmer, speculated that he would save fellow Sydneysiders Spofforth, Murdoch and Alick, but none of the Victorians.

Already the stitches binding private enterprise and the responsibilities of representing a 'nation' were splitting. Conway sought the New South Wales Cricket Association's support to 'promote what is in reality a national undertaking' by giving the Australian Eleven's games precedence over the intercolonial match between NSW and Victoria. The NSWCA and the Victorian Cricketers' Association declined, but offered Conway

10 per cent of the gate for the intercolonial match if he released his players to participate. They also offered him fundraising matches after the intercolonial. Conway replied that 'the members of the Australian team are resolved not to disunite and play against each other' — he, and they, feared that the success of the tour could be compromised by reigniting intercolonial rivalries. He also wondered if the intercolonial might threaten the profitability of the Eleven's matches. The associations, he said, 'ought to be proud to lend their assistance' to the Australian Eleven. The associations were having none of it: they saw Conway's team as a private circus, not a 'national undertaking', and the impasse remained: the stars did not take part in the intercolonials.

Public opinion, as expressed in the newspapers, was against the Conway–Gregory team. The senior Victorian player Dan Wilkie, writing as 'A Bohemian' in the *Australasian*, said 'we have had too much said about the self denial and patriotism of these eleven or twelve gentlemen … it cannot be denied that it is nothing more nor less than a speculation which the promoters hope to carry through without a loss and possibly with a fair margin of profit'. Spofforth later said that 'the public generally seemed to regard the scheme with coolness … The sporting papers again ignored our movements almost entirely.'

But wider public opinion was, not for the last time, gravitating towards the superior entertainers. The Eleven's farewell games in Sydney and Melbourne drew crowds of 10,000. Charles Bannerman, Horan, Gregory and Spofforth were spurring hopeful pressmen to write that 'everyone looked forward eagerly to hear with what measure of success they would face the Elevens of Old England'. The tantalising thought that a team of colonials could compete at home was beginning to override antagonism towards the cricketers' profit motive.

The Eleven's departure, on 29 March 1878, was a shambles. Gregory's initial plan was to sail on the *Chimboraso* from Melbourne, but it was wrecked on Point Perpendicular, so the Eleven had to rush to Sydney to board the *City of Sydney* to San Francisco. Garrett wrote: 'This was the only hope we had of getting to England in time to play our first match.' They left Melbourne at 6 am on the Friday, and three train and coach rides later arrived at Circular Quay at 7 am on Saturday, to embark at 3 pm.

Among the 128 passengers on the *City of Sydney* were singing troubadours, businessmen and emigrants. Gregory's men put in two hours of daily deck practice. They reached San Francisco, still rolling with the sea as they slept in the Palace Hotel, took a seven-day train journey to New York, and left on the *City of Berlin*, farewelled by a local cricket team, on the nine-day voyage to Liverpool.

There they were met by Conway, who had preceded them on the Suez mail boat. He escorted them to Nottingham where 'an immense crowd of people had gathered at the railway station, and a splendid band was playing "Auld Lang Syne", but so great and long-continued was the cheering, that the music was completely smothered'.

In Nottingham they met up with their secret weapon, 'The Sandhurst (as Bendigo was then known) Infant' Billy Midwinter, who had bolstered Australia with bat and ball in the Melbourne 'Tests' and had since followed Lillywhite's team back to England, improving his game under W.G. Grace in his United South Elevens. Born in Gloucestershire, Midwinter regarded himself as an Australian – on the cricket field, at least – and was made a shareholder by Conway. Yet the presence of this mercurial character, a wonderful all-round sport as skilled at billiards, shooting and archery as batting and bowling, could not counterbalance a sudden depression in the Eleven's spirits. The journey had given them too much time to ponder the task ahead.

The 1878 spring was proving even wetter than the previous year's record drenching, and colder too. The innocent Australians had packed silk shirts but no sweaters. They shivered from cold and nerves as eight thousand lined the streets of Nottingham to cheer them to the Maypole

Hotel in their omnibus drawn by four grey horses. A surprised old-timer was quoted saying, 'Why, they bean't black at all; they're as white as wuz.' The speaker, apparently, could not square this mob with his memories of the 1868 Aboriginal troupe.

Two hours after a champagne civic reception, the Eleven arrived at Trent Bridge. They remarked on how small the ground seemed, how green was the turf and how the red roofs of the surrounding flats hemmed them in. The wind blew chilly, and their heavy brown brogues slipped on the sloppy turf.

Cricket in England was undergoing rapid transition. William Clark's All-England Elevens, which had dominated cricket as a spectacle, touring the country and taking on all-comers, mostly at odds, for the benefit of bookmakers and punters, had fractured under commercial pressures. Since the 1860s the Marylebone Cricket Club, based at Thomas Lord's ground in St John's Wood, London, began to aggregate control over laws and playing conditions. The professionals lost their grip on the game as the county clubs, run by amateur committees, began to organise a national competition. By 1873, the professionals' freedom to ply their trade was constricted by a rule that they could only play for one county per season.

Beneath these power shifts lay centuries of English tradition. Professionals were working-class or lower-middle-class men who coached, curated grounds, bowled to amateurs in the nets, and, when they got a chance, played for poor wages. The touring English professional cricketer didn't enjoy a high reputation. Lillywhite's wicketkeeper, Ted Pooley, for instance, had missed the famous Melbourne matches because he was in a Christchurch jail, having got into a fight with some punters who thought he had tricked them. (Pooley had cleaned up by 'predicting' the batsmen's scores in the match; he put them all down as zero, and enough Christchurch batsmen made ducks to leave Pooley well ahead. His 'victims' accused him of scamming them, and when he tried to collect his winnings, blows were exchanged.) On tour the professionals were, wrote Alan Gibson, 'too fond of diddling an innocent colonial, and of looking upon the girls when they were bonny, and the wine when it was red – even more when it was sparkling.'

A mid-level professional in 1878 earned no more than an unskilled labourer – around £85 a season – and lived a life that was nasty, brutal and often shortened by a soaking in alcohol and brawling. This did not characterise all professional cricketers, but it encouraged amateurs to wrest away control of the game.

The amateurs were drawn from aristocratic and middle-class ranks. Not necessarily rich, they did not depend on cricket for their living – at least, not in theory. Amateurism was more a distinction of symbol and ethos than of money. As Anthony Trollope wrote, 'To play Billiards is the amusement of a gentleman; to play Billiards pre-eminently well is the life's work of a man who, in learning to do so, can hardly have continued to be a gentleman in the best sense of the word.'

Amateurs supposedly played for the love of the game, and brought it a dash and joy that professionals could not afford. Naturally, they were almost always batsmen, leaving the hack work to the lower orders. Amateurs were received in good society, dressed in better-appointed rooms, went by their full titles on scoresheets (giving rise to an immortal team of the 1880s, 'The Gentlemen of England, and Pougher'), and played only for 'expenses', though the actions of Grace and others boosted expenses far above professional wages.

It was not until they were in England that the Australians could witness Grace's full impact on the game. His average, in many years of the 1870s, was twice that of the next batsman. He was, says Rae, 'the greatest draw ever known; the man whose popularity required the introduction of turnstiles and then set them clicking so merrily that, it was said, he provided half the bricks in the cricket pavilions of England'.

The 'look' of cricket was also being revolutionised. When the 1878 Australians arrived, on-field vestiges of olden days were still common: top hats, striped, checked or spotted shirts, boots that were black or brown, and flannel jackets. The pitches and grounds were, to put it kindly, variable. As Frederick Gale had written about a match at Lord's in the 1860s: 'Had I been a wicket-keeper or batsman at Lord's I should have liked (plus my gloves and pads) to have worn a single-stick mask, a Life Guardsman's cuirass, and a tin stomach-warmer.'

In many grounds boundaries were still yet to be allowed — every hit had to be run out. Among bowlers, the great mid-century dispute between round-arm and under-arm had been resolved in the round-armers' favour, but they were soon to be superseded by over-armers, the most educative of whom would be the Australian Spofforth.

The Australians did not initially want to play Nottinghamshire, the famous nursery and proving ground of professionalism. The local team would feature the father of Notts professionals, Richard Daft, the two best bowlers in England, Alfred Shaw and Fred Morley, and the rising batsman Arthur Shrewsbury. Due to the cold and the danger of being thrashed, Conway asked for a postponement, so that Australia's first match could be against the MCC and Ground, at Lord's on 27 May. Fearing failure, Conway wanted to play the big game at Lord's, the moneymaker, before his men lost their gloss.

Lillywhite told him that Nottinghamshire had advertised the match and a postponement was impossible.

Three days' practice deepened the Australians' trepidation, and on a grey, squally 17 May the Bannerman brothers' blue and white caps and scarfs were the brightest thing about them as they walked onto Trent Bridge.

All England awaited. Seven thousand hardy souls braved the rain; elsewhere, *Wisden* reported, 'the interest of cricketing England centred on Nottingham ... and the enquiries that day on other grounds of "Do you know how the Australians are getting on", were earnest and frequent.'

Australia flopped for 63, routed by Shaw and Morley. Then

they bowled with what Garrett called 'a ball like a lump of mud', and conceded 153.

Among the crowd, there was still confusion about their racial characteristics. What did Australians look like anyway? Spofforth heard a comment: 'They bean't furriners after all.' Garrett explained: 'Evidently the locals expected a team of black men. One of them remarked to his neighbour, "They bean't black, Bill" but as he spoke Dave Gregory, Billy Murdoch and Jack Blackham appeared on the scene, and he exclaimed, "but those three chaps have black blood in them".'

Such comments would follow them throughout the tour; Lord Harris, the president of Kent and Lord's, sniffed that 'the ignorance of Colonial ethnology and geography was in those days lamentable'. His fellow amateur Allan Steel showed similar sentiments, but with a sense of humour, when he introduced Spofforth to friends as 'the demon nigger bowler'.

By the end of day two, Australia, batting a second time, had lost four wickets and were still 46 runs behind. Gregory, who made a pair, said they hoped to make a game of it on the third day. Instead Shaw and Morley humbled them for 76. Enough time remained for a single-wicket, four-a-side match to compensate the crowd.

At a dinner at the George Hotel, the Notts secretary, Captain Jack 'Hellfire' Holden, graciously predicted the Australians would win more than they would lose. Gregory thanked Nottingham for the unexpected turnout. Privately, he was questioning whether the whole venture was worthwhile. Some players were talking about going home, and Spofforth, who had taken one wicket to Shaw's eleven, said, 'our confidence in ourselves [was] rudely shaken'.

They spent a day sightseeing around Nottingham before taking a train to London, where no crowds met them. As they bumped into the Horseshoe on Tottenham Court Road, they wondered if they had bitten off more than they could chew: the fabled MCC awaited. *Wisden* applauded them for their 'pluck' in presuming to take on 'the well seasoned skilled cricketers of old England', but Charles Alcock, the secretary of Surrey, said 'the idea of a visit from an Australian team … was at first treated as something of a joke by our English cricketers'. Grace was 'not very much alarmed about being defeated by them … [We] never for a moment thought of classing them with an English representative team.'

A week into their tour, Gregory's Eleven was in danger of vindicating an Australian newspaper which had called it 'a presumptuous adventure calculated to dampen the ardour of the most enterprising speculator'. But Spofforth, so shaken after Nottingham, would on his deathbed 49 years later say, 'I made my reputation in May.' To be precise, 27 May, the day cricket changed forever.

The Marylebone Cricket Club and Ground Eleven seemed chosen for the purposes of humiliation. Garrett said it 'was almost a representative English team'. Grace, of course, headed the batting, and the bowling featured the Trent Bridge destroyers, Shaw and Morley. Among the rest were the cracks from several counties: Lancashire's 'Monkey' Hornby, Middlesex's 'AJ' Webbe, Notts's Fred Wyld and Wilfred Flowers. George Hearne, the top wicket-taker for Kent, would back up Shaw and Morley. Making up the numbers was George Vernon of Middlesex, a future England captain.

The Australians were driven to St John's Wood at 11.30 am. A storm had lashed Lord's at 10 am, and another blew in soon after their arrival. Fewer than 500 spectators were present, 'failing to recognise the team'. When it became clear that a game would start, more filtered in — eventually 4742, handing £119/7/- into the tourists' kitty.

The rain was interspersed with warm sunshine drying the wicket stickily, so the toss, in modern parlance, was a good one for Gregory to lose. There was no question that the MCC would bat. Even on wet wickets the captaincy adage was, 'Always bat. Sometimes consider bowling; and then bat.'

Grace liked to start with a swing to the leg boundary, setting the tone, and this he did to Allan at 12.03 pm. He often said he didn't like defensive strokes 'because you only get three for them'.

Gregory left square leg open; as Allan ran in again, Dave indicated to Midwinter to shift into the space. Sharp practice by our standards, but not in 1878. Grace duly pulled the ball again and found Midwinter. His shock was profound, but the crowd, hoping the underdogs could put on a show, cheered. 'It seemed the applause would never cease,' reported the *Argus*. The stands rang with cries of 'Bravo Allan!' and 'Well done, Australia!'

Hampshire's Clement Booth fell in Boyle's first over, but Hornby crashed one over square leg, breaking the fanlight of the billiard-room door. The crowd recovered their patriotism and cheered Hornby and Arthur Ridley to 2/27 before Gregory brought on Spofforth for Allan.

The most significant bowling change ever? The Demon proceeded to take the MCC apart. He gave up two runs in his first over, but in his next five, of four balls each, he took six wickets for two runs. He bowled Hornby in his second over and Webbe in his third. In the first three balls of his fifth over, he caught and bowled Flowers, bowled Hearne, and had Shaw stumped. Next over, Murdoch ended the innings by stumping Vernon.

Incredible. MCC, all out 33. 'The rush to the gate to view the wonderful Australians as they reached the pavilion was something to be remembered,' the *Argus* wrote. 'The public were fairly stunned by the performance.'

Wisden was only a little more measured: 'Spofforth and Boyle [were] thoroughly mobbed ... The fielding of the team was smart and effective, all working together admirably, their backing up being the very perfection of our cricket, and quite a pleasure to look at.'

But Australia still had to bat on the gluepot. In Morley's second over Charlie Bannerman was caught by Hearne, a running catch with the sun in his eyes. 'It was a remarkable catch, and the crack Sydneyite was highly chagrined,' said the *Argus*. Garrett and Midwinter survived to lunch, but soon Australia fell to 8/24. Gregory, with another duck, still waited for his first run in England. Allan came in, his style triggering great laughter around Lord's, but he 'clung tenaciously to his bat' and, with Murdoch, eked out a nine-run lead. Alfred Shaw bowled 135 balls in taking 5/10.

It was 3.57 pm when Grace went back out, expecting to set matters aright. The *Argus* reported: 'Every one said that W.G. would make up for it in the next innings.'

Spofforth stood at the top of his short run, his 'beak nose, high cheekbones, heavy eyebrows, piercing eyes and cleft chin', in Ralph Barker's re-creation, seeming 'to exude a pathological hatred of all batsmen'.

The MCC were out by 4.50 pm.

It was, said the *Argus*, 'the most extraordinary bowling triumph ever witnessed in a great match. The first ball from Spofforth completely puzzled the great batsman, and his uncertainty was quite apparent to the spectators. The Sydneyite's second, a beautiful breakback, just lifted the bails, and a perfect storm of applause, lasting till the Leviathan reached the pavilion, greeted the bowler.'

The bail flew 30 yards. In surprise as much as glee, Spofforth cried: 'Bowled!'

He knocked down Webbe's stumps first ball and hit Hornby in the midriff, causing him to retire hurt. Boyle removed Booth, Ridley and Flowers, and the MCC were 7/17 when Hornby returned, with W.G. as his runner, to great cheering. But Boyle bowled Hornby before Grace was needed, and the MCC were all out for 19, Boyle having taken 5/3 and Spofforth 5/16.

Twelve runs later, Horan ended the game by slicing Morley through slips. It was 5.30 pm, five and a half hours after the start.

The thousands burst their banks, rushing the players and applauding them to the pavilion in what *Wisden* called a 'maddened crowd' that included MCC members 'who shouted themselves hoarse before they left to scatter far and wide that evening the news, how in one day the Australians had so easily defeated one of the strongest MCC elevens that had ever played for the famous old club'. Except for 400 Australians, they were Londoners, little understanding the historical magnitude of what they had witnessed but knowing a great spectacle when they saw one.

Spofforth would 'well remember that, when we left Lord's and returned to our hotel, we could scarcely realise our victory, and all the evening callers kept pouring in with congratulations. It is impossible to over-estimate the importance of this victory in its effect on the future matches and the destiny of Australian cricket, for another defeat like that at Nottingham might have made us lose heart, besides giving the English public a far lower idea of our merits than we deserved.'

The telegraph flashed through England and Australia. The *Globe* said the MCC team 'was as good as could be found to represent London and England, and probably nearly as good as the Club has ever turned out'. The *Home News* agreed: 'it was clear that our Antipodean cousins could more than hold their own with the best cricketers in this country.' *Punch*, in a parody of Byron's *The Destruction of Sennacherib*, sang:

> 'The Australians came down like a wolf on a fold;
> The Marylebone Club for a trifle were bowled,
> Our Grace before dinner was very soon done,
> And Grace after dinner did not get a run.'

The win supercharged Australian nationalism. *Punch* praised the victory as proof of 'more than gold, Australian beef and kangaroos'. Reserved at first about Gregory's Eleven, *Wisden* said the victory was applauded 'tumultuously so by the thousands of other Englishmen present, whose bones will have mouldered to dust long, long before the cricketers of the future — Colonial and English — cease to gossip about the marvellous short time match played by the Australians at Lord's on the 27th of May, 1878.'

And the tour's fortune was made. A happy Garrett said, 'The match undoubtedly placed Australian cricket on the map.' A century later, even though the game was never given the status of a Test match, Alan Gibson summarised its significance: 'It had more to do with the development of international cricket than any other that has been played.'

Wherever the Eleven appeared, crowds converged. Of a night train trip from Yorkshire to London, the *Argus* wrote: 'At most of the stations on their way back to London hundreds of people assembled to have a look at them, and the windows of the saloon carriage set apart for their use was darkened by the faces pressed against it. The team had innumerable instances given them of the general ignorance of Australian geography, very few persons appearing to understand that Sydney, Melbourne, Adelaide and Brisbane are hundreds of miles apart. Some one inquired about a Mr Blank, at Ipswich, and a Mr Dash in Western Australia, and one of the cricketers stated that even their fellow-lodgers looked steadfastly at them, surprised to find them fashioned as they were, and their customs and habits the same.'

When they played Surrey at the Oval, 'so great was the pressure of the crowd that the turnstiles could not admit half of them. Small doors were broken open in the fence, and money-takers were placed who received one shilling and half a crown, and neither gave nor were asked for change. It was evident that the crowd would give anything so long as they could get in and get a sight of the play.' The playing surface was shrunk by the numbers pressing over the boundaries. *Wisden* said 'the throng was simply marvellous in its numbers, the pavilion seats and steps were chock full; the spacious rows of seats, dignified by the title of "Grand Stand", were literally packed with people, who willingly parted with extra coin to obtain the "coign of vantage" that those seats certainly gave; the little terraced embankment, that so happily hides the hideously ugly "Skating Rink", was crowded to inconvenience.' *Bell's Life* estimated the first-day crowd at 20,000.

At Leicester – the only county to guarantee the Australians a lump sum upfront – the *Argus* said: 'The spectators crowded around the tent and called lustily for them. They were hand-shaken and questioned in the most confidential manner. It was evident that they had also made an impression on the ladies, for one fair one was heard to remark that they were really as nice-looking as the English people.'

After worrying about insufficient fixtures, Conway tried to cancel some to give his players a rest, 'but the fame of the Eleven had become so great that every town had made its arrangements, and did not want to be disappointed'.

Though they played in East Melbourne colours, they were the 'Australian Eleven', the words painted on their huge canvas carry-all known as the 'caravan'. They lugged it democratically, drawing lots. In New Zealand, Spofforth and Murdoch had hauled it 'a mile and a half ... to climb fences and scramble over gates with the huge thing in tow'. The 'caravan' went through Australia to New Zealand and back, by steamer to San Francisco then rail to New York, over the Atlantic to Liverpool, to Nottingham and finally London, where, Spofforth recorded, 'it was lost, and no man knows its burying-place'.

The men lasted longer than the 'caravan': only thrice did they need a replacement. They were acknowledged as England's superior in fielding: sharp movers, aggressive throwers, inventors of new attacking positions. *Wisden* admired them for 'demonstrating, as they frequently did, how a well placed thoroughly disciplined Eleven, working with a will all round, could at times win matches by their splendid abilities in saving runs – the most beautiful and enjoyable portion of our good old game.' Their bowling revived the over-arm style, which before 1878 had suffered under the batting punishments of Grace and others. They introduced England to the fast off-break, which would dominate cricket for decades, spitting off uncovered wickets and flying off gloves or bat-shoulders to specially-set catchers on the leg-side.

Though Charlie Bannerman justified his reputation as the crack batsman, making centuries in four countries (Australia, New Zealand, Canada and England), the bowlers were the celebrities. Boyle invented 'Boyle's mid-on', which we call silly mid-on. Against an Eighteen of Elland, in west Yorkshire, when Boyle took seven wickets in eight balls, one spectator called out: 'Send a man in!' Another replied: 'Send in three or four at once: one's no use!'

Allan, whose strange batting style caused great mirth and earned him the nickname 'Crouching Panther', played some useful innings and had great days with the ball, delivering it from 23 yards to allow more time for swing. He offered entertainment to the English crowds, though Lord Harris observed 'an unhappy, ungainly cricketer, and I shall never forget the contemptuous "You crab!" hurled at him by one of his indignant comrades for some bungle in the field'.

The 1878 tour had one genuine superstar, one true colonial hero at the dawn of the age of celebrity. The late Victorian age was a time of heroes: General Gordon, David Livingstone, Florence Nightingale, the two Charleses – Darwin and Dickens – and, of course, the Queen herself. Australia's heroes were Ned Trickett – cheered home by 20,000 after winning the world sculling championship on the Thames – and Spofforth, who advertised Australia's health and vitality to British eyes.

Whenever the train pulled into a new town, crowds pressed against the windows crying, 'Which be Spoffen?' When the masses packed the county grounds, there was one Australian they wanted to see, the bowler whom Altham would rate after a half-century of peerless Test bowlers – Barnes, Lohmann, Richardson, Turner, Bosanquet, Trumble, Noble, Jones, Gregory and McDonald – as the greatest of all.

He earnt his garland of nicknames on that tour. 'The Windjammer', for his yorkers. 'Loup', for his wolfish mien. 'The Express', 'The Electric Spark', and, most lastingly, 'The Demon'. Under this name he was caricatured in the *Vanity Fair* 'Spy' series, the 1878 version of the cover of *Time*. Among cricketers, only Grace had been similarly honoured.

Though he 'frightened batsmen out', Spofforth encountered little hostility from the English crowds, who were fascinated by this long, lean, theatrical devil. Only at Keighley, in Yorkshire, did he hear disparagement, and as a form of grudging respect: 'I'm afraid I was bowling very fast indeed, and was knocking men about a little – a fast bowler has to frighten a batsman sometimes. Suddenly an old Yorkshireman rose up among the crowd, and, amid a dead silence, called out in his loudest tones, "Chain t'long beggar up; he's trying to kill 'em.'''

Yorkshire also produced an unfriendly atmosphere in another encounter, at Bramall Lane in Sheffield, the *Argus* commenting:

'The spectators had ringed in until the slightest tap gave the Yorkshire batsmen 4 runs; the Australian Team were thus heavily handicapped, and its members had the satisfaction of hearing many remarks about themselves as they ran through the crowd after the ball; many were heard to remark in astonishment that they were so white; for the smoke of Sheffield certainly gives the skin a dull leaden colour which is foreign to all Australian natives. A rougher assemblage could scarcely be imagined, their applause was very one-sided and very rough language was used when the Australians met with any success. Every member of the Eleven had been very disagreeably nick-named long before the day was over. The smoke from the factories of Sheffield completely smothered the ground, the smut rested upon their clothing and the cricketers were right heartily glad when they got back to their hotel at Wharncliffe and could indulge in a bath.'

Success had its price, and as the tour went on the stresses built up. Garrett complained in a letter to a friend: 'Everywhere we go it is the same style of thing. They do all they can to beat us.' After Trent Bridge, Gregory's Eleven were considered easybeats. After Lord's, the top English players stalked them from fixture to fixture, guesting for whatever club or county was opposing them. Between games, Garrett said, conditions were trying. 'The travelling in those days was most difficult. Matches had been arranged without regard to distances. One day we would be playing in the North of England, knowing that on the morrow we would have to start another match somewhere in the south. There was no comfort in travel, either – no sleeping berths – and we generally arrived at our destination in the early hours of the morning, and started to play the same day.' Even more challenging for Garrett, his father, the colourful Sydney parliamentarian Thomas Garrett Senior, joined the tour, and his high-living habits meant that while the Australians earned a lucrative pay-out for their £50 investment, young Tom would later confide in his friend Banjo Paterson that his debts from the 1878 trip took him years to pay off.

Besides being the most significant sporting venture in our history, the 1878 Australians were involved in controversies that set the tone for what would follow.

On 20 June, Midwinter was padding up at Lord's for the match against Middlesex. Horan, whose eyewitness account has been taken as the most reliable, detailed the 'very unpleasant affair' that followed.

W.G. Grace, regarding Midwinter as a Gloucestershire teammate, 'was very vexed to hear there was a chance of losing so good a man' and 'resolved to try his best to get him to remain' with his county, who were playing Surrey at the Oval. Conway went to the Oval to tell Grace about Midwinter's decision to continue playing for Australia all summer. 'This seems to have mightily riled Grace, and he openly told Conway that the Australians were a lot of sneaks to try and entice Midwinter away. High words, of course, followed on both sides.' Conway drove back to Lord's 'where Midwinter was dressing to go in with the Australian eleven. Shortly, however, arrived on the scene [James] Bush [Gloucestershire's keeper and Grace's best man] and W.G., and after about a quarter of an hour's pressing from the two of them, away walked Midwinter with his bag.'

The 'kidnapping' of Midwinter, then, seems only to have been a mild matter of 'a quarter of an hour's pressing' from Grace and his teammate Bush. But in a second report, Horan expanded: 'That Grace lost his temper and sadly forgot himself there can be no doubt, while the indecision of Midwinter, who did not seem to know his own mind for two minutes together, cannot be too strongly deprecated ... Nothing can justify Grace's passion and language, nor his conduct in coming to Lord's and almost forcibly leading away the captive Middy, when the latter was ready to go in with Bannerman to commence batting for the Australians.'

Conway, with Boyle as wingman, gave chase and confronted Grace at the Oval. They accused Grace of bribing Midwinter with an offer of eight pounds a game. Grace, says Simon Rae, 'may have bullied' Midwinter into returning, 'but he was in no position to bribe him'. Indeed, Grace's claim was that the Australians had offered the bribe, a share in the joint-stock company and a benefit match back in Australia, 'a much larger sum than we could afford to pay him', according to Grace's elder brother E.M.

Unable to persuade Midwinter to come back or Grace to let him go, Conway and Boyle returned to Lord's.

'A great deal of unpleasantness arose from this untimely interference,' reported the *Argus*, 'and as if bent on creating mischief, Grace said on leaving [Lord's], 'You haven't the ghost of a show with Middlesex.' Perhaps the result of the match surprised him somewhat; and then to complete the halo of success which surrounded the team, Surrey, whom the Australians beat by 5 wickets, defeated the Great Western County with all the cracks, including Midwinter, by 16 runs.'

Gregory, fired up by the incident, produced his best innings of the tour. The *Argus* summarised: 'His 11 previous innings had only secured a total of 23, and most persons had come to the conclusion that he could not bat even a little bit. This coming out of his shell created intense astonishment; his form was magnificent, and from first to last he did not give the slightest shadow of a chance. The way in which the crowd cheered him as he returned to the pavilion, was something to be remembered ... The enthusiasm of the spectators, and especially the ladies, must have been very gratifying to the captain.'

Conway wrote a letter of complaint to Gloucestershire, threatening to cancel Australia's game at Clifton. To save the match, which would bring hundreds of pounds to Gloucestershire, W.G. Grace wrote to Gregory (not Conway, whom he detested): 'I apologise that in the excitement of the moment I should have made use of unparliamentary language to Mr Conway.'

Grace is a dominant figure in this book, and Rae captures the essence of his relations with Australia: 'If sport is war without the shooting, Grace was cricket's natural warlord, and though his antics sometimes appalled them, the Australians kept coming back with wave after wave of superlative bowlers to try their skills against him ... For all his faults, Grace was a difficult man to dislike for long, and for the vast majority of his contemporaries, playing with him was a privilege.'

Neville Cardus once asked a Gloucestershire veteran, 'Did the old man ever cheat?' The reply was: 'No, sir, don't you ever believe it – he were too clever for that.'

But there was no ruse he was not above. In 1878, for instance, in the Gloucestershire–Surrey match, while he was taking a run, the return throw lodged in his pocket. He kept running until the fieldsmen could stop him. Even then, he refused to hand it back, fearing an appeal for handled ball.

The Grace stories are often like this: outrages that went beyond seriousness. The Australians did go to Clifton to play Gloucestershire (Midwinter had an injured thumb), and inflicted the county's first-ever home defeat.

Ultimately, Grace would be the early Australian teams' most influential friend in England. Born into a doctor's family in the backblocks, never able to earn a large living from his medical practice, Grace was not part of the amateur establishment, much less an aristocrat. For forty years, although he was the pillar of the Gentlemen of England, he was a Player by temperament, one who played for keeps and was prepared to push his market value to the limit and beyond. He was not the only shamateur in English cricket, but nobody's income approached his, which Kynaston estimates at £120,000, or many millions in today's money.

If the Australians learnt the game from anyone, it was from Grace, and not just in his perfection of the dual front-foot and back-foot technique of batting. Gregory and Conway took 80 to 90 per cent of the gate from their 40 matches in 1878, to which their opponents agreed because the residual 10 to 20 per cent was ample.

Following Grace's example, the 1878 Australians were neither amateurs nor professionals, strictly speaking. They mixed in gentlemanly company and were allowed the run of the best facilities. They did not live solely from cricket. In Australia there was no traditional professional class of cricketer. As Pycroft had wryly reported, 'Australians did not readily develop a race of professionals to do the hard work for them.'

On the other hand, they received gate money in such quantities as to make paupers of every English cricketer except the Champion.

Historian David Montefiore says Gregory's team 'occupied a status on tour that was entirely on their own construction' – a new, distinctly Australian hybrid of entrepreneur-amateur. They were not shamateurs, who played for inflated 'expenses'; they were capitalists, speculators in their own success.

On 23 July, the banqueting highpoint of the tour, the Duke of Manchester hosted them at Willis's Rooms in London. Toasting the guests, the Duke said: 'I am ashamed to say that I am ignorant, disgracefully ignorant, of the game of cricket, and as the eyes of so many experts are on me, I will not venture to say much on that subject; but there is one point to which I can most sincerely advert, and most cordially remark upon, and that is the plug and spirit which have induced the Australian cricketers to come half-way around the world to play an old English game on the soil of Old England (cheers). I am happy to know that they have not been altogether unrewarded (hear,

hear). They, of course, did not expect to come all this way, encountering all the risk of times and seasons, and win every match they played in; but I am happy to hear that they have won ten matches against five lost, whilst three have been drawn (cheers). I think that is an ample success and reward for the enterprise, and I will add also, the patriotism they have shown in coming to England. (Hear, hear). I take it as a proof that our colonists are ready to share with us in any enterprise which England, or any portion of the Empire, may be called upon to undertake in more serious rivalry, if unhappily we should have to enter the lists against a foreign enemy (cheers). That is a spirit which we all admire in them, and that is the spirit in which we all welcome them to "Home, sweet home."'

Gregory replied: 'We shall carry back nothing but agreeable recollections of our trip across the ocean to visit the dear old country from which we all sprung ... I am sure in one thing we are quite as English as you, and that is, in our love of cricket; and on that point I may say that we did not come here with any idea of defeating your best men ... Our idea was to measure our strength against your county elevens, and against such antagonists we have more than held our own.'

The banquet, said the *Argus*, 'was the most largely-attended affair that has ever met before in London, where Australia was concerned. The company numbered about two hundred, and would have been very much larger but the capabilities of the room prevented, and many coming up to the last moment for tickets had to go without them. The charge for admission was two guineas, and the banquet will be a red-letter day in Australian annals.'

By September, when the Australians were due to meet the Players of England at the Oval, the local professionals had had enough. As Rae says, they 'would have been prepared to go along with the fiction that they were playing their social superiors had the tourists been willing to share the proceeds of the proposed match a little more generously', but the Australians were not.

Surrey had given the Australians free use of the Oval, guaranteeing their profits. So the Players demanded £20 a man – double the going rate for a representative match (for ordinary matches the rate was £5 to £6), approximately what each Australian would earn. The Players drew on a precedent. In the 'Tests' in Melbourne in 1877, the Victorian Cricketers' Association had charged Lillywhite £20 for each Australian player's 'expenses'. The Players of England were now asking no more than that. But Conway refused, and many of the Players boycotted the game.

The Australians played so poorly that a virtual Third Eleven of Players needed only 18 runs to win with five wickets in hand. Gregory gave the ball to Spofforth and said, 'Loup, we are going to be beaten by a lot of second-raters.' Spofforth took three wickets in the next over and Australia won. Afterwards, to make a point to the boycotters, Conway paid the Players £20 each, the umpires £10 pounds each instead of the standard three, and doubled the wages for the ground staff.

That might have settled matters for a day, but the boycott was the beginning of a 35-year argument. As Montefiore puts it, the cultural clash was between 'two dominant factions' – 'one which subscribed to the largely pre-modern value system and economic priorities of the English game' and 'one which was spectator oriented, economically pragmatic and which recognised the potential to unite colonial cricket's fragmented popularity successfully in the international arena ... In adopting cricket, the Australian colonies also adopted its contradictions and perhaps its most glaring yet enduring contradiction was the "gentleman-professional".'

The 1878 Australian tour was not just the birth of international cricket in England but the beginning of a challenge to the amateur-professional system. On 2 November, after the Australians had left, the MCC stated: 'That no gentleman ought to make a profit by his services in the cricket field, and that for the future no cricketer who takes more than his expenses in any match shall be qualified to play for the Gentlemen against the Players at Lord's.'

Furthermore, it stated, this had always been the case. A sceptical Lillywhite wrote: 'Cricketers … know, as well as we do, this statement is, to use a mild term, hardly consistent with the facts.' He accused Grace in all but name: 'Ninety-nine out of every hundred cricketers know as well as we do that … one well-known cricketer in particular has not been an absentee from the Gentlemen's eleven at Lord's for many years past, and that he has made larger profits by playing cricket than any Professional ever made.'

The MCC could not legislate shamateurism out of existence, but the Australians' tour, having shone a light on the contradictions and hypocrisy within the status quo, was the first crack in the paternalistic edifice.

When the Eleven farewelled England from the *City of Richmond* on 17 September, they had won 18 of 40 games, losing only seven. Their rate of completing matches was high, considering a summer in which Harris was 'sure my boots were never dry from early in May to late in August'.

Improved pitches, technique and equipment would be legacies of the 1878 Originals. Acknowledging their responsibilities as colonial ambassadors, the Australians donated £100 to the Thames Calamity Fund after two steamers collided on the river on 3 September – more than 600 people died – though they turned down an invitation to play a charity match. H.S. Altham and E.W. Swanton, in their history of cricket, comment that 'a decided tribute [was] paid to the resolution, discipline, and training of the eleven; their punctuality and smart appearance, and the automatic way in which they fell into their places, whatever change of bowling was made'; although, they added, 'the whole-hearted enthusiasm of our visitors sometimes involved impatience and resentment at the umpires' decisions when unfavourable to themselves.'

Most importantly, the traditional appeal of domestic English contests now had to take a back seat: *international* cricket had arrived.

The chip on the colonial shoulder began to ease. Press coverage reflected complex emotions. London's *Town and Country Journal* was earnest in its botanical reference: 'The manly qualities of the parent stock flourish as vigorously in these distant colonies as in the mother country.' But the *Illustrated Sydney News* declined to gloat. 'We must, though, all remember that we are from the old stock, perhaps improved by grafting on Australian soil.'

On 5 October when the team left England, the *Illustrated Sydney News* concluded: 'If it had done nothing more than to prove to the millions of our friends at home that the climate of Australia had no enervating influence on the Anglo-Saxon race that would have been a great deal.'

By the time they returned to Sydney, via USA and Canada, in November, Gregory's Eleven knew they were something more than mere cricketers. In their game at Montreal, Gregory and Garrett were taking a walk round the ground when they met a 'middle aged gentleman' who said 'the Australian cricketers had set an excellent example to Australian statesmen by federating'. He introduced himself as Lord Dufferin, the Governor-General of Canada. The Australians saw themselves as personages of national significance. It was a big step up for cricketers since 1862, when one of H.H. Stephenson's professionals, Roger Iddison, said of Australians that he 'didn't think much of their play, but they are a wonderful lot of drinking men.'

When they returned to Sydney, Gregory's Eleven were asked to stay aboard until a fitting reception could be organised. By the time a launch took them to Circular Quay, one-tenth of Sydney's population, or 20,000 people, had turned out. Flags and banners decorated buildings in George and Pitt streets as the team was driven from Circular Quay to the Town Hall for an official function. Garrett said: 'A half-holiday had been proclaimed, and amid great cheering we were driven to the Town Hall, where the Premier, Sir John Robertson, made most eulogistic speeches ... Altogether we had a royal welcome that day in Sydney!'

Spofforth remembered: 'All the crowded steamers met us outside the Sydney Heads to welcome us back.' They proceeded into town to have 'one of the greatest nights I have ever seen ... I shall never forget the reception – an immense contrast to our cool "send off" ... The old motto "Advance Australia!" seemed to span every corner.'

Conway wrote that 'the reception exceeded anything they could have anticipated, all classes doing their utmost to show how genuine was the appreciation of the fellow-colonists ... On no previous occasion had Sydney been so moved.'

While the prestige of being heroes could not be measured, the financial rewards could. When Conway did the final accounts, he netted £1200 for himself – 7.5 per cent of the gross plus his share. The players received approximately £750 each. To put that into perspective, it was five times Garrett's annual salary as a clerk of the Supreme Court, and two and a half times Gregory's salary as a senior accountant in the audit office. It was more than ten times Alick Bannerman's salary in the Government Printing Office, though his agreed set fee of £200 was three times his salary.

Firmly on the front foot, Gregory asked the NSW government for the payment of his salary for the time he had been away – and likewise for Garrett, Bannerman and Henry Gibbes, Conway's assistant. Richard Driver, president of the NSWCA and a member of parliament, petitioned the premier, Henry Parkes, on Gregory's behalf. Parkes refused, but, on further pressing, agreed to make good Gregory's £160 of unpaid salary. In future years, 'Handsome Dave' would head the NSW Treasury and refuse an invitation to become the Commonwealth's inaugural Treasury secretary. With his efforts in 1878, he had shown himself eminently qualified to handle high finance. But he had left behind a legacy of commercial-mindedness that would cause untold problems between Australia and England.

'GO BACK, YOU WERE NOT OUT'

The 'Australian Eleven' was a club within a club, a travelling enterprise loyal to itself rather than any higher authority. When Gregory's Eleven returned from their world tour, they did not disband, go back to their separate colonial teams, and vie for selection on the next tour. As they continued to play against the colonies for gate money, celebration quickly gave way to resentment.

During 1878 the Melbourne Cricket Club had issued an invitation to a prominent England amateur, Isaac Walker, to bring a team of gentlemen to Australia. The amateurs (Grace aside) were falling behind the professionals as a representation of cricketing strength, but the Melbourne club was keen to elevate the tone of Anglo-Australian cricket. Word having filtered back about the 'mercenary spirit' of Gregory's team, the *Australasian* of 26 October 1878 editorialised: 'Cricket, unfortunately, is becoming now-a-days too profitable an investment of skill and muscle to be carried out in the same friendly spirit that characterised it fifteen or twenty years ago. Then the play was the thing, now it is £.s.d. also; and when the two come into collision the £.s.d. spirit is bound to carry the day.'

But Grace, no stranger to the £.s.d. spirit, was in the thick of his medical studies, and Walker had trouble rounding up enough interested amateurs. 'Several other gentlemen who had undertaken to go,' Altham wrote, 'were later obliged to cry off.' No gentleman was keen to spend an antipodean summer bowling on parched wickets, so the two Yorkshire professionals, George Ulyett and Tom Emmett, were invited to carry the bowling. No first-class wicketkeeper could be found. Then one of Walker's brothers died, and he pulled out of the tour. Lord Harris stepped in.

George Robert Canning, the fourth Lord Harris, descendant of Britain's Prime Minister in Napoleon's time, would serve English cricket until 1930, though he appears to have had as great a gift for *being* served. No one ever accused him of suffering fools or colonials, but he would perform impressive deeds as a legislator of the game and as its missionary into India, where he governed Bombay. Perhaps the best inference about his character is contained in his *Wisden* obituary: 'Unbeknown to some, he was the kindest and most affectionate of men.' As Alan Gibson comments, that 'sounds rather too much like the character in *Oklahoma* who loved everybody and everything — "only he never let on, so nobody ever knowed it".'

Harris's arrival in Adelaide in December 1878 put local society into such a tizz that the grand welcome dinner had to be cancelled because no caterer could be found quite grand enough. The local gentry turned out in great and well-dressed number to watch Harris's team play an Eighteen of South Australia. As many as 750 ladies attended, hundreds of carriages were arrayed around the Oval, and an enormous unpaid lunch account was fobbed off to the South Australian Cricket Association. The South Australian cricketers did the right thing and lost, but their improvement since 1876–77 was noted and attributed to Jesse Hide, a 21-year-old protégé of Lillywhite who had come from England to coach the locals for £200 a year.

When Harris's team travelled east, their place in Adelaide was taken by Gregory's Eleven, now into the twelfth month of their tour. They saw the Englishmen not as guests but as commercial competitors. Who could blame them for wanting to cash in? There were enough cautionary tales to remind them of the folly of playing cricket on the cheap. Tom Wills was in an asylum, Charles Lawrence was working on the railways in Newcastle, and Sam Cosstick, curating a ground in Maitland, needed handouts to afford train trips to Sydney. Pioneering the game was not its own reward.

Gloom and staleness had set in among Gregory's men, however, and they lost to South Australia. They should have been in good odour with the locals, as Conway was only asking for 12.5 per cent of gross receipts, allowing the SACA to make a good profit. But they were in a surly temper and complained about the local umpire, without, the South Australian *Register* said, any reason. 'Mr Kennedy, the Australians' umpire, made three bad mistakes in one day – all in favour of his own side – and two of them so palpable as to be condemned by nine-tenths of the spectators.'

After the grandeur of Lord Harris's amateurs, no Australian team could have created a worse impression.

Two big matches were arranged between England and Gregory's Eleven. The first, at Melbourne, started with a downpour and a fight between Conway and an MCG gatekeeper who wouldn't let him in to the Members' Stand. Harris would blame the weather and light for England's performance. Something was certainly wrong, as they were 7/26 by lunch. Spofforth completed a hat-trick, the Reverend Vernon Royle and Emmett sandwiching the wicket of Francis Mackinnon, the Mackinnon of Mackinnon, 35th chief of the clan of Mackinnon.

The weakest of all 'official' England teams was out for 113 and 160, no match for Australia's 256 and 0/19. 'Not for the last time,' said Altham, 'were Englishmen to find that the best of fieldsmen at home were only too liable to drop catches in the strange atmosphere of the Antipodes.'

While the Englishmen went off to Tasmania, Gregory's Eleven played a game at Inglewood, in rural Victoria, before disbanding at a triumphant dinner at Trumps Hotel in Melbourne on 13 January. Alick Bannerman, the only non-shareholding member of the party, received a £90 bonus for good behaviour.

The storm was, however, gathering. In the third week of January, a NSW team was preparing to play the English at the Association Ground, soon to be renamed the Sydney Cricket Ground. Gregory, no doubt mentally spent after running a tour in four countries over fifteen months, did not show up for practice. As he did not provide an explanation, he was dropped for the match, which NSW won by five wickets.

Harris was bemused by the playing conditions. 'The turf at Sydney was so rotten that special arrangements were made to avoid playing on the same wicket all through a match. A parallelogram was marked out, and within that each Captain would choose a new wicket.'

Recalled for the return fixture, Gregory was exhausted and distracted. After friction with umpires on four continents, he now had to stomach George Coulthard, a ground bowler from the MCG travelling as England's umpire, giving Harris not out to a caught-behind appeal. The decision, said the *Sydney Morning Herald*, was 'admittedly a mistake'. When he was finally out, Harris was seen throwing his bat across the width of the pavilion.

England made a good 267. Billy Murdoch, who had scored 70 and 49 in the first match, was the home side's pillar again, making 82 not out, but their 177 disappointed the thousands of spectators, many of whom were betting on the game. The *Herald* decried the 'impunity with which open betting was carried out in the pavilion' in defiance of signs prohibiting it.

For NSW, the follow-on was compulsory, as their deficit was more than 80 runs. They collapsed again, and, late on the Saturday, Murdoch, battling to survive, was given run out by Coulthard.

Murdoch had been backed to make runs; the gamblers started, or participated in, a hail of outrage. Coulthard had been chosen by the English; he appeared to have favoured Harris in the caught-behind decision; but worse than that, he was a Victorian.

Murdoch 'walked away like a man', the English player Emmett said, and the visitors waited in the middle with Coulthard, the not-out batsman Charles Bannerman, and the NSW umpire Edmund Barton – Australia's first Prime Minister 22 years later. But in the members' pavilion, the *Sydney Morning Herald* said, there was 'a large betting element' and it 'was from that quarter that the first shouts of "not out" proceeded and that the player, who had quietly accepted the obnoxious decision, was greeted with shouts of "go back".'

Gregory emerged from the dressing room, planted himself at the gate and said to Murdoch, 'Go back, you were not out.' Harris walked to the fence and asked if Gregory might send out a new man. Gregory refused.

Harris said he 'asked Gregory on what grounds the objection was raised and he said, at first, general incompetence, but afterwards admitted that the objection was raised on account of the decision in Murdoch's case. I implored Gregory as a friend, and for the sake of the NSW Cricket Association, which I warned him would be the sufferer by it, not to raise the objection, but he refused to take my view of the case.'

A commotion swelled around the captains. Harris turned to see that the ground 'had been rushed by the mob and our team had been surrounded. I at once returned to the ground, and in defending Coulthard from being attacked, was struck by some larrikin with a stick. Hornby immediately seized this fellow and in taking him to the pavilion was struck in the face by a would-be deliverer of the larrikin, and had his shirt nearly torn off his back. He however conveyed his prisoner to the pavilion in triumph. For some thirty minutes or more I was surrounded by a howling mob, resisting the entreaties of partisans and friends to return to the pavilion until the field was cleared, on the grounds that if our side left the field the other eleven could claim the match.'

Ulyett's account of the riot was similar. He said Murdoch was run out 'by a good two yards', then, when the crowd came on, 'I got behind the stumps, thinking they might be useful, and took up one in each hand ready for an emergency. One man struck at Lord Harris, and I elbowed my way to him and said, "Let me have a go at him, my lord." "No, no, George," he replied, "we are going to do nothing wrong."' Then Hornby dragged the man away 'though he had his shirt nearly torn off his back. He was a game 'un!'

Taking the view that possession is nine-tenths of the law — as Greg Chappell and Dennis Lillee would on the same turf 92 years later, when it was England who walked off after crowd trouble — the Englishmen stayed in the middle. Emmett said two thousand of the 10,000 spectators were on the ground 'and we had a lively time ... Someone must have struck at [Harris] with a stick, for I saw his Lordship let go with his fist.'

Harris didn't think Gregory would try to claim a forfeit, 'but I determined to obey the laws of cricket'. For the next hour and a half, negotiations shuttled between the captains. At five o'clock, police cleared the field of the invaders, mostly flashy young larrikins but also some members, and Harris's assailant had been locked up in the committee room. Harris asked his team if they should comply with Gregory's request and change Coulthard. Emmett said: 'Not likely. We ought to go straight home if we did and never play another match.'

Harris recounted: 'It was decided *nem com* that there were no grounds for the objection, and that we should decline to change him. I informed Gregory of the decision, whereupon he said, "Then the game is at an end."'

Barton told Gregory that the game would indeed be forfeited if he did not send out a new batsman. Presumably Gregory's competitive juices overcame his other considerations, and he sent out Nat Thompson. But before the restart, the crowd invaded again and the batsmen fled. Harris asked Barton if England could claim a win. Barton said, 'I'll give it to you in two minutes if [Bannerman and Thompson] don't return.'

Harris and Gregory were now like a warring married couple, speaking through go-betweens. Harris asked Barton to ask Gregory what he planned to do. Barton came back saying the batsmen would resume. They came out, but the crowd invaded for a third time. Harris said: 'I remained on the ground until the time for drawing the stumps, surrounded as before.'

A humorous incident happened after the Englishmen repaired to the dressing rooms. Emmett said Harris was looking for him, to be told by Ulyett that 'the crowd had given me such a fright that I was last seen running like a madman towards Sydney, and that they had sent a cab after me!'

The following day, the rest day, Harris wrote his report on the incident for Lord's. He said the riot was begun by the bookmakers and accelerated by Gregory, and some in the NSWCA were 'uncricketlike' in their behaviour towards the English.

It rained that night, and on the Monday morning NSW were quickly bundled out, losing their last six wickets with the score stuck on 49. Emmett thought this was ironic justice, the riot having saved England from likely defeat. 'Had we been sent in to get 80 runs, eleven Graces could not have got them on that wicket ... it was another instance of an unruly mob doing harm to the side they desire should succeed.' He had another reason to be pleased: he and Ulyett had put £20 on England to win at 2/1 with the bookmakers in the pavilion.

What has rarely been reported is a secondary riot, on the Monday, which Ulyett spoke of 19 years later. He said that, following the Saturday incident, the Commodore of Sydney gave his tars the Monday off and 'if they saw anyone attempt to molest the English cricketers they were at liberty to "go for them". Well, on the Monday, the tars were in groups of a dozen a few yards apart among the crowd ... After the match a couple of hundred loafers waited for the poor umpire [Coulthard], who asked us to stand behind him while he fought the best man in the crowd. While we were getting ready for the fight, however, a dozen of the Sydney Commodore's men arrived, and seeing what was happening, they went for the crowd and polished them off with their fists in double quick time. Then we and the umpire got away without further trouble.'

In the immediate aftermath, every instrument of public opinion came down against the Saturday rioters. The *Sydney Morning Herald* called the incident 'a national humiliation'; the riot pushed Ned Kelly's raid at Jerilderie off the front page. The *Herald* said a 'large majority of the public were deeply humiliated' by what happened, especially that it originated among the members. 'The pavilion is supposed to be the rendezvous of the elite of the cricketing community and it ought to give the tone to the opinion of the ground.' A NSWCA delegation apologised to Harris, though he 'could not say that the events would be easily forgotten'.

The NSWCA subsequently banned betting at the ground. Two men, one a bookmaker from Victoria, were charged and banned. They both pleaded guilty and, said the *Herald*, 'expressed deep regret for what had occurred, and it was in consideration of this rather tardy contrition, and the good character given them by the police, that the Bench fined them 40 shillings, and to pay 21 shillings professional costs and 5 shillings costs of the court.'

The prosecutor was Richard Driver, President of the NSWCA and Gregory's confidant. It was insinuated in some newspapers that Gregory egged on the rioters because he had some link with the bookmakers. A *Sydney Mail* journalist wrote: 'I believe Gregory was coerced by certain persons in the pavilion not to send another man in when Murdoch was given out.' Charles Absolom, an England player, alleged the same. But nothing stronger than rumour was produced to support this, and it would have been a fiendish twist indeed if, were Gregory corruptly involved, his ally Driver would have prosecuted those responsible. Gregory's competitive drive was unquestioned, and he had earnt a reputation for disputing umpiring decisions around the world. But no other allegations of corruption were made against him, and his later career as a head mandarin of the NSW Treasury suggests that his character was, outside his hot-headed cricket moments, unimpeached.

The NSW authorities bent over backwards to placate Harris. The *Herald* oozed: 'The Bench referred to the kindly hospitable treatment the Australian cricketers received in England, expressing deep regret that Lord Harris and his team should have met such a disagreeable experience.'

But Harris was implacable. He cancelled the second scheduled Test match, and even managed to antagonise the friendly, even toadying, Victorians in the second of two matches against them following the riot. Although the agreed stumps time was 6.30 pm, Harris refused to play after 6.00 pm due to bad light. Fred Ironside, an early Australian cricket chronicler, reported that 'an angry altercation ensued between both captains, but matters having been amicably arranged, what at one period promised to end in an unseemly termination resulted in the resumption of the match on the Monday following.'

Happily, Johnny Mullagh, the most accomplished of Lawrence's 1868 Aboriginals, starred in Victoria's second innings, scoring 36, whereupon the crowd raised a collection which was 'invested in the purchase of a watch'.

Harris's team had played five first-class matches, winning two and losing three, which may have had some effect on their leader's dyspeptic mood. After the Melbourne Cricket Club paid out the 'enormous and unexpected incidental expenses' for both the English and Australian cricketers, it was looking at a deficit of £153. Harris in his farewell speech rebutted English press concerns that the tour would be 'a gate money affair' and said it was 'contradicted at the earliest opportunity', but it was also a fact that while England's two professionals received £200 each, the amateurs received more than twice as much in 'compensation' for their expenses.

The riot was over, but the controversy was just beginning. Harris had written a candid letter relating the Sydney incident to Isaac Walker. Walter Hadow, who had been on Harris's tour to Canada, wrote a letter to the peer. Both were published in London's *Daily Telegraph* on 1 April, 1879. The letters revealed an underlying anger and resentment. Harris concluded: 'We never expect to see such scenes of disorder again; we can never forget this one.'

Hadow was still stewing over Gregory's 1878 team. 'It is sincerely to be hoped that we have now seen and heard the last of Australian cricket and cricketers; at any rate until they have learned the true spirit in which the game should be played.'

The Australian reaction was righteously indignant. The NSWCA – on which Gregory was a committeeman – sent a reply to the *Telegraph* pointing out how strongly the Australian press and public had condemned the riot. The riot's leaders had been convicted and punished. 'Lord Harris, by what we feel to be a most ungenerous suppression of these facts, has led the British public to suppose that in New South Wales, to quote his own words, "a party of gentlemen travelling through these colonies for the purpose of playing a few friendly games of cricket should have been insulted and subjected to indignities", while the Press and inhabitants of Sydney neither showed surprise, indignation, nor regret. We cannot let a libel upon the people of New South Wales so unfounded as this to pass without challenge. The country upon which such a reproach could be fastened would be unworthy of a place among the civilised communities, and the imputation is especially odious to Australians, who claim to have maintained the manly, generous, and hospitable characteristics of the British race.'

As for the incident itself, Sydney's response was that the rioters had never been targeting the Englishmen, but rather the Victorian umpire. Coulthard's appointment, the NSWCA's letter said, 'had created real, though suppressed, dissatisfaction, and one, giving Lord Harris a second "life", was openly admitted to be a mistake, and when Mr Murdoch, the hero of the hour, was, at the crisis of the game, given run out by what a large proportion of the spectators both in the pavilion and round the enclosure, as well as the batsman himself, whether rightly or wrongly, took to be a most unfair decision, the excitement and indignation of a section of the spectators led by the juvenile element unhappily broke through restraint. The present demonstration was against the umpire whom Lord Harris still considers competent whilst admitting he had made mistakes. It was certainly not against our gallant visitors. The betting men to whom Lord Harris alludes, and of whom only one or two were present, were not members of this Association at all, and it is completely unjust to assign the demonstration to any such agency. Bad as it was, it sprang from no mercenary motive.'

Three influential Australian voices came out saying Harris had overreacted. Spofforth, who would become a friend of Harris's, wrote in 1895: 'I should like to point out that the feeling aroused was almost entirely due to the spirit of rivalry between the Colonies ... The umpire was a Victorian, and the party spirit in the crowd was too strong. "Let an Englishman stand umpire", they cried; "we don't mind any of them. We won't have a Victorian." There was not the slightest animosity against Lord Harris or any of his team; the whole disturbance was based on the fact that the offender was a Victorian.'

Spofforth doubted 'if Englishmen will ever understand the spirit of rivalry that runs high between the colonies of Victoria and New South Wales. The spirit is not limited to the field, it extends to politics, to society, to every side of life, indeed, in which the two are brought into contact with one another.'

Among the Englishmen, Emmett seemed to understand the NSW–Victorian rivalry. 'If it were a game of marbles,' he said, 'they would fight over it almost to the death.'

Two months after Harris's letter was published, Tommy Horan wrote in *The Australasian*:

'Lord Harris is a pretty good cricketer, but we cannot congratulate him on his appearance in print ... [His] version of the treatment experienced at the hands of the "howling mob", as he termed it, of Sydney, is certainly not written in good taste, nor does it evince those finer sentiments of good feeling and tact that we might expect to find in an English gentleman and a peer of the realm. No one condemned more strongly than we did the treatment Lord Harris's eleven received in the match at Sydney. By none could it be more regretted that the fair fame of Australian cricket should be sullied by an outbreak of popular feeling at Sydney, but a certain individual [Gregory] may be painted in too dark colours, and we think the strong expressions of indignation, bordering on vindictiveness, that the press in England have indulged in are due principally to the one-sided manner in which the case is put by the Kentish peer. The ground was rushed, the game stopped, and a disorderly scene ensued, but, beyond rowdyism of voice and gesture on the part of the mob, we do not think the English gentlemen were exposed to any personal danger. It was the Victorian umpire that was struck, and in defending him Mr Hornby, it is acknowledged, had his shirt torn off his back. (We hope the MCC made him a present of a dozen new ones.) Lord Harris owns to "a sly kick or two", but as he came out of the howling mob safe and sound after 30 minutes' detention, and afterwards remained "an hour and a half" on the ground amidst this "howling mob", why it is pretty evident the noble cricketer did not incur so much danger (!) as he would imply. Victorian cricketers have experienced rougher treatment more than once on Sydney cricket fields, but they took it like men, and real gentlemen.'

In his annual booklet *World of Cricket*, Ironside wrote a chapter titled 'The great Cricket fracas rationally reviewed', in which he said, 'Harris and his team were not wholly blameless.'

'The spectators, none the less enthusiastic nor unmixed in character than is to be found in all large public gatherings in other parts of the world, believing that a palpable error of judgement had been made, gave vent to expressions of disapproval, first taking the office from a number of excited individuals who gesticulated wildly in the pavilion. From this out came the contention, a stoppage of the game, and demands all round, not that Murdoch should go in again (as has been stated), but for another umpire.'

Ironside felt that a routine dispute was escalated by the English captain.

'Lord Harris and team determined upon one course, and the public bent upon another. Prompted by curiosity, and wishing as some people do to be in the thick of any dispute, however much they are best away, some three lads first leisurely paced their way towards the wickets; presently a few more ventured, and gradually the numbers increased to somewhere about 300. Intermixed with the crowd were the English players walking about the ground, some unwisely arguing with mere youths, and evidently losing temper, while a few others with more discretion paced about as if indifferent which way things went. Presently some few blows were struck, but having been equally well repaid both by Lord Harris and Hornby this method of retaliation was freely commended. Suddenly something had happened which made 'confusion worse confounded', and an ill-guarded remark by one of the [English] Eleven about "sons of b---- convicts", flying as it did from one to another, worked irremediable mischief, and fortunately ended in nothing further than dispelling all hopes of reconciliation for the time being. It was indeed a bloodless battle, positively one of words rather than blows, if excepting the above and the blow given on a lad in error by one of the English players, and which afterwards led to an apology from the latter.'

Emmett and Ulyett, the professionals who found themselves accused of uttering the 'convicts' insult, wrote a hot denial to the *Herald*. Barton backed them, writing that he believed them 'honest and incapable of having acted or spoken in such a way'. But the next day, the paper's cricket reporter maintained: 'I now have a letter before me from a well-known citizen (and one who has for years taken a deep interest in cricket), in which he says "I can tell you that I heard the remark, and that it spread like wildfire round the ground." The writer is one of those who went on the ground to pacify the mob.'

Ironside, 'taking an unbiased view of this so-called disturbance', tried to steer a conciliatory line. 'There was undoubtedly a "little wee blame" on both sides, in that (1st) the public had no right to interfere, and (2nd) in the English team's want of discretion in not taking the lesser of two evils, by consenting to a change of umpire not in itself without a precedent. The adoption of this would certainly have ensured peace, and saved that which was anything but a good example from "folks of high degree".'

Ironside thought the NSWCA did everything to smooth things over until Harris's letter, 'which held them irresponsible'. 'The difficulty was here supposed to be at an end, but not so, the dignity of this gentleman had been confronted and must be atoned for. His statement was "one-sided" and the NSWCA met on 4 June. And they replied, noting "important details which had been forgotten by 'my Lord'"! The little sympathy hence which was shown him proved in the end undeserving, his wailing rejoinder forming a ready subject for caricaturists in more than one of the pictorial journals of the day.'

The seriousness of the initial incident was magnified by subsequent actions. Harris's refusal to play a second Test — which may have been due to the superiority of Spofforth and the Australian batsmen more than the crowd's behaviour — elevated the temperature. Soon Horan began to fear for the consequences: '"Give a dog a bad name" etc holds good in cricket as in other things, and our chief regret that Lord Harris wrote so ungenerously is that it may prevent the resumption of international matches for some time.'

Ironside was more sanguine: 'No sulks are eternal. It is only a question of time, and Australian cricketers will play against the best that England can furnish — if not this year, then another. Ever since games have been games they have led to disputes. They grow up easily under the excitement of emulation and competition. But the games remain while the disputes are forgotten!'

That remained to be seen.

Murdoch's 1878 tour had been his apprenticeship in batting. As his subsequent performances at home showed, he was about to solve Australia's principal weakness.

Cricket was to assume a central role in redeeming his troubled personal life. He had invested heavily in a shipping venture that failed when a vessel sank in the South Pacific, bankrupting himself and the legal firm he owned with his brother. Murdoch & Murdoch was dissolved in June 1879 with debts of £775. The young batsman-wicketkeeper's only assets were clothing worth £10 and a bank account of £25. His brother Gilbert lent him money to live on, and for the next two years all of Billy's surplus earnings from cricket would go back to Gilbert.

Notwithstanding the wealth they had gleaned from the 1878 tour, some of the veterans were stepping aside from cricket. Gregory was in the NSW Treasury, Bailey had a banking career in Tasmania, and Horan had a new full-time job writing for the *Australasian*. Garrett's legal studies and Allan's farming would also stop them from taking the next international tour — whenever that happened to be.

Spofforth's availability was also fluctuating. In the summer of

1879–80, the *Sydney Mail*'s 'Square Leg' criticised him for 'coquetting with the [NSW] selection committee' and choosing to play against his home colony, for a Combined Fifteen, because he was still owed money from 1878, a 'latest phase of eccentricity on the part of "the demon".'

Spofforth replied angrily: 'I am not going to play cricket all my life, and I think it is about time I turned my attention to more serious pursuits; besides this, I cannot afford time to practise so as to do myself and my side justice.' He hinted he would retire unless local cricket was organised better.

'Square Leg' retracted his criticism – partly. 'It is rather curious, though, that if Spofforth's firm intention was not to play, that he should have attended practice regularly at the Association Ground.'

Spofforth played for the Fifteen and demolished the Eleven. Two weeks later, on 3 January, he quit his job with the bank. He had another overseas venture coming up.

'A BRIDGE WHICH WILL ENDURE FOREVER'

For all the doubts about relations with the English and the commercial viability of inbound tours, the 1878 tour to England had been too lucrative not to repeat. In 1879 Conway began talking to Boyle and Murdoch about going again. Meanwhile, Driver and the NSWCA were trying to promote a rival tour. The remaining members of the Eleven held the upper hand over the associations, threatening to boycott the 1879–80 intercolonial matches, but they saw Conway as an impediment to good relations with both Lord's and Sydney and Melbourne. Boyle and Murdoch obtained joint support from the NSWCA and Victorian Cricket Association, and sidelined Conway by choosing George Alexander, a Victorian all-rounder, as manager.

Conway's fall was swift. In 1878 Gregory had issued this testimonial: 'We shall ever be grateful to our friend John Conway, from whom the idea emanated; but for his idea the majority of us probably would never have seen Old England.' Garrett wrote: 'Jack Conway was the originator of the idea.' But their successors felt Conway was a liability.

Spofforth, the Bannermans and Blackham – the remaining nucleus of the 1878 team – accepted invitations, along with the rising Victorian stars Joey Palmer and Percy McDonnell, barrister William Moule, Tom Groube, Jimmy Slight and George Bonnor. Alexander would step in to play when needed.

Although the team was announced in early January 1880, Lillywhite, again their agent in England, only heard in February that they were definitely coming. He conveyed the counties' frosty reply: they had arranged their fixtures. Lord's would not be available, either for a Middlesex match or any fixture involving the MCC.

Historians have repeated the assertion that the 1880 Australians were hampered by their late organisation and arrival. Altham, in his *History of Cricket*, writes: 'The story of the [1880 tour] makes very curious reading. In the first place it was not apparently until late in the spring of that year that anyone in England knew for a certainty that the trip would take place.' Altham was usually authoritative enough to be repeated ad infinitum, but in this case he mistook a fob-off for the truth. The Eleven of 1880 arrived in England two weeks earlier than the 1878 and 1882 teams, both of whom obtained fixtures at Lord's. Moreover, in 1880 the MCC said Lord's was unavailable for the Australians because of a commitment to a touring 'Gentlemen of Canada' team – which did not play at Lord's until 10 June and arrived nearly a month after the Australians. In any event, the Canadians, many of whom were English and American, were a shambles. Their captain and best player, the Yorkshireman Thomas Dale, travelled under the alias of Thomas Jordan because he was wanted for desertion from the Royal Horse Guards in 1873. He ran the gauntlet by coming to England, and was unmasked and jailed. He escaped, but was arrested by a citizen, court-martialled and jailed again. In his absence, the Canadians' performance fell apart dramatically.

The truth about Lord's and the counties' supposed unavailability was, the Australians would soon find out, that Lord Harris was still sulking. The lack of fixtures was a concerted boycott by English committees, not a timing problem.

Ironside, as usual through his chronicling of cricket and collection of statistics, had high-quality information: 'The prevailing and very general opinion was that [the tour] was somewhat premature, and that it would have been more polite to have deferred it for a few years to allow of the subsidence of any probable bad feeling which the Lord Harris dispute might have engendered, but this was overruled. The initiators, in all probability not desirous of being deposed in their intentions of another antipodean venture, which in the case of Gregory's Team was so successful, both pecuniarily and practically ... declined to bow to public feeling in the matter.'

The Eleven began their tour with a fundraising circuit of Australia. Two matches in, they suffered a blow when Charlie Bannerman came down ill. Richard Cashman suggests: 'Drinking and gambling appear to have played a significant role in his rapid loss of form after 1878.' Bannerman, who also had a coaching offer from the Melbourne Cricket Club, retired from international cricket.

Few niceties had been paid to cross-colonial sensitivities — the squad had nine Victorians and three New South Welshmen — but a new round of intercolonial horse-trading gave Bannerman's place to South Australia's first representative, the wicketkeeper-batsman Affie Jarvis.

Bannerman's withdrawal left a young team, three — Jarvis, Palmer and McDonnell — still teenagers. But a bold Spofforth said this team was 'much stronger than the last', contradicting most public opinion.

Early results also contradicted him. Whereas the 1878 team had lost one of their 22 warm-up games, the 1880 team lost four of nine, all played against the odds, twice to Horan-inspired Fifteens of Victoria, to a Twenty-Two of Daylesford and to an Eighteen of South Australia.

The second match against the Victorians was noteworthy. Victoria was chasing a win in the fourth innings when Horan could not be found to come in to bat. Ironside recorded: 'at 44 seconds over the orthodox time (2 minutes)', Horan was allowed to come out, and won the game with his batting. 'Had the Eleven been so inclined they could have claimed the match, and no argument could have stood against it. Personally, if I had been in Mr Boyle's position the match would have been one more victory for the Eleven.'

This was nothing, however, compared to the bombshell that had arrived on the eve of the match. A 'staggering cablegram', as Ironside put it, 'reached here to the effect that certain gentlemen would decline to meet the Eleven, and that they would be regarded in the light of professionals.'

Even decades later when he wrote his memoir, Harris was coy about revealing the reason for his vendetta against the 1880 Australians. He wrote that they 'asked no one's good-will in the matter, and it was felt that that was a discourteous way of bursting in on our arrangements; and the result was that they played scarcely any Counties, and were not generally recognised. We had to make some protest against too frequent visits.' Too frequent visits or professionalism? Uncouth manners or a peer's temper tantrum? Either way, the fig leaf of 'late timing' was blown away.

Boyle's Eleven sailed uncertainly from Adelaide on the SS *Garonne* on 19 March. Boyle wrote of an eventful voyage: 'The skipper of the vessel, Captain Hillkirk, is a fine, jolly fellow and did all in his power to make us comfortable. We went in for shinty very strong, till at last we were compelled to stop it, as all our fellows were getting chipped hands and broken shins. Our next game was ship cricket, the balls we used being made of oakum, which we purchased from the sailors. It was rather an expensive amusement, as though we only paid 3d. each for the balls, yet we managed to lose 10 or 12 overboard every day.'

By April, the difficulties awaiting them in England had become depressingly clear. The only confirmed fixtures were against non-county Fifteens and Eighteens. Hopes of taking on the MCC again, or even a representative England Eleven, were slim. For the few fixtures he had been able to organise, Alexander obtained 75 per cent of gate money, but in return the Australians would be classified as 'professionals'. The *Australasian* said defiantly, 'It may be necessary at Lords to define a "professional" and to prohibit his presence in the "pavilion", but we have not come to that here yet.'

The Eleven may not have liked it, but what could they do? If they stuck to their guns, they faced financial ruin and perhaps an abandonment of the fragile Anglo-Australian enterprise. An English newspaper called them 'a money-hunting crew' and Alexander made a speech on board telling the players: 'We have to live down a bad name.' In the Suez, a team meeting was held. It was decided that Boyle, one of the strongest characters from the 1878 tour, might not be the best leader. The more emollient character of Murdoch was seen as a diplomatic choice. Boyle, who had no great desire to lead, appears to have accepted the decision without demur.

The Eleven made several stopovers in the Middle East and Mediterranean. The King's Palace at Naples, wrote Boyle, 'must have cost a mint of money ... One of the staircases which is built of solid marble, our guide said, had cost over half a million.' He had every reason to think about money: the tour, at this stage, posed a lifetime financial risk to the player-investors.

After six weeks, the *Garonne* put in at Plymouth on 4 May. Boyle said he and Alexander went ahead to London 'to select quarters, &c.' They arranged lodgings at the Tavistock Hotel, near Covent Garden, 'and we have since found it a very comfortable place to stay at'.

But there was little else to comfort them. Lillywhite told them that 'much to our disappointment' no matches had been arranged in London. The *Australasian's* columnist 'Robin Hood' said it was 'difficult to get anyone to say a word about the team – good, bad or indifferent. A desire to ignore it exists, especially in London.'

Alexander and Boyle visited the MCC, which told them the program 'had been settled and could not be altered'. Lillywhite reckoned it was payback not for the Sydney riot, but for 'the commercial spirit which had inspired' the 1878 team, memories of which 'were still disagreeably fresh in the minds of Englishmen'.

Harris said gentlemen would only play Australia if they 'would admit that their trip was only one of pleasure'.

The Australians were being pincered by both English classes. Whereas in 1878 it had been the professionals who complained about the money the Australians raked in while maintaining the status of amateurs, now it was the gentlemen who refused to recognise them at all unless they played for free.

'Unwilling to compromise and do that which would be contrary to facts,' Ironside said, 'Mr Boyle very politely declined to make any such admission, and for the nonce the interview ended.'

A disconsolate Boyle wrote home: 'The feeling here is very bitter; but it is only nursed up by Lord Harris, Hornby, Hadow, and some more of that kidney ... We could not be treated worse if we were a set of blacklegs ... We have been assured that if the Marylebone club had met us, then all the counties and the gentlemen too would have played, but Harris, Hornby and [Frank] Penn being on the committee of the club, spoiled all show for us.'

Ironside, back in Australia, waxed indignant: 'As if to add to the little feeling then existing in England against the Australians they had scarcely landed before a few turbulent scribes through a certain section of the London Press, styled them "Commercial Cricketers". As undoubtedly ignorant of the above little pecuniary incident in connection with

International cricket ... they have o'erstepped themselves, and in matters of cricket at all events, in future would do well to quietly "take a back seat".'

Not every English voice was against the Australians. Why should the visitors give up their economic model when Lord Harris's amateurs had accepted handsome 'expenses' in Australia? Why should they accept the meagre fate of the professional class? *London Society* admitted: 'Few of the English professionals have a shilling left when winter has drained their store, and the spring has come again with new engagements to the public schools or country clubs. Yes, and some of the same Australian [English] Elevens, who happily landed with money awaiting them in the Bank, would but for the happy trip, have been borrowing as many pounds to start with on some Club engagement for the season as they then had hundreds to their credit awaiting them in the Bank!'

Boyle and Alexander had conceived a plan B, which might at least publicly embarrass the amateur committees into giving them a game. 'As the feeling of the London cricketers seemed to be against us, and to show the public we were willing to meet them,' Boyle said, 'we instructed our manager, Mr Alexander, to write to all the papers, stating that we were very much disappointed at no first-class match being arranged in London and that we were willing to play any team that they liked to bring against us, the whole of the takings, as far as we were concerned, to go to the English Cricketers' Fund.'

It would seem a public relations coup, a selfless gesture to advance the credibility of the Australian Eleven while taking no money.

It backfired. Boyle said the 'letter brought forth a perfect deluge of correspondence in reply, but as none of them suggested any match but simply abused us, we took no notice of them'.

While Alexander and Boyle were seeking fixtures, the others practised at Mitcham Green, in south London, where the professional James

Southerton had a wicket and a pub. The immediate drawcard for curious onlookers was George Bonnor, who had not played a first-class game but had attracted attention with his hitting for the Bathurst and Albert clubs. His mother, Sarah Ann, came from a prominent Yorkshire cattle-farming family. When she and her husband, also George, emigrated from Hereford, their herd of pedigree cattle was stolen by bushrangers. But they had prospered through hard work and produced, in George, a boy who A.A. Thomson claims 'was reckoned among the handsomest men of his time; a time, you understand, when there *were* handsome men'.

'Bonnor's admirers,' among whom Thomson clearly numbered himself, 'said that he was six feet six in height and even his detractors allowed him six feet four and a half. Despite his enormous height, his proportions were so near to perfection that he was incapable of a clumsy movement. For so big a man, he was as active as a cat and a remarkable sprinter. Ruskin, with less originality than you might have expected from a master of English prose, called Bonnor "a young god", while E.V. Lucas, writing long years afterwards, lovingly recalled "the mighty Bonnor, immensely tall, with golden hair and beard ... this superb figure, like a god from another planet ..."

'An English peer who visited him in Australia said that he was the most perfect physical specimen of humanity he had ever known. Not that peers are necessarily experts on standards of physical beauty, but this one was in a better position than most to know what he was talking about because, when his lordship paid him his historic visit, Bonnor was in his bath.'

Bonnor had been chosen as a hitter. His reputation, said Thomson, 'preceded him to our shores, for the Australian temperament seldom cripples itself with understatement'. Nor did the English, when it came to slogging. Their biggest was C.I. 'Buns' Thornton, who once hit Allan Steel from Scarborough Cricket Ground into the neighbouring Trafalgar Square. A lady asked Thornton, years later, if he'd been batting at the Oval or Lord's.

At Mitcham Green, Bonnor put on a show, hitting one ball that Southerton measured to carry 147 yards. Thomson wrote: 'The report of this stroke echoed round the country. On every ground that he visited spectators waited for him, cheered him wildly when he appeared and were bitterly disappointed, as though he had deliberately deceived them, when he failed. For him a tour of our country became a royal progress of violence.'

Another towering shot hit a small boy on the forehead, knocking him out. Bonnor was extremely upset until the boy came to. Bonnor's sensitivity pointed to a contradiction between temperament and talent, as Thomson wrote:

'Bonnor was by nature a friendly soul, with malice towards none. With his happy nature, he bore no ill-will towards person or object, except a small red ball. Like many another giant, he was shy in the presence of women, but warmly approved of by dogs and children. He would take his turn at ship's concerts or pavilion sing-songs and when he "rendered" in his pleasant tenor voice "The Tear in Every Eye" he quivered with honest emotion, all six foot six of him. He had another trait in common with many a famous man: he longed to be famous for something else. Your comedian secretly sees himself as a Hamlet and Bonnor cherished the ambition to be known not as a slogger, but as a stylist. It is one of the sad things in life that such dreams are misunderstood and his attempts to acquire elegance filled his colleagues not with sympathy, but with rage. What, they demanded, had got into Bon? Who did he think he was? His sacred mission was to massacre the bowling, not to prance around like a dancing master.'

By 13 May, it was time for cricket. Lillywhite had arranged a game in Southampton against an Eighteen of St Luke's Club. Murdoch, 97, set the foundation before Spofforth's 17 wickets and Boyle's 14 sealed an innings win before 8000 spectators over the three days.

More significantly, two of the Grace clan, W.G.'s brother Fred and his cousin William Gilbert, played for St Luke's. The Graces' nominal county was Gloucestershire, but they topped up their cricket incomes by freelancing. As Rae writes, 'the two young mercenaries made no secret of their general availability. The Australians proved a very acceptable source of income, and they followed them up and down the country making guest appearances for local teams.' Gilbert and Fred were, of course, amateurs.

Aside from scoring more than half of St Luke's runs in each innings, Fred opened a channel of communication between the Australians and W.G., who did not belong to the Harris-Hornby-Hadow clique. The Champion saw the financial opportunity in an Australian tour and offered them a match with Gloucestershire, breaking the effective Lord's embargo. His liberality and pragmatism on the subject of money was a first, vital step towards recognition.

The St Luke's match was followed by a rare first-class fixture, Australia beating Derbyshire by eight wickets on a pitch 'which bumped considerably', favouring Spofforth, who took 13 scalps. 'We had again a very large attendance of spectators,' said Boyle, 'and they were a very impartial crowd, cheering every good bit of play.'

Fred Grace and Gilbert followed them to the Longsight club near Manchester, who had beaten the 1878 team 'and were sanguine of doing so again', wrote Boyle. But Blackham 'played a magnificent innings of 81', Bonnor hit a ball into an adjacent field that 'must have reached 160 yards', Spofforth bagged 18 wickets and Australia won again.

A four-day break followed – not from choice, but from the thinness of the program – enabling Murdoch, Bannerman and Boyle to go sightseeing in Paris and the rest to see the Derby at Epsom. Back in Manchester, a win over an Eighteen of Rochdale, and some social acceptance, followed. Boyle recounted: 'They gave us a grand banquet in the evening, and the President of the Club said that they really thought they would defeat us on this occasion, but that we were too good for them. We were very kindly treated, and shown through all the large Manufacturing Flannel Factories. The people here, the poorer classes, nearly all wear clogs, and the women never seem to use bonnets or hats, but make a shawl their covering for the head.'

Two wins and a rained-out draw against northern Eighteens took Australia through early June, when a 'rebel' Yorkshire Eleven took them on. Officially the county maintained the boycott, but most of the regular players took part – except one. 'They had their best team against us,' said Boyle, 'with the exception of Ulyett who, we believe, was not allowed to play on account of the English team who visited Australia under Lord Harris having engaged him to play at Lord's against the Canadians. We believe this was done to injure us. The Yorkshire people were very wrath that he did not play, and they expressed their opinion on the subject very strongly.'

Boyle, by his own estimation, 'fielded magnificently, and caught five men out at short mid on'. Australia were left with 91 to win 'and as the wicket was greatly cut up, it was considered doubtful if they would do it'. McDonnell's 47 ensured they did. 'There was a very large attendance on the ground at the finish, but they were very one-sided in their applause; in fact, we don't think there was twenty who cheered us on our victory.'

Their next eight games, of which Australia won five and drew three, were against Eighteens. In Belfast, 'after a long and weary journey of 25 hours, without sleep ... the sons of "Ould Erin" treated us very kindly, and we soon felt at home'. In Dublin 'we were made royally welcome. As the Australians had contributed a large amount of money to the Irish Famine Fund, they did all they could to make us feel at home. We were told that Australia had contributed more than England, twice as much as Canada, and four times that of India. We had the free run of all the theatres and amusements, and one night we visited the Queen's Theatre, where our old friends Baker and Farron were playing. On our entrance the band played "Come Back to Erin" and "Rule Britannia", and the audience rose en masse and cheered us heartily. In the interval between the third and fourth acts Mr Wallace, the manager, from the stage gave us welcome to Dublin. They had a special box for us gaily decorated, and we were the lions of the evening.'

In Northampton, against an Eighteen including Fred Grace, Gilbert, Emmett and Harry Jupp, players 'gathered from all the counties in England, it was expected that we would receive a crushing defeat. The match was played on a new ground, which was very rough,' wrote Boyle. 'The result of the match [Australia winning by eight wickets] was a great surprise to the knowing ones, who thought it was a certainty for the local team.'

They won again in Harrogate, 'famed for its medicinal waters, which are said to be good for all sorts of diseases', and Newcastle, where 'We visited the great Tyne Bridge, which is considered one of the finest in the world.' During a win over an Eighteen of Middlesborough, Boyle went on, 'A curious circumstance took place during our innings. Slight was injured while batting, and Murdoch was running for him; in backing up to get a run the ball was thrown in from the field, and struck his (Murdoch's) bat. The umpire gave him out for obstructing the field – a most curious decision!'

London remained a pebble in their boot. When they played an Eighteen of Crystal Palace Club on 19–20 July, Boyle said, 'It was expected that the attendance would be enormous, but the promoters of the match had given but little publicity, and it was not known except by a few that we were to play there.'

Another unofficial match with Yorkshire sparked talk about Lord's relaxing its embargo. 'The result of the [Yorkshire] match caused great excitement throughout England, and it was suggested by many writers in the newspapers that England should select her best team to meet us.'

England's north remained welcoming. The Australians crushed an Eighteen of Hull, Bonnor won a throwing contest, and the Eleven toured the London and North West Railway Company's locomotive works at Crewe, the biggest in the world. They almost missed their train south to Gloucestershire, piling aboard in their whites, and 'the spirits of our boys fell to zero' as, weary after their northern circuit, they contemplated facing W.G.

The Champion was Australia's greatest friend in 1880, but after losing to them in 1878 he was also hell-bent on beating them. Gloucestershire, treating the occasion as a true international, turned out in force, 'a large and fashionable crowd, who seemed to have especially laid themselves out for a real day's enjoyment,' Boyle said. Australia soon fell behind, W.G. bowling his deceptive round-armers and winkling out batsman after batsman, and the swashbuckling E.M. scoring 65 before being bowled, which made him so angry he smashed all three stumps out of the ground. In Australia's second innings McDonnell 'hit out manfully, and we must say, had a little luck', to score 79, and set Gloucestershire 166. A typical dispute arose when W.G. had the pitch rolled between innings on the second evening, then, illegally, again on the third morning. Murdoch protested, but this was Clifton, so Grace got his way. Riled, Spofforth bowled one of his best spells of what was already a superb tour and dismissed W.G. lbw for 3, E.M. caught and bowled for 41, and Fred bowled for 10. Spofforth took 7/54 'on a perfect batsman's wicket' and Australia won by 68, bringing congratulatory cablegrams from the NSW and Victorian associations.

This was the highpoint of the tour. The team went back north to defeat Eighteens of Hunslet, Bradford and Sunderland, watched by large, enthusiastic crowds. They took three days off at Scarborough, 'which the boys took advantage of to see all the fine scenery,' Boyle wrote. 'Some of our team amused themselves by riding donkeys on the sand, and the spills they got were certainly amusing.'

All that was missing, still, was a nod from St Johns Wood. 'A well-known cricketer', possibly Horan, wrote in *Boyle & Scott's Australian Cricket Guide*: 'At the present time we have a second Australian Eleven carrying all before them in the cricket grounds of England, but who, we regret to add, have been, and are being, met in such a hostile spirit, and treated in such an unfair and unsportsmanlike manner by the cricketing "powers that be" in the old country, that it would appear as if the love of fair play supposed to be inherent in the British race, has completely ceased to exist. One thing is certain, and it is that in all departments of scientific cricket, Australians furnish standards of comparison not surpassed in any part of the world, and there is no fear that a period of degeneracy is likely to set in.'

After the Clifton match, W.G. went to Canterbury to represent the Gentlemen of England against Harris's Gentlemen of Kent. In front of a full deck of amateurs, Grace pressed Harris for a match in London between a fully-representative England and Australia, something never put on before.

Harris had started to soften. The Australians had given no quarter to his demand that they play for 'pleasure', but the passage of time and the inconsistency of his position were weakening the force of his tantrum. Over the next fortnight, he and Grace spoke to the secretary of Surrey, Charles Alcock, who was enthusiastic about staging an England–Australia match at the Oval. A date was found when Lord Sheffield, the president of Sussex, agreed to postpone the Australians' match at Hove, for compensation of £100. The Australians would receive 50 per cent of the outer-ground receipts from the Oval (which would come to £2600). On the morning of 21 August, when Australia were entering the third day of their match with an Eighteen of Scarborough, the news came through: Grace and Alcock had succeeded in swaying Harris, and England would play Australia at the Oval over three days from 6 September. Harris's recollection was sniffy: 'C.W. Alcock implored me to help to make things pleasant before they left.'

The Australians had not lost a match; Spofforth had ripped apart what was admittedly questionable opposition. The personalities in the team had also made a great impression, as one expat wrote in a letter to Boyle: 'The remarks I heard in some instances were very amusing.

One of the crowd said to his neighbour that it was not surprising the Australians fielded so well, as in Australia they got the natives to throw the ball at them, and to save themselves from being hit, caught the ball ... They called Spofforth the demon emu, and said that the reason he was such a good bowler was that he was an emu hunter, and made his living by catching emus, his mode of operation being to knock them over with balls made of wood, the same size as cricket balls. I enjoyed the conversation of the yokels muchly, but made no remark. I may mention that the members of the Australian team are much stouter than when they left Victoria. Bonnor now weighs about 17 ½ st [III kg]. [He] has suddenly found himself on the pinnacle of fame. He has lately been promoted from simple, unassuming George, to such appellations as the giant, the Hittite, the six-foot-sixer, and the latest is that it has been discovered by the Australasian that he can really play cricket ... Besides, if he shouldn't come off in the cricket field, he would be of immense advantage to Canon Smith, in the latter's proposed lectures on the advantages of New South Wales. Only fancy our worthy Canon having such a trump card as Bonnor to show at the conclusion of each of his lectures. We can imagine the rev. gentleman concluding thus: "And, ladies and gentlemen, to show you that the English race is not degenerating in the colonies, I will introduce you to a real live specimen of an Australian native. Observe his height! Look at his general build! He can hit a cricket ball from Liverpool to New York, and stride over the Atlantic to catch it! He once retaliated upon a man who insulted him! That man was cremated on the spot, and his ashes are kept in a corn-sack in the town of Orange ... If you can show me an Englishman that can compete with him in anything, I'll give in.'"

But then, when the Australians had every reason to rejoice, the worst happened. Within half an hour of the Oval match being arranged,

Spofforth went in to bat at Scarborough. He had taken 12 wickets in the match, and was bowling at his peak, proving to be even more destructive than in 1878.

Near the end of Australia's first innings, Scarborough had put on a bowler named Joseph Frank. His eight overs convinced the Australians that he was a 'shier'. Spofforth asked the local umpire if he would no-ball him if he bowled like Frank. The umpire said, 'Yes, you try it.' When Spofforth retorted, 'Why wasn't Frank no-balled?' the umpire answered: 'That's my business.'

'Before we started our second innings,' Boyle wrote, 'Murdoch asked the Scarborough captain [Henry Charlwood] not to put on Frank, as we did not consider he bowled fair. His remonstrance was of no use, however, as when our two first men made a stand he was put on.'

After facing one ball, Bannerman refused to take any more from Frank. At the fieldsmen's urging, Frank threw the wicket down, to great cheers. Murdoch 'again asked them to take him off, but this they would not do. Bannerman had his finger nail knocked off by him, and shortly after retired. None of the rest made a stand, as it was not safe to bat against such dangerous throwing.'

Sections of the crowd jeered the Australians, crying 'Go on!' and 'Another Lord Harris affair!' Murdoch wrote that Frank was hitting his team 'so frequently and with such force, that it caused them to limp about the ground in the most painful manner. This seemed to give the spectators no end of amusement, judging from the laughter that burst out after each knock.'

Then Spofforth came out, and suffered a 'very serious accident': 'he got the middle finger of his right hand broke by Frank, and was unable to bowl in any more of our matches in England. We suffered our first defeat at last, after playing 26 matches without losing one. Many old cricketers on the ground said Frank did not bowl fair, and the umpire cautioned him, but would not "no ball" him. Spofforth was not the only one who met with an accident, many of the others being injured.'

The impact was catastrophic. Without Spofforth, the Eleven were a very different proposition. They beat a weak Eighteen of Yeadon (enjoying their first official reception of the tour, from the Mayor of Leeds), but lost to an Eighteen of Stockport and, after a long trip south to the Sussex coast, drew with an Eighteen of Hastings. At the worst possible moment, with the great Oval match approaching, Boyle said, 'Our men were now getting very stale, and no wonder, considering the continued travelling and playing we had for nearly four months.'

Murdoch and Alexander met Grace, Alcock and Harris, and agreed to put the 1878 and 1879 incidents behind them. Harris relented on his demand that Australia renounce a share of the gate, and selected and played in the England Test team, because, he said, Australia's 'splendid form and consistently sportsmanlike conduct had led me to bury the hatchet'.

Harris's backdown, under great pressure from Grace and public opinion, has been represented as a noble concession. Rowland Bowen, in his history of cricket, wrote: 'Had it not been for that reconciliatory attitude by Lord Harris, the tour would have been a certain flop, and the first Test in England would never have taken place when it did (and it came late enough in the season, in September) and arguably might never have occurred. For there might not have been another tour to this country from Australia for many years, and if the second Australian tour had ended in financial and social disaster, there would have been sufficient ill-feeling engendered to inhibit the frequent English tours to Australia that were to occur in the near future. It is, in short, by no means fanciful to suppose that Test cricket as we know it would have developed along quite different lines, and very much later – and might even never have developed at all.'

If exaggerated, Bowen's summary does acknowledge the importance of Harris's concession. International cricket would have been retarded if the 1880 tour had ended without a representative match. But Harris was only stepping down from a row he had done much to create. In truth, the MCC had backed the wrong horse, the disastrous Gentlemen of Canada, in preference to the 'mercenary' Australians. In his history of early cricket, John Major presents a more sensible interpretation of Harris's motives: 'It is possible he thought the Australians had learned their lesson, but he may simply have wanted to play and beat them.' This would be easier now that Spofforth was out.

The hatchet was not fully buried. Ulyett, Emmett and Hornby, who had played in the Sydney riot match, refused to participate. Hornby cannot be blamed for harbouring a grudge after his personal involvement in the riot, but it must be added that the England rugby three-quarter was an aggressive fellow who confronted critical journalists so vigorously that, A.A. Thomson wrote, 'Why he was not regularly sued for assault and battery I cannot imagine.'

Other gentlemen, off on grouse-shooting holidays, felt inconvenienced. Allan Steel later told Home Gordon 'what a rotten journey he and Alfred Lyttelton had from Scotland, where they were having some splendid shooting, in order to take part in the game'.

England fielded a strong team, even without the northern trio. W.G., Fred and E.M. Grace were in, as were the great Notts professionals Billy Barnes, Shaw and Morley, and the star amateurs 'Bunny' Lucas and Steel. So crucial was Spofforth's absence that Murdoch asked for a delay. Ironside reported that 'under the circumstances in which the match was brought about it could not be well postponed, and they trusted to the chances of cricket to pull them through. To a certain extent Spofforth's not playing lessened the Colonies' interest in the match, the conclusion arrived at by 9–10ths being that All England must win.'

On 6 September, the Oval gates were open by 8.00 am and before 11.00 am it was, said Boyle, 'an impossibility to get a seat at any price; such a large crowd was never before seen at any match. We were heavily handicapped through the absence of Spofforth who was anxious to play but was unable to do so. The whole of our team were very stale.'

Still, he felt that this was 'the greatest match in the annals of cricket'. The 'attendance was enormous, about 100,000 visiting the ground during the three days over which the match lasted'. It was more likely to be 65,000 – 48,000 paying fans and 17,000 members – but in any case no such crowd had ever watched a cricket game.

Harris said to Murdoch at the toss, 'You will find the timber and we will find the workmen to build a bridge which will endure for ever'. Harris won, and the Australians took the field to applause soon drowned out by the roar for W.G. and E.M.

The day was W.G.'s – a debut Test century after a decade of total cricket domination. Palmer nearly yorked him early, but he did not give a chance until he was dropped on the boundary on 134. His 152 in just over four hours from 294 balls was, he said, 'one of the best I ever played'. Boyle rued the absence of Spofforth: 'our fielding was first-class but our bowlers were stale, and the wicket was so good it was almost impossible to make the ball do anything.' Alexander, Moule and Bannerman, the latter two rarely used as bowlers, took eight of the wickets.

Rain on the first night deadened the wicket, making 'our chance of reaching their score very remote'. England, with 420 on the board, were eager to bowl, and by lunch Australia were 9/126. Bonnor had skied a ball from Shaw 'upwards with almost superhuman force. Up and up it rocketed into space. The batsmen ran one, ran two,' wrote Thomson. 'They were embarking on a third when the ball started coming down. With flawless judgement Fred had run round to a position in front of the second gas-holder. His heart almost stopped beating as he watched the ball swooping downwards, but he held onto it and Bonnor was out.'

The ball was measured to have travelled 115 yards from the wicket, plus a fair few into the atmosphere. As Bonnor came off, teammates commiserated. Fred's had been a fine catch. 'Hard luck nothing,' said Bonnor. 'I should have hit the perisher.'

The game seemed destined to finish within two days when, following on 271 behind, Australia lost 3/14. But their two best batsmen, Murdoch and McDonnell, added an attractive 83. Perry McDonnell was the London-born son of a barrister, the Honorable Morgan Augustine McDonnell, who had emigrated to join the government of Victoria. Percy, educated at St Patrick's and Xavier colleges in Melbourne, had studied Greek and mathematics and chosen teaching over medicine as his career. In 1880 he set himself up as Murdoch's heir as Australia's best batsman.

By stumps, Australia's 6/170 at least guaranteed a gate for the third day. Grace and Murdoch, who had become firm friends at Clifton, had bet each other one sovereign on who could make the highest score. Murdoch's first-innings duck had been precisely 152 runs off target. Now, when he was 79 not out at stumps, Grace congratulated him on his innings but predicted he'd run out of partners before he could win his bet.

The next morning, Bonnor and Palmer were soon out but somehow Alexander, who was to manage Ivo Bligh's team in Australia two years later, and Moule, a future Victorian County Court judge, hung on with Murdoch. Hit painfully in the groin by Morley when he was 99, Murdoch survived to add an astonishing 140 runs with the Victorian bunnies. To make England bat again was a great feat. Murdoch passed Grace by one run, and was not out, winning his sovereign, which he wore on a chain for the rest of his life. He also received a bat, as a prize, from Surrey.

Murdoch's 153 in 316 minutes from 358 balls was the first great knock by an Australian in England. It broke new ground, because for all their admiration of Australia's bowling and fielding, the English didn't think a lot of the Colonials' batting. Newspapers described Murdoch's innings as 'beyond all praise' and 'unsurpassed in England, played without a chance', ranking Murdoch 'with the batsmen of the age'. Fifteen years later, Grace wrote that Murdoch's innings 'will always stand in the history of cricket as one of the most heroic performances that has ever been achieved by a batsman'.

Complacently, Harris sent out Fred Grace, who had a cold, and the Hon. Alfred Lyttelton to chase down the required 57. Palmer dismissed Fred and Lucas, and when he bowled Lyttelton, Boyle said, 'the excitement was now very high at the possibility of the Australians pulling the match off'. Two years earlier they had dismissed the MCC for 33 and 19; why not England for less than 56? Barnes and E.M. fell to Boyle, and England were 5/31 when W.G. finally went in to sort out a crisis of his captain's making. He and Penn collected the rest of the runs, which took England 33.3 overs.

The match had satisfied all hopes. The Australians, said Altham, had given 'unmistakable evidence of that power to play an uphill game which has since been perhaps the hall-mark of their cricket. It was a game full of variety, incident, and sensation'. Behind the stumps, Blackham and Lyttelton gave 'the finest exhibition of the [wicketkeeping] art ever known'.

Boyle wrote: 'Had Spofforth been in the team, it was the expressed opinion that the Australians would have been victorious.' But for diplomatic purposes, a gallant loss was better all round.

From the Oval pavilion, Harris called for three cheers for the Colonials, and proposed to 'bury the hatchet'. Boyle said, 'It was very gratifying to us to find that all bad feeling had entirely passed away, and everything was done during the remainder of our stay to make us comfortable, which is as it should have been.'

Australia played six more times, still taking games wherever they could find them, subjecting themselves to a punishing schedule that later teams would find all too familiar. The day after the Oval Test they caught a train to Scotland, where they drew over two days with an Eighteen of Clydesdale at Glasgow's Titwood ground, then bounced south to Sussex, 'a terrible long journey, and which knocked us up very much', said Boyle. 'The team by this time was getting very stale, the continual travelling and playing knocking us clean out of time. The stumps were drawn before the usual time to allow us to catch the express for Edinburgh, where our next match was to take place. By the time we got to Edinburgh we had travelled over 1700 miles in nine days, so that there is little wonder at our being a bit stale.'

Glasgow, Hove ... of course, Edinburgh would be next. They started their match against the Gentlemen of Scotland an hour after getting off the train. They did enjoy the beauties of Edinburgh, even if, Boyle said in grand understatement, 'unfortunately we had little time to spare'.

First-class fixtures, so sparse in four months, now came thick and fast: a draw with the Players of the North, a loss to Nottinghamshire, and a win over the Players of England at Crystal Palace. By now the Eleven was down to Ten, as Slight needed an operation to remove a fistula. Spofforth played in London, but batted only. The Australians wore black crepe to signify Fred Grace's funeral: the cold he'd had during the Oval match had swiftly turned to lethal pneumonia.

After five months, this strange tour was over. The 1880 Eleven played 37 matches in the British Isles, winning 21, losing four, and drawing 12. Only 11 of those matches were first-class. Australia could, said Altham, 'look back with pride on a tour infinitely more successful than its initial stage had promised'.

They were given a luncheon at Holborn Viaduct by colonial expatriates who presented 'handsome silver cups, suitably inscribed, and in addition Murdoch was presented with a very handsome silver loving cup, weighing 120 oz, in recognition of his splendid batting performance in the great match'.

At Mansion House, the Lord Mayor threw them a farewell dinner. An Australian wrote to Boyle of the 'servants in gorgeous dress' who received him, then 'an official presented me with a gold embossed plan of the tables'. 'Subdued and delightful music was going on all the time. Thinking I was now free, I turned about to admire the luxurious rooms and the splendid appointments, when I was suddenly requested to fall in and be introduced to his lordship, who was simply covered with furs and gold chains – his insignia of office. He was shaking hands with everybody, and fortunately got tired before my time had arrived, and retired. By the time he returned, the doors of the banquet-room were flung open, and a voice that would have silenced 20 steam pianos told us dinner was ready, and we marched in to music. Two minutes after I was lapping up the most heavenly turtle soup imaginable. It was a royal fest, and no mistake. The Lord Mayor sat with the eleven on either side of him dovetailed between successful colonists, aldermen, &c. Our little friend Alick Bannerman was supported by two of the most distinguished guests robed in velvet and fringe ... Plate dishes were filled with water from huge golden jugs, which were then laid down on their sides in the dishes, and the whole thing pushed round the table, everyone taking a dive in it as it passed him ... It is said by the cognoscenti that the magnificent hospitality of the Lord Mayor has been the means of smothering the last drop of illfeeling between the cricketers of England and Australia.'

Harris and Murdoch made friendly speeches, and, according to Ironside, the following day the team 'hied homeward, better impressed with the treatment shown them with the latter part than any other portion of their trip, a measure of hospitality won by their courteous demeanour all through their engagements'. Boyle agreed, leaving England 'well pleased with the kind treatment we had received at the close of our tour, which was so different to what we received at the commencement'.

'WHATEVER THE SCHEME ACTUALLY WAS, IT FAILED'

Boyle's – now firmly Murdoch's – Eleven came home with their pockets filled, and they returned their sponsors' investments. The Melbourne Cricket Club made a £531 dividend on the tour, the East Melbourne Cricket Club £434 and the Victorian Cricketers' Association £119 minus £10 for a celebratory luncheon.

Outside the Melbourne clubs there was not the same public enthusiasm as for the 1878 tourists, however, and the *Bulletin* reported that the Eleven were 'displeased by the absence of a public reception on their arrival in Sydney'.

But they were still a draw. The *Australasian* said 'it is candidly admitted by the team that £.s.d. is the goal at which they will aim, and that, while gate-money rolls in to swell their already large credit balance, the cohesion of the team members will continue to exist'. When they finally disbanded on 12 May 1881, their payout was only a little less than the Gregory Eleven's £750. For their last matches, against a Combined NSW-Victorian team, the VCA decided to charge the Eleven a fee of 7.5 per cent of the gate – the same amount which it had charged Lord Harris's team. If they were going to behave like a touring team, they would be treated as such. The Eleven flexed their muscle by pulling out of the intercolonials, an act the NSWCA's secretary Phillip Sheridan called 'a breach of faith which could not be too strongly condemned by the association'. 'Umpire' in the *Weekly Times* complained that club and colonial cricket was declining because the best players were always on tour, but the crowds followed the Eleven's matches, enjoying their big hitting and fast bowling.

In their last game together, in March 1881, they were flayed by the tall young banker-batsman Hugh Hamon Massie, which gave 'Square Leg' the opportunity to proclaim sourly that the Eleven was 'not by any means the strongest team that the colonies can produce'. Whether it manifested itself in the jibes against the Eleven (on both sides of the world), or in the gambling-fuelled Sydney riot, money was seen as the root of all cricket evil.

Cricket was, like horse racing, still indivisible from gambling. The 1870 version of the MCC's laws of the game included four rules on wagering: one saying bets were only payable at a game's conclusion, and three governing player-versus-player 'exotic' wagers. While chiding the Eleven for not playing in club matches, 'Umpire' also condemned the number of 'close results' in those games, suspecting that betting activity (bookmakers turned over more money when contests were tight) was driving the players.

Betting could only flourish if the punting public was confident in the incorruptibility of the players. Such confidence was shaken by an incident during the tour of English professionals who followed Murdoch's Eleven to Australia.

Having lost money touring America in 1881, the Shaw–Lillywhite professionals arrived in Australia down on funds. They engaged John

Conway as their local agent. Upset at having been dumped by the Australian Eleven, Conway was willing to play hard in negotiating the gate share and fixtures. In previously unpublished letters in the possession of cricket historian Ronald Cardwell, Conway can be seen pressing the NSWCA's John Gibson and Phil Sheridan for fixtures. When they fobbed him off with evasions and excuses, Conway turned to flattery, talking of Sydney as the colonies' best 'show town' and stroking the administrators' experience in 'show business'.

He got what he wanted — two Combined Australia–England matches in Sydney, and two in Melbourne — but only after encountering hostility over Ulyett, whom the Australians did not want to play after his behaviour during the 1879 riot and his refusal to play them in England. In August 1881, Gibson asked for Ulyett to be replaced. Conway replied that it was probably too late, but that he had told Lillywhite about 'the feeling there is about Ulyett in the colonies'. Lillywhite, he said, had replied that it would be 'folly' to bring out a team without the Yorkshireman. Cricket in the colonies had improved, and early defeats by Victoria and NSW would doom the tour to financial failure. 'In their desire to witness high class cricket,' Conway wrote, 'the Australia public will with their usual forgiving spirit overlook Ulyett's action as they passed over that of Midwinter and Coulthard. Ulyett no doubt acted unwisely but it is well known he was merely an instrument in the hands of Hornby and Lord Harris.'

He pointed out that the 1878 and 1880 Australian Elevens had not wanted anything to do with Midwinter after his defection to Gloucestershire, but subdued their hostility when he came to Australia to play in 1880–81. On Ulyett, he pressed hard: 'If any members of the last Australian Eleven refuse to play against him they will not only act in a childish spirit but they will irreparably reopen the breach between English and Australian cricketers ... It depends entirely on the treatment the English professionals will receive whether the next visit of the Australians to England is a success or not.' Without Ulyett the main matches would have 'no value whatsoever' as 'the Players of England without the Yorkshireman would be like a representation of Hamlet with the omission of the character of the Prince of Denmark'.

With Ulyett on board, the Englishmen contested half a dozen country matches, and one against a makeshift NSW, before settling in Melbourne for a game against a Victorian team with all its stars.

A weighty sporting and social occasion, it was hugely attended. Robert Twopenny wrote in *Town Life in Australia*: 'In Australia, not to be interested in cricket amounts almost to a social crime.' The 20,000 crowd on the second day was, said Shaw, 'the largest number seen at a cricket contest anywhere in Australia up to that date'. For the first part of the match, the locals were happy. Victoria's 251 was an overwhelming first-innings target for England, who were unable to cope with the cut of Palmer and Allan. Following on 105 runs behind, England fared better in their second innings thanks to a fine unbeaten 80 by Arthur Shrewsbury, the young Notts batsman fast becoming one of England's finest. Shaw, meanwhile, was given out by Lillywhite. 'Good gracious, Jim,' he cried, indicating all the difficulties that arose with the appointment of a 'team' travelling umpire who was also a promoter of the tour, 'you've lost us the match!'

A storm, gumming up the MCG wicket, meant the Victorians would have to fight to score the required 94. There were doubts about the players' ability to finish the game by the end of the third day. Shaw wrote: 'We had arranged to sail for Adelaide at one o'clock on the morning of the last day of the match, December 20th. The Victorians were very keen on having the game fought to an issue, and naturally they thought they stood an excellent chance of scoring an easy victory. I consulted Lillywhite, and we came to the conclusion that it would be wise to avoid any cause for unpleasantness if we could do so. We therefore told the Victorians that if they could arrange to have the departure of our boat delayed, we were prepared to stay and play the match out.'

To their surprise the ship was delayed, 'an illustration of the remarkable keenness manifested in cricket in Melbourne even in those days'.

It wasn't just keenness to see a result. Massive sums had been wagered on a Victorian win both before and during the game. As England's most successful bowler of the summer, Ted Peate, wrote, 'The bookmakers were standing up doing business as if they were in Tattersall's ring.'

To Shaw's astonishment, during the last day the bookmakers were so sure of a Victorian victory that they offered 30/1 against England.

'It came to our knowledge that there was a great deal of betting on the result of the match', he wrote later. 'Most extravagant odds were offered on the Victorian team, in spite of the fact that the weather was wet, and there was a possibility of the home batsmen having to play on a sticky wicket, to which they were unaccustomed.'

One of his players was the mercurial Midwinter, an Englishman again since the 1878 'kidnapping', for the moment, anyway; as the *Bulletin* put it, 'In Australia he plays as an Englishman; in England, as an Australian and he is always a credit to himself and his country, whichever that may be.'

Midwinter, who scored 1 and 0 in the match and only bowled a handful of overs in Victoria's first innings, reported the odds to Shaw.

'It was a very rare thing for me to have a bet, but I said I was prepared to have 1 pound on those terms, and Midwinter accepted 30 to 1 pound for me, and the other members of the team invested 1 pound each on the same absurdly extravagant terms. This was after we had followed on, and before our second innings was completed.'

But Midwinter had a bigger bombshell: he said he had been asked by Ulyett and John Selby to participate in a fix. He said, according to Shaw, that they 'had received a promise of a "Bet" of 100 pounds to nothing on the Victorians winning'. William Scotton, the Nottinghamshire stonewaller, was also allegedly involved. Midwinter said Selby had asked him to join in, but when Ulyett overheard the conversation he threatened to 'jowl' the pair.

Shaw gave Midwinter's allegation 'no credence' until on the field he 'came to the conclusion that the rumours were not without foundation'. As the Victorians chased the 94 runs – a task which, on the sticky dog, was troubling them considerably – some Englishmen kept dropping chances, and took one by accident, Shaw said. 'A remarkably curious circumstance was that after one ridiculously easy catch had been dropped, a batsman was out by the ball going up inside the fieldsman's arm and sticking there – not, I have reason to think, with the catcher's intentional aid.' This was most likely Selby's catch of Boyle for a top-scoring 43, which turned out to be the matchwinning dismissal. Shaw gave neither Midwinter nor Ulyett the ball.

'Whatever the scheme actually was,' Shaw said, 'it failed.' England won by 18 runs in one of the great comebacks, providing the first instance in Australia of a side winning after being forced to follow on. There was drama right to the end, when Victoria's last man, Allan, was apparently run out. Peate said: '[Dick] Pilling had taken the bails off, and was walking away, considering the match over, when the umpire called, "Not out!" Luckily, Barlow bowled him in the same over.'

Peate would later repeat a rumour that the bookmakers had paid the steamship company £300 to delay the boat. Sam Grimwood, a Halifax expatriate watching the match, took the odds on England 'and did so well that he finished up by rushing down to the boat and presenting us with a £10 note each. The bookmakers were very badly hit by the result of the match. Certain of their schemes failed, much to the satisfaction of most of us.'

A contented Shaw said: 'The modest sovereign which I and two others put on at odds of 30 to 1, odds that were duly paid to us, were but straws showing the direction of the betting wind. I should not have accepted such a bet at all had it not been with the hope of showing that cricket is not a game on which extravagant odds can be laid. I have only made two bets on cricket in my life, and this was one of them.'

But Shaw still had to investigate Midwinter's accusation against Ulyett, Selby and Scotton. 'It was Midwinter who informed me of the offer made, and he it was who was afterwards maltreated, a quarrel taking place on ship-board. The players implicated in the unsavoury business are, as I have said, both dead, and it is but justice to their memory to say that both indignantly denied the allegation made, and that though my co-managers and myself made every effort to probe the facts and find out who it was that had offered the alleged bribes, we were unable to obtain any information to which credence could be given, and the whole matter was therefore allowed to drop.'

Or not entirely. After the tour, in April 1882, the *Scotsman* reported that the Nottinghamshire and Yorkshire committees had received letters saying two of their professionals (Selby and Ulyett respectively) tried to get a third (Midwinter) into the scam and, when he refused, 'assaulted' and 'seriously maltreated him'. While no findings were made against Ulyett or Selby, the latter never played for England again, and the *Australasian* reported piously that the 1881–82 English team's general behaviour did not help them when the rumours got about: 'Professional cricketers who keep late hours, make bets to some amount, and are seen drinking champagne at a late hour with members of the betting ring when they ought to be in bed, must not be surprised if people put a wrong construction on their conduct. They have only themselves to blame.'

Shaw, the honest pro and manager, continued to put a positive spin on things, reporting warmly on 'Happy Jack' Ulyett's play and character. He did not appear to harbour any suspicions that the Yorkshireman was habitually corrupt.

After the controversial match, and a drawn first Test, England's tour went swiftly downhill. They battled their way through New Zealand, and only won one more first-class game (the return fixture against Victoria). The four-Test series went Australia's way 2–0. Altham says the Englishmen 'found the playing conditions most primitive, and the outspokenness of the local critics only equalled by their ignorance'.

The local critics were cocky, patriotic cheerleaders for their champions. Murdoch's 321 against Victoria, the highest first-class score in Australia until the 1920s, gave them plenty to boast about, and Horan and McDonnell scored centuries in the Tests, while Palmer and Garrett excelled with the ball.

The Englishmen straggled home in three different groups. Possibly ill-feeling over the Victorian game lingered. Scotton and one of his teammates were also involved in a dispute over a woman. Cricket tours always foment division, but they never look worse than when the key matches are lost.

'FAMOUS FOR ALL TIME'

As early as 1881, the Melbourne lawyer and cricket enthusiast Charles Beal had been organising an Australian tour of England in 1882. The happy ending to the 1880 tour, and its financial success, had transformed suspicion into enthusiasm, and now the cash-hungry counties were lining up in welcome.

An Australian Eleven's status – amateur or professional? – remained a vexed issue. In 1881, the columnist 'Umpire' called on the VCA to decree the players' status. But it wasn't that simple.

In the Australian colonies, where cricket had evolved quickly and recently, if an entertainment raised money, the entertainers believed they were entitled to share in it. They were nearly all amateurs, in that they didn't play cricket full-time for a living, yet they also took gate money in the style of English professional Elevens.

This hybrid status confused the English greatly. The teams of Gregory and Murdoch had found, to their chagrin, that the professionals regarded them as of their own class, unfairly given access to the bars, lounges and privileges of the gentlemen; meanwhile the amateurs were happy to invite them into such premises *as long as* they didn't take gate money. In truth, the Australian Elevens were a third kind of cricketer – democratic entertainers – which the English class system didn't yet know how to deal with. *Lillywhite's Cricketer's Companion* opined: 'If the Australians did not make cricket their profession in their native land, they most decidedly did when they came to this country, for all who had anything to do with them soon found out how keen they were about "pounds, shillings and pence".'

Beal, cleverly, reverse-engineered a compromise for the Eleven of 1882. With 38 games planned, all first-class, it was to be the first fully-sanctioned tour. To keep the English happy, Beal accepted 50 per cent of the outer-ground gate money – not grandstand money – which was lower than the 75 per cent of all receipts taken by the 1880 Eleven and the 80–90 per cent from 1878. Having made the goodwill gesture of asking for a lower cut, Beal now had to find some acceptable status for them.

On the earlier tours, Beal wrote, 'An endeavour was made to stamp our men as pros. When it was decided that a team should go in 1882, it was determined that things should be altered, and that instead of the players pooling any money towards expenses, a dozen or so of cricket enthusiasts should contribute £100 each, and thus form the fund for expenses.'

He wrote to Henry Perkins, the MCC secretary, informing him of the new terms, 'and asked him to put the matter before Lord's committee with a view of ascertaining definitely whether that body would receive the team as amateurs'.

He told Perkins about the team members' jobs – proving they were not 'cricket professionals' in the English sense – 'and informed him that on the termination of the tour the promoters proposed to divide whatever surplus there might be after repaying themselves amongst the members of the team in equal shares, as recompense for loss of time, salaries, &c. Of course, if a loss occurred, well the promoters would suffer. I received a cable telling me Lord's would gladly receive us as amateurs, and then we arranged the tour. The team would not have gone had Lord's cable been different.'

The investors included wealthy businessmen who travelled with the team: Arthur Blake of the Melbourne legal firm of Blake and Riggall, the Sydney businessman Frederick Dangar, Edmund Parkes, Superintendent of the Bank of Australia, Caleb Peacock, an Adelaide businessman and James Cooper Stewart, of the solicitors Malleson, England and Stewart. In March 1882 Beal drew up a deed of partnership, under which the first £1500 of profit went to the investors, the rest shared between the players, except for Alick Bannerman, who would travel, as on the earlier tours, for a set fee. The signatories also agreed that 'inebriety' or 'misconduct' would draw a fine of five pounds for the first offence, ten pounds for the second, and dismissal for the third.

The main players selected themselves: Murdoch, Blackham, Horan, Bannerman, McDonnell, Bonnor, Spofforth, Boyle, Garrett (who had finished his legal studies and was available again) and Palmer. Massie was picked on the basis of his strong hitting when he was able to take time out of his banking career. South Australia's rock-hard young all-rounder, postal worker George Giffen, had come into the Australian team during the home series and, in his first Test innings, put on, with Horan, the first century partnership in international cricket. Giffen gave an insight into how becoming one of the 'Eleven' had become the aspiration of all cricketers:

'I began to indulge in day-dreams, and to wonder whether there was any possibility of my being selected ... Shortly after I had concluded my [first Test] innings, I was strolling about the members' reserve, when Murdoch asked me if I would accompany the Australian Eleven to England, if the selectors chose me. Had a thunderbolt struck me I would not have been more astonished, although I had so often built castles in the air about a trip to the Old Country. However, I found my tongue at last, and it was, of course, to signify assent; but I was very anxious until the team was finally selected.'

Acknowledging the heavier schedule, the Eleven, which had grown to Twelve in 1880, would now be Thirteen. Ted Evans, the NSW bowler many thought superior even to Spofforth, was invited. But, the *Sydney Mail* said, 'Evans dreads the sea voyage, and apart from that, family reasons act as a bar to his joining the team.' His employer, the NSW Government, offered him leave, but he stayed at home due to his wife's poor health, which made him responsible for the care of his five young children. The *Mail* said it was a pity, for 'there can be no doubt that if he did [tour], his performances with the ball would open the eyes of cricketers at home'.

When Evans pulled out, Midwinter — who but Midwinter? — offered his services, but some players were worried about his loyalties if Grace should try to poach him again. His offer was rebuffed, but later in the year he would declare an aim to resettle in Australia for good.

The last chosen, then, was Sammy Jones, a young sporting all-rounder from Sydney, described by *Boyle & Scott* as a 'good change bowler and fine field' but 'rather an ungainly batsman'.

On 17 March, Murdoch's Thirteen left Adelaide on the SS *Assam*, taking the more expensive but faster route via Suez. McDonnell, suffering from sunstroke and possibly flu, was taken aboard on a stretcher. His health did not improve as expected, and a game of deck cricket saw him bedridden again.

The crossing of the Great Australian Bight was rough, Horan and Bannerman becoming so seasick they ate only one apple each in a 24-hour period. Teammates taunted them by offering rich delicacies. Bonnor was bruised when thrown against a bulkhead, but 32 dozen plates were not so hardy, being smashed before the *Assam* rounded Cape Leeuwin.

The routines of shipboard life, with their concomitant bonding effect, were well established from 1878 and 1880. There was fishing in King George's Sound, Boyle catching five dozen, and colourful stopovers in Point de Galle (Ceylon), Port Said and Malta. Regular night-time concerts showcased the comic talents of Murdoch and Beal, playing Bones and Tambo in a minstrel show. Jones impressed with his tenor voice, and Blackham sang 'See My Grave's Kept Clean'. Spofforth appeared on stage as Mephistopheles, Murdoch as a monk and Bannerman as a naval officer. Horan said Bonnor appeared 'as a Roman soldier of ye olden time, but, instead of looking the character, he gave one the idea of a man who had jumped out of bed in a hurry, and thrown a seedy blanket over his shoulders. His appearance was laughable in the extreme.'

Giffen, one of the new boys, loved every minute. The original 'Mr Cricket', soon to gain a reputation as Australia's answer to W.G., Giffen said: 'What a delightful voyage we had in the *Assam!* Rough enough it was at first, but when one is once accustomed to the rolling of the boat, what pleasanter mode of travelling can one imagine than sailing on the bosom of the mighty deep?'

He did not mention the controversy of the voyage, Spofforth being challenged to a duel by an insulted Frenchman named Thomas. The reason for the duel was not made public, and indeed it wasn't until 53 years later that Jones, in a letter, revealed Murdoch's clever way of settling the matter before anyone got hurt.

'Spofforth had the choice of weapons, and when the challenger formally issued the challenge, Murdoch, Spofforth's second, named "buckets" as the blood-letting weapons. These mysterious duelling weapons had not come within the ken of the French and, consequently, the matter was dropped.'

Since the 1880 tour, Spofforth had been something of an enigma in domestic cricket. In August 1881, the *Bulletin* reported, he had almost killed himself on a horse at a family farm in the NSW countryside.

'Spofforth, the Demon bowler, narrowly escaped death the other day, near Cassilis [outside Mudgee]. He was mounting a fresh horse, and having his gun in one hand and pipe in another, was unable to control him, when he suddenly dashed off. Spofforth was half mounted and was by degrees getting into his seat, when the horse collided violently with another throwing the Demon very heavily, severely injuring the side of his face, breaking a bone in the right jaw, and apparently a bone in the left wrist. Spoff is recovering!'

After the incident, Spofforth remained in the bush and did not play in the intercolonial or the first three Test matches in 1881–82. The press chided him for 'wasting his sweetness on an up-country station'. The *Australasian* voiced the anxieties of a nation: 'What has become of our demon Freddy?'

Spofforth's biographer, Richard Cashman, suggests that he was probably extending his rest in knowledge of the ardours of an England tour. He also enjoyed keeping the press guessing. But the press, Cashman says, found 'a simpler and more convenient explanation': 'the hero had become big-headed, frequently behaving in an erratic and eccentric manner. Whether [or not] this was the case, there is no doubt that Spofforth was well aware of his prima donna status. He knew that his presence in the Australian side was so vital he could enter and exit at a time of his own choosing.'

That was all very well — as long as he survived the voyage.

The last act of the voyage on the *Assam* was performed by Bonnor, challenged by another passenger for 100 sovereigns to prove his boast that he could throw a ball 120 yards. When they reached Plymouth, Bonnor threw a ball from the ship onto the first park he saw, and won his wager.

Following established routines, Murdoch's team stayed at the Tavistock Hotel in Covent Garden and practised at Mitcham under

Southerton's hand. 'Don't I just remember the lunches we used to have at Southerton's Hotel!' Giffen wrote. 'What beautiful slices of roast beef and what foaming tankards of bitter!'

They also went sightseeing in London, but they had not played much in the capital on previous tours and were less than impressed. Horan said 'the unanimous opinion of the time is that the said city is much too big. During this stroll several members of the team lost themselves in the maze of streets, but the ever courteous London constable invariably put them on the right road to Covent Garden.'

The opening games were first-class, eleven-a-side fixtures against Oxford University, Sussex, the Orleans Club, Surrey and Cambridge University. Charles Pardon, a *Bell's Life* journalist embedded with the team, gave an insight into daily life: a three-hour train ride from London to Oxford, luncheon at the Clarendon Hotel, a visit to the Christ Church cricket ground 'as a matter of course', dinner with 'a small Sunday evening college wine', and finally 'a fire lighted in the smoke room of the "Clarendon" and [talking] cricket till bed time'.

The 1882 Australians immediately showed themselves worthy of their program. Massie opened affairs with an unbeaten 206 at Oxford, the highest debut innings in England before Bradman, even penetrating a stacked off-side boundary. Horan said: 'It is almost needless to say that our hero on returning to the pavilion met with a ready and spontaneous burst of applause, and it is also equally needless to observe that the bright eyes of the ladies in the reserve – and they were not a few – were bent upon the said hero as he entered the pavilion gate with his blushing honours, or rather runs, thick upon him.'

Murdoch's team was well-oiled. Jones wrote that 'there were "no restrictions to a 'modest quencher'". I shall always remember breakfasting at Magdalen College before our first match of the 1882 tour. Champagne cup was sent round with monotonous regularity, with old Oxford Ale as a sort of topper to the function.' Jones asked a waiter for 'Starkey's Stone Ginger Beer', a Sydney brand that he didn't realise was unknown in England, and earned himself the nickname 'Starkey'.

At Sussex, Murdoch bettered Massie, hitting 286. Sussex offered him membership. He accepted – a decade later. But in 1882 the devils of throwing and bad umpiring were returning to dog another tour. Murdoch protested against the bowling of William Blackman, who, Horan said, 'throws in an undisguised manner'. Pardon agreed: 'I don't suppose the Sussex amateur intentionally and knowingly throws, but I have no doubt in my own mind that he does not bowl fairly.' Reverend Frederick Greenfield, captain of Sussex, refused to take Blackman off, and Murdoch put his head down to bat the county into submission. Australia finished with 643, a signpost to how 'scientific' batting was gaining hold in the Australian team. Blackman's fate was to die of consumption in Melbourne three years later at the age of 22, a few months after migrating for the sake of his health.

Murdoch was building on the advances he had made in 1880, tormenting bowlers with his dog shot, a glance he played beneath an upraised front leg. Off the field he was known as a shooter, a dressing-room wit, a drinker and a diplomat. Charles Fry, who would play with him at Sussex, wrote that he was 'a square-round – the double term applies – powerful, well knit figure, as active as most men half his age and every bit as keen; a man who would enjoy a Klondike or a Mansion House dinner ... His spirit would refuse to be unfortunate; his body scorns incapacity for meat and drink. No wonder he led Australia well in the old days – a fine Odysseus to meet our mighty bearded Ajax.'

The mighty bearded Ajax had had mumps in the spring, and his diminished size shocked the Australians in their third match, with an England-strength Orleans Club at Twickenham. So seriously did the Englishmen now take these Australians that the Orleans game was treated as a Test trial. Australia had much the worse of a draw salvaged by another Murdoch century.

Taking the field for the first time in their tour caps of crimson, black and yellow, the colours of the 96th Regiment, the investors' choice,

Australia defeated Surrey. The majestic Studd brothers of Cambridge University then crushed the Australians. In what A.A. Thomson calls a 'near-classic age' of English names which 'were to remain legends for half a century', Charles Studd was 'the golden lad'. The three brothers combined for 297 runs against 'the lean, grim fighters who later tumbled English cricket in the dust and reduced it to Ashes'. Charles also took 5/64 in the first innings and hit the winning runs in the second after John and George had led off with a century opening stand.

If these Australians enjoyed a respect and prestige denied to earlier tours, they were still not above cavilling. There was Murdoch's objection to Blackman at Hove, and now, after being given out to a ball which 'did not touch his bat, but simply grazed the batsman's shirt sleeve at the elbow', Horan complained about H.H. Stephenson's umpiring at Cambridge. Spofforth was given out stumped, 'a very erroneous decision, and admitted to be so by the Cambridge men themselves'.

Australia had a bigger concern than umpiring or throwing. As *Wisden* reported on Studd's Cambridge innings, he was 'particularly severe on Spofforth'. A 'facetious young gentleman' observed that Spofforth 'wasn't going to be the prima donna on this tour'. Spofforth didn't like it, but the taunter had some evidence: the Demon had only taken eight wickets in five games at nearly 40 apiece. On previous tours, by this stage, he had taken more than 50 wickets.

Spofforth was stung into life. Morose after their loss to Cambridge, the Australians boarded their train at 7.40 pm and did not arrive in Manchester until 2.30 am. After an understandably late breakfast at the Waterloo Hotel, they had to go to Old Trafford to play the champion county, Lancashire. Summoned by adversity, Spofforth took 6/48 and 6/109 in a four-wicket win. The Demon was back; Australia would not lose another match until mid-August.

They were happier when they won. Horan wrote: 'It affords me much pleasure to say that from start to finish the [Lancashire] match was played as cricket should always be played – that is to say, without the slightest sign of bickering or unpleasantness — and our fellows, one and all, agree that we shall have very pleasant matches indeed if we continue to meet such genial and thorough cricketers as we have met here in this great city of Manchester.'

The schedule was designed partly to repay favours from 1880. The Australians' loyal friends in Yorkshire and Gloucestershire were rewarded with five and two games respectively. Rae comments: 'These were valuable favours. The Australians were the biggest draw in English cricket and, barring rain, any match in which they played was guaranteed to generate healthy revenues.'

Bonnor showed that kindness stopped at the boundary, whacking five sixes in his second innings of 35 in the first of the games against Yorkshire, at Bradford. Sixes, not fives — they had to fly out of the premises, not just over the rope. Giffen spoke of the team's relief: 'We often used to wish that Bonnor would not get the idea into his head that he could, if he chose, bat as scientifically as any one. This was generally after he had heard some one say, "Oh, Bonnor is nothing but a slogger." Then he would go in and play his "sweetly pretty" game, and sometimes last a while too; but it was painful to watch a giant of six feet and a half playing the barndoor game when we knew that if he chose, and got going, he could pulverise the bowling and disorganise the field.'

Nottingham was the nursery of English cricket professionalism, the home of William Clarke, George Parr, Richard Daft, Shaw, Morley, Shrewsbury, Billy Barnes, the Gunn brothers, Selby, Scotton, and later Harold Larwood and Bill Voce. In 1881, the Notts professionals had led a strike. They took a principled position against the discrimination exercised by amateurs. Bundled in with this was an opinion that the Australians were having their cake and eating it too, getting gentlemen's privileges while being paid more than the pros. Nottinghamshire had defended their opinions on the field, too, beating both the 1878 and 1880 teams.

Professionals earned £5 a home match, £6 away, £10 for a representative, with a pound bonus per win. The annual wage for a good pro came to little more than an unskilled labourer's — which is what many cricketers became during the winters. The Nottingham strike, a direct result of Australian tours, had failed, however, to win any increases. 'Thereafter,' concludes Kynaston, 'the game settled down into a daily ritual of class-based apartheid.'

Australia's match in Nottingham started badly. The night before, the team had endured a four-hour train trip from Bradford, not arriving until 1 am. Their hotel had not kept their reservations, and it was 3 am before they were settled in another, so, as Pardon wrote with some understatement, 'the Colonists could not expect to be as fit as usual'. They were lucky to bat first, but at the luncheon interval the Notts secretary Captain Jack 'Hellfire' Holden refused the Australians lunch in the dining room, as, in his opinion, they were professionals. He suggested they buy beer from the tent outside, along with the Notts players, but, said Pardon, 'there was no possibility of obtaining anything reasonable to eat. They had, consequently, to do without.' Bonnor 'became so angry he had to be restrained', according to Cashman.

The *Bulletin* reported that Holden took out a cigar and said: 'Will some Englishman give me a light?' Bonnor thundered: 'I can tell you, sir, I am as much an Englishman as you or any gentleman present; I can trace my family back for six generations, and perhaps you cannot do more.' Then he went out and launched a huge hit over Parr's Tree.

The Australians won, took £238 in profit, and got an apology from the Notts committee.

Seven wins in seven matches followed. At Bramall Lane in Sheffield, the crowd honoured them with nicknames. Bonnor was 'Jumbo', Bannerman 'Little Jumbo' and 'Quicklime', Horan 'Features', Palmer 'Ribs', Blackham 'Darkie', and Spofforth 'Spider'.

There were always quibbles over umpiring, and the Australians accused Derbyshire's William Mycroft of chucking, but Murdoch's teams expressed their dissent more acceptably than Gregory's. Giffen explained a general tolerance: 'We have had, I say unhesitatingly, to put up with many very bad decisions, and I know that at first we used to entertain strong opinions on the matter, but I think that, after further acquaintance with most of the umpires with whom we had to deal, we came to the conclusion that, though they were naturally enough influenced in time of great doubt in favour of their countrymen, they were always conscientious.'

The eleventh match of the tour, against the Gentlemen of England at the Oval in late June, was, said Boyle, 'looked upon as a test match'. Giffen stepped into the spotlight with 8/49, delighting the leading English umpire, Bob Thoms, who exclaimed, 'Beautiful ball, my boy, would have beaten anyone', and 'Splendid, splendid! Stick to it – great future!' Once, when Giffen appealed for lbw, Thoms got the giggles, wandered towards mid-off, and said 'Not out, not out. The ball broke a furlong!'

Thoms was also unusual in that he explained decisions, Giffen said. 'It is much nicer for [the bowler] to know that, even though he had made a mistake, it would have been a close thing, than to have to be content with a sharp "No", uttered in such a tone as to make him feel that in appealing he had committed a crime.'

The Gentlemen, at this time, thanks largely to Grace, the Studds and Steel, had the better of the Players. Australia's win over them, by an innings and one run, was a significant milestone, Horan said. 'Before the match it was confidently predicted that we had not the ghost of a show … but if you go by results we had much more than the ghost of a show; in fact, we had the whole body and substance of a show. And now that we have won so easily, letters are appearing in the papers to the effect that the Gentlemen team was weak and not nearly representative. We, however, can smile at this sort of thing …' He recalled the innings loss to the Gentlemen in 1878. 'What about the whirligig of time and its revenges?'

Speaking of time and its changes, the Australians were keenly aware of improvements in their social status. They did not just see themselves as a cricket team, but as representatives of the success of colonisation itself. In their match at Northampton, the mayor spoke at lunch and, said Horan, 'remembered the time when New South Wales and Van Diemen's Land were mentioned only in places associated with the worst type of convict life; but now all that had passed away, and the Australian colonies were sending forth men capable of holding their own against all-comers, not only in athletics, but also in that which is far more important in the development of a nation – namely, intellectual power'.

Progress! Civilisation! Lord Harris, and Lord's, hadn't yet advanced. The MCC again refused a gate share for any match Australia played at Lord's. Instead the club offered a set fee of £210, which would be lower than at nearly all other venues. Had Gregory been the leader, Australia would not have played. Murdoch was a compromiser, though, and his Eleven played Middlesex and the MCC in successive matches at headquarters in July, winning the former and drawing the latter when Charles Studd flayed them for another century.

The unbeaten run – which raised the 1882 team into the pantheon shared with the teams of 1902, 1921 and 1948 – continued into August, but understandably the punishing schedule was draining the players. At Liverpool, Spofforth strained his thigh and missed the next three games. They won two, over Grace's Gloucestershire and Harris's Kent – who went to conspicuous trouble in decorating Canterbury with banners saying 'Let Cricket Flourish' and 'Welcome to the Australians' – but succumbed to the Players' attack of Peate, Ulyett and Morley at the Oval. Although Spofforth returned against a combined (but not Test-strength) Eleven of England at Derby, Horan remarked: 'The hard work that we have been doing since the 14 May last is beginning to tell on certain members of the team. Giffen has given way in the knees. Palmer is very much prostrated, and Garrett is fast becoming stale and done up.'

A narrow loss followed to Cambridge Past & Present at Portsmouth, where Bonnor hit 66 in half an hour and splintered the sightscreen, but the Australian crankiness in defeat re-emerged. When given out,

Bonnor 'expressed his mind pretty freely to the umpire'. A decision against Bannerman 'was strongly commented upon by Murdoch. He asked [umpire] Wrigley why he had given Bannerman out, and the reply was – For a catch at the wickets. Afterwards Wrigley, in the hearing of more than one of our men, said to Major Luard, the hon secretary to the Portsmouth Club, that he had given Bannerman out leg before wicket,' Horan said. 'If the umpiring had been as it should have been, we would have won the match easily.'

Stale, injured, form and good temper slipping, the Australians were hardly in the mood for the biggest match of the tour: against England at the Oval. An unnamed player wrote in the *Sydney Mail*: 'I am very sorry to say that the incessant toil has interfered sadly with the physique of our men, and if we win Australia will have cause to be proud of her broken-down champions. I wish heartily that this great match had taken place about two months ago instead of now, when the men are all knocked up.'

Spofforth trained for the match, for the first time in his life, but they were nowhere near the peak they had enjoyed between June and early August.

The story of the match has been told so often, by players, witnesses, historians, even poets and mock-obituarists, that there is no hope of adding to it by repetition. The skeletal facts are enough for the imaginative cricket mind to feel the tension. On an Oval wicket that was best when drenched and diabolical when drying, Australia collapsed for 63. Spofforth cut England down for 101, a lead that was wiped away by Massie's 55, the only individual score in the match to exceed 32. Murdoch, unluckily run out, helped Australia to 122 and a fourth-innings target of 85 for England. '85 to Win', as John Masefield's poem had it, captures the dread that hung over England's pursuit. Grace and

Ulyett seemed to have it, then Spofforth and Boyle reeled them in and, as they had at Lord's in 1878, squeezed the nerve out of the best batsmen in cricket. Reginald Brooks's mock obituary in the *Sporting Times* would be the first part of the diptych that made up the legend of the Ashes.

One reason the Oval Test holds such a fabled place is the strength of the England team. In all frankness, no England team that toured Australia could be considered representative until 1891–92, Grace's first trip as a Test player, and no full-strength England team *ever* came to Australia before the First World War. The 1880 England team had been weakened by the professionals' boycott. The Oval match of 1882 was, then, the first true contest of the full strength of the two cricketing countries. As Altham comments, England's 'batting seemed overwhelmingly strong'. England's bowling had no great pace, as Morley was injured and Harris, a firm activist against throwing, would not choose Lancashire's pacy John Crossland. Pardon remarked that 'his delivery is considered unfair by many of our leading cricketers, several of whom have openly told me in correspondence or conversation that in their opinion Crossland is a thrower'.

That said, an attack of Barlow, Ulyett, Peate, Studd, Barnes and Steel was the pick of the combined Gentlemen and Players.

After Australia's first-innings collapse, uncomplimentary remarks were uttered in Spofforth's hearing. He was already angry about his teammates' batting – 'I might speak for myself, and say I was disgusted, and thought we should have made at least 250' – but, like all great fast bowlers, he found a more productive channel for his passions.

Spofforth bowled heroically in England's first innings, during which there was an interesting and provocative incident. While Spofforth was bowling, England's captain, 'Monkey' Hornby, was backing up too far at the non-striker's end. Spofforth warned him: 'I could stump you now – you're out of your ground.'

Hornby replied: 'Yes ... but surely that's not your game, is it?'

'Well, no.'

It is not often Australian teams were able to occupy the moral high ground, but Spofforth's restraint would come to seem most sportsmanlike. Umpire Luke Greenwood, who umpired for the Australians on the 1878, 1880 and 1882 tours, later said: 'They always behaved like gentlemen to me, and I never saw teams work better together.'

The second day brought the incident that ignited the match. Murdoch, battling with Sammy Jones to eke out some kind of lead, popped a ball from Steel towards square leg. Umpire Greenwood takes up the story:

'The Hon. A. Lyttelton, who was keeping wicket for England, ran for it and threw it in to Peate, who was at short slip. The run was made safely enough, and Peate made no attempt to take up the ball. Mr Jones thereupon walked out of his ground to pat the wicket where the ball had risen at the previous delivery, and W.G. Grace coolly picked up the ball, walked to the wicket, dislodged the bails, and cried, "How's that?" Thoms, who was the umpire appealed to, gave him "out", and out Mr Jones had to go. Mr Murdoch, on seeing what had occurred, remarked, "That's very sharp practice, W.G."; and to this day I think it was. Had I been appealed to I should not have given Jones out, for the ball was to all intents and purposes dead, and there had been no attempt to make a second run.'

Here was one of those grey areas, contained in those bland words, 'to all intents and purposes'. Grace could, and did, point to Law 29, which said: 'After the ball shall have been finally settled in the wicket keeper's or bowler's hand, it shall be "dead".' As it had gone to neither the wicketkeeper nor the bowler, nor even Peate, the man near the stumps, Grace believed it wasn't dead.

Horan, watching from the pavilion, wrote: 'Thoms, the umpire, it appears said: "If you claim it, sir, it is out."' Jones, of course had to walk to the pavilion, and so displeased were many of the lookers on at W.G.'s action that they groaned, and hissed him not only at this time but when he was returning to the pavilion at the completion of our innings. In strict cricket no doubt Jones was out, but I do not think it rebounds much to any man's credit to endeavour to win a match by resorting to what might not inaptly be termed sharp practice.'

Horan implied that Thoms hesitated over the decision, giving Grace the chance to back out – 'If you claim it, sir' – but Thoms later told Pardon that Grace's action was within the law and 'denied having said anything more than the necessary word "Out!" Thoms told me the point was a very simple one, the ball was not dead, and the batsman was run out. If Grace, instead of going up to the wicket and putting off the bails, had thrown at the stumps and missed them, the batsman could, and probably would, have run again, and then every one would have said what a smart thing the Australians had done. Jones did a foolish, thoughtless thing in going out of his ground, and he paid the penalty of his rashness. Grace did what he was perfectly justified in doing, and there can be no doubt the run out was legal and fair.'

But there is law, and there is cricket – or so we would like to think. 'It was strict cricket but it was taking advantage of a young player's thoughtlessness,' Pardon said. 'I personally cannot say I approve of what Grace did ... I am sorry that anything should have been done to give any one a chance of saying with any basis of truth, however small, that a member of the picked eleven of England played a discourteous game.'

It was the type of thing Grace did on a weekly basis for 50 years. He was the gamesman's gamesman. He got away with it, because cricket needed him so badly, because his competitive intensity had something disarmingly lovable about it for those who knew him, and because, as Kynaston writes, quoting Shakespeare, 'Nice customs as ever, curtsey to great kings.'

What Grace had no hope of realising was that something he might do without a second thought in a match for Gloucestershire or the United South was given a whole new context in this new game, this *Test cricket*.

What of Jones, the victim? He was a young man struggling through an unfulfilling tour. *Wisden* said 'the affair left Jones without ill-will'. The almanack's account of the affair was mostly pro-Grace: 'after the excitement had cooled down a prominent member of the Australian Eleven admitted that he should have done the same thing had he been in Grace's place'. *Wisden* also approved of 'a gentleman in the pavilion' who had said, 'Jones ought to thank the champion for teaching him something.'

However, as Jones's biographer Max Bonnell reveals, 'students at Auckland Grammar School [where Jones became a teacher] recalled that Jones expressed "great admiration for Grace as a batsman but, even fifty years later, became quite emotional when describing how he had been dismissed". Somehow this account is more convincing than the rather sanitised version preferred by *Wisden*.'

The Australians were incandescent. They were representing their *country* – or what would become a country in 1901. Moreover, as Massie's son said in a letter 74 years later, Grace had not just taken advantage of Jones's inexperience, but had wilfully tricked him. When Grace had the ball, Jack Massie wrote, 'Jones nodded to Grace', thinking it was all right to leave his crease. Then 'to the amazement of the Australians, the umpire gave Jones out'. This added a new element: calculated deceit. 'I have no reason to doubt what my father told me,' Massie junior wrote; 'he was not given to romancing.'

According to Massie's letter, 'When the Australians were all out and the English team left the field, [Spofforth] went into the Englishmen's dressing-room and told Grace he was a bloody cheat and abused him in the best Australian vernacular for a full five minutes. As he flung out of the door his parting shot was, "This will lose you the match."'

Spofforth then returned to the Australian room and uttered his immortal line: 'This thing can be done.' If one verbal formula can knit together every bowler from Spofforth through to Warne and McGrath, it is those five words.

Spofforth later wrote, rather mildly, that the incident 'seemed to put fire into the Australians, and I do not suppose a team ever worked harder to win.'

The truth was far more colourful. Garrett wrote that the Australians 'were very much incensed' by what Grace had done. In Australia's dressing room, Spofforth said, 'I'm going to bowl at the old man. I'm going to frighten him out.'

Meanwhile, a sad event was taking place in the terraces. Forty-seven-year-old George Spendler, of Brook Street, Kennington, 'complained of feeling unwell', records Ralph Barker. 'He got up, and almost at once fell to the ground, suffering an internal haemorrhage. He was carried to a room next to the pavilion and examined by several doctors, but already poor George Spendler was dead.' That at least put paid to the theory that Spendler had a heart attack during the doomed England chase that was so suspense-filled that an Epsom bookmaker, Arthur Courcy, chewed halfway through the handle of his brother-in-law's umbrella, the English players opened their champagne early not to celebrate but to use as a 'tonic', the scorer's hand so trembled that he wrote Peate's name as 'Geese', and a Surrey member said to Charles Alcock, 'I don't know whether to cry or be sick.'

That immortally tense afternoon still lay ahead. Garrett said, 'When we went out in the field W.G. Grace came in first. Bonnor walked up to him and in the most dramatic manner said: "If we don't win the match, W.G., after what you have done, I won't believe there is a God in Heaven."'

Grace apparently 'gave as good as he got' verbally, and proceeded to play an innings of 32 that, Rae judges, was 'a splendid innings hovering on the brink of greatness. If the early afternoon had shown him at his belligerently competitive worst, the last hour had seen him at his incomparably competitive best.'

As Grace and Ulyett steered England towards victory, the ever-present bookmakers quoted Australia as 6/1 outsiders.

Then Spofforth took over. His final spell was mesmerising. Umpire Greenwood said: 'I never saw such excitement in my life as the match produced when one English crack after another fell.' With 19 to win and six wickets in hand, Lyttelton and Lucas were becalmed for maiden after maiden until Spofforth advised Bannerman to misfield intentionally and get Lyttelton on strike. Greenwood said facing Spofforth must have been like 'standing on the edge of a tomb'.

Inside the England rooms, C.I. Thornton reported later, the mood was far from confident. 'Charlie [Studd] was walking round the Pavilion with a blanket around him; Steel's teeth were all in a chatter; and Barnes's teeth would have been chattering if he had not left them at home.'

The Australians benefited from some strange captaincy from Hornby: Studd had scored three centuries against Australia that summer, but Hornby said, 'I want to keep you up my sleeve.'

As A.A. Thomson puts it: 'So Charlie went up the sleeve and, alas for England, stayed there.' Studd went in at number ten and didn't face a ball, watching aghast as Peate, who said he 'couldn't trust Mr Studd', took a swish and missed Boyle's match-concluding ball.

What seems truly modern in the match, as well as the action between Grace and the Australians over the Jones run-out, was the response at the end. After a few moments' silence, the crowd mobbed the Australians. The cult of celebrity was one of the Victorian Age's most durable inventions. Charlie Beal's mother grabbed the first player she saw, George Giffen, and embraced him. 'I am only speaking the truth,' Horan wrote, 'when I say that we were as heartily cheered as if we had won the match on an Australian ground before an Australian public.'

Grace, taciturn about his teammates – 'I left six men to get thirty odd runs and they could not get them' – was full of praise for the Australians. 'The shouting and the cheering that followed Spofforth's performance I shall remember to my dying day, as I shall remember the quick, hearty recognition over the length and breadth of the land that the best of Australian cricket was worthy of the highest position in the game.'

He did not comment on his running out Jones, or on how it motivated Australia. Rae concludes: 'It is impossible to know what would have happened had he not broken Jones's wicket. Jones might have batted on with Murdoch and taken the game out of England's reach; he might have been bowled next ball. What is certain is that by running him out in what the Australians thought an unsporting manner, Grace roused Spofforth to produce one of the greatest bowling efforts of all time.'

The winners did not hold a grudge against Grace. Thomson writes with poetic flourish: 'He never let the sun go down upon his wrath, though there were some colourful sunsets while it lasted.'

In victory the Australians were beside themselves, knowing instantly what this meant. They had never before beaten an England team that was, truly, the best. Spofforth 'stood on a table to make a speech, but I never remembered what I said'. Hornby produced a 'loving cup' for all to share, filled with champagne, lemon juice and seltzers. The Australians got into their carriages. Horan marvelled at 'how the crowd around our conveyance cheered us to the echo; how they almost took Spofforth off his legs in their desire to pat him on the back, how the ladies from the windows in the Kennington-road waved their handkerchiefs to us, and how all the way back to Tavistock the passers-by looked at us as if we had done something to make us famous for all time.'

Another tradition started in that Test match, which was the English press's relish for turning on their own. Brooks's 'obituary' was the least of it. *Lillywhite's Companion* noted: '"The Decadence of Cricket" was the theme of leader-writers in a hundred papers.' The *Sportsman* accused the English batsmen of playing like 'so many tailors' dummies'.

An amused Horan would later mark the fickleness of the commentary: 'The very papers which, in dealing with the first day's play, said, in effect, that the English cricketers were the noblest, and bravest, and the best; that, like the old guard of Napoleon, they would never know when they are beaten, now turn completely round, and, with very questionable taste, designate these same cricketers as a weak-kneed and pusillanimous lot, who shaped worse than eleven schoolboys. This seems to me both unfair and unmanly.'

He thought the Australians deserved more credit. Spofforth had, after all, been 'breaking the ball back quite six inches and towards the end of the second innings the ball probably broke as much as a foot'.

In *Bell's Life*, Charles Pardon agreed: 'Though England for the first time had to lower her colours to Australia at home, we were beaten by a magnificent eleven, before whose prowess it was no disgrace to fail.' Presciently, he added: 'At least three matches should have been arranged between England and Australia as one contest … can hardly be looked on as a real test.' This was one of the first uses of the term 'test' for a cricket match between England and Australia, and the first recognition of the necessity of a series. That is the legacy of the match of 1882, still the most history-making Test ever played.

Murdoch's Eleven played eight more matches, winning four, drawing three, and losing to the North of England at Manchester, where Crossland threw and Peate bowled them out twice. A late-tour highlight was at Scarborough versus I Zingari, where Bonnor hit 122 in less than two hours, including 20 off one four-ball over. He protested at having to bat with his polar opposite, Bannerman, whom he didn't like running with. 'Catch me going in first with Lord Alec again? First it's "Come on, Bon, are you asleep?" Then "Go back, you fool!" And when you've done everything he's called for, he'll come half-way down the pitch to read the Riot Act at you!'

The pair put on 167, and Bannerman made two fewer runs than Bonnor in *five* more hours of batting.

The stonewaller was invaluable in a sometimes flighty batting order, however, and his fielding was prized. He had no little courage, crouching in close when the fiercest hitters tried to intimidate him. In a match at Harrogate, Bannerman was fielding very close for Tom Emmett, who asked, 'Are you married?'

'No.'

'Oh, then, you're all right,' Emmett replied. 'It doesn't matter if I kill you, but if you had been married I should have advised you to get back a bit.'

A reception at the Crichton Hotel in London concluded the tour on 28 September. Murdoch made a warmly received speech in which he acknowledged the debt his team owed to their 'educators', the English. He wasn't just being magnanimous in victory. There was a double edge to his words, for not only had the Australians learnt much of their cricket from the English, but also the art of shamateurism.

On 30 September they left England on the SS *Alaska*, the 'greyhound of the Atlantic', for Ireland and New York. They raised money for the Shipwrecked Mariners' Fund and enjoyed what Giffen called 'a picnic trip across America' and Hawaii, winning games and, happily, avoiding the unpleasantness of the 1878 tour. A crowd of several hundred met them in Sydney when they arrived on the *City of New York* on 18 November, and they toured Australia for banquet after banquet. In the Sydney suburb of Cremorne, streets still bear the names of Spofforth, Murdoch, Bannerman and Boyle.

How good was this team? Of their exhausting schedule of 38 first-class games, they won 23, drew 11 and lost 4. Boyle said, 'The great win against All England will amply compensate for these defeats.' The *Times* said they were 'the finest eleven ever collected'. In Grace's view, they were 'the best team sent to the mother country. So brilliant were their achievements, and so completely did they captivate the British public, county cricket suffered complete eclipse.'

Over time, this opinion would consolidate. Altham, writing his *History of Cricket* more than 40 years later, comments:

'In the opinion of three of the greatest of contemporary judges – W.G., A.G. Steel and Alfred Shaw – the 1882 Australian Eleven was positively the best that ever visited this country,' though only Murdoch among the batsman would probably have made an England Eleven. 'Nevertheless they had now made an immense advance upon the rather primitive methods of their first tour.' Giffen and Horan were highly thought of. Of the three hitters – Bonnor, McDonnell and Massie – one always came off. And the bowling was 'as strong as any that has ever figured on any side'. Blackham's keeping 'was once again the theme of universal admiration'.

But the gloss of success did not entirely mask the sore that still festered. A poem, 'The Australian Eleven', written by 'Wattle Blossom', made optimistic reference to it:

'The friendly relations of old are resumed,
And all the unpleasantness deeply entombed;
For England is proud of that tie that endears –
Is proud of the sons of the old pioneers.'

Optimistic, because it wasn't fully correct that the unpleasantness had been 'entombed'. The truth was that the 'commercial' spirit of the Australians, even though they were taking a much smaller cut, was as offensive to English amateurs and professionals in 1882 as it had been in 1878 and 1880.

Altham writes: 'The Australians took their cricket in deadly seriousness; they were keen enough about their success to place it above all the minor distractions that, often in the name of hospitality, threaten the form of a touring eleven; they were – it is permissible to say so at an interval of forty years – equally keen, too keen, about financial considerations. These had dictated their over-weighted programme of thirty-eight matches, extending, with but one solitary break, from the middle of May to September 26th, and accounting in its turn for their persistent refusal to play before noon or after 6 pm. A writer in the contemporary *Lillywhite* records his considered opinion that, "Unconsciously, and perhaps without any suspicion on their part that such is the case, the Australians have seriously and perceptibly aggravated the symptoms of a commercial spirit in cricket."'

Within two years, those symptoms would break out into full-blown disease.

'I COME OUT HERE FOR CRICKET, I DID NOT COME OUT TO FIGHT'

The Australian Eleven's return coincided with a new group of English tourists arriving. Their contrasting fortunes through the early summer of 1882 illustrated a remarkable reversal of public sentiment towards Murdoch's travelling troupe.

The England team, invited by the Melbourne Cricket Club, was no more representative than the earlier groups but its mostly amateur composition made it stronger than the previous summer's professionals. In Charles and George Studd, Allan Steel and Walter Read, it had England's best batsmen outside Grace, who, buckling down to his new medical practice and family commitments, was never a chance of touring. As usual, the amateurs (except Steel) didn't care for too much bowling under the antipodean sun, so the work would be done by Fred Morley, the Billys, Bates and Barnes, plus Dick Barlow.

The team's journey on the SS *Peshawur* was marked by seasickness, romance and tragedy. The first afflicted most of the team but definitely not the sturdy Peate, who joked that he could 'never manage more than five meals a day'. The captain, Ivo Bligh, the future Lord Darnley, met the family of Sir William Clarke, a Victorian grandee, and fell in love with their governess, Florence Morphy. There was much joking about the 'Ashes' of English cricket taken by Murdoch's Eleven, and Bligh's hopes of bringing them back home, whatever 'they' were.

Off Colombo, the *Peshawur* smashed into another boat. The liner did not sink, but Morley broke his ribs and damaged his internal organs so severely that he would do little bowling in Australia. Two years later, he would die, supposedly from complications from his injuries.

On arrival, Bligh's men were treated in grand style in Adelaide. The city radiated hope. Giffen, its favourite son, had distinguished himself on tour, South Australia was now a full-fledged third member of the intercolonial circuit, and, most excitingly, Ben Wardill, secretary of the Melbourne Cricket Club, had written to the South Australian Cricket Association (SACA) offering one of the four Test matches.

While Bligh took his popular team around the country playing odds matches, speaking publicly of his aim 'to recover those Ashes', Murdoch's Eleven began to suffer a public backlash. The torchlit processions, commemorative medals and banquets soon grated with players who wanted to return home after so long on the road. The *Bulletin* criticised them for agreeing to play money-spinning matches for the Eleven but not for their clubs: 'The amount of real patriotism about them can be judged by their refusal to play. There are a good many points about this team which the public should know. As soon as all the "fizz" has gone flat, we shall endeavour to bring these arrogant athletes to their proper level. It is no use casting mud at demigods, so we shall refrain for the present from expressing our opinion of their conduct until they subside into normal insignificance.'

At a reception in Adelaide, Murdoch told the SACA that a Test would be played there. But the negotiations with Wardill were taking a wrong turn. Wardill offered the SACA just five per cent of the gate, the rest going to Melbourne and the Australian and English players. The SACA made a counter-bid of 10 per cent. They did not hear from Wardill until he announced that two Tests would be played in each of Sydney and Melbourne. He then ignored the representations of John Creswell, the South Australian Football Association (SAFA) secretary, who made a brief and unsuccessful attempt to bypass Melbourne and negotiate with individual players. In 1883, the SACA would bring a breach of promise action against Melbourne; Wardill accepted responsibility and the club paid compensation. Creswell was to become secretary of the SACA on 22 October 1883 and just over a year later, the inaugural Adelaide Test match would be another flashpoint.

The background to the 1882 negotiations was that the Australian Eleven had come home with much less silver in their pockets than the 1878 or 1880 teams. Horan wrote that they received £270, minus expenses, for the tour. *Cricket* reported on 25 October 1883 that the tour profits were £3563, or £254 a player. 'Mid On' in the *Argus* said, 'the English clubs have had them very cheap and know too much of them in business, if not in cricket'. Beal was criticised for having agreed to outer-ground money, not the more lucrative stands. One reason for the 1882 Australians' popularity in England was clearly that they lost out financially. As a result, the Eleven were keen to control the income from the home Tests against Bligh's team. The result would be a handy bonus of £495 per man, taking their overall income back up to the levels of the previous tours, and a residue of ill-will against them.

Meanwhile, Bligh's team was ready to play what the *Sydney Morning Herald* was calling 'the first of the great test matches' in Melbourne. Bonnor, with the bat, and Palmer and Giffen, with the ball, did most of the damage in Australia's easy nine-wicket win. After the match, though, the Australians were criticised in the press for 'drinking champagne in the bush'. In fact, the English were doing much the same in Tasmania, according to a report by R.D. Beeston: 'Whether it was owing to the Tasmanian climate, the bright eyes of the Insular ladies (unsurpassed in any portion of the globe), the extreme soundness of the beer brewed in the locality, or all three causes combined, deponent sayeth not; but it is certain that [in the second Test] the seekers after the "ashes" were all in tip-tip form.'

England's matches outside the big cities were arranged commercially. A local association would offer the Melbourne Cricket Club — as tour promoter — a set fee, then recoup its costs by selling vending rights inside the ground and charging gate money. These games were mostly lucky to break even; the tour's financial success depended heavily on the gate money from the Test matches.

Refreshed from Tasmania, their captain having spent some extra time at Sir William Clarke's homes in and around Melbourne, the English went back to the MCG full of pluck. They beat Australia by an innings, Bates taking a stunning 7/28 and 7/74 with his tweakers, including a hat-trick for which he received what Steel called 'a very smart silver hat'. He had not troubled high-class batsmen like this before. So what had changed?

The Australians had a ready answer, believing that at the other end Barlow had been gouging a 'spot' on the wicket with his boots. Before the third Test in Sydney, a week later, Murdoch complained to Bligh about the plates Barlow was wearing. Bligh had Barlow remove the plates, over the bowler's objection that he had always worn them and now resented the imputation that he was a cheat. There was some history to this, too: at certain times on his England tours, Spofforth had been accused of cutting up the pitch, most recently for Giffen in the match against the Gentlemen in 1882. Indignant, Spofforth brought evidence, said the *Sydney Mail*, 'to show that he only used one nail and a spike — less than any other cricketer uses — in the present match. Spofforth does not use more spikes in his boots than are necessary for him to obtain a fast hold when delivering the ball, but with his extraordinary movements when delivering the ball he would cut up the turf even without spikes.'

It was not much of a riposte. As the England player C.F.H. Leslie put it, Spofforth 'did not ... deny that [his boots'] effect was similar to those worn by Barlow, though he did deny that he caused this effect purposely'.

Rather like Grace at the Oval, Spofforth was playing within the letter but not the spirit of the law. There was no prohibition on bowlers following through on the wicket, but they could be cautioned for unfair play. As Spofforth's actions were unintentional and his boots were not enhanced with extra spikes, he got away with it. But that is not to say he didn't give his team an advantage by gouging the turf. Leslie wrote: 'Mr Spofforth, notwithstanding our remonstrance, cut up the wickets very badly ... It ought not to be left to the umpire to say whether it is fair or unfair play, but rather whether the effect caused is fair or unfair. The Australian umpire, when appealed to, decided that as Mr Spofforth had denied the damage to the pitch to be intentional, it was fair play.'

Bowling angrily, Spofforth returned to his best in Sydney, taking 4/73 and 7/44. But England made their runs before rain drenched the wicket, and Australia, chasing 153, fell 70 short. The drying, chopped-up wicket made every bowler lethal. Even the slow-medium Horan, taking 3/22 in England's second innings, was hard to handle. Bligh wrote in *Lillywhite's Annual 1884*, 'the wicket being cut up at both ends by Spofforth's heels to such an extent that Horan became an unplayable bowler; perhaps, if we would, we could say no more than that'.

But more than that had been said already. 'After the match was over,' the *Age* reported, 'an allusion was made in conversation to Spofforth having cut up the wicket with his feet. This so annoyed the demon bowler that he struck out at Mr Read, of the English eleven. Fortunately for Spofforth, the genial Surrey secretary is as good tempered as he is muscular and contented himself by smiling upon his ill-mannered adversary.'

Four days after the Test match, the *Bulletin* ran a satirical poem called 'Song of the Spike', which said, in part: 'Spoff cut up rough on Barlow, 'cause he cut up rough the ground.' In the dramatic, pun-filled rendition of events, Spofforth and Barlow 'shaped quite quick for the affray; All thought that spike would cause a great Spiketacular display'.

> *'Then Read appeared, and said — "Oh, bosh!*
> *Of this spike we're all full;*
> *To fight about a spike is not*
> *A bit respiketable."*
> *"I'll go for you!" then howls out Spoff,*
> *But Read said — "No, not quite,*
> *I come out here for cricket, I*
> *Did not come out to fight."'*

Read's intervention then stopped 'a fracas this of fools'.

This version – that Spofforth and Barlow were ready to fight until Read stepped between them – was supported in the *Sydney Sportsman* 33 years later, citing players who were there: 'One word led to another, and Barlow made some insulting remark to Spofforth and the Demon replied with a blow which knocked Barlow over the seat. A big fight seemed imminent, but friends dragged Spofforth inside, and Walter Read (a champion amateur boxer) stood in front of Barlow to protect him.'

It might have been an exaggeration, abetted by the Demon himself, that he actually hit Barlow. Bligh wrote, in a letter to his father, that 'Spofforth rather nearly came to fisticuffs with Read and Barlow but I think he was excited a little above himself at the time.' He wrote that 'our fellows were very angry' about Spofforth's effect on the wicket and Spofforth 'struck out at' Read. Bligh said he 'wrote a very strong protest to the Sydney committee and to Murdoch telling them that if it occurs again we shall appeal to the umpires'.

The altercation was a blot on an otherwise popular tour. Indeed,

Bligh's team did much to restore the reputation of England's amateurs. When the professional teams of Lillywhite and Shaw had lurched and gambled drunkenly around the country, little more was expected: they were *players*. But when the amateurs of Grace and Harris had offended their hosts, there was moral outrage. Bligh's hope, after the 'spike' dispute, was that 'there will be no serious row as our trip has been so thoroughly harmonious as yet – the only awkward thing in fact being the very marked comparisons made in the papers between our team and Harris's and W.G.'s in our favour'.

The quarrels that erupted over throwing, umpiring, 'sharp practice', gambling and running on the wickets show how passionately these men were playing the game, how fervently they were being supported, and how much – a quasi-national pride, no less – was at stake. By contrast, a matter that was not contested until decades later was the abstruse question of whether England 'won' the 'Ashes' in 1882–83.

With Australia trailing 1–2, a fourth Test was played. The first three had been between England and Murdoch's 1882 Eleven. The fourth Test, in Sydney, with an experimental rule of each innings being played on a fresh wicket, was between England and a 'Combined' Australia. Out of Murdoch's Eleven went the out-of-form Massie, McDonnell and Garrett. In came Ted Evans for his overdue Test debut, Midwinter – now an Australian again – and Boyle. The introduction of Evans and Midwinter made this the strongest Australian team of the summer, and a Test-first brace of half-centuries by Blackham saw them home by four wickets.

Midwinter had come back from England with Murdoch. The public's welcome was cautious. The *Sydney Mail* said in December 1882 of 'this very slippery character':

'Last season he played with England against Australia, and wanted badly to go to England immediately after as a full-blown Australian cricketer in Murdoch's team. Failing to induce the Australians to take the giant to their arms, he journeyed back to the old country with Shaw's team and played for his county Gloucestershire during the whole of their last cricketing campaign. In order to ingratiate himself with the colonial cricketers, who will not forget his base desertion of the first Australian Eleven at Lord's, he returned to Australia with Murdoch and his companions, announcing his intention of "never never" returning to the old country.'

With Midwinter and Evans, the Australians squared the series. Did this mean they retained the 'Ashes'?

Historians have argued to and fro, but a loose consensus has been settled that England recovered the 'Ashes' by beating Murdoch's Eleven 2–I. As the *Argus* put it:

'The avowed object of the visit was to wrest, if possible, from Murdoch's victorious Australian team the title of supremacy in the cricket-field which on Kennington Oval they had just won from a representative eleven of England. A series of matches with Murdoch's team was made the primal condition of the tour, and as far as this ruling object is concerned the Hon. Ivo Bligh and his companions can in the future look back with a feeling of pride on this particular portion of their expedition. Three matches were played. In all of them the verdict was unmistakeable, and at the end the balance of power rested with the English team.'

The notion that 'Australia' retained the 'Ashes' by winning the last Test is to misunderstand the nature of Anglo-Australian cricket in its early years. There was not a unified 'Australian' team as there is now. There was 'Murdoch's Eleven' which had toured England, and it was against that team that Bligh was contesting the 'Ashes'. Florence Morphy and her friends presented Bligh with a pouch of burnt material – its origin now unknown – after the third Test. Bligh, Murdoch and everyone involved would acknowledge that the 'Ashes' were a gimmick, at stake only in the three 'revenge' games. Thereafter, the 'Ashes' were more or less forgotten for twenty years. Clarence Moody, the Australian journalist who retrospectively compiled and validated a list of 'official' Test matches in the 1890s, referred to the 'Ashes' as having been constantly up for grabs since 1882, but they were not. They were only contested in the first three Tests of 1882–83. The next mention of them by a cricketer was not until 1891–92, when the 'ashes' were those of a decidedly sick Australian game.

'THE ROVING, RESTLESS SPIRIT'

Today's cricketers would keel over with exhaustion simply to think about the program followed by the men of the 1880s. After a 12-month tour during which, tempestuous boat voyages aside, they played tough competitive cricket in sometimes dreadful conditions for six or seven days a week, often arriving at their new destinations at two or three in the morning of match days, they had 10 or 11 months at home before the planning started again. Those who went on the first four tours – Murdoch, Blackham, Spofforth, Boyle and Alick Bannerman – were truly cricketers with constitutions of iron. Bonnor, McDonnell and Palmer went on three of those tours, while Giffen's 1882 tour was the first of three straight before his resources became overstretched. Little wonder that their status, amateur or professional, was a grey area.

But how much was too much? In its report after each tour, the NSWCA noted the harm being done to lower levels of cricket. Its 1881–82 report said: 'The question of the visits of Australian teams to the mother country has arrived at a stage which calls for special attention. The refusal of members of returned teams to take part in the intercolonial contests has shorn these matches of much of their wonted interest.' In 1883–84: 'The constant visits of Australians to England and of Englishmen to the colonies are proving disastrous to club cricket.' And in 1885–86: 'The visits of Australian elevens to England and of English teams to the colonies have become so frequent that they threaten to exercise a prejudicial influence on local cricket.'

But no association yet had power to restrain the Elevens, who travelled to England as private enterprises. What could hold them back was a decline in profits. From 1878 to 1882, their gate-money share had declined from 90 per cent to less than 50. The players' profits had dropped from £750–800 to £250. Horan, having missed the lucrative 1880 tour and gone in 1882, was the unlucky man. He made himself unavailable to tour in 1884 and, in his newspaper columns, campaigned against it:

'The laurels gained by the 1882 team, and which we still retain, would, it was thought, have caused a long interval to elapse before another team would visit England, especially as the last trip was not a monetary success. But a roving, restless spirit has taken possession of some members of the old teams. They cannot content themselves to settle down to quiet humdrum business life, and so they have resolved once more to leave these shores and fight their bloodless battles over again on classic English fields.'

That 'roving, restless spirit' animated Murdoch and company in late 1883. Most of them were up for another tour, as long as they could claw back the profit share. There were delays in naming the team until after Christmas because employers still had to grant leave 'to two or three players in whose absence no Australian Eleven could be termed representative'. Massie and Evans were unavailable, for business and family reasons respectively. Spofforth and Garrett were chosen but the promoters had 'so far failed to get a definite answer from either',

Horan reported. Garrett was 'unable to decide for private reasons, and Spofforth, who, I understand, is sheepdroving in Queensland, still shows all his old weathercock mutability. Of course, everybody expects that the "demon" will be on the deck of the steamer with the rest of the team when they say goodbye to us in March.'

Spofforth was playing cat and mouse again, but this time he had a grim personal matter to deal with. In September 1883, his 35-year-old brother, Edward, died of 'nervous exhaustion'. Through January, when the Eleven began its Australian leg with an unprecedented 'trial' match, putting the last places up for grabs, in Melbourne, then toured the local circuit to raise funds, Spofforth didn't play. On 9 February the *Sydney Mail* reported that he had 'positively declined' to tour but 'if Spofforth can be induced to alter his determination, a place will be found for him at the last moment'.

He played on 15 February for a Combined Eleven *against* Murdoch's team – taking 4/101 and 1/10 in his first bowl in twelve months – but didn't join the swing through Queensland, Victoria and South Australia. On 23 February the *Sydney Mail* said 'four out of five persons one meets in the street say he is sure to go, yet he himself says otherwise'.

In the end, it was not until 15 March, after the boat had left, that the *Sydney Mail* reported that he had joined the team.

Spofforth clearly needed rest, knowing how much bowling awaited him in England, and a period of grieving for Edward. But Richard Cashman suggests the showman might have been heightening the tension: '[I]t is hard to escape the conclusion that Spofforth relished playing out the drama for the benefit of the press and public, who seemed to have sensed that he enjoyed generating media copy and was never really taken in by his act. They knew that Spofforth was never a person who would walk away from a challenge. The weight of evidence suggests that Spofforth was always likely to tour but wanted to do so at his convenience and with maximum publicity. Spofforth enjoyed the limelight. As the star turn he was a law unto himself.'

The team was more than just the Demon, however. Murdoch had returned to his best, scoring 279 against the Combined Eleven to follow 158 in the intercolonial. Giffen took 10/66 in an innings in the second trial. New to the Eleven were a young Melbourne medical student, Henry Scott, and a bearded Victorian leg-spinner, William Cooper, while the manager George Alexander and Midwinter returned after missing the 1882 tour.

The players embraced touring because, for all its ardours, there was an experience of a lifetime in being part of a famous team playing to big crowds. Giffen wrote of one night during the team's stay in Tamworth:

'The atmosphere at night was stifling, and we could not get to sleep. Three of us – Percy McDonnell. Jack Blackham, and myself – wandered about the hotel in pyjamas praying for a breath of air. We were idle, and like many other idle fellows, we had occupation found for us by the Imp of Mischief. Some silk hats invitingly hung in the hall, and each donning one, we boldly marched into "Paradise Gardens", down the street, where a fancy dress ball was being held. We found our way to the platform, and one of us collaring a bell, started to ring for the next dance to start. Up rushed the Master of Ceremonies, frantic, and without attempting to expostulate, started to bundle us out. At his heels, however, ran Charlie Bannerman, who was one of the dancers. Charlie whispered to the MC, 'Don't you know who they are? They are three of the Australian Eleven.' You should have seen how that man's countenance changed! No longer irate, he became most apologetic. Instead of being regarded as intruders we were lionised, and became honoured guests. Such is fame!'

Murdoch's 1884 team finally sailed from Melbourne on the P&O steamer SS *Sutlej* on 11 March. They departed with a clear mission of playing good cricket and returning a profit. Thanks to the respectability and fine play of the 1882 team, they were now being offered three Test matches, at Old Trafford, Lord's and the Oval. Lucre beckoned. Alexander asked for half the gate, stands and outer included, but was knocked back by every county. The final agreement was for 50 per cent of outer-ground takings plus the entire gate for a Test match at Lord's. *The Field* was 'surprised, if not disgusted' at Alexander's demands. The *Sporting and Dramatic News* said the Australians 'have undertaken the enterprise less for honour than the filthy lucre ... we most heartily and earnestly deprecate another infliction upon us next year'. Harris deplored 'the formation of a class of semi-professionals'.

Cutting costs, the tour only took 12 men and Alexander. Horan criticised a plan he saw as dangerously avaricious:

'The 1880 team had 12 men and the manager of the present team, and they had to play Nottingham with 10 men, and lost the match partly by reason of this, and partly by reason of Bonnor's bad fielding. Then they had to send cripples into the field to oppose England in the great match in which Murdoch played his grand innings for 153 not out ... The 1882 team had 13 men and a manager, and they found it all they could do more than once to send 11 men into the field.'

He urged them to take 13, predicting that nine matches on the program 'will be against teams very little inferior to the full strength of England, so that it is clear, unless our men be thoroughly fit each time, they will stand a good show of being defeated'.

The *Sutlej* arrived at Plymouth on 29 April, but not before some onboard action made Horan's words ring true. In a game of shinty — they had not learnt their lesson! — Cooper tore ligaments in the spinning finger of his right hand. It was a particular blow for the 35-year-old, who had only taken up cricket at 27 under medical advice to exercise after an illness. 'He never thoroughly recovered the use of the finger,' said Giffen, 'and a bowler who we thought would, on account of the vital variation of his style from that of Spofforth, Boyle, Palmer, and myself, have been of great service to us, was nothing more than a passenger.'

Eighteen years later, Cooper had the consolation of becoming the singles lawn bowls champion of Australia.

Knowing they had to get fit and stay fit, many of the players, including Giffen, got into the routine of rising at six o'clock each morning to feed the ship's furnaces, before appearing on deck covered in sweat and coaldust. 'I shall never forget the first shovelful I put into the furnace. I had not mastered the knack of it, and, slipping, instead of getting the coal through the door, I very nearly went in myself.'

Giffen's voyage was not without accident, including one which 'annoyed me very much at the time. We were in the Mediterranean and it was a bitterly cold day. A party of us were enjoying some luscious oranges, and I proceeded to throw a handful of peel over the rail into the sea. To my consternation, two diamond rings, one of which had been presented to me as a trophy by the Norwood Club, the other a gift from my brother, slipped off my finger, and went the way of the orange peel. Some of the peel struck the taffrail, but unfortunately none of the rings came back to the deck.'

When they arrived in England and saw the strength of their opposition, several of the Australians warmed up with London clubs. Bannerman and Giffen played for the City Ramblers at Battersea Park 'and, as a joke, the other side were not to know who we were'. Giffen took a hat-trick. The pair opened and 'notched a good many runs', including an all-run eight.

'The amusement came at the conclusion of the match, when our bags were placed prominently in the tent, so that the other fellows might be sure to see them. At first they resented the joke which had been played at their expense, but the resentment was only momentary, and over the parting glass they laughed as heartily as any of the Ramblers.'

They weren't going to be able to get away with such frivolity against first-class cricketers. The *Standard* exemplified the seriousness with which England was now taking an Australian visit, calling on cricketers 'to sink all county, university and club considerations, and combine to form practice teams, to check, if possible, the advance of the Australian invader'. In Australia's first match, against a hot welcoming committee of Grace, Shrewsbury, Ulyett, Barnes and Shaw playing for Lord Sheffield at his estate in Sussex, the locals demanded the width of McDonnell's and Bannerman's bats be run through a four-and-a-half-inch gauge in front of the crowd. The Australians were bemused, as the bats were English-made. Giffen reported: 'I know Percy Mac's was found to be a trifle too wide, but no more so than a bat often becomes after severe usage, for the faces of many blades have a tendency to spread. But annoyed though we were, a little fun was extracted out of the incident, when somebody suggested that one of W.G.'s bats should be put through the gauge, and the very first one would not pass muster.'

The Australians won the game, but lost to Oxford University, the MCC & Ground and the Gentlemen of England. On a dangerous wicket at Birmingham, they defeated an Eleven of England in less than a day: 76 and 6/33 beating 82 and 26. Spofforth took 14/37 in that farcical fixture, but a few days later was hit in the arm by a drive from Walter Read at Lord's 'with such force,' wrote *Cricket*, 'that he was only able to finish the over by rolling the three remaining balls along the ground'.

The first month was already the worst yet for an Australian tour, even if the opposition was the strongest. Against the MCC, they became only the second bowling team to concede three centuries in a first-class innings: Grace 101, Steel 134, Barnes 105 not out. Moreover, the Australians had risked playing Cooper, and Grace belted him out of the attack — effectively, out of big cricket. Murdoch made two golden ducks in the first three matches, and by late May Bonnor had scored 32 runs in eight innings. Only the openers, McDonnell and Bannerman, had shown any consistency.

After the loss to the Gentlemen, the team gathered in the Tavistock and reviewed their progress in a 'crisis meeting'. 'Were the adverse critics right after all?' Giffen asked. 'Were we going to lower the reputation of Australian cricket?'

They defeated a weak Derbyshire, then went to Manchester to play the champion county. Rain interfered, but finally the key batsmen showed some fibre, Murdoch scoring 39 and 64, and Giffen 113. Giffen followed up with a hat-trick and Australia had the better of a draw.

Notably, in that match, they faced John Crossland, the alleged chucker who had caused anxiety in 1882. Led by Lord Harris, some English counties were moving against throwers. Umpires were not calling them, as an element of class solidarity existed between former and playing pros. Bob Thoms said, 'We are not going to do anything, the gentlemen must do it.'

But throwing had become a contagion. Harris would not choose Crossland for England, but Hornby kept picking him for Lancashire 'to the disgust of many in the game'. In *Lillywhite's Companion 1884*, R.H. Lyttelton appealed to Hornby, but the latter's refusal 'produced considerable ill feeling around the county circuit'.

It reached absurd proportions in the Roses match at Old Trafford. When umpire Wootton didn't call Crossland, Peate promised to throw one himself. He did, and Wootton didn't call him. Peate said: 'There, that shows what you umpires are all worth!'

Grace, always deft at compromise, submitted to Lord's that the square-leg umpire should be empowered to call a thrower. The charge was adapted, but it was several years before the epidemic was brought under a semblance of control.

The Australians, while they had sometimes suffered from individual chuckers such as Crossland and Frank, were able to look on the controversy with an air of smugness. In his official report on the 1882–83 tour, Bligh had written, 'Throughout the whole tour not only was there not a single thrower met with, but not even a bowler to whom the slightest suspicion of an unfair action could be imputed. And whence this result? Simply because in Australia not only would anyone who threw be no-balled, but anyone about whose action there could be the slightest doubt. Does the solution of the problem that has been so voluminously discussed lie in this excellent example set us by the younger cricketing community of Australia?'

Murdoch's Eleven went on a mostly victorious swing through the north, defeating Yorkshire, Nottinghamshire (where they ate in the dining room) and Cambridge University, losing only to the North of England by an innings at Old Trafford. In that match they were dismantled by Ulyett (7/92) and Peate (10/51), while Crossland also took two wickets. Giffen said: 'A good story is told about an Australian batsman, and his dislike for Peate's bowling. The Yorkshireman beat him with a clipping leg break in one innings. The batsman, determined that it should not happen again, got hold of a bat in his room at the hotel, and began to make strokes at imaginary balls. At one he would play back and mutter, 'That's the way to play you, Peate.' Then he would play forward, remarking, 'Not this time, Peate, my boy.' At last, he ventured on a big hit at a leg ball, and, swinging round with a 'How do you like that, Peate?' sent the toilet set, which he had forgotten all about, in fragments to the floor. Later on in the day, confident that he would make a score, he faced the real Peate and was clean bowled first ball.'

An inspection of the scorecard shows that the one Australian who was bowled first ball by Peate in the second innings, after being dismissed by him in the first, was Giffen himself, though Charlie Turner later claimed that the unnamed batsman in the story had been Murdoch. Suffice to say that the very best of the Australians were frightened of Peate, first in a long line of deadly Yorkshire slow left-armers.

While in the North they received a letter from a 'Well-Wisher' saying Murdoch deserved to lose every game for not picking Scott as opener. 'Of course the genial William, and all the rest of us, were duly thankful for the advice thus tendered,' said Giffen.

It wouldn't have been an Australian Eleven tour without an edge creeping in. Fed up with some of the umpiring, Murdoch forced Walter Price to stand aside from the second Gentlemen's match after bad decisions earlier in tour. But after umpire Farrands disallowed a catch in slips, Spofforth bowled angrily, his fastest ever, with six men in the cordon, and took 7/68 to inspire a come-from-behind win by 46 runs.

After the relative harmony of 1882, money was again becoming a vexation. Shrewsbury, Barnes and Flowers refused to play Australia for the Players at Sheffield for £10 each. As with the 1880 Players' boycott, the fee was standard, but they knew the Australians would be making much more. In the event, 60,000 spectators paid to watch Spofforth (13/123) wreck the Players' batting and Bonnor (70 and 95 not out) come good in a tight win. But the revival of feeling against the Australians' 'commercial spirit' was gaining momentum.

England's selection for the inaugural Test match in Manchester was disrupted when Harris adopted a 'him or me' stance on Crossland, who had thrown out 11 Australian batsmen for 79 at Liverpool. The bowler was stood down but Harris also boycotted the match, possibly for his own safety in Crossland's home town. Hornby led England again in what would turn out to be his final appearance.

Manchester's first day as a Test venue was rained off, and the weather had the last say in the match. *Cricket* said Murdoch's Eleven 'deserved the highest credit for the way in which they worked at the finish in hopes of a victory', but the stubbornness of Grace, Lucas and Shrewsbury and the 'lucky hitting' of Tim O'Brien meant Australia did not have time to chase a small victory target.

Spofforth, Boyle and Palmer were at their best in wins over Leicestershire and Middlesex before, as Rae puts it, the MCC 'climbed onto the Test bandwagon at last, agreeing to stage a match' at Lord's. Harris was back to lead England. Murdoch called 'Woman' correctly and Australia might have made more than their 229 if the captain himself, fielding as England's substitute for Grace, hadn't caught Scott for 75. The Australian bowlers were bested again by the fine amateur Steel whose 148 would prove decisive in the series. When Harris was bowled by Spofforth, England were in peril at 5/135. Seeing Barlow — the man for whom the term 'stone wall' was invented — Harris exclaimed:

'For Heaven's sake, Barlow, stop this rot!' He did, helping Steel put on a matchwinning stand of 98.

Australia batted again, starting 150 behind, but now the 'spot' caused by the third step of Spofforth's follow-through came back to bite them. Ulyett took 7/36, catching Bonnor in remarkable fashion, as A.A. Thomson described:

'With all his giant strength Bonnor hammered it murderously back at the bowler. Happy Jack shot out a hand. There was a crack that echoed round the ground like a pistol shot and, by some miracle, the ball stuck. Ulyett said afterwards that it came back at him as if it had been attached to elastic. *Punch* with plantigrade humour suggested that he should be specially engaged by the Army to catch enemy cannon balls and hurl them back. The oldest MCC member called him up, handed him a sovereign and told him that it was the catch of his (the oldest member's) lifetime. W.G. Grace, whose opinion was only partly medical, called Ulyett a dam' fool for attempting anything so foolish; he was lucky to have any fingers left.'

Giffen, the non-striker, said that when Bonnor hit his 'mighty drive' everyone on the field 'looked down the ground to see where the ball landed, and the spectators began to open a space in the ring'. Ulyett quipped, 'The ball was no sooner out of my hand than it was back again.'

England had every right to feel pleased, but the money issue was boiling over. Alexander had negotiated the entire gate — £1334 from 35,411 paying spectators. Meanwhile the four English professionals, Barlow, Ulyett, Shrewsbury and Peate, took home £10 each. A week later, when the Australians were programmed to play the Players at the Oval, the indignant Nottinghamshire committee banned their professionals, reserving them instead for a game against Gloucestershire. This 'robbed the [Players] match of much of its interest', said *Cricket*, but not of the underlying anti-Australian mood. Spofforth (14/96) and Bonnor (68) starred in getting Australia to the point where they only needed 28 in their second innings. Just before two o'clock, when the lunch bell rang,

Bonnor was out for 12 and the score was 17. 'It was generally thought,' said *Cricket*, 'that as there were only 11 left to win, the game would be completed before lunch. The bell rang, though, and this gave rise to a very disorderly scene.'

The Players' captain, Tom Emmett, asked Murdoch to finish the game. Murdoch declined. Sections of the crowd, thinking Murdoch was engaged in a cynical ploy to wait out the lunch break so that more paying customers might be lured through the gate, converged, shouting, on the pavilion. 'When the bell rang for a renewal at half-past two, their attitude became still more hostile, and the middle of the ground was not only occupied, but the stumps sent flying.'

The Australians' interpretation was, as reported by Giffen, quite different. He said it was the ground authorities who wanted the break, for the benefit of the caterers. Murdoch 'agreed to stop, on condition that no charge was made for admission after two o'clock. All he received for his pains was abuse.'

When the crowd was protesting, Giffen appeared at the pavilion door and got a cheer. Alcock said, 'You seem to be all right with them, Giffen. Just go and explain things. Perhaps they will hear you.' '[N]ot having been in the habit of addressing large crowds, [I] made myself scarce,' recalled Giffen.

Alcock then asked Peate to calm them. Peate replied: 'I didn't come here to quell a riot; I came to play cricket.'

Ultimately, the police were needed to clear the way for Murdoch and McDonnell to go out, another hour later, to finish the game.

It is unlikely that Murdoch was prolonging the match to increase the gate. The scheduled interval only went for half an hour, and the numbers who might have come in to watch Australia score 11 runs would be negligible. In addition, there is Giffen's testimony that Murdoch insisted that no latecomers be charged entry. What is more significant is that the crowd jumped to the conclusion that the Australian captain was acting cynically and greedily. They were incorrect, but by now the prevailing opinion was so negative towards the Australians' motives that every doubtful action was interpreted in the worst light.

After a surprise loss to Kent and a draw with Gloucestershire (Grace scoring a century a week after the death of his mother Martha, the only woman before Rachel Heyhoe-Flint to be in *Wisden*'s Births and Deaths), Murdoch's Eleven tried to square the Test series at the Oval. A dry summer was ending with a perfect wicket. 'We were in our element', Giffen said. 'It was so warm that several of the spectators fainted.'

Murdoch won the toss and again showed his capacity for concentration, scoring 211 in just over eight hours, from 525 balls, the first double-century in a Test match – and, as events would determine, the last of his great innings. McDonnell made 108 and the in-form youngster Scott 102. *Cricket* said of Murdoch's innings: 'A more remarkable display of accurate timing and judicious batting has never been witnessed.'

His problem was that the laws did not permit declarations. The Surrey club had only allowed three days for the game, a day fewer than in Australia. So, while he wanted to make the most of the batting conditions, he was also running out of time. All eleven Englishmen bowled, the wicketkeeper Alfred Lyttelton taking 4/19 with his lobs while Grace wore the gloves. The innings ended comically, Midwinter swinging at a Lyttelton ball going down the leg-side which lodged in Grace's gloves. Grace said Midwinter hadn't hit it, 'but I had no time to prevent the umpire giving his decision, so Midwinter had to go'.

Thanks mainly to Palmer, the Australians still looked likely to force a win when England were eight down and 370 behind with more than half a day to play. Walter Read, incensed that Harris had listed him at number ten, came in and smashed 117 in 113 minutes (still the highest Test score by a number ten) while the opener Scotton, who had come in 24 hours earlier, blocked up the other end, his 90 taking nearly six hours. Harris showed the better side of his sportsmanship when, with the crowd encroaching so far onto the Oval that the Australian fieldsmen were impeded, he announced that if they did not move back he would forfeit the game. 'That is the spirit,' said Giffen, 'manifested at the time of keenest rivalry, that one can admire and hold up as a pattern to young players.'

After the match was drawn, the *Sunday Times* said England had won the series under 'false pretences' because the three-day limit was a relic of times when wickets were worse and scores lower. Australia certainly had the better of the draws at Old Trafford and the Oval. In the final analysis, though, this Eleven was rated weaker than 1882. They did not have the relentless consistency of 1882 or even 1880, but, that said, England were putting up high-quality opponents regularly. Also, the dryness of the wickets in 1884 made it hard to compare the statistics with previous tours. Spofforth ended in a flurry, taking 12 wickets against the South of England and finishing his tour with a hat-trick. Cashman has argued that Spofforth's 205 wickets (more than a hundred better than the next man, Palmer) at 12.50 made this the best of all his tours, considering the conditions and the opposition. That is a fair judgement, but in the Test matches Spofforth was ineffective, his wickets costing just over 30 apiece.

Reviews of their cricket were mixed. The *Standard* rated the tour 'fairly successful'. *The Daily News* said it was 'brilliantly successful'. Giffen noted 'a far more formidable programme than the 1882 Eleven, and it was, therefore, doubly unfortunate that one of our bowlers [Cooper] was useless ... If we had only been able to secure a couple of wins, instead of two draws in our favour, with England, I fancy the 1884 team would have been ranked equal to, if not higher than, the previous Eleven.'

Eleven being the operative word. Horan's warnings were justified, as 'for exactly four months the team were kept at the full tension', said *Cricket*. Australia concluded with 18 wins, seven draws and seven losses. In the tour-closing Smokers versus Non-Smokers match, Bonnor hit 124 for the Non-Smokers, including a six off Spofforth, then celebrated, to general amusement, by walking around the field puffing on a cigar.

The Australian Eleven's commercial attitude left a deeper impact than their cricket. The *World* said: 'The Australians' visit has made all other matches seem tame and insipid, for it has introduced a bloodthirsty spirit. The Australians make their own terms, insist on them, not always very gracefully, and play too obviously for the money's sake. They arrogate to themselves the rank of "gentlemen" and yet are only "professionals".'

A cartoon in *Entr'Acte* showed Spofforth as a kangaroo with a pouch full of money. The lion says, 'Well you don't mind a good licking, so long as you get the gate-money, do you?'

The lively resentment of the Australians' amateur status returned. Scorers made their statement by dropping the honorifics from the Australians' names. The press compared the Gentlemen of Philadelphia, who were touring at the same time, favourably with the Australians. The Philadelphians, it was pointed out, barred professionals from their matches and donated their income to their home association. Murdoch commented wryly that their generosity showed 'the Gentlemen of Philadelphia apparently know how much it is worth to see them play'.

From Australia, the *Argus* took up the team's defence: 'We have been constantly reminded this season that the Australians take gate-money and the Americans do not, but it has yet to be insinuated that they obtained any of that money under false pretences, by not giving full value for it in a cricketing sense.'

The *Argus*'s 'Observer' said: 'The attitude of the English Press has not been at all generous ... Australia is a working community, and young men with their own future to mould cannot afford the time and expense of an English tour without some return.'

Horan, writing in the *Australasian*, took his countrymen's side. The team 'had one and all been subjected to spiteful criticism from certain portions of the English press … As a specimen of narrow-minded and insulting abuse its remarks outstrip anything that has yet been levelled at the Australian cricketers.'

The bottom line was that the 1884 team went home with £900 per man – more *in nominal terms* than any Australian team would take home for the best part of a century. In purchasing power – £900 could buy two houses in a good part of Sydney – these riches have still not been surpassed.

The *Illustrated Sporting and Dramatic News* declaimed: 'These Australian adventurous spirits have undertaken their enterprise less for honour than for filthy lucre, demanding a sort of commission for their services: and a seemingly correct and uncontradictable report has it that each player returning to the vast colonial regions of Australia took away £900 in his pocket. Win or lose, they accept their expenses all the same. The present generation of lovers of the once noble game must have seen enough of the Australians to last them for life, and their intrusion into the mother country will henceforth be regarded as a veritable nuisance, carried out to its bitter end.'

Was the English reaction hypocritical? Given that Grace had been paid £1500 to go on his 'honeymoon' tour of Australia in 1873–74, and the prevalence of shamateurism, the Australians had every right to dismiss the protests. The problem of remuneration for cricketers was England's, not Australia's. But that would not stop it becoming Australia's by the end of the year.

'STUPID, PALTRY
AND SELFISH'

L ove and death accompanied the Australian and English teams as
they sailed south in October 1884.

Already the Australians had left Spofforth in Derbyshire, where
he was courting his sweetheart Phillis Marsh Cadman, daughter of a
successful merchant. Cupid was busy; aboard the SS *Mirzapore*, Murdoch
met Jemima Watson, whose Scottish-born father John Boyd Watson,
a Bendigo gold-mining magnate, was one of Australia's richest men,
with holdings in banking, real estate, rail and tramways, a steamship
company, and farming. Watson also helped fund the launch of the
Daily Telegraph newspaper in Sydney. By his death in 1889 he would be a
veritable Croesus, worth possibly £2 million.

Within a few weeks, Spofforth would be engaged and Murdoch
married. John Watson, unhappy about the whirlwind romance, did not
give Jemima away; George Alexander did.

An England team had left Plymouth three weeks before the Australians, on the SS *Orient*. It was a reversion to the Shaw-Lillywhite-Shrewsbury professional model, only this time the players' strength had overtaken the gentlemen's. The team contained nine of a first-choice England Eleven. Only Grace and Steel of the amateurs would have dislodged any of them. It was by common consent the most representative England side to have come to Australia.

In Adelaide, they received terrible news: Morley was dead. 'We did not recover from the shock for a long time,' wrote Shaw and Shrewsbury, 'for although poor old Fred had been ailing for many months, none of us had thought when we left home that his end was so near. Everyone had some recollection of the Notts bowler, and "Poor Fred" were words that were frequently uttered, and which meant a very great deal.'

Morley had been Shaw's partner in the famous Nottinghamshire attack, causing Australia problems on all their tours. Less exalted was his batting, which brought him just 130 more runs than his 1274 career wickets. It was said that when Morley padded up, the horse that pulled the roller at Trent Bridge knew to walk around the ground and stand between the shafts.

Waiting for the Englishmen at Port Adelaide, loitering at the dock for 24 hours, was the persuasive and persistent John Creswell. Nine months earlier he had written to Conway, who would be the Englishmen's local agent, negotiating a Test match in Adelaide. South Australia's performances in the intercolonial matches had been fair, and Giffen's feats in England raised their reputation further. Creswell had thought he was getting a Test in 1882–83. Now he would not let Shaw, Shrewsbury and Lillywhite disembark from the *Orient* until they had signed a contract. Then he travelled to Melbourne to secure Murdoch's and Alexander's signatures when they docked on the *Mirzapore*. So far, thought Creswell, so good.

Initially there was little hint of the pending earthquake. Shaw's men were given public welcomes by the Adelaide Mayor and other dignitaries, and after two odds matches against South Australia they sailed to Melbourne for a game against Victoria. There they learnt that the Victorians in Murdoch's Eleven were not going to play them, and nor would the NSW members play in the following week's game in Sydney. They claimed to be unfit after their sea journey.

Their unavailability was not unusual, as we have seen. The Elevens, when they returned from England, did not disband until after Christmas, continuing a home tour in effective competition with the intercolonials. In 1882–83, these home matches had saved their bacon. The 1884 team wanted to repeat the exercise, but the latest Englishmen had a harder commercial edge than Bligh, and the Eleven viewed them as rivals for gate money. Charles Pardon wrote in *Wisden* that 'from the moment Murdoch's team landed ... it became evident they were animated by a feeling of bitter hostility towards Shaw and his party.' Having claimed to be unfit, they announced a rival match in Sydney. Lillywhite was disappointed, writing: 'Ill will seemed from the first uppermost with [Murdoch's Eleven], as immediately on arriving home if they had been allowed, they would have signally spoiled our first match in Sydney. Being annoyed at this, the Victorians refused to play for their Colony against us at Melbourne, on the plea of being out of practice, although they would have commenced the same day at Sydney to do us an injury. The same feeling was also shown by Murdoch and [Alick] Bannerman in the New South Wales Match.'

England won both matches against the weakened colonies, but behind the scenes was a total breakdown of relations. One reason was that the Nottinghamshire members of the England team – Barnes, Flowers and Shrewsbury – had boycotted the Players' match against Australia in Sheffield. There was also a falling-out between Alexander and Murdoch, on the one side, and Conway, whom they had dumped in 1880. When the *Age* reported that the English team did not want to play Murdoch's Eleven, Alexander wrote to Conway asking for an explanation. Conway passed the note to Lillywhite, who did not reply.

The real issue was, of course, money. Murdoch and Alexander felt that as they were continuing as the Australian Eleven, they were entitled to the terms they had enjoyed in England: that is, half the gate. This would be unprecedented. A touring team bore much greater expenses than a home team, so the convention had always been for generosity to err on the tourists' side. But Murdoch and Alexander considered their Eleven to *still* be a touring team.

England then played at Windsor, Parramatta and Grafton. Ulyett 'fell' out of boats in Sydney Harbour and the Clarence River, showing off his diving and swimming ability through shark-infested waters. He said he only fell into the Clarence after he had been trying to 'bleed' a local doctor, who pushed him away. Ulyett just avoided the propeller, then saw a shark. A teammate held a spear in case the shark went for him, and Ulyett had his knife out, but he made it safely onto the boat. On board, the doctor promised £100 in apology for pushing him off. He gave Ulyett a possum rug, but the money never eventuated.

In the game at Parramatta, Shaw had an unusual meeting. 'Among our visitors to the ground was a detachment of harmless people, who were patients in the Parramatta Asylum. I had a long talk to a decently-dressed Englishman, who was never suspected of being one of the afflicted, the conversation turning on trade and other matters in the old country, but much to my surprise I learned afterwards that I had been talking to Thomas Cresswell, an inmate of the asylum, who is said by some to be the real Arthur Orton of the Tichborne romance.'

This was a rare light moment during what Shaw described as 'a chapter in Anglo-Australian cricket that it is not pleasant to recall'.

Negotiations for the Test in Adelaide, and two to follow in Melbourne and Sydney, became deadlocked. Murdoch's demand for half the gate, wrote Shaw and Shrewsbury, 'coming from a team supposed to be composed of amateurs, and playing at home, staggered us. We replied that 30 per cent was the utmost we could afford to give. We held that it was absurd, not to say ungenerous, to expect the same sum for playing at home as would be paid to a team who had travelled thousands of miles in pursuit of their profession. Melbourne, Sydney, and Adelaide were the only places where we could hope to realise a substantial profit, and to give half of this profit to a team who had been making a handsome profit in England, when playing against professionals who received only £10 per man, was most unreasonable. Our offer of 30 per cent was refused, and I made a personal offer of £20 per man, which was rejected with contumely.'

Lillywhite wrote that even 30 per cent was 'far too much when taking into consideration the pay these men (i.e. the English eleven) had when playing against you in so many of these large money-making matches'.

The England manager threatened to 'rouse' public opinion against the Australians, but it was happening anyway. On 22 November, the *Sydney Mail* noted 'great indignation' at the Eleven's 'grasping policy'.

For the first Test, Alexander said he would accept 40 per cent and give 10 to charity. Shaw rejected this. Fearing the cherished, long-awaited Adelaide match would fall victim to the squabbling, Creswell offered each team a flat fee of £450 plus one-third of any profits, which the teams accepted. Shaw said, 'We thought it very hard that we should have to submit to the demand of the Murdoch combination – for that is what the playing on equal terms amounted to – but had we not done so there would have been no match.' Brokering the compromise was an enormous risk on Creswell's part, and the SACA set prices at a high four shillings per seat in the stand and two shillings in the outer.

While the Englishmen prepared, the Australians were hopelessly distracted. Giffen wanted to make a success of the historic event in his home city. He, McDonnell and Blackham 'practised assiduously for a fortnight to get into form, but none of the others took the interest they should have in the match, and some of them played without having had more than a day's practice since they left England'.

Four days before the match, Murdoch married Jemima and practised little, if any, cricket. Spofforth, meanwhile, had only just arrived from

England, and said he had an ankle injury. Aside from not having bowled for two months, he had other reasons not to play. His brother-in-law, Charles Farquhar Clive, had died a month earlier, and he wanted to go back to Cassilis, this time to comfort his widowed sister, Anna.

When Horan met him as he got off the SS *Ganges* in Melbourne, Spofforth revealed that he did not share the Murdoch–Alexander position on gate money. Spofforth, wrote Horan, 'does not intend to play with the Australian Eleven against the Englishmen in Adelaide, and he regrets very much the position taken by his comrades in connexion with the now fully ventilated question of gate money. The want of tact and good management on the part of the executive of the Australian Eleven has surprised the "demon" not a little.'

An expectant South Australian government declared Friday 12 December, the opening day of the Test, a public holiday. But the high ticket prices kept the crowds away, and a disappointing 7000 showed up on what Shaw nevertheless called 'a grand [day] for cricket'.

Any expectations of peace were quickly shot down. At the last moment, Murdoch objected to Lillywhite standing as England's umpire. Forced to accede or abandon the match, the English backed down. 'As it was then too late to get any thoroughly competent men from either of the two great centres of cricket,' Shaw and Shrewsbury wrote, 'we had to put up with two unknown men [Tom Cole and Isaac Fisher], one of whom proved by his decisions that his knowledge of the game was limited.'

The Englishmen didn't make the umpires' life any easier, according to the *Advertiser*, which said 'the English have the irritating habit of appealing in chorus at every possible opportunity, presumably with the motive of discommoding the batsmen. The sooner this undesirable habit is corrected the better.'

The Australians were the first to suffer, Bannerman getting a bad lbw decision. The home players were not, said Shaw, 'slow to express dissatisfaction'. Murdoch and Scott followed, and then Blackham joined McDonnell, who had made a fine start. Soon Blackham was given out lbw, but made such a commotion – enough to earn him a long holiday today – that the umpire changed his mind. 'Then it was our turn to grumble,' Shaw said. 'An over or two after Blackham had been allowed to keep his place, the same umpire asked [Billy] Barnes why he had not appealed for the batsman's dismissal in a similar way to another ball. "Why," asked Barnes, "should you have given him out?" "Certainly," replied the clever judge. And this was to a ball that was pitched two or three inches off the wicket.'

Blackham went on to 66, the only support for McDonnell's 124, made out of 190 while he was at the crease, in Australia's 243.

The next day, Creswell halved the admission and 10,000 attended. A dust storm blew up, and Boyle, Giffen and Palmer bowled over after over on the dry wicket while Cooper was again ineffective. Showers turned the wicket sticky for the third day, but Barnes made 134, Scotton 82 and England led by 126. The 'practisers', McDonnell, Blackham and Giffen, were the only contributors to Australia's second innings. McDonnell looked set to become the first Test cricketer to score two centuries in a match when, on 83 and the score at 125, he called Giffen for a run. 'I wish I were anywhere but in the middle of the ground', said the sickened South Australian, whose indecision ran McDonnell out.

After more rain, England won by eight wickets. Shaw said 'every member of our party felt as if he had obtained personal satisfaction for an unpleasant business.'

Nobody could have known that the Test match was the beginning of a dark age for cricket. Creswell must have been wondering what he had got himself into. His gamble had failed: gate receipts of £792 left the SACA with a loss of several hundred pounds.

This only hardened the VCA's and the Englishmen's resolve for the second Test: they would not let the Eleven push them around. Lillywhite offered Alexander 30 per cent of the gate for the January Test in Melbourne and a February Test in Sydney. Alexander rejected it, and Lillywhite threatened to play against a replacement team: 'I have not the slightest doubt that both matches will pay us better than playing you at 30%.' The local press had now swung behind the Englishmen. Horan, who was hosting Shaw and company in Melbourne, appealed to Murdoch's Eleven to 'make what you can in the old country' but in Australia 'act a little generously towards our visitors'.

The Englishmen toured the rich Victorian gold-mining centres of Maryborough, Sandhurst (Bendigo) and Ballarat, plus the pastoral town of Benalla where local entrepreneurs funded their matches. Ulyett and Scotton won mining shares as prizes, which they auctioned off, said Shaw, for 'a useful sum'.

When the English returned to Melbourne, eight of Murdoch's Eleven, including the captain, were playing in the intercolonial. Murdoch made 97 for NSW, Blackham a century for Victoria. Horan played, but not Spofforth. To the Englishmen's surprise, the Australian stars mixed amicably with them. This convinced Shaw and Shrewsbury 'that many of the side were willing from the first to meet us in the field, but they were very badly advised by their captain and the secretary, Alexander, who, as many of our English readers will know, was wonderfully keen in the commercial department throughout the whole of the English tour'.

The Australians had overreached fatally in Adelaide. By taking £450 and scorching the SACA, they had pushed the VCA and the Englishmen together. When negotiations again stalled over the second Test, the VCA refused to underwrite a loss. Conway and Lillywhite offered £20 per man, which Alexander and Murdoch rejected. Seeing the public and VCA were backing England, Alexander and Murdoch asked for 40 per cent of net profits, which they would hand over to Melbourne charities after deducting their expenses. When this ploy was rejected, the members of the Eleven boycotted the match.

On 27 December, Horan wrote that the VCA 'should show some backbone in this matter and take notice of these refusals. If every member of the recent Australian team disappeared from the country tomorrow, cricket would still flourish in the land. Indeed, according to their action since they came back, it would be a good thing for Australian cricket if they never played here again.'

It was an extraordinary outburst by a man who had been on two tours of England and was a good friend of the Eleven. The press, the visitors, the administrators and many Australian players were now arrayed against Murdoch and Alexander.

In addition to the members of the Eleven who boycotted the match, Midwinter said he was sick, Giffen could not get leave from the Adelaide Post Office, and Spofforth was still in Cassilis. He did, however, send a letter to an English friend stating his 'thorough disgust' with the Eleven.

Asked to explain why they would not play, the Victorians in the Eleven — Boyle, Blackham, Bonnor, Palmer and Scott — sent a message saying simply: 'Because Conway is manager.' Lillywhite said this was a 'despicable excuse' and a 'ridiculous subterfuge'. It might have been true that Murdoch and Alexander didn't like Conway, but nobody bought this as a reason. Horan said the message was 'so feeble, frivolous and absurd that a schoolboy of 12 would hesitate to sign it'. The real reason, he said, was gate money. He launched into a defence of Conway against the objections, which were 'of the lamest and most impotent description'. The Eleven, he wrote sarcastically, would happily play in a Conway-organised game for 50 per cent of the gate, but at 30 per cent he was suddenly a man they could not stand. He called attention to Conway's history as a founding force in Australian Test cricket:

'Mr John Conway was made the stalking horse, and, believing some tittle-tattle that had been carried to them by some meddling busybody, they pronounced him solely responsible for their refusal to play against the Englishmen. Poor Conway! Had it not been for him there would have been no Australian Eleven for years, for it was to his energy and judgement that we owed the existence of an Australian Eleven, and had it not been for his pertinacity some of those who were members of the first eleven and are now his bitterest enemies, would not have accompanied the team.'

The president of the VCA, Mr Justice Hartley Williams, had 'dispersed to the winds the assertion that Mr Conway was the obstacle ... This move was aptly described by his Honor as 'drawing a red herring across the trail'. No one had been more loyal to the Australians than Mr Justice Williams. He had fought their battles at home and abroad, but he expected, as we all expected, that, having done well in England, they would on their return fight for the honour of their country, apart from all monetary considerations.'

What upset Horan most was that after the Australian Elevens had had to defend themselves against English accusations that they were mercenaries, now, at home, they were proving the accusations correct.

'Many a time and oft have we resented what we considered the ill-natured remarks of the English press when denouncing the Australians as mercenary men, and had we considered them in the right upon this occasion we should have written our pen to the stump in their defence. But they were clearly in the wrong, and it grieves us to think that those who were so ready in England to take every opportunity to twit them with being mere money grubbers will now consider that they have strong corroborative evidences in the demands they have made in their own country.'

Things got even worse when it was rumoured that Murdoch and Alexander were trying to bully some waverers into maintaining the boycott. Alexander went to print refuting this, and wondered where the rumours had come from. Horan replied: 'If he is very desirous of knowing [who], let him ask the members of his own team. Let him ask them, and see if each one can lay his hand upon his heart and honestly say that not one of them used any expression, did anything, or caused anything to be done in any way that would tend to influence any player against the Englishmen, and keep him from playing in the combined team.'

Now worked up to outrage against his former teammates, Horan revisited the November dispute, when the Australian Eleven had talked of staging a match competing with England's game against Victoria.

Horan thought that was 'the meanest thing ever done in the history of Australian cricket … in one breath the members of the Australian Eleven [said] they could not play for Victoria in the first match against the Englishmen because they were out of form after their long voyage. In the next breath they wired up to Sydney to arrange a match a week before the Englishmen, so that they might keep all the money out of the pockets of the latter, and so destroy their match. That indeed was a noble action, was it not?'

The VCA chose Horan to lead Australia in the Test, and banned Boyle, Palmer, Scott, McDonnell, Blackham, Bonnor, Cooper and Alexander from any matches under their jurisdiction. Horan and Sam Jones were the only Australian players at the MCG with Test experience, and five of the debutants were appearing in what would be their only Test. One, Harry Musgrove, had only ever played one first-class match – three years earlier. Musgrove, a theatre manager with a reputation for creative financial doings, would resurface in Australian cricket a decade later.

England despatched the tyros by 10 wickets. 'Altogether,' said Shaw, 'the match was a very pleasant one'. The attendance of 23,000 over four days was well down on the 50,000 who had gone to watch three days of the corresponding Test two years earlier.

The strikers became outcasts. Shaw and Shrewsbury wrote: 'Everybody we met condemned the stupid, paltry and selfish conduct of the team, and the press generally sided with us, and expressed sympathy towards us, while they were unsparing in their denunciation of the behaviour of the men who had been so well treated and had made so much money in England.'

On 3 January, Horan again let fly at his old mates: 'That the members of the fourth Australian Eleven have since their return lost all the good opinion they gained by their splendid play in England is patent to any ordinary and impartial observer. On all sides their action as a team has been condemned in the strongest terms. And now that they act not as a team but as individuals they are pursuing exactly the same course which called forth the well-merited censure of the press ... these men, who have all their time at their disposal, and could easily play, deliberately slight the association and the cricket public of the colony. The public desire to see the best team in Australia meet the Englishmen but rather than please the public these men prefer to vent their petty spite by doing all in their power to keep the pounds out of the pockets of our English professional visitors who make their living by cricket ... They have done all they can to destroy the good feeling between English and Australian cricketers ... They have shown no manliness, no courtesy, no spark of kindly feeling whatever to our English friends. I wonder how our men would feel if they were similarly treated in England. What would they think if W.G. Grace and the best men of England refused to meet them at Lord's or Kennington Oval?'

Shaw's team resumed their country odyssey. They endured an alarming voyage on rough seas from Nowra to Sydney, some players preferring the long road trip. Johnny Briggs got kicked by a horse, nearly toppling off a cliff at Fitzroy Falls, and six weeks later at Armidale his pipe stem stuck into the roof of his mouth when he fell off his bucking mount. He was unconscious for four hours and reports spread that he'd been killed. Shaw said: 'The poor fellow was so skinned and bruised that he could not recognise his own face.' Another time Briggs killed a venomous snake as it was about to bite him, while walking from a match to the team hotel.

Meanwhile, the Australian cricketing landscape rearranged itself. On 17 January, Boyle, Blackham, Palmer and Scott signed a letter to the *Australasian* detailing their objections to Conway. Softening, Horan wrote, 'Everybody would like to see them playing again.' Shaw, Shrewsbury and Lillywhite removed Conway as agent, as an olive branch. It was a sad end to the relationship between Conway and Murdoch, who would remain unreconciled. When Conway died in 1909, only Horan and Allan of the 1878 team went to his funeral. Horan wrote a tribute calling on the

MCC to put up a memorial 'to keep green the name and work of the dead and gone old warrior'.

On 24–27 January the English recorded a hollow victory over NSW, but none of the Eleven appeared. Murdoch did not even answer his invitation. Three weeks later, the return intercolonial was staged in Sydney. Again Murdoch stayed with his bride in Cootamundra, and the VCA's ban still kept out Blackham, Boyle, Scott and Palmer, but there were some surprising faces for NSW. Spofforth was back, opening the batting. Alick Bannerman was 96 not out when NSW won, after Charlie had top-scored with 83 in the first innings. And Bonnor was now playing for NSW after he and McDonnell had moved north. McDonnell's shift seems to have been genuine, as he was offered a position with the NSW Education Department, while Bonnor appears to have been trying to dodge the ban. In response, the associations imposed a four-month residential qualification period.

With the proposed third Test in Sydney a week away, the VCA appealed to the NSWCA to support its ban. The NSWCA did not, regarding it as a 'domestic Victorian matter', and said of its players' refusal to play for NSW against England, 'this committee does not consider that it comes within its province to demand any further explanation, or to take any further action with regard to such refusal'.

Lillywhite intimated that the NSW move 'was no doubt owing to a very powerful party in Sydney secretly siding with what the Colonists had done, and outvoting those who condemned their actions'. It is quite likely that Dave Gregory, a 'powerful party' in NSW cricket, was squarely supportive of 'the Colonists'.

So the NSWCA, which selected the Australian team for the Sydney Test, chose a mixed bunch: four members of the Eleven (Bannerman, Scott, Bonnor and Spofforth), four players from the second Test (Horan, Jones, Affie Jarvis and Billy Trumble), and three NSW veterans (Evans, Garrett and finally Massie, whom, for good measure, they made captain). An exciting, low-scoring Test match

NEVER A GENTLEMEN'S GAME

ensued, punctuated by a hailstorm on the first day that blanketed the ground in white, and Spofforth's ten wickets had the final say as Australia won by six runs.

Sydney staged another Test match in mid-March, a reconciliation affair in which Palmer, McDonnell, Giffen and Blackham were brought back, to play alongside the 'strike-breakers' such as Horan, Garrett and Spofforth. Only Murdoch was unavailable. On financial matters, Lillywhite wrote that the Australians had 'come to their senses' and played for their 'bare expenses', 'except Bannerman and Giffen, who charged an exorbitant price'.

The excitements were on the field, for a change. Giffen starred in England's first innings with seven wickets, then Bonnor crashed his only Test century, 128 in 115 minutes. The English complained that Giffen and Horan bowled at the 'spot' created by Spofforth's follow-through. The Demon and Palmer shared nine second-innings wickets and Australia squared the series.

If there was a feeling that peace had descended, it was cautious. The rancour that had built up over seven years was not going to dissipate in a few weeks. A *Bulletin* cartoon on 24 January showed the Eleven gathered under the banner of 'Professional players who keep a sharp eye on the Gate Money' while standing on a mat titled 'Gentlemen Amateurs'. Another on 7 March showed an octopus of '£.s.d.' dragging down the body of 'Australian Cricket'. It mocked Murdoch as 'the giant' and 'the Australian Great Man', and welcomed his absence. 'It's about time that William resumed his profession as a gentleman', it said, and 'gave the gate-money racket a rest'. 'We consider him a bore.' He had 'had his day ... Billy is getting too fat'.

Yet at another point in the season, the *Bulletin* remembered its nationalist leanings, saying Australians 'would never consent to be spat upon by dirty little cads whose soap-boiling or nigger-murdering grandfathers left enough money to get the cads' fathers "ennobled" and to enable the cad ... to live without working.'

By March, Lillywhite wrote that the tour had been 'unsuccessful ... financially up till now'. Little wonder. Hoping for an increased gate for a newly scheduled fifth Test match in Melbourne, he asked the VCA to lift the bans on the Victorian stars. It refused, but promised the Englishmen 100 per cent of the gate. The match was a bizarre one. It had seven umpires, due to ill-health, walk-offs and the teams' objections. Elliott died the day before the match and was replaced by Hodges, Phillips replaced Lillywhite on the morning of the match after the latter decided to concentrate on his managerial duties, Garrett stood after tea on the third day when Hodges objected to remarks made by the Englishmen about his competence, and Lillywhite came back to stand on the last day. Allen of the Melbourne CC stood for the last two days when Phillips fell ill. Even Massie, visiting Melbourne as a spectator, had a hand at umpiring. Spofforth scored his only Test fifty, but England won by an innings, spearheaded by a Shrewsbury century and seven wickets from Ulyett.

Widespread relief greeted the end of the season. The English promoters left with a bare profit of £150 each, but gained some compensation by winning opportunities to sell sportsgoods. The Australian public had responded appropriately: the five Tests drew 98,000 spectators compared with 175,000 for the four Tests of 1882–83. This would start a decline that would soon threaten the very viability of Anglo-Australian cricket.

In mid-1885, the participants tried to play the dispute down. Shaw said it was 'an unpleasant family jar' more than 'a serious international quarrel'. He wondered 'if the cricket rivalries of England and the Colonies might not have a lamentable influence upon the more vital relations between the Mother Country and its off-shoots'. It was pointed out in the press that the cricket quarrel hadn't stopped NSW and Victoria supplying men to Britain's war in the Sudan.

Horan, summing up a season in which he had made a surprising and not entirely happy return to Test cricket, wrote on 25 April 1885:

'Never in the history of Australian cricket has it fallen to the lot of cricket scribes to make a retrospect so full of unpleasantness and discord as that of the season which has just terminated. In bygone years we have had occasional dissensions, but they were usually of a mild and evanescent type. Those troubles left not even the faintest speck to tarnish the lustre of our cricketing fame. They passed away as speedily almost as the cloud shadows that flit across the turf we play upon. But in 1884–5 there came a deep and lasting shadow, which cast a universal gloom upon our manly game.'

'BLOOD-SPATTERED CARRIAGES'

The gloom was only just beginning. Would an Australian team ever be welcome in England again? As historian David Montefiore notes, the rise of Test cricket in Australia was 'anything but certain' – after 1884 there was 'a near total collapse in support for the emerging institution of Anglo-Australian cricket'.

Lillywhite summarised: 'The real cause of all this disturbance was money; nothing but money! And no explanation on the part of the Colonists will prove any other motive. The fact is the wondrous success of these men in England was too much for them, and in their conceit, considered what they proposed must be law, and their admirers in Australia also fostered this idea; consequently, when proposals from them were met by a blank refusal, their dignity was roused, and vengeance in the shape of, if possible, spoiling the monetary success of the tour was resolved upon … I hope it will be a lesson to the rising players in this Country and Australia, that such a grasping policy is hardly likely to conduce to harmony.'

In 1885, there was doubt whether another Australian Eleven could be formed. The *Sportsman* suggested that the next tour should wait until 1887. On 14 March 1885, the *Bulletin* reported that Lord's had sent a cable stating that only Spofforth of the 1884 Eleven would be welcome, and Australia would not be allowed to play at Lord's, the Oval or Trent Bridge. It would 'serve em right' as they had 'wrung the neck of the goose that laid their golden eggs'. The *Sydney Mail* added: 'Murdoch's Eleven, in their thirst for gold, have brought the stigma on themselves.'

Lillywhite wrote to the *Sydney Mail* that the Australian team must 'bring Spofforth, even if they have to give him a thousand down', but 'they must not bring any of Murdoch's late team, even if each of them offered to give 100 pounds to be selected. They would only spoil the trip.' The *Mail* opined that if Spofforth came back to England, he would 'find himself 10 times more popular than he ever was, all in consequence of his conduct in the late cricketing dispute'.

But Spofforth announced he would not be taking another tour. In June 1885 he moved to Melbourne, becoming officer-in-charge of the National Bank of Australasia branch in Moonee Ponds. His boss was Frank Grey Smith, vice president of the Melbourne Cricket Club, which Spofforth joined. Bonnor, meanwhile, returned to Melbourne but would play the next summer for NSW. Murdoch refused to play cricket outside Cootamundra. Derek Carlaw comments: 'It seems to be generally acknowledged that Murdoch decided to retire and concentrate on his [legal] practice because he had had enough of press criticism and cricket politics in general. Given his essentially easy going outlook on life, it seems likely. On the other hand, pressure from his new father-in-law might have played a part, as could the need to earn regular serious money. It would not be very surprising if he was anxious to be seen to be capable of keeping his new wife in the style to which she was accustomed.'

Murdoch and Jemima moved to Victoria in 1885, where he practised law and rebuffed Boyle's pleas to play against NSW.

For all the comings and goings, the festering issue remained. Lord's, the Oval and Trent Bridge would only welcome an Eleven if they played truly as amateurs. It was back to 1880.

Justice Williams asked for a court to deem the banned Victorians as amateurs, but failed. The VCA lifted its ban on 10 November, but the players were told they would not be invited to England on the same lucrative terms as in 1884.

By December, Harris, Hornby and Bligh wrote that a team comprising 'amateurs' would be better received than a privately backed one like the previous tours. *Cricket* said the team would be 'coldly received' if it contained professionals, after the 'unwise and unsportsmanlike action of the leading spirits of Murdoch's combination', and Lillywhite wrote that 'the best interests of the game were not consulted when the trip was merely speculative undertaking on co-operative lines run by the players themselves, as a show'.

Horan saw both sides of the issue: 'Englishmen scoop the pool in Australia, and Australians scoop the pool in England.' He reminded readers that another Eleven going to England would be good advertising for Australia. The Elevens, he said, 'have been the means of bringing Australia and its resources very prominently before the English public in all parts of the kingdom ... When the people see and come in contact with real flesh and blood – strong, active fellows from the home of the kangaroo – the case is different. Australian elevens travel the length and breadth of the island, they play in every county, thousands flock to see them everywhere, hundreds of questions are put to them and letters written about Australia, and whether it is a good country to settle in. In this way the thing strikes right home.'

Creswell suggested that a combined SACA, NSWCA and VCA committee should choose a team of amateurs who would be accountable to that joint committee. It was a revolutionary idea – the first seed of a controlling cricket authority – but the VCA would only back it if NSW did, and NSW declined. When Creswell's proposal fell through, the

Melbourne Cricket Club took over, organising the tour with a fund of £1000 in its 'All England Eleven account', the profits it had made from Test matches in Melbourne. It was also trying to raise money for a new grandstand after its reversible one burnt down on 31 August 1884. With 1800 members subscribing more than £3000 per year, Melbourne was the most cashed-up cricket body in Australia and the nearest thing to an antipodean Marylebone.

The fallout was apparent in the team selection, announced on 12 December 1885. Murdoch, Bannerman and McDonnell refused to tour as amateurs, while work commitments kept out Horan, Boyle and Massie. Giffen, Bonnor, Palmer, Scott, Jarvis and Blackham backed up from previous tours, agreeing to go for a nominal upfront fee. Jones and Garrett prevaricated, but by late January both agreed to tour. Spofforth was picked but, as the *Sydney Mail* reported on 9 January, 'as usual, avers that he will not join the team; but when the "Demon" says "no" he generally means "yes", or rather he does the reverse of what he says!'

The newcomers included Victorians Billy Trumble, John McIlwaith and Billy Bruce, but the most noteworthy was Evans, who finally accepted his fifth invitation at the age of 37. He fell ill with sunstroke which 'affected poor Evans' mind', or so said the *Sydney Mail*, in November 1885, but recovered by January. The *Mail* said, 'this popular cricketer' who was a 'really good bowler' on wet wickets could emulate Boyle in England. Spofforth finally agreed to tour in mid-January; then, putting ego ahead of camaraderie, told Horan he would back himself to take 100 more wickets than Evans. Provocatively, Horan wrote: 'If Evans shows anything like his old intercolonial form when he used to beat the demon time after time in bowling average, Spofforth's chance of winning the wager will, I fancy, not be particularly bright.'

The other discussion point was the captaincy. Giffen spoke for many players when he said Murdoch's unavailability was 'a decision which every Australian regretted'. Murdoch was the natural leader, able to harmonise several headstrong characters. His batting remained the lynchpin, and without him, Bannerman or McDonnell, the 1886 team looked short on runs.

The *Mail* said, 'one cannot but be struck by the want of players in the team suitable to fill the position of captain. It is very strange that out of 13 good cricketers there is not one who possesses that tact, judgement and discriminative faculty which are required in the leader of an eleven.'

The colonial captains were Blackham (Victoria), Garrett (NSW) and Giffen (SA). Giffen would have too many responsibilities holding together the batting and the bowling. Blackham was seen as introverted and too close to Murdoch, as well as being busy enough behind the stumps. And in the first NSW–Victoria match, when Victoria scored 471, Garrett was widely criticised for not handling the bowling well. He had led NSW twice, and both times they lost by an innings. In the second intercolonial of 1885–86, he marched onto the ground to argue with an umpire about whether a shot had gone over the boundary or not. He later apologised, but the Victorians were resentful.

As if by default, the captaincy devolved to Scott. Although a paid-up member of Murdoch's clique, he appealed as the right type. He was 27, Toorak-born, Wesley-educated, a medical student at Melbourne University, and a representative of St Kilda and East Melbourne. He had a strong tour in 1884, when he picked up the nickname 'Tup' for his habit of taking twopenny bus tours sightseeing in London.

The early auguries for the 1886 team were unpromising. Trial matches fell through when the NSW players refused to play in the first, for money reasons, then the Melbourne Cricket Club refused the SCG's ground rental for the second. Scott had his work cut out.

Charles Pardon in *Wisden* would begin his report on the 1886 Australians with a simple statement: 'The fifth tour of Australian cricketers in

England was emphatically a failure, whether we regard it as an event of itself, or compared it with the previous visits.'

Given the background politics and the missing players, how could this tour *not* have been 'a feeble and spiritless thing'? At its outset, however, optimists tried to hype up the tour. Murdoch and some others from 1884 were in decline, fresh blood was called for, and here it was. Spofforth, Palmer and Garrett gave bite to the attack. Scott and McIlwraith had made centuries in Australia, while Giffen, long touted as 'Australia's Grace', was poised to prove the boom with figures in England.

Three thousand well-wishers gathered at the MCG to celebrate Scott's Eleven with fireworks, coloured lights and a military band. Seven of the team left Adelaide on 28 March, while the other six, detained by various personal commitments, left with Ben Wardill, secretary of the Melbourne Cricket Club, on 10 April. The two groups met in Naples and arrived at Plymouth on 4 May.

According to Altham, the team 'was heralded with something of a flourish of trumpets' because it was organised by the Melbourne Cricket Club. 'The almost unanimous verdict of the Australian Press had hailed it as at least the equal, if not the superior, of any of its predecessors.'

After nine days of practice at Chiswick Park in west London, Scott's Eleven turned out at Sheffield Park in the red, white and blue of Melbourne in front of an 'immense attendance' of 13,000 – and were bowled out for 98. Scott, who had top-scored with 23, dropped Scotton early in Lord Sheffield's Eleven's innings, and the Australians began to bicker in the field. Garrett's 6/22 kept the home team's lead down, but another ignominious collapse for 70 sealed a poor eight-wicket loss.

Rain plagued them through the spring, preventing a result at Trent Bridge and any play at Lord's. In between, they lost to Surrey, then had what might be described as a humiliating victory over Oxford University. Dismissed for 70 and 38, Australia – chiefly Spofforth with 10 for 36 in the match – put the students out for 45 and 38.

A heavy defeat to the North of England followed with dreadful cricket on a wicket only bowlers could love: Australia made 45 and 43, the North 34 and 1/15. In nine completed innings, Scott's Eleven had only passed 100 once, when they totalled 109 against Nottinghamshire.

England was sodden. From sunny Melbourne, Horan wrote sympathetically about Evans: 'Can we not figure him going to the front door of the Grand Hotel after breakfast each morning, when in London, and gazing in a hopeless, mournful way at the leaden, cheerless, weeping heavens, and wondering whether the weather will ever be fine again? ... Evans, doubtless, by this time thinks the whole island a gigantic watering-pot.'

The seventh match was crucial, not so much for the result – Australia registered a win over the Gentlemen – as for an injury to Spofforth while Lord Harris was batting. Spofforth 'followed up his ball very far, and as I probably jumped in, he was very close, too close to put his hand in exactly the right place'. Harris's drive broke the third finger on Spofforth's right hand. To that point, Spofforth had been averaging just under seven runs a wicket, and had dismissed Grace that morning.

Giffen said that without Spofforth's injury, 'I feel sure the record at the close of the tour would have been a very different one.' Spofforth went off to The Cedars, the Derbyshire mansion of the Cadman family, where he recuperated and courted Phillis. Her father Joseph had expanded a grocery store into the Star Tea Company, a big business with shops, warehouses, cafes and hotels throughout England. It listed publicly in 1892, by which time Spofforth would be the son-in-law and managing director.

While Spofforth was out, the pitches dried. Garrett, Palmer and Giffen had to carry the attack. Garrett's first son, Thomas, was born at St John's Wood on 24 May. His wife Helen had sailed over and taken lodgings, and his spendthrift parliamentarian father Thomas was also in tow. Garrett was working on a new approach to bowling, with far-reaching consequences. His biographer, Max Bonnell, writes, 'Garrett's innovation was the realisation that on good pitches, good batsmen were more likely to be caught than bowled.' Garrett was the first fastish bowler to use off-theory as a form of attack. On his previous tours, more than half of his wickets had been bowled. In 1886, of his 123 wickets, 80 were caught. The novelty of 'off-theory' would eventually become orthodoxy.

Giffen was in irresistible form, taking 6/71 in the Gentlemen's second innings, then 7/41 and 9/60 against Derbyshire, 8/56 against Cambridge University, 8/23 and 8/42 against Lancashire, 4/91 against the Players, and recording four half-centuries in those matches, before finally, in Spofforth's return against Lord March's Eleven at Chichester, taking 3/22 and 7/21. Giffen was the only Australian player on the tour to write a memoir, and his recollection is infused with his personal achievements: he regarded the tour as successful. By June, he wrote, 'our record was almost as good as that of any team which had preceded us'. In that spurt after Spofforth's injury, when he took 51 wickets at 9.35, Giffen said that 'that fortnight's bowling was the best I ever did'.

His optimism was an island, however, in a sea of gloom. Only Scott, Jones and Bruce made centuries before the first Test. The batting was consistently bad, and that old wound of Australian cricket, NSW–Victorian relations, had turned septic. Scott had to adjudicate in disputes, and there were reports of 'bloodstained carriages' after team members came to blows during a post-game train ride.

One reason for the discord, argues Bonnell, 'was Scott's treatment of Evans. It was obvious from the outset that the captain had a low opinion of Evans's bowling. Evans was given two long spells in the match against Surrey, but otherwise he bowled only nine overs in the team's first nine games ... Inevitably he was not as penetrative as in his younger days, but he posed a greater threat than Billy Trumble, Scott's friend from Melbourne University, who was given more bowling. Sometimes Scott's reluctance to use Evans was conspicuously perverse.'

Giffen supported Scott, saying Evans was 'only a shadow of

what he had been as a bowler six or eight years before'. By the first Test match, at Old Trafford starting on 5 July, the Australian team was limping. Spofforth was complaining about his finger, unable to impart his old cut and spin; most players agreed with Harris that the Demon 'was never the same bowler'. The ranks were so thin that Roley Pope, a Sydney University player who had been called up as one of the lambs to the slaughter in the second Test of 1884–85, before studying medicine at Edinburgh University, was asked to play. When his term finished in June, he met up with the Australian Eleven and followed them around as a fan. While watching them play Middlesex, he said, 'to my utter astonishment I was called to put the pads on'. He helped Blackham seal a one-wicket victory, played three more first-class games, and answered the call to field 18 times. Grace called him 'the Universal Substitute'.

Before the first Test, the England side was also mired in dispute. Grace, having his most prolific season against an Australian Eleven, was still denied the England captaincy. After putting Hornby and Harris ahead of him in previous series, now England chose Hornby again. When he withdrew with a leg injury, they chose Steel. Rae writes: 'Grace's behaviour in Australia [in 1873–74] may have counted against him, and his abrasive competitiveness was always likely to spark an incident ... As long as there was a credible alternative, the authorities were clearly determined to play safe.'

There was also Grace's closeness to Murdoch, and his apparent encouragement of Australia's 'mercenary' approach on previous tours. Moreover, recently he had been linked to some unpleasant business. In the first week of June 1886, his cousin Walter Gilbert, who had been so involved with Australia's 1880 tour, turned professional because he was in need of regular money. But a week later a sting caught him thieving from his Gloucestershire teammates' clothes hanging in the dressing room, and he was sacked, then convicted in court. He served 28 days' hard labour before being sent to Canada where he led a blameless life for another 38 years. For Lord's, though, it was another black mark against W.G.

A tour's success was now judged by Australia's performances in the big matches. The 1878 and 1882 tours had been lionised because Australia had won the centrepiece contests. The 1880 and 1884 teams were as good, but their glister was dulled by their failure to beat England in the Tests.

In 1886, a win on the Test stage was needed to save a crumbling venture. In Manchester, large crowds watched three unusually dry days. Australia's batsmen, led by Sammy Jones, dominated the early sessions, but a late cascade of seven wickets for 24 runs kept them to 205. England took an 18-run lead, Barlow scoring 38 not out before he grabbed the ball and decimated Australia for 123. As the pitch broke up Australia took early wickets, but Barlow, having the match of his life, guided England home by four wickets.

Heartened by their brave uphill struggle, the Australians had the better of a draw with Nottinghamshire, beat Yorkshire and drew with Liverpool and District before the second Test at Lord's. There, in the litmus test of the tour, they were crushed. Before 33,000 paying spectators over the three days – defeat never harmed Australia's pulling power – Shrewsbury played one of those innings that had Grace exclaim, when asked who was the greatest batsman he had played with, 'Give me Arthur!'

England won the toss but rain spiced up the wicket. 'The wicket was none too clever,' Giffen recalled. 'It was a fiery Lord's pitch, and most first-class batsmen know what that means, but [Shrewsbury's] defence was perfect, and he played all the bowling as though it were simple as ABC.'

In nearly seven hours over the first two days Shrewsbury scored 164 on what Altham calls 'three different types of pitch – fiery, slow and sticky'. Harris and Barlow judged it the best innings they saw, and Altham, nearly four decades later, after Trumper, Ranji, Hill, Hobbs and Macartney, said it was 'possibly the greatest innings that has ever been seen'.

Shrewsbury was the greatest of the professional batsmen at a time when they overtook the amateurs. His batting for Nottinghamshire helped make them the champion county through the decade. In 1903, believing he had a terminal illness, he committed suicide at the age of 46, having topped the national averages the season before. Four years later, a dying Alfred Shaw said: 'Put me under the ground twenty-two yards from Arthur, so that I may send him down a ball now and then.' The story – unfortunately apocryphal – went that he was buried 27 yards away, to allow for his five-yard run.

At Lord's, England's 353 was insurmountable for the brittle Australian batting, which could not handle Briggs's left-arm spin. The only bright note was that Lord's gave them 80 per cent of the gate, or £650, for 'expenses'. Giffen concluded: 'It is strange how badly Australians have on the whole shaped at Lord's ... Australia have more than once shockingly failed on the ground in a most unaccountable way ... I think the failures are due more to imagination than to anything else. Our batsmen have got the idea into their heads that Lord's is one of their "unlucky" grounds, and with such a superstition dominating them, stupid though it may be, they have not done themselves justice ... Perhaps the particular goddess who controls the destinies of cricketers is making Australians pay, whenever they appear at Lord's, for having in 1878 trailed the Union Jack of English cricket in the mud on that famous ground!'

Bonnor was injured at Lord's. Cricket teams all have cliques who protect their less-gifted friends, and Bonnor's record – 17 Tests, average 17.08 – suggests he was lucky to take five tours. His occasional spectaculars masked the fact that mostly he was a passenger. But he always drew a crowd – perhaps the real reason he was selected – and he was worth many good stories. On this tour, he showed that at last he had become a proud Australian. Accused of not knowing who Dr Johnson was, Bonnor said: 'I come from a great country where you can ride a horse 60 miles a day for three months and never meet a soul who has heard of Dr Johnson either.'

Having lost the Test series, the Australians' morale was shattered. August brought a sequence of drawn matches and the humiliation of being thrashed by Surrey by an innings and 209, and Yorkshire by 10 wickets. Then, before more big crowds at the Oval, they suffered another innings defeat to England. They dropped Grace at 6, 23, 60, 93 and 169 during a four-and-a-half-hour slaughter. Giffen said: 'As I stood there watching him bat, I would think to myself, "What a difference to Australian Elevens it would make, if there were no W.G. to go in first and kill our bowling!"'

Grace scored 170 of the 216 while he was at the wicket, the highest proportion for a century in Ashes cricket. It was helped by the fact that his partner for most of it was Scotton, who scored 34 runs in nearly four hours. *Punch* could not resist a parody of Tennyson's 'Break, Break, Break' which concluded:

> 'And the clock's slow hands go round,
> And you still keep up your sticks.
> But, oh, for the lift of a smiting hand,
> And the sound of a swipe for six.
> Block, block, block,
> At the foot of they wickets, ah, do!
> But one hour of Grace or Walter Read
> Were worth a week of you!'

England ended up with 434, with Evans bowling 13 overs for six runs, and Giffen bowling 62, Garrett 99, and Palmer and Trumble 47 overs each. Of Australia's reply – 68 and 149 – the less said the better.

Their losing margin, an innings and 217 runs, was the heaviest by either team until 1934.

For the first time in a Test, the Australians were destroyed by the true heir to Spofforth. George Lohmann's 7/36 and 5/68 eclipsed the Demon, who was used sparingly in what would be his last Test match in England. Lohmann's appearance captured the imagination. Altham calls him 'the very personification of cricket. With his fair moustache and hair, his wide blue eyes set rather far apart, his broad shoulders, yet lithe and supple frame, he was a wellnigh perfect example of the Anglo-Saxon type; his whole heart was in the game, which, indeed, he loved not wisely but too well, crowding into thirteen years more work than even his magnificent physique could stand.'

Grace and Charles Fry said Lohmann was the best medium-pace bowler they faced. For Altham, 'he was the first English bowler really to master the revolutionary lessons of Spofforth, and to make length the handmaid of variety in pace and spin and flight'. He had the full repertoire: high delivery, subtle flight, ability to break the ball either way, tricky slower ball. Ralph Barker locates his art in deception and variation: 'The four-ball over was still in force at this time, but bowlers like Lohmann welcomed the increase in the number of balls per over when it came, because it enabled them to bring more and more variety and deception into the same over.'

Lohmann would retire with the lowest average of any English bowler against Australia, 77 wickets at 13, though his average, if not his skill, was helped by the swift deterioration in Australian batting and some poor pitch preparation.

After the Oval Test, the tour dragged on for another 13 matches against mainly composite teams. Grace, who ended up taking 812 runs off the Australians, said the program was 'too long for all practical purposes ... Towards the end of their thirty-nine matches public interest in their doings somewhat dwindled away.'

By universal consensus the 1886 tour ranks among the worst. The Tests were lost 3–0, still the only whitewash for an Australian team against England, and of the 39 tour fixtures, 9 were won, 8 lost, and 22 drawn. Even the relentlessly positive Giffen admitted that the tour 'somewhat tarnished the escutcheon of Australian cricket', though most of the 22 draws 'were in our favour, so that I don't think we did so badly'.

In Australia, the reaction was predictable. Horan wrote that Evans did 'very badly' but had 'not been given a proper chance'. The team 'were absolutely, hopelessly, irretrievably crushed'. The *Sydney Mail* said, 'our old players are not to be relied upon' as 'they are getting stale, and their retirement is necessary for the restoration of our cricketing prestige'. It named Garrett, Evans and Spofforth, and said, 'there can be found more trustworthy batsmen than Bonnor in our junior ranks'.

More dispiriting than the results was the lack of fight. Altham said that 'for the first time we saw an Australian side at its worst under difficult batting conditions, and liable to "crack" at a crisis'. Charles Pardon, in *Wisden*, said any strong county team could have toured England and done better than Australia. 'Instead of an energetic, skilful, determined, bustling game, we saw on too many occasions a mere playing-out of time, and on one or two days a failure of nerve and an exhibition of weakness which those who had looked upon the Australians at their best – as we saw them in 1882 – found it difficult to believe possible.'

Perhaps the key players had other things on their minds. Spofforth, between games, married Phillis Cadman at Breadsall Church near Derby. Bonnor, his best man, was the only Australian cricketer present, while Lord Harris sent a timepiece as a gift. Spofforth and Phillis, Garrett and McIlwraith and their wives would sail home separately from the other Australians.

The captain, Scott, retired from international cricket and stayed in England to pursue his medical studies. When he returned to Australia, he became a heroic country doctor, Mayor and Chief Magistrate of Scone, in the Upper Hunter Valley of New South Wales, and a friend of Banjo Paterson, before dying of typhoid caught from a patient in 1910. He was buried alongside his boon companion and fellow Mason, William Blomfield Pulling, headmaster of Scone Grammar School, who had collapsed and died in front of his class in 1894.

As with many a losing Australian team in England, the 1886 tourists were immensely popular. None of the players got rich from this tour, but the Melbourne Cricket Club made £1083: its report said 'the financial results of the trip were fairly successful'. In every other way, however, it marked the beginning of Australia's doldrums.

'A PERIOD OF DECADENCE'

Until 1885, international cricket's squabbles had grown out of Lillywhite's words, overheard by Conway, in 1877: 'There'd be plenty of money in it.' The enrichment of the early Australian Elevens produced secondary contests between the players and the local associations, between the players and the English authorities and professionals, and between the players themselves. But always it was a contest over how to divide the unexpected spoils of a great public entertainment.

There was never any question that if the best of Australia and England took the field, crowds would flock in. But as the squabbling worsened, the public changed its mind about cricket. The years Altham calls 'the doldrums' and Horan 'a period of decadence' threatened the very future of the international game.

Cricket's financial strength always rests on the pulling power of the key players – not on administrators, not on marketing visionaries, not on 'structures'. So it shouldn't be forgotten that the main reason for Australia's decline after 1884 was the disappearance of Murdoch, the fading of Spofforth, the ageing of Boyle, Palmer, Garrett and Horan, and, apart from Charlie Turner and Jack Ferris, the scarcity of new talent to replace them. Up to 1886, Australia led the completed Test matches by nine to eight. Of the next 11, England won 10, raising a belief that the era of Murdoch and Spofforth had been a historical anomaly, an interruption to the natural order of English superiority.

During the unhappy 1886 tour, Ben Wardill had been negotiating with England's leading amateurs about bringing a team to Australia the next southern summer. Their hope was to replicate the successful Bligh tour. But during the Australia–Gloucestershire match in August, Wardill learnt, probably from Grace, that a rival professional tour, organised by Shaw and Shrewsbury, was going to Australia.

Horan reported that two English teams competing for 'official' status and crowds in the colonies was 'unknown simply because from the outset cricket speculators were well aware that it would not pay to bring two teams out together'. The Shaw-Lillywhite-Shrewsbury professional enterprise, which had brought every England team but one to Australia since 1876–77, understandably thought it 'owned' the Australian territory. But the acrimony of 1884–85 and the Melbourne Cricket Club's organisation of the 1886 'amateur' Eleven had led to competition. Horan asked: 'How then has it come to pass that we are to have two teams now, when cricket is not as great a public attraction as it used to be? The answer is easy to give, but by no means pleasant to dwell upon.' He blamed the 'opposing agencies' of Melbourne and the English professionals – 'each body wishes the other to retire, and ... neither will do so. It is quite clear that there is room here for only one English team in one season, and hence if two teams come the effect will be decidedly detrimental to both. There is sure to be financial failure, coupled with much unpleasantness and heart burning.'

Faced with the inevitable, Wardill started talks with Shaw, saying his club would shelve its plans if the English would play their Melbourne games on the MCG. It was a last gamble to prevent disaster. *Wisden's* Charles Pardon reported: 'We shall say very little about this matter, because there was a good deal of ill-feeling displayed at the time ... It would have been simply deplorable if two English teams had competed with each other for the favour and countenance of the Australian public.'

A deal was struck, and two months later the professional English team was ripped apart in Sydney by Charlie Turner and Jack Ferris. Turner, nicknamed 'The Terror', had been in first-class cricket for several seasons. As a youngster, he had taken 10 wickets in an innings against Shaw's team in Bathurst, but had done little for NSW. It all changed in 1886–87. Bowling medium-fast off-breaks, targeting the stumps, Turner believed bowling was 'a pure gift ... that some men possess. It is no good saying that any man can be a bowler, as some people do.' 'Gift' or not, he did not fully discover it until he had Ferris at the other end. Ferris, nicknamed 'The Tricky', was a medium-pace left-armer of great accuracy, a containment bowler with subtle cut and spin who could play foil to Turner. Needless to say, each helped the other with footmarks on the desired length on the wet and poorly prepared pitches they enjoyed in Sydney.

Two weeks later the Scott-free Australian Eleven returned, 'jeered and chaffed' for their defeats in England. Ralph Barker comments: 'The Australians, it was clear, felt this series of defeats keenly and they were in a mood to discard their entire team and find a new one. "No one speaks of the team who have represented them in England," wrote one correspondent, "except to reproach them for their want of success".'

The English touring professional Maurice Read observed a contrast between Australian and English selections. 'If you have a bit of bad luck and make nothing two or three times, you are not of much account in

Australia, and out of the team you should go, even if you have scored excellently on occasions.' In England, however, 'if you are a recognised player, half a dozen successive noughts will not exclude you from a team'.

The Melbourne Cricket Club organised three games between the Australian Eleven, now led by Garrett, and the Englishmen, which the tourists won 2–0. The Australians' batting had improved little. Spofforth's decline coincided neatly with the arrival of Turner, who took ten Victorian wickets in the intercolonial including a hat-trick of Palmer, Horan and Trumble.

McDonnell, who had finalised his move to Sydney and scored 239 against his erstwhile teammates in the intercolonial, was elected captain for the match between a combined All-Australian Eleven and England at the SCG starting on 28 January. This, and not the previous three matches, was designated 'Test cricket' by Clarence Moody because all Australian players, not just the 1886 tourists, were considered. (The same logic would have excluded the watershed Adelaide Test match of December 1884. Perhaps Moody was not inclined to deprive his home town of its glory.) With Australia's sharp deterioration in quality and organisation, some so-called 'Test matches' became more and more questionable.

Play began at 1.45 pm with McDonnell making a splash by sending England in to bat. In the return intercolonial, which had only finished that morning, Turner had taken eight wickets and Ferris nine for NSW, Spofforth seven for Victoria. The highest individual score was Garrett's 28, and no team made more than 89.

With the SCG in a frightful state, the Test match was played on four separate wickets. In 35 four-ball overs Turner (6/15) and Ferris (4/27) dismissed England for 45. Australia made 119, and the match seemed won. But the English extended their second innings to 184. Spofforth, not needed in the first innings, took his last Test wicket by bowling Briggs. The *Sydney Mail* paid him one farewell compliment, saying the 'ball, especially when coming from Spofforth, often rose as high as the batsman's head, and several of the Englishmen were seen to drop their bats and wring their hands after something extra had found its way into their fingers'.

After his dismissal for 32, a bristling Billy Barnes 'walked away from his wicket a few yards and then, going back to the pitch, began to pat down the ground with his bat, implying by his action that the ground was not in a proper condition to play on', said the *Sydney Morning Herald*, which chastised him for his 'impertinence'. When Lillywhite wrote defending Barnes, the *Herald* replied from its high horse that he had done precisely what a 'cricketer' would not do.

Amid heavy betting activity, Barnes took six Australian wickets for 28, winning the match for England by 13 runs. At a function after the game there were accusations of cheating on both sides – most likely to do with bowlers' footmarks – and Barnes, no doubt well-oiled in victory, threw a haymaker. Some stories said it was McDonnell he was aiming at, but Barnes later told *Cricket* that his adversary was Hugh Hiddilston, a skilled boxer and occasional NSW cricketer who had been mouthing off about the game. In 1889, Hiddilston would be sentenced to 10 years' jail for forging receipts and embezzling while working as a cashier in the NSW Registrar-General's Department. Whoever his target was, Barnes missed and hit a brick wall, hurting his hand badly enough to put him out of the second Test. Robust self-expression was nothing new for Barnes, who had once been reprimanded by Nottinghamshire for being so drunk he was 'staggering out to the wicket'. He had scored a century, after which he said to the members, 'How many of you Gentlemen could score a hundred, drunk or sober?'

The Sydney Test had laid bare the farcical state of Australian cricket. Altham argues, 'The unfortunate quarrels that had marked the winter of 1884–1885 were the prelude to a black period for Australian cricket; year after year they cropped up again in one form or another, and year after year, not merely in England but even on their own grounds, the Australian Elevens were sapped of their proper strength by intestine faction.'

At no time was this 'sapping' more apparent than in the second Test, when five debutants were brought in for selected players who rejected the 'loss of time' payments the NSWCA was offering them. Giffen, Blackham, Palmer, Bruce and Trumble pulled out, while Spofforth and Bannerman were dropped. Sammy Jones was picked, but did not show up on match morning. On the last day, Turner would take a catch for England as substitute for William Gunn, who was umpiring in place of the Australians' absent official Jim Swift. The *Herald* called Australia a 'mongrel' team, 'little better than a scratch team', and the *Mail* said, 'we must only hope that the Englishmen will never talk of having beaten Australia's best'.

The English professionals won easily, despite 18 more wickets for Turner and Ferris. Lohmann, wearing a black armband after hearing of his mother's death, was unplayable in the first innings with 8/35 from 27 overs.

A dismal summer, in which each Test attracted fewer than 10,000 spectators, could not finish soon enough. A proposed third Test was cancelled when the NSW contingent refused to play, and the tour ended with a match between Smokers and Non-Smokers, held at the East Melbourne Cricket Ground to compensate that club for the loss of its planned fixtures to the MCG. A woeful gathering of 1600 – possibly an inflated figure – attended over four days, while at the MCG 20,000 watched the Austral Wheel Race. England's wicketkeeper, Mordecai Sherwin, wrote to Horan: 'We were surprised at the poor attendances in Melbourne, and it seemed to some of us that Victorians do not attend a sport in large numbers unless the sport is associated with betting and gambling'. The cricket match, and the tour, ended with Scotton being given out handled ball by Reg Wood for picking up the ball to keep as a souvenir.

Shaw, Shrewsbury and Lillywhite had invested £450 each, roughly the same as in 1881–82 and 1884–85. They paid their players £250 each plus expenses and free champagne on Sundays and after victories.

On the first tour, the promoters had made £2100. On the second, they made £450. On the third, this one, they lost £750. Touring Australia was now literally not worth the effort.

Against this background, it was only commonsense for no English team to come in 1887–88. As the associations had been warning, the grassroots had been eaten away by international cricket and needed some fallow time.

Instead, two English teams came.

Horan had heard the rumours that the Sydney Cricket Ground Trust had approached Shaw, Lillywhite and Shrewsbury to tour yet again as a prelude to an Australian Eleven it was planning to finance in England in 1888. This time it promised to underwrite the English promoters' losses. Horan was flabbergasted by Sydney's temerity. 'In the history of Australian cricket New South Wales have never once organised an Australian team for England. Whoever dreamed that New South Wales would now suddenly wake up and make up its mind not only to invite an English team to Australia, but to send an Australian team to England.'

He said that 'Shaw, Lillywhite and Shrewsbury had not the slightest intention of bringing out an English team next season. They think there should be an interval of two years between visits of English teams to Australia. But in the present case the offer made by the New South Wales trustees was so liberal that, as businessmen, Shaw and Co could not refuse. Besides, they were told that if they did not take the matter up someone else would. They were absolutely secured against loss, and profits, if any, would be theirs ... It is none the less a fact though that the Melbourne club was first in the field, and hence if two teams come the MCC will merit public sympathy and support.'

Horan believed all Australian players, including those from NSW, shared his view that an amateur English team, sponsored by Melbourne, was the legitimate one. 'New South Wales cricketers are animated by a spirit of fair play, and they know it is not fair play to have any other but the Melbourne Cricket Club English team here in 1887–88.' He turned out to be wrong: the Australian Elevens would, as always, base their decisions on self-interest and the highest bidder.

Melbourne's claim to having been 'first in the field' was based on Wardill's aborted approaches to the amateurs in 1886. Meanwhile, the SCG Trust said it believed the amateur tour had been 'abandoned', not 'postponed'. The rivalry between the organisations prevented any genuine communication. Melbourne considered postponing its tour again, but the president, Frank Grey Smith, said it would not 'stand aside a second time in succession for the benefit of those who make these visits purely as a monetary speculation'.

So two England teams were coming, when Australian cricket was not strong enough to host one.

The amateurs and professionals sailed on the same boat, the SS *Iberia*. Just to confuse matters further, the Melbourne-sponsored amateur team, led by George Vernon (who fell down a companionway and split his head badly) and captained by Yorkshire's the Hon. Martin Bladen Hawke, had four professionals – Bobby Abel, Bobby Peel, William Attewell and Billy Bates – while the Sydney-backed professional team had four amateurs, including C. Aubrey 'Round the Corner' Smith, their captain. Smith would become a Hollywood character actor, playing the standard English gentleman, and helped introduce cricket to California. His house in Los Angeles was called 'Round the Corner'. A.A. Thomson explains his nickname: 'He was a slow bowler – slow to the point of slow motion – who used to start his run about mid-off and then, as though by an afterthought, bowled round the wicket.' Once when he dropped a catch, Smith ordered his butler to bring out his spectacles, only to drop another and exclaim: 'Egad, the dam' fool brought my reading glasses.'

When both teams arrived in Adelaide on 25 October 1887, the SACA had an awkward moment. Only the amateurs (with their four professionals) had been invited to the welcome party. To save the blushes, the ever-pragmatic Creswell invited the professionals (with their four amateurs) to join the party. Hawke made a speech replete with the amateur spirit, saying: 'We have come here just to enjoy ourselves and we mean to do it. But the real point is that it does not matter to us whether we win or lose, though, of course, we should like to win for the sake of England.'

Clearly the Vernon-Hawke team aimed to restore, or introduce, the idea of international cricket as a pure, non-commercial pastime. Lord's was still trying to stem the flow of money that had gushed since 1878. But it was hard to do so with a professional English team also in the colonies. The Australian press was fascinated by the fine delineations between amateurs and professionals, noting that in Adelaide the amateurs stayed at the South Australian Club and the professionals at the Prince Alfred Hotel. There were reports of a scuffle in Melbourne, when cabbies wouldn't take the amateurs from St Kilda to the city. The Hon. Timothy O'Brien had a fight with one driver, after which the English gentleman ended up travelling by train.

Hawke, a stickler for good manners, later wrote: 'It is rather curious that the Australians themselves do not realise that our professionals prefer to be on their own off the field rather than to be in the same hotel as the amateurs. Indeed, I know that some of our professionals would prefer to have second-class passages on board ship rather than having to dress each night for dinner. This is not in the least diminishing the perfect accord between English amateurs and professionals.'

'The Baron', as Hawke was known, came in for great ridicule in Australia for his justifications of the class system. His declarations — 'Pray heaven a professional will never captain England!' and 'Amateurs are the moral backbone of a county team' — would be hurled back at him by a press that took strident pride in Australia's 'egalitarian' spirit.

In any event, his father died early in the tour and he went home, succeeding to the title of the 7th Baron Hawke. Vernon took over. Hawke described the summer as 'a prominent case of folly', and it was. Vernon's and Shrewsbury's Elevens trailed each other through Australia for four months, playing a glut of matches, 51 in all. At a time when cricket was already losing popularity, this flooded the market and caused its near-total collapse.

The packed summer was not without incident, much of it unedifying to Australia.

For a mid-December match, eight Victorians, including Blackham, Midwinter, Bruce and Spofforth, decided not to play Shrewsbury's team. The result was Victoria's heaviest defeat ever: 624 beating 68 and 100. Horan, who played for Victoria, wrote a piece that captured the dismay and frustration:

'Cricket in Victoria has come to a pretty pass. We have just had one of the finest English elevens here in Melbourne to meet us, and nobody would play against them. The selector of teams was at his wits' end when best man after best man refused to play. The upshot was that Victoria was not represented at all. It is true that eleven men went into the field, but what an eleven! Shades of Tom Wills and other good men and true of our elder days, what do you think of our cricketers of today? They have grand spirit, have they not? They come down to the pavilion, and under its graceful shade watch the novices at work against a combination of amateurs and professionals, such as never before visited us. One would think that as these beautiful Victorian cricketers refused to play they would have stopped away altogether, instead of coming down to gloat over the misfortunes of and to laugh in their sleeves at the embryonic cricketers who met the Englishmen in the match.'

Mishap followed misery. Practising in Melbourne with Vernon's team four days before Christmas, Bates was hit in the eye, and his sight damaged permanently. The Yorkshireman was finished as a cricketer, after five tours of Australia, a Test batting average of 27, and England's first Test hat-trick.

The same day, in response to the chaotic season and the calls from Shaw and Horan for a single authority to start selecting and financing tours, officials from NSW, Victoria, South Australia and Western Australia met at the Oriental Hotel in Melbourne. They resolved to withhold patronage from any English visits for the next three years and from tours of England for the next four years. For 'amateur' players, they capped loss of time payments at 10 shillings a day. They recommended a program of regular home-and-away matches between the colonies (though nine months later NSW backtracked, saying the program was 'impracticable'). They also recommended a change in the lbw law so that a ball pitching outside the off stump could take a wicket, and brought in the six-ball over.

It had taken utter chaos to prompt the first meeting of a central Australian body, but it was soon revealed to have no authority. The repudiation of international cricket for three to four years was logical, but unbeknown to the meeting, one of its delegates, Charlie Beal, who had managed the 1882 tour, was already making inquiries about a tour to England in 1888. It was not the last secret he would keep.

Vernon's team left Bates in hospital in Melbourne and travelled to Adelaide, where unusual circumstances awaited.

England amassed 382 against South Australia, who replied with 143 and were 0/11, following on, on the second evening. The next morning, having received a distressed message from the Adelaide Oval curator that the pitch had been sabotaged, Giffen rushed to the ground and found Vernon, Read and O'Brien, 'who were much annoyed, but no more so than I and other South Australians were, that such a deed had been perpetrated. We found the wicket at 11 o'clock sticky. Pieces of the turf had been lifted out by a man's heels, while the centre of the pitch was uneven through the roller's not having completed its midnight work.'

The English wanted to abandon the match. Giffen suggested making a new wicket. The English would not have that, but agreed 'for the sake of the promoters of the tour to play upon the apparently ruined pitch'. Bobby Peel said, 'Oh, let them play; they will be out before lunch.'

They weren't. Although the wicket 'played queerly' at first, Giffen batted for most of the next two days to score 203. 'A handsome reward was offered for the discovery of the perpetrator of the mischief,' he said, 'but he was never found. Whatever his object could have been was a mystery. If he had backed the Englishmen he did not need to damp the pitch to ensure victory, for they already had us under the whip, while if he was a South Australian backer he was not likely to improve our chance by watering the wicket. The match was drawn.'

Joe Darling, an Adelaide schoolboy at the time, later heard that the sabotage was probably 'done by some lads in a spirit of bravado, as they could not by any means have reaped any advantage by doing it'. A night guard was subsequently installed at the oval.

Various quasi-representative Australian and English teams played each other through 1887–88, until in February the NSWCA managed to organise a 'Test' match between a combined Shrewsbury-Vernon Eleven and an All-Australia team to celebrate the centenary of European settlement in Australia. The England selection was indubitably strong. Australia, predictably, was decimated by withdrawals. Unable to get time off work or the money to compensate, Giffen, Jarvis, Bruce, Horan and NSW's John Wood declined to play.

The game was a debacle in every sense, though notable perhaps for the first Test appearance of Andrew Stoddart, destined to become one of England's most popular and tragic captains.

On the first day, in front of 1173 people, England fell to Turner and Ferris for 113, but Australia's reply was 8/35, courtesy of Lohmann and Peel. Then it poured for three days. Resuming before 700 onlookers, Australia advanced to 42 all out, England made 137 (Turner 7/43), then Australia's batting collapsed once more, Shrewsbury taking three popped-up dollies at silly point to add to his three in the first innings. On the third day, Australia could thank Garrett's 25 not out for getting them to 82. The attendance was estimated at 100.

As the worst match ever given Test status, the 1887–88 game has no rival. The total gate, and what everyone had been fighting over, was £117. For the next four years it would be the last Test match in Australia, if, as Altham asks, 'such a title can fairly be attributed to the unrepresentative and disgruntled elevens that took the field'.

The interminable summer continued with more matches before pathetic crowds. Turner became the first and only man to take 100 wickets in an Australian first-class season, thanks to rain as heavy as the programming. The last day of the Vernon tour was a testimonial for Bates but the minuscule crowd meant that the stricken all-rounder received no benefit.

Having underwritten Vernon's tour, the Melbourne Cricket Club lost £3583. According to the club's annual report, Walter Read (along with his wife) had cost £1137 in 'expenses'. Meanwhile Lillywhite's tour lost £2400, and the SCG trustees welshed on their promise to indemnify its losses. To rub salt into Shaw and Shrewsbury's wounds, Lillywhite later defaulted on making up his share of the deficit.

Shaw wrote with great bitterness: 'The cricket rivalries of Melbourne and Sydney were our undoing. The least that can be said of the blunder is that it was such a stupendous folly that a similar mistake is never likely to occur again ... The Melbourne Club by inviting a team out in opposition to ours succeeded in entirely wrecking the enterprise upon which Shrewsbury, Lillywhite, and I had embarked. They have handsomely recouped themselves since, while we have had to look on and whistle for our lost money.'

After so many good and profitable years, this disaster was the last Lillywhite-Shaw-Shrewsbury tour. They cancelled their planned New Zealand leg. Cricket was not worth it. Seeing a different opportunity,

Shaw and Shrewsbury organised a rugby tour of Australia in 1888. Stoddart, who had batted handsomely for Vernon's Eleven, stayed on and played the winter game, becoming captain when Robert Seddon was drowned in a sculling accident on the Hunter River at West Maitland.

'A CHORUS OF
GLOOMY PROPHECY'

At the beginning of the second century of white settlement, cricket in Australia was rotten. Although six versions of Australia met four versions of England through 1887–88, Australia no longer had a representative team worthy of the name. At the intercolonial level, none of the authorities trusted each other enough to act in concert. In Melbourne, the MCC and VCA were as friendly as Capulets and Montagues, while Sydney quaked as Dave Gregory, unable to stand his fellow selectors, quit as chairman of the panel. Even at club level, things were dire. On 30 April 1887, Turner had dismissed the once-great Albert club for 10.

Tours to England, which had created the problems, remained the only hope of income and redemption. But the colonial associations didn't see it that way. Having 'banned' all tours to England until 1892, they turned their backs on Beal when they discovered he had secretly organised a venture for 1888.

Beal hoped to generate some of the 1882 spirit around Turner and Ferris, but even though this tour would be back under the players' management, man after man declined Beal's invitations. Giffen, Bruce and the beanpole young Victorian off-spinner Hugh Trumble opted out. Harry Moses, who had scored 297 not out in an intercolonial for NSW against Victoria during the season, stayed home to tend to his banking career. Most damagingly, Giffen, the mainstay of 1886, would not tour. His chief reason, he wrote, was neither financial nor, as had been written, that he had been denied the captaincy. Nor was it that his brother, Walter, was left out. George did not tour because 'I did not consider we were strong enough to tackle the cricketers of the old land, with reasonable hope of success.' He had also been worn out by his 'gruelling of work' in 1886. 'I have heard all kinds of absurd reasons suggested for my withholding from the 1888 and 1890 teams, but none were more ridiculous than that I would not go unless I was elected captain. Such a thought never entered my head.'

A veteran rump of the great teams was selected: Alick Bannerman, Blackham, Boyle, Bonnor. Much would depend on McDonnell and Jones, the only batsmen near their peak. The debutants were South Australian hitter Jack Lyons, Victoria's pair of Jacks, Worrall and Edwards, the Melbourne postal worker and leg-spinning all-rounder Harry Trott, plus Turner and Ferris. Never, said *Lillywhite's Annual*, 'did a party of cricketers set out on an extensive tour under circumstances so thoroughly calculated to discourage'. Altham notes that they 'embarked amid a chorus of gloomy prophecy'.

The colonies refused to play them in the late summer, so they arranged three games with the English teams. Vernon's Eleven beat them twice, Shrewsbury's once. Turner continued to plunder wickets, but there was precious little else.

Even at sea on the SS *Oceanien*, things went against them. The recommended change to the lbw law had been sent to Lord's for ratification. Horan wrote that this would advantage not only Turner and

Ferris but the vital third bowler, Trott, against whom 'many a batsman has saved his wicket by his legs or body'.

'I remember well his expression of delight when he heard that the law was to be altered,' Horan wrote. 'The thought of that change was sweeter to Trott than the falling leaves of autumn, the perfumed breath of spring, or the delightful note of a thrush in his favourite walk through the gardens. I can figure him pacing the deck of the *Oceanien*, contemplating with pleasure the prospect before him, the good time he will have on English grounds with his leg-breaks under the new law.'

But during the voyage, Lord's decided not to endorse the change.

'Poor Trott!' Horan continued. 'How he will chafe when he reaches England and finds the law unaltered, and that confounded leg and body play in the same full swing that he so hated here.'

Beal did his best. Accompanied by his wife and mother (Lyons and Bannerman, too, were permitted to bring their wives), Beal clad the team in the lucky red, black and gold of the 1882 team, lodged them at the same hotel, and trained them at Mitcham Green. Against all forecasts the Sixth Australians started with five straight wins. Blackham, Bonnor, Trott, McDonnell and Turner made scores, and Turner and Ferris tore through county after county. They suffered a narrow loss to Lancashire before Grace (165) and Walter Read (109) tamed Turner and Ferris at Lord's for the only time on tour. A rare Bonnor century saved the draw for Australia, and at the end of May they had, against all prognostications, as good a record as any tour before them.

In their next game, against the Players at the Oval, things started to wobble. Australia lost by ten wickets, and Jones, who had been in good form with bat and ball, felt weak and said he was 'unable to get rid of the feeling of cold'. He played on, but in the next game he left the field with a fever. While Australia was losing heavily to Nottinghamshire, Beal called a doctor. Smallpox was diagnosed, and Jones was put up in a private house in Nottingham. Smallpox, fatal in 40 per cent of cases, had no cure. The only treatment was rest and care of the sores.

Given the normal incubation period, Jones had probably caught it in Manchester or Sheffield, where there had been outbreaks.

So virulent was smallpox that if Jones's illness had become public knowledge the team might have been quarantined and the tour cancelled. So Beal announced that Jones had rheumatic fever. Later, when Jones's smallpox became known, *Wisden* still approved of Beal's deception: 'No risk was run, no danger was incurred, no steps were taken to which the strictest purist in morals could have objected; but, acting under full medical authority and sanction the secret of the highly contagious nature of Jones's illness was strictly and faithfully kept.'

Meant to calm everyone, Beal's concealment had an inadvertently opposite effect. The week Beal announced Jones's illness, a British politician, Colonel Robert King-Harman, died. The cable back to Australia said, confusingly: 'Obituary, King-Harman; SP Jones, Australian cricketer, rheumatic fever.' An evening paper in Sydney reported that Jones had died.

In fact, he was improving quickly from what turned out to be a minor case of smallpox. The *Bulletin* reported: 'A Sydney daily killed Sammy Jones over a week ago by cable, and now they have reluctantly brought him to life again.' The *Times* reported he was 'much better' by 1 July. He would return to the field against Kent in August, but exhausted himself with a laboured 24 not out, and scored five runs in eight more innings. Having averaged 27 before his illness and been anointed by *Wisden* 'the best batsman in the side', the unfortunate Jones ended the tour with an average of 16.

Replacements were always ready but of questionable quality; the exuberant Cambridge undergraduate Sammy Woods was called up in Jones's place. His bowling had given the Gentlemen a sensational victory over the Players at Lord's, with Aubrey Smith his partner, and he uttered the line of the season when, after bowling Grace, he said to the batsman: 'I shouldn't go, Doctor, there's still one stump standing.' (This quote was also attributed to Charles Kortright in 1898, when, in successive deliveries, he had a plumb lbw and an appeal for caught behind off a blatant snick turned down, and finally uprooted two of the doctor's stumps.) Woods, who got on very well with Grace, captured him better than most when he called him, affectionately, 'an artful old toad'.

When Australia were going well in May, Spofforth announced that he, with his pregnant wife Phillis and their son Reginald, would be emigrating to England to run Joseph Cadman's Star Tea Company.

Would he join the Australians? Whether or not they wanted him was one thing. Whether he was up to it was a matter for hot debate. 'Point' in the *Sydney Mail* said that as the veteran Boyle was the 'weak spot' in the team, 'I would like to know whether our old friend Spofforth has been asked to go. He was the backbone of former teams, and if he be judged on recent performances in Victoria, his arm does not seem to have lost any of its former cunning ... Turner may fill Palmer's place, but Spofforth's never.'

In the same paper, 'Cricket Gossip' disagreed: 'Anyone who has followed Spofforth's career must see that his day for cricket has gone by.' The *Bulletin* chimed in: 'If Turner keeps up his present form with bat and ball, the Britishers will forget about Spofforth, who at his best was only one part demon.'

Murdoch made an appearance at a function at the Melbourne Cricket Club, giving Spofforth a farewell speech and suggesting the Australian team — or even England! — might call him up. With typical bravado, Spofforth agreed with Murdoch that he would arrive in time 'to be of some service to the Australians', and would consider playing against them too, 'if England paid him the compliment of picking him'.

'If as a member of an English eleven [I am] instrumental in beating an Australian eleven,' he was reported as saying, '[I] would feel all the more proud of it for the sake of Australia.'

While Phillis gave birth to their second baby on the SS *Orizaba*, Spofforth exercised vigorously in case he got the call for the first Test match, at Lord's. When he disembarked on 15 July, the English press's speculations provided great entertainment but had little substance. He was not chosen for either country. At the end of the season, *Cricket* asked if Australia might have used 'the valuable services of Spofforth', and another *Sydney Mail* columnist, 'Anglicanus', said he would have been better than Woods, as, when he did finally turn out for the Gentlemen and his adopted county Derbyshire, Spofforth 'bowled very finely, and showed plainly that the demoniacal right arm has by no means lost its cunning'.

But the unexpected truth was that the 1888 Australians were making a reasonable fist of their program, McDonnell leading the batting with some help from the old guard and the Turner-Ferris combination causing nearly as much terror as Jack the Ripper. 'If figures go for anything,' writes Altham, Turner and Ferris were 'definitely the most successful [pair] that ever appeared together in any touring side, whether English or Australian, in the whole history of the game.' Turner's speed was measured at Woolwich Arsenal at 55 mph, making him, in our terms, a fast off-spinner, though it's likely the technology underestimated him. Turner's 'terror' came less from his pace than his ability to probe batsmen's weaknesses. His workload, and Ferris's, were phenomenal: in first-class matches on the tour Turner delivered 9702 balls for 283 wickets – 188 bowled – at 11.68. Ferris's 8321 balls gave him 199 wickets at 14.74. These quantities have never been surpassed. *Town and Country Journal* said their achievements 'stamp them as equal, and we are inclined to think superior, to any of the bowlers of the present day', even to Lohmann, who was enjoying the first of his three 200-wicket seasons. He took 209 at 10.90.

Most importantly, as *Wisden* said, Turner and Ferris were 'scrupulously and irreproachably fair'. There was not a hint of throwing or deliberately scuffing up the pitch; 'their action was free from tricks of any kind'. The summer provided a welcome break from past controversies.

At Lord's, Turner and Ferris were largely responsible for the lowest-scoring Anglo-Australian Test in history. The summer was turning out wetter than usual, and *Wisden* said that while confidence in England's batting would have been 'almost unlimited' on a dry wicket, the constant rains made the course of the match 'so fluky, that victory would depend almost entirely upon success in the toss'.

English followers were in a state of high anxiety when McDonnell won the toss and batted – 'all concerned, from batsmen, bowlers and umpires down to the merest spectators, felt the importance of the issue, and how much was at stake. We ought, however, to say that to the best of our knowledge there was little or no betting of any consequence, and certainly, with all the eagerness and keenness of feeling, there was no bitterness or acrimony on either side.'

Better behaved, more modest in their ambitions, McDonnell's team snatched victory through some bold hitting and opportunism. Ferris was the hero, smacking 14 and 20 not out and producing match figures of 8/45. Australia's 116 and 60 beat England's 53 and 62, Grace's second innings 24 being the highest score of the match. On the second, and final, day, 27 wickets fell in three hours. A huge crowd massed in front of the pavilion, said *Wisden*, and 'cheered with a spontaneous and genuine heartiness that could scarcely have been exceeded if the Englishmen had made the runs instead of being badly beaten. So ended a game that will never be forgotten in cricket history, and one which practically ensured the fame of the Australian team.'

It was a great victory by an admittedly inferior team; but it ensured no one's fame and was quickly overshadowed by the batting debacles that followed.

The talk of the second Test at the Oval was that Grace, cresting his fortieth birthday, would at last become England captain. Steel's magic had run out and he retired to concentrate on his career at the bar. The decline of amateur cricket was such that Grace remained the only Gentleman who merited a place in England's strongest Eleven, and therefore assumed the captaincy by default. Ironically, after the class snobbery that had promoted Harris, Hornby and Steel ahead of him as captain, it was now another side of the same prejudice that delivered him the job. Had he been an Australian, he would have been his country's captain since 1880. He was certainly the most popular cricketer in England and the most famous private individual. When he arrived at a match at Edgbaston that summer, the crowd chaired him around the ground *before* the start.

McDonnell's Australians, in *Wisden*'s view, were now taken very seriously, comparing with not only England's best at the Oval but the record of the 1882 team. 'This game it was, more than any other, which took from the Australians their chances of rivalling the fame of the team that came over six years before. Whatever the results of the less important games had been, if the McDonnell-Beal combination could have beaten England twice out of the three times, the tour would have been regarded in Australia, and with a great deal of justice, as a triumph.'

The wicket was good, but Australia's weak batting was exposed by Briggs's left-arm spin, which reaped 10/57 in the game. A total of 80 was indefensible, and Abel and Barnes built a lead before Lohmann hit an extraordinary unbeaten 62 in 55 minutes with ten fours and just one single. England romped home on the second day, and *Wisden* commented (unfairly to Ferris but otherwise on the mark) that only three of the Australians, Turner, McDonnell and Blackham, would warrant selection in a World Eleven. Comparisons with the 1882 team were swiftly discarded.

Nottinghamshire, Gloucestershire and an Eleven of England thrashed the Australians in the next two weeks as morale slid. Before the decisive third Test, Manchester's rain did enough to soften the wicket but not drown out the match, which was completed within six and a half hours. England's 172 was enough for a comfortable innings victory; in the entire series Australia's 116 at Lord's and 100 at the Oval were the only times they attained three figures, and McDonnell's 32 in the latter stood out like a triple-century. The weather contributed, but the state of Australian batsmanship was so dire as to renew the calls for a suspension of Test cricket.

Throughout the tour, dreadful losses were followed by magnificent wins, and the running joke was that Beal would be called up before the Jockey Club to explain the Australians' form. They ended up with a creditable 17 wins, six draws and 14 losses, and, as *Wisden* said, 'did not deserve a quarter of the contemptuous things said about them by newspapers of their own Colonies'.

McDonnell's captaincy waxed and waned. Pardon felt his conduct 'was by no means unanimously approved by the team or by English cricketers ... and it is an open secret that but for Beal's tact, the loyalty and level-headedness of Turner, and the unswerving obedience of Ferris, there was now and then a possibility of the same sort of muffled mutiny which in some former teams has been unpleasantly apparent. Now the tour is over, and there can be no harm in speaking all one's mind, we may say that we think on many occasions McDonnell showed want of judgement. We do not mean in his batting, though after the marvellous Manchester performance [against Lancashire] his rashness was apparent to anyone; but in the general management of his bowling. He never seemed happy unless he had Turner on at one end and Ferris at the other ... it was a Turner and Ferris trip or nothing.' McDonnell can hardly be blamed for over-reliance on the magnificent pair, and if he only used the other bowlers to give his aces a rest, he was employing the same basic strategy as Armstrong in 1921, Bradman in 1948 and Waugh in 2001, all lionised as the captains of the greatest Ashes tours.

Giffen later wrote that 'if Moses, Bruce and myself had been with the 1888 Eleven, when Turner and Ferris, being new to English batsmen, were so deadly, a great fight would have been made against England's best Eleven'. That might have been true, but Giffen had prejudged the 1888 team, as he would the 1890 team, as failures. The brief glow around the 1888 tour was deceptive. Australian cricket still had some way to fall before hitting the bottom.

'OUR BOYS WILL BE BOYS'

It was hoped that the absence of English touring teams would allow cricket in the colonies to grow again. Time would tell. In the short-term, what grew was the resolve of cricket authorities to squabble, and of the public to shun the game.

Attendances were dismal for the eight first-class matches of 1888–89. Only once, during the intercolonial at Melbourne, did a crowd exceed 10,000, and most days were so badly attended that official figures merely registered an adjective: 'poor', 'sparse', or 'meagre'.

Cricket was also commencing its struggle against competing sports. A.G. Spalding brought out a popular American baseball troupe, while the *Sydney Morning Herald* reported on the popularity of sailing, saying, 'many young men abandon the willow for the tiller'.

Cricket did little to help itself. Virtually broke, the VCA tried to ban the MCC from club competition when Melbourne took over the organisation of intercolonial matches. The South Melbourne, Carlton and St Kilda clubs defied the ban, and the VCA had to back down. All this did was reinforce the idea that Australian cricket administrators had no effective control.

Control was tested in another way in the 1889–90 season opener in Adelaide. Giffen, on 9, survived an lbw appeal off Hugh Trumble, but 'in making the stroke I slipped down, and while in the act of rising again, was said to have knocked the wicket with my foot, and a bail fell off. The fieldsman at cover appealed, and Mr [Tom] Flynn, of Victoria, gave me out. I knew, however, that I had not touched the wicket, and, moreover, I had got into my head the idea that the ball was dead, and that a second appeal could not be made, so I declined to leave the crease.'

The Victorians were outraged, but Giffen stayed. Blackham exchanged strong words with him and said he would only continue the game 'under protest'. Giffen went on to score 85 before Trumble bowled him.

That night, Blackham and Victoria's manager, Robert Greig, sent Creswell an official letter of protest. They also wrote to Lord's. The SACA made a counter-complaint about umpire Flynn and requested that the VCA submit umpires' names for pre-match approval. The brawl dragged on into the winter until, 'in my calmer moments', Giffen 'realised that I had acted wrongly, no one regretted my action more than I did, and I was not sorry when our last wicket fell at the end of the match with the Victorians 18 runs to the good'.

The matter was not fully resolved until late in 1890. The VCA passed its 'Giffen' motion: 'if any cricketer refuses to obey the rules, and to concede to the judgement of the umpire, he might be disqualified for a particular term.' It repudiated South Australia's request to submit umpires' names ahead of matches. Giffen finally asked his association to back down. In the peace-making match at the MCG in January 1890, he scored 237, took 12 wickets and won a trophy.

Intercolonial cricket barely had a pulse. South Australia had been invited for its first match in Sydney, but the players were haggling over loss of time payments. Giffen said, 'it is not every player who can secure leave [from work] for more than a month'. For a four-day game, the players needed compensation for a nine-day trip. The SACA eventually conceded — it was pay up or have no game — but it lost £234 on the match, and their team was annihilated on a grassy SCG strip.

A lighter note was struck when a Sydney enthusiast presented two bronze shields, valued at 25 guineas, to the best bowler on each side. Fred Jarvis won South Australia's. Giffen said the shield was 'large enough to hide a fair proportion of the wall of an ordinary-sized room ... We had no end of fun in getting the gigantic trophy home. It would have been an effective protection if bush-rangers had chanced to fire upon the train ... Trouble began, however, when the South Australian border was reached. Fred was informed by the business-like Customs sentry that he was importing a work of art, upon which he would have to pay 25 per cent duty. He would not pay the six guineas demanded. The shield was impounded and if that duty had been insisted upon, might have been in pound to this day; but representation of the circumstances to headquarters led to a remission of the tax.'

There were some green shoots of cricket recovery. Receipts from the intercolonial match between Victoria and NSW at the MCG were £977, more than double the 1887 figure. But it was assumed the English would not want another Australian Eleven going 'home' any time soon. Horan wrote: 'It was thought when the last team returned that our cricketers would no longer follow the habits of the happy birds that change their sky and "live their lives from land to land".'

But cricket was integral to Pax Britannica. An official England team toured South Africa, playing what would be recognised as the first Test matches involving that country. Vernon also took a team to India and Ceylon, and Parsee teams had toured England in 1886 and 1888. As Grace wrote, cricket tours 'helped to deepen British interest in our colonies and to bind us in closer harmony with other nations ... and I am disposed to think that the good fellowship born on the cricket-field has done more than is recognised to knit together the various sections of the British Empire and to advance the cause of civilisation'.

By late 1889, contact had been made between England and Harry Boyle, who would select and manage a private group of Australian players. The 'veteran swallow cricketer', as Horan dubbed him, invited the best cricketers. Giffen again declined because he didn't think the team was good enough to turn a profit to justify his unpaid leave. His absence would be critical, as he was then by some distance the best cricketer in Australia. 'Were it not for more important considerations, my desire to excel might have induced me to visit England in 1890, for at that time I was playing as well as I ever did.'

Affie Jarvis and Alick Bannerman also declined, and Moses pulled out again for employment reasons. Blackham, Turner, Ferris, Jones, Lyons and Trott would form the nucleus, backed up by NSW debutants Percie Charlton and Syd Gregory (son of Dave's brother Ned, born in the hut alongside the SCG where Ned lived while curating the ground), Victorians Frank Walters, Hugh Trumble and Dr Jack Barrett, and Tasmania's Kenny Burn. Bonnor, finally, was left out of a tour, despite staking his claim with 267 in a club match in Bathurst.

Boyle's coup was to entice Murdoch out of retirement. For five years he had been vainly begging the great batsman to play for Victoria. Now, in Australia's crisis, offered the prospect of advancing his interests in Britain, Achilles came out of exile.

One crucial factor in swaying Murdoch was the death of John Boyd Watson in June 1889. 'At least one Australian paper,' notes Derek Carlaw, 'unkindly suggested that Murdoch would not have dared to return to the game had his father-in-law still been alive.'

Murdoch and Jemima sailed several weeks before the rest of the team, who left Melbourne on 14 March. Either before or during the tour, the Murdochs had decided to move permanently to Sussex.

At a farewell dinner at the Melbourne Cricket Club, Boyle spoke optimistically about the team's chances, but already he was trying to sort out a mess over who should tour as Blackham's deputy wicketkeeper. The NSW players, led by Turner, wanted Syd Deane, their 24-year-old gloveman who had made his debut that season. The Victorians wanted Jack Harry, 32, who had stood in once for Blackham in 1884 and occasional off-breaks. Deane travelled with the NSW players on the SS *Liguria* from Sydney to Melbourne, where he faced the humiliating news that he was no longer wanted.

Horan commented: 'The Deane and Harry battle is still raging. Boyle is sending telegrams to Turner at Bathurst, Turner is sending telegrams to Boyle in Melbourne, and so far the issue is not at all satisfactory. There is no doubt whatever that Blackham is the man who should be chiefly consulted in the selection of an assistant wicketkeeper; yet the Sydney men when they picked Deane never dreamed of asking Blackham's opinion. The veteran wicketkeeper knows well that in Melbourne alone we have many better men than Deane, better not only in wicketkeeping but in every department of the game.'

Blackham finally came up with a compromise. He told Boyle that he had heard 'Burn, from Tasmania', was a good wicketkeeper.

The touring players knew Burn – or thought they did. Kenny Burn, 27, a maintenance engineer with the Hobart tramways, had trialled with the 1888 Australians. Horan had pushed for his selection, but he did not make runs in the two trials. Now he rushed across Bass Strait to join the team in Melbourne, and Horan was happy.

'At last the team has been finally chosen, and Boyle no longer dreams of telegrams, no longer sinks back in his chair with a nervous clutch at his forehead to feel for the extra furrows begotten of the recent weary time he had had. I am glad for Boyle's sake that it is all over, for his appetite was gradually failing, while his wonted gaiety had almost completely left him. That last notion of sending for Kenny Burn I like very well ... Indeed the very man (Blackham) who has now got Burn into the team was one of the very men who rejected him in 1888 ... He is a capital batsman and a fine field.'

But no wicketkeeper. In Melbourne, nobody told Burn that he had been picked as Blackham's back-up or, if he was told, he chose not to reveal his secret until they had left.

The team was strolling around Adelaide when, said Horan, 'it was discovered that Kenny Burn had, to use his own words, "never kept wickets in his life". This caused considerable amusement at the expense of the crack wicketkeeper [Blackham], who had solved the Deane-Harry puzzle by suggesting the inclusion of the crack Tasmanian. The mistake was the result of a curious misconception. Blackham had seen in print that "Burn" had stumped men in Tasmania, but that Burn was Kenny's brother, and quite an inferior player [James Burn, by then 40 years old, who never played a first-class match]. However, the team was consoled by the reflection that the Tasmanian has the reputation of being a fine batsman, a fair bowler, and a good field. Extraordinarily heavy work will fall on Blackham's shoulders, or I should say his hands, but, like the keen cricketer he is, he looks forward cheerfully to his task.'

Interestingly, even though the mix-up was discovered in Adelaide, it did not make it into the public domain until the team had arrived in England. There would have been time to recruit Harry or Deane, but clearly Boyle and Blackham preferred to let sleeping dogs lie. Deane consoled himself by going on to a successful career as a stage and film actor, appearing in more than 40 Hollywood films including the first adaptation of *Treasure Island*.

Sailing without their captain, their greatest cricketer and their most experienced opening batsman, the Seventh Australians seemed doomed from the start. Lyons fell off a trapeze and injured his hip. Then the *Liguria* collided with French and British ships while coming to anchor at

Gibraltar. But these were minor compared with what was awaiting them on the cricket field.

As Australia had gone into decline, England had flourished. Lord's had a smorgasbord of talent to pick from: Grace, Stoddart, Walter Read and Cambridge undergrad wicketkeeper Gregor McGregor from the Gentlemen, and Shrewsbury, William Gunn, Maurice Read, Ulyett, Abel, Peel, Barnes and Lohmann from the pros. Two of the greatest names of English cricket, Stanley Jackson and Archie MacLaren, would emerge from the north that summer. It was a bad time for Australia to be weak; a bad time for cricket to become one-sided. The great revelation since 1878 – that games between Australia and England were a bigger attraction than games between Englishmen – was in danger of being thoroughly unwound.

Turner and Ferris could yet redeem things as they had in 1888. Blackham was Blackham, and it was hoped and prayed that Murdoch was still Murdoch. Trott, Lyons and Jones had shown potential in 1888, Barrett had the ability to stonewall in the manner of Alick Bannerman, and Hugh Trumble, the towering lantern-jawed off-spinner, was clearly a cut above his brother Billy.

On paper the team did not appear any weaker than those of 1886 and 1888; perhaps, given Murdoch's inclusion, it was stronger. But during practice at Chiswick Park, Blackham confided to *Wisden*'s Charles Pardon that 'while he thought the side would be strong enough to beat any of the counties, the batting was not sufficiently powerful to offer much hope of defeating England on a hard wicket'.

Blackham proved, for once in his life, to be an optimist. As Pardon said, 'When it came to actual play, however, the batting fell below even Blackham's moderate estimate, and the contrast to the form shown in 1882 and 1884 was very marked indeed.'

The high point was the very first game, against a side in which Lord Sheffield, perhaps unkindly, had included Grace, Shrewsbury, Stoddart, Walter Read, Peel, Briggs, Lohmann and Attewell. Murdoch announced he had not missed a beat by scoring 93; Turner (6/50) and Ferris (12/88) did the rest. Such an emphatic start had never been made, even by the heroes of 1882. England was in total shock to see its best men rolled for 27 (of which Grace scored 20) and 130. Game, as it were, on.

A few days later, Turner and Ferris did the same to Warwickshire (38 and 51), the Terror taking 12 wickets to his partner's six. However, reversal was not long in coming. A Test-strength team picked by cricket patron W.H. Laverton defeated the Australians at Westbury, home of the famous White Horse, in Wiltshire, and soon not even Murdoch could pull the tourists out of the low-scoring mire they had been bogged in since his first retirement. They became the first touring team to go through June without a win. Billy Gunn racked up 228, a record innings against an Australian touring team to that point, as the Players trounced them at Lord's. When they eventually won matches again, it was only against non-first-class Staffordshire and Leicestershire. By 21 July, the start of the first Test at Lord's, Australia had won two of their previous 14 games. Sheffield Park seemed a very long time ago.

The most harmful result of the team's performances was the Test's diminished status. Middlesex pulled Stoddart out for what it judged a more important fixture at Tonbridge against Kent. The *Pall Mall Gazette* reported: 'the fact of the present Australian team having been found weaker than some of its predecessors does not, in our opinion, excuse the Middlesex executive for departing from a proper and well-established plan.' Perhaps so, but tours by Australian Elevens were slipping behind the newly organised county championship.

For Australia, Jones was ill with what was reported as a 'severe chill' (and, for most of the tour, said Pardon, was 'quite useless'). Sammy Woods declined the call-up from Cambridge, and Walters was out of form, so Kenny Burn became one of the luckier Test cricketers.

Although 'no other game was looked forward to so eagerly', as *Wisden* said, anticipation for the first Test was founded more on past glories than present form. Australia would be forgiven if they could 'make a fresh start to their trip', and 30,279 turned up over the three days.

The match was studded with some batting highlights. Lyons reprised Massie, smashing fifty in 36 minutes — a Test record. The evergreen Ulyett's 74 gave England a lead, overcoming the surprise bowling packet of Lyons who took five of his six career Test wickets. In Australia's second innings Barrett (67 not out) became the first opener to carry his bat in a Test match. Set 137, England were carried home on the shoulders of W.G., who put paid to all the nonsense with 75 not out. Blackham, who had played every Australian Test match bar one, and McGregor, making his debut, did not concede a bye between them.

The tourists were commended for their fight, and Murdoch went to his favourite county, Sussex, the next day to score 158. Sussex had invited him to join them a decade earlier; now, having shown all his old style, he was prepared to sit down and talk.

By the second week of August, seriously hampered by injuries, the Australians again sent an SOS to Roley Pope. Since his cameos in 1888, Pope had remained in Edinburgh, playing occasional first-class cricket for the MCC and even representing Scotland against Canada, becoming a dual international, if somewhat differently from Midwinter. Pope had gained his Bachelor of Medicine and Bachelor of Surgery on 1 August, then travelled south to watch Murdoch, who asked if he could play against Cambridge Past and Present. Pope did everything, none of it well. He took the gloves from Blackham, who had a sore hand, and twice dropped Edward Streatfeild early in his innings of 145. Blackham was rushed back on to replace him. As the Cambridge score piled up, Murdoch asked Pope if he could bowl.

'Somewhat diffidently I said that I could bowl lobs a little,' Pope reported.

'Just the thing,' said Murdoch, 'I think we'll try an over of lobs.'

'Only one run was scored off me in the first over, for I fancy Streatfeild was looking out for some peculiarity about the lobs which was not discoverable.

'At the end of the over I said, "What do you think, Billy? Shall I have another one?"

'"I should think so," he replied, "why, you stuck 'em up!"

'I went on. Eighteen runs were made off that over and at the end of it I said, "What do you think about it, Billy? Shall I —"

'"Come out of that," he said, "you're a fraud!"'

He then opened the innings and was bowled for a duck by Streatfeild.

The game, as a cricket contest, was quite remarkable. Cambridge Past and Present scored 389 and dismissed Australia for 218. Following on, Murdoch hit 129 and Trott 186 to get Australia to a declaration of 6/355. The university, with 185 to win in an hour and 25 minutes, 'instead of playing carefully for a draw, went in for reckless hitting' and nearly collapsed to a 'well deserved' defeat, in Pardon's view. They hung on desperately to finish at 8/78.

That gave Australia heart for the second Test at the Oval, a match which showed how fine was the line between a successful tour and one that *Wisden*, among others, pronounced a complete failure.

Again the Test's prestige was marred by county cricket, a dim reflection on the Australians. Middlesex, playing Yorkshire, requisitioned Stoddart again. When Lord Hawke heard the news, he recalled Ulyett and Peel from the Test team. Peel would dismiss Stoddart cheaply in both innings of a rained-out draw.

At the Oval, Australia played another doughty uphill game. Trott, as he would throughout his career, batted best on a rain-affected wicket, and his 39 was the heart of his team's 92. The destroyer was Peel's replacement, the left-armer Frank 'Nutty' Martin, called up by Lord Harris from the Kent ground staff. Martin's 6/50 and 6/52 would not be overtaken as a Test bowling debut until Bob Massie's 16 wickets at

Lord's 82 summers later. Martin's reward was to be given just one more Test, against South Africa.

Ferris had Grace caught first ball as England stumbled to an eight-run lead on the still-sticky wicket. Australia, however, could do little better; Trott again stapled them together with 25 out of 102.

Ninety-five to win raised memories of the same ground eight years earlier. There was no Spofforth, but with Turner and Ferris this thing could surely be done. First ball, Grace sliced a cut straight to Trott, who for a decade was so good a catcher he was called a 'strong-point'. The ball went in, and out, of his hands.

Grace might have avoided his only pair in four decades of first-class cricket, but by the time the score had reached 32 he was out, along with Shrewsbury, Gunn and Walter Read. Interest, wrote Pardon, was now 'reaching a very acute point'. James Cranston, on debut, and Maurice Read pushed the score to a safe-looking 4/63 when Read chipped a catch to Murdoch at mid-on. This too was dropped. If not, Pardon thought, 'Australia would in all probability have won'. Cranston and Read added another 20, then, with 12 to win and six wickets in hand, 'there came a collapse that recalled the great match in 1882'. At 8/93 Jack Sharpe joined McGregor 'and five maiden overs were bowled in succession, Sharpe being beaten time after time by balls from Ferris that broke back and missed the wicket'. Overwhelmed by frustration, Sharpe and McGregor decided to run on the next hit. Sharpe struck the ball to Barrett and ran. McGregor didn't. The batsmen were virtually at the same end, the match was there for the taking, but an overanxious Barrett hurled the ball over Ferris's head and the batsmen took the winning single. Trumble sympathised, 'Barrett was positively broken-hearted, and for many days was in the depths of dejection.'

The match, largely forgotten now, is worth recalling in detail because it illustrates how sweeping judgements can be reduced to a moment's luck. Had Peate connected with that ball from Boyle in 1882, there would have been no Ashes obituary, no Ashes, no 'famous for all time'. Had Murdoch or Trott held their chances in 1890, had one or two of those breakbacks from Ferris clipped a bail instead of skimming over the top, had Barrett performed the simple task of throwing the ball accurately, the 1890 team, instead of being consigned to the lowest rank of Australian tours, would be acclaimed as heroes. That, as every cricketer knows, is cricket.

Murdoch's fourth team had no chance to redeem themselves. The third Test was drowned. Rain also dogged the last first-class matches, and while Turner and Ferris continued to amass mind-boggling statistics, the animating spirit had gone out of the tour. The final matches were distinguished by poor batting, scant crowds and low morale. Murdoch had always been a liberal kind of leader, which worked well when he had a team of stars. Now he seemed to be dining out, or drinking out, on past glories. Factions were rife, as ever in a losing team, and Boyle and Lyons reportedly came to blows. The *Bulletin* said the Seventh Australians made 'a fortune for the brewers', and mocked their loose ethic: 'The Australian cricketer in England, batting the day after a banquet, sees at least two balls approaching. One is dead on the wicket. He smites at the other and sees four bails flying about, two wicketkeepers looking the other way, two prostrate and two erect stumps. Then he retires to two pavilions, makes 22 excuses, and another cable about bad luck and wet wickets is dispatched. The Australians always play on a wet wicket after a banquet.'

Pardon's summary in *Wisden* despaired: 'The tour was a disappointment, and the players themselves made no attempt to minimise their failure. They fell far below their expectations, and they did not scruple to admit the fact.'

History has condemned the 1890 Australians as a quarrelsome touring group, but there were moments of levity, as Trumble recalled of a trip with Burn, a keen musician, to the Albert Hall. After the concert, Trumble asked what Burn thought of the cornet player: 'Not b-bad,' said

Burn, who spoke with a pronounced stutter, 'but we've got a b-b-bloke in Hobart t-t-town who could b-b-blow his b-b-blooming head off!'

The team was the first Australian Eleven to go through England with a losing record. Among 34 first-class matches, they won 10, lost 16 and drew eight. They played four other eleven-a-side matches, winning three and drawing one. Several of their wins were against opposition which, Pardon wrote, was 'scarcely worth while to bring an eleven a sea voyage of fifteen thousand miles' to play. Murdoch headed the averages for a fourth time, but in the Tests he scored 9, 19, 2 and 6, betraying a decline in his reflexes. As a captain he followed McDonnell's example, bowling Turner and Ferris into the ground. Ferris took 186 wickets at 14.28 and Turner 179 at 14.21. Lyons, Trott, Barrett and Trumble gave glimpses of promise, but their overall performances, along with those of Jones, Charlton and Walters, paint a vivid picture of a tour that turned none of its younger men into better cricketers. Blackham was yet again a marvel, with one comical exception. At Manchester, Ferris lured Bill Attewell out of his crease; Blackham took the ball and appealed for the stumping. Umpire Farrands said, 'Chuck it up', denoting it was out. Attewell scampered back to his crease and said to the umpire, 'You old crack-pot; he ain't broke wicket.' He was right: Blackham had forgotten to effect the stumping and Attewell was not out. After seven tours in 12 years and barely an error to show for it, Blackham's oversight was forgiven.

Sammy Jones's long absence from the tour, with no reported illness worse than the 'severe chill' that kept him out of the first Test and an abscess he had removed at St Thomas's Hospital in November, attracted scrutiny. When he failed to take the field against the Lyric Club in a match at Barnes, the *Athletic News* hinted at more than just illness: 'This young gentleman's career all through the tour has been so erratic that I think the team would benefit not a little if he were sent home. His vagaries only tend to demoralise the others. It is hardly fair to his comrades to act as he does.' Jones's biographer, Max Bonnell, concludes that Jones 'drank too much, and spent too much of his time at parties and dinners', speculating further that Jones, who did not return to Australia until January 1891, might have required extended treatment in England for a sexually transmitted disease. The *Bulletin* did comment, allusively, that 'Our boys will be boys, apparently ... The genial Jones seems to visit England solely for the purpose of picking up the ailments fashionable during his stay.' The record is silent on whether he was the first Australian Test cricketer brought down by an STD, but it wouldn't have been the first time he carried a disease that was kept secret.

Trumble alluded to the temptations of touring life when he said, years later, having lived through the transformation into a more disciplined age: 'It is really a case of self-denial, or avoidance of the many pleasures and entertainments that are offered, and of taking scrupulous care of oneself when off the field, so as to be always physically fit and able to do justice to one's game and the side.'

Notwithstanding the closeness of the two Test matches, the Seventh Australians were a dismal team. In 22 Test innings since 1886, Australia's average score was 108, and only once had they reached 200. Nine times they were out for less than 100. As Ralph Barker wrote decades later, 'the truth must be faced that the Australian batting in this period was deplorably weak, weaker perhaps than at any other time before or since, so that interest in the matches began to wane, as interest will always wane when a contest is one-sided.'

The Australians had hoped to improve their finances by playing 10 matches in South Africa, on an invitation by the Wanderers Club, but it fell through. Plan B was a tour of India; that also fell through. Eventually they stopped for a game in Colombo, which they drew.

Not all were on the boat. Barrett stayed in England to continue his medical studies, while Murdoch signed with Sussex. He became an MCC member the next year. Pardon was complimentary: 'It was rather a risky experiment for the greatest of all Australian batsmen to come back to first-class cricket after such a long interval, but the result proved that he had not misjudged his powers.' Murdoch enjoyed another good decade of cricket for Sussex and Grace's London County club, and toured South Africa as an Englishman, playing a Test as wicketkeeper-batsman in 1891–92. As captain of Sussex, he said, 'These dear lads would eat lemon out of my hand and swear it was sugar but my old lot [the Australians] would swear that treacle was sour.' Allan Steel said he was too soft and allowed too much 'talking back', but Charles Fry liked him immensely, saying Murdoch was always confident of scoring a century, regardless of whether he had scored any runs in the previous month. Another Sussex charge, Billy Newham, called Murdoch 'a mighty man at shifting liquor', though during matches he consumed only a sandwich and a glass of water.

Like Spofforth, Murdoch settled down as an English gentleman – still the ultimate measure of status for an Australian – but in another extraordinary twist in his extraordinary career, Murdoch would press for inclusion on the Australians' next tour of England in 1893. For the last time, he was rebuffed.

Ferris had also played his last Test for Australia. Early in the season, W.G. had approached him with a proposal to join Gloucestershire, whose committee arranged for Ferris's immediate qualification. Competitors smelt something fishy, Steel writing in *Wisden*: 'We are told that Ferris has taken a house or cottage of some sort near Bristol in order to secure some so-called qualification for Gloucestershire, though from all accounts he himself is at present in Australia.'

Qualification rules were a sham, as riddled with hypocrisy as payments to amateurs. The next season, when Sussex asked Gloucestershire's permission to field Murdoch, E.M. Grace replied, with a temerity that ran in the family, that Gloucestershire 'feel bound to uphold the Rule of Residential Qualification for County Players'.

Ferris dramatically lost his bowling skills after a Test appearance alongside Murdoch for England in South Africa. He returned to Australia in the late 1890s and played three undistinguished matches before joining the British Army in the Boer War. Typhoid killed him at Durban in 1900, much experience having been crammed into his 33 years.

On 11 November, Murdoch's 1890 Australians arrived home as they had left: leaderless. There was no suggestion of a banquet or parade; they came in like fugitives, unable to answer the question those serious about Australian cricket wanted to ask, which was how much lower it could sink.

A FALL FROM GRACE

One benefit to come out of the 1890 tour germinated in conversations between Boyle and Henry Holroyd, the third Earl of Sheffield and cricket patron who hosted the Australians on his ground in Sussex. After a four-year break, with the sport losing participants and supporters, and the colonies falling into economic depression, Boyle and Sheffield talked about the revitalising effect of an English tour to Australia.

When he returned, Boyle canvassed opinion and wrote to Sheffield that a tour would indeed be welcome – but begged him to bring W.G. Grace, at any cost.

Sheffield would take him literally. Grace, about to turn 43 and breaching 18 stone (115 kg), had no great appetite to revisit the spiteful days of 1873–74. But Grace, as ever, had his price. He refused and refused, then relented for an extortionate £3000 – double what he had taken for his 'honeymoon' tour – plus free travel and expenses for Agnes and their two youngest children, thirteen-year-old Bessie and nine-year-old Charles. It would be, as Rae calls it, the 'holiday of a lifetime' for the Grace family. It would also guarantee a financial loss for Sheffield.

In the meantime, the depleted Australian colonies played five first-class matches in 1890–91. The touring Eleven, for the first time, were not worth keeping together for a local circuit. New South Wales made their first trip to Adelaide for a win inspired by Ferris's 14 wickets, but lost in Melbourne in a game disrupted by dissent towards the umpires. After Alick Bannerman refused to leave when given out caught behind by umpire Denis Cotter, Horan remarked with asperity that 'some men require to be told half-a-dozen times that they are out before they will move away'. Giffen hit 237 and took 12 wickets against Victoria in Melbourne, but the season underscored the fragile state of Australian cricket. Even the NSW–Victoria match in Sydney was played before crowds described as 'limited' and 'very small'.

Lord Sheffield's tour, to be managed by Alfred Shaw, was considered a last chance for Australia. The excitement of Grace's inclusion finally had the local associations acting in concert. Ben Wardill of Melbourne, Frank Illingworth of East Melbourne, the NSWCA, VCA and SACA all agreed to cooperate in arranging fixtures. So harmonious were they that Dave Gregory, retiring as secretary of the NSWCA, suggested the formation of an Australian Cricket Council.

Things were not so sweet on the English side. The old guard of Nottingham professionalism, Shrewsbury and Gunn, were appalled at Grace's fee. Shrewsbury warned Shaw that on the 'amateurs' tour led by Lord Harris in 1878–79, the gentlemen had cost the promoters twice as much per man, in 'expenses', as the professionals. Sheffield now was offering the professionals £300 each plus expenses ('exclusive of wine and cigars') and a share of post-tour profits. Shrewsbury and Gunn didn't think any profits were possible – Shrewsbury thought Grace's presence might add £1500–2000 to the takings – and declined to join the group. During the tour, when Shaw wrote to Shrewsbury complaining about escalating costs, Shrewsbury wrote back, 'If he hadn't taken Grace out, Lord Sheffield would have been £3000 better off at the end of the tour, and also had a better team.'

For Grace himself, the wine and cigars would be included. This also rankled with Shrewsbury, who said, 'I told you what wine would be drunk by the Amateurs. Grace himself would drink enough to sink a ship.'

Shrewsbury and Gunn aside, the team was, as Grace claimed, the strongest to come to Australia. The professionals Lohmann, Briggs, Bobby Abel, Peel, Maurice Read and Attewell, plus himself, Stoddart and McGregor as the best amateurs, made up a team Grace believed could go through the summer undefeated.

Sailing on the P&O liner SS *Arcadia*, the English played in Malta and Colombo. According to Shaw, the voyage was enjoyable, with Grace blackening his face for a Christy minstrel show, and Peel and Attewell having great fun exploiting Abel's phobia of rats, dragging a piece of string across his bunk at night to frighten him awake. In the Colombo game, there was an inversion of the many stories of Grace's habit of putting his bails back on and refusing to walk when he'd been bowled. This time, the match was played in such searing heat that the Englishmen lined their pith helmets with cabbage leaves. Grace was 14 when a ball cut back. One of his bails fell, but nobody saw him or the ball hit his wicket, and the umpire gave him not out. 'That's all right,' Grace said, setting off for the shade, 'I'm going anyway.'

On arrival in Australia the team lunched at the Adelaide Oval and witnessed Giffen play the second of those performances that have never been equalled: this time scoring 271 runs and taking 9/96 and 7/70 in an innings defeat of the poor Victorians. Grace said generously that 'you have the best all-round man'. Sheffield told Creswell that he would like to see more regular home-and-away matches between all the colonies, governed by a single administration, intimating that he might even donate funds to make it possible.

Wardill and his fellow Victorian William Ryall now acted as local agents, after the first choice, Illingworth, an employee of Harry Boyle, went unaccountably missing. England went on a victorious swing through Adelaide, Melbourne and Sydney, with Lohmann, Attewell and Jack Sharpe in fine form. A newspaper asked, 'How is it that our batsmen against them are like so many prostrate, nervous, weak-kneed, palsied specimens of the genus homo?'

There was no questioning who was the drawcard. Billboards announced, simply: 'W.G. Grace.' Against Victoria, he didn't disappoint, scoring an unbeaten 159 out of 284. 'Considering his great weight and his 43 years, it cannot be expected that he would be as quick on his feet as of old,' Horan observed. 'His excellent exhibition delighted everybody, especially the individual who sent him a special letter requesting him to be sure and stop in until after luncheon on the Saturday, as the individual would not be able to get down before luncheon ... I doubt whether he ever met with an ovation more thoroughly enthusiastic, more genuinely sincere, than that which was accorded him on Saturday by the 15,000 persons who had assembled to witness his skill and prowess.'

Horan repeated the comment of an 'old cricketer' who had seen Grace 18 years earlier: 'Why, he is just the same as ever, except that his chest has slipped down a little.'

He seemed better behaved, too – so far. On 5 December, Sheffield made a rare speech. A shy man, he had left most of the public speaking to Grace and travelled separately from the team, but in Sydney he told a gathering that if he deserved any credit it was for transforming Grace's name 'into a real living presence, and for clothing that name with real good flesh and blood, and thus enabling the younger generation of Australians to see for themselves the hero they have worshipped from afar'.

It was during that very game, however, that the real living presence was starting to revert to type. England had brought Denis Cotter from Melbourne to be their umpire, but Harry Moses, the NSW captain, objected. 'On what ground none of us could understand,' said Shaw. 'An hour was wasted in argument as to who should stand as umpire ... and in the end my unwilling services were accepted by both sides.'

The most likely reason was that Cotter was a Victorian, like George Coulthard. It was also Cotter who had given Bannerman out in the dispute in Melbourne the previous season. But once they saw Grace arguing with Moses, the Sydney crowd began barracking for the Champion. As Shaw saw it, 'There was a free and easy element among the Colonial supporters, to whose pleasantries perhaps more attention was given than there ought to have been. Certain umpiring difficulties also arose, for which, possibly, both sides were equally to blame.'

From there, Grace became increasingly caught up in petty quarrels, even in minor games. When the English went to Parramatta to play an eighteen of Cumberland, he insisted on taking 12 men into the field. Cumberland responded by batting 19. Grace even argued with the Cumberland captain over who had won the toss, and said he would 'break things' if the man didn't apologise. The local paper said W.G. 'may be a very good cricketer, but he has some decidedly funny ways'. He got a duck in the first innings and refused to bat in the second.

The *Bulletin*, predictably, hopped in. It mocked Sheffield as 'merely a non-aggressive representative of deplorable social and political systems ... a simple-minded old fellow who runs a wholesome show for his own glory.' Of Grace, the magazine said: 'We smile. £3000 and exs for a pleasure trip ... He played the game like a professional card-expert; the veteran is master of every form of "bluff", and appeals on the slightest pretext.'

A slide towards the old acrimony was on. Before the first Test in Melbourne, Creswell threatened to withdraw Giffen and Lyons unless Adelaide was guaranteed the third Test. Sheffield finally agreed, but, annoyed by the threat, would have no more to do with Creswell.

Quarrels were put aside in the thrill of New Year's Day 1892. A crowd of 20,110 turned out at the MCG and Australian cricket received its shot in the arm. New Year's Day, said Giffen, was 'the dawn of a new era in Australian cricket'. Horan compared the scene with Lord's, the Oval, Old Trafford, Bramall Lane and Trent Bridge, but 'I have never seen any cricket gathering to surpass the picturesqueness and brilliance' of Melbourne.

Australia would be led by the players' choice, Blackham. His contribution so far, over 16 years of Test cricket and seven tours of England, boggles the mind. For those thousands and thousands of balls pounded down by Spofforth, Boyle, Allan, Garrett, Palmer, Turner, Ferris, Evans and Trumble, 'the prince of wicketkeepers' had been behind the stumps. For day after day of cricket and travelling – more than seven years of cricket, if each day were added up – Blackham had been there, gloving the ball safely, leading Australia's fielding. His cricketing contribution had no equal for endurance and excellence. Now he had the captaincy – not his strongest suit, as it would turn out, but due recognition for a pillar of the game.

He had a problem straightaway. Grace was objecting to his lucky penny, claiming it was so worn that heads and tails could not be distinguished. Blackham tossed it, and Grace called incorrectly. Australia would bat. But Grace kept testing the coin to see that it wasn't 'loaded'.

The Test match, still in the timeless format, was the first to use six-ball overs in Australia, and the first to last five days. The loss of Murdoch, Spofforth, Boyle, Palmer and McDonnell had convinced many that 'Australia could not replace them', said Giffen, but the 1891–92 team showed 'Australia had produced another generation of cricketers, who were worthy successors to the Tritons of former days'.

Australia's weakness since 1884 had been its loose batting. Now Bannerman (for whom it was no imposition) and Lyons (for whom it certainly was) knuckled down to defend against the very good English attack of Attewell, Sharpe, Lohmann, Briggs and Peel. The crowd barracked Lyons – 'It'un over the chains, Jack!' – but he refrained. Bannerman let ball after ball pass, but the crowd took the Sydney man's side, shouting, 'That's right, Alick, don't touch them', 'Why don't you bowl at the wicket, Lohmann?' and 'Watch him, umpire, he's bowling wides.'

This bemused Horan, who a few days earlier had seen the same crowd abuse Bannerman for the same tactics against Victoria. 'How is it that stonewalling for Australia against England is all right in the opinion of the crowd, while for New South Wales against Victoria it is wrong?'

Nationalist fervour expressed itself noisily during the five days. Australia made 240 – Bannerman top-scoring with 45 in 195 minutes – before England, led by Grace's 50, batted through a violent dust storm to take a 24-run lead. Melbourne's Bob McLeod, who took 5/53 on debut, nearly bowled the Champion, and W.G., ready to tease the crowd, wagged his beard as if to curse his luck and started walking. 'Twenty thousand pairs of hands are clapping,' said Giffen, 'but the old man turns round and asks for block for the next stroke. Then the crowd is silent and crestfallen, for a rise has been got out of them, and they don't like that.'

Grace could never be accused of shrinking from public intimidation. When Billy Bruce caught England's debutant George Bean, Grace challenged the catch, saying the ball had bounced, and the crowd ripped into him once more.

Bannerman again top-scored, this time with 41 in 230 minutes, and Australia set England 213. Grace told Giffen they would get the runs for the loss of six wickets at most. But Turner and Trott bowled superbly, the home team held every catch, and a 54-run win resulted. Giffen said the match was the highest standard he had ever played in, and great entertainment for the 63,652 who watched.

Horan was quick to announce the rejuvenation. 'Those who were under the impression that the visit of Lord Sheffield's team would not be beneficial to Australian cricket have changed their minds, and it is now the concurrent testimony of all that the visit has caused a cricket revival which has surpassed even the most sanguine anticipations ... To the Earl of Sheffield the vast gathering was a pleasure and a surprise. He thought the attendance would be really good, but he never dreamed that a total of about 70,000 persons would be counted as having witnessed the contest.'

The great contrast between the teams was in their approach to batting. For the match, England had scored 422 runs off 174 overs, 47 of them maidens. Australia ground out 476 runs off 343 overs, blocking out 159 maidens. Giffen heaped praise on the defensive effort: 'The batting of our men was the soundest all round we had ever exhibited. It had taken twenty years for the English batsmen to teach us that, on good wickets, matches were to be won by sound, rather than risky, batting.'

Grace saw it differently, making a public statement in favour of attacking cricket. 'Matches are played to be won, not lost, and slow defensive play is against that, and in my opinion opposed to everything that is conducive to the welfare of the game.'

He was in a bad mood anyway, after his first Test loss as England's captain. He complained about the 'dazzling' light England had batted in, and, according to the *Bulletin*, 'grossly insulted a newspaper man who asked him in a civil way' for a post-game comment.

His mood was little improved by the second Test, in Sydney three weeks later. Blackham's penny landed favourably again, but Lohmann bowled one of his great spells to take 8/58 and dismiss Australia for 144. Harry Moses, who had strained his leg during the first Test, had not fully recovered, and Grace had stated, quite fairly, that he would not consent to a runner. Moses aggravated his strain, and Grace stood his ground. Moses had to hobble from end to end and the crowd let Grace know what they thought of him. Then Giffen's brother Walter, on debut, hit a return ball to Lohmann, who scooped it up. There was doubt about whether it had carried, but Lohmann flicked it to Grace, who threw it triumphantly into the air. The umpire gave it out, though the *Australasian* said Grace 'assisted in the deception by tossing up the ball'. Grace was obviously carrying on the dispute from Melbourne, where he thought Bruce had caught Bean unfairly.

England's jockey-sized opener Bobby Abel, who had almost killed himself on a kangaroo- and emu-hunting trip between the Tests when his horse bolted, batted through England's innings of 307, scoring 132 not out. Raised hard in south London, a model of persistence and practice, Abel, in the words of Charles Fry, 'gathers runs like blackberries everywhere he goes'. The tiny pro was loved by the crowd at the Oval, who called him 'The Guv'nor'.

Only after watching Moses limp around the field did Grace relent, but he wouldn't accept substitution by Syd Gregory, the twelfth man and Australia's best fieldsman, instead insisting on the considerably less agile Tom Garrett.

On the rest day, Sunday 31 January, the *Truth* newspaper confirmed the Champion's poor opinion of the Australian press by reprinting the so-called 'Grace letter' from the 1873–74 tour. On that occasion, Richard Egan Lee had marked Grace's departure by composing a pretend letter in which 'Grace' stated his real feelings about the country: 'I didn't want to fraternise with the tinkers, tailors and snobs who are the great guns of your cricket world. To take their money was a fair thing in return for work done, but to hobnob with a lot of scum was a far different thing. Fancy the chance of a greasy butcher on his travels walking up to me one day at Lord's with "How d'ye do, Mr G; I lunched with you in Australia"?'

In 1874 it had been read as it was intended – tongue in cheek. But Lee was dead by 1892, and the *Truth* republished it as if it were authentic, under the headline 'Dr Grace Extraordinary Behaviour. He Abuses and Insults Australians.' It called him 'the famous professional English cricketer, who calls himself an amateur, while making fortunes at the game', which was about the only truth in the article.

Grace had not behaved well, but he didn't deserve this. He insisted on a correction and retraction, which was published in the more reputable *Sydney Morning Herald* on 3 February, the day the Sydney Test match finished.

After the rest day, England resumed in an apparently unbeatable position. Bannerman and Lyons set about climbing the mountain 162 runs behind. Australia's innings was arguably their finest Test batting performance to that point, up with the Murdoch-inspired second innings at the Oval in 1880. Lyons scored 134 in three hours, returning to his freer style. 'Much as one admires and commends steady batting,' Giffen said, 'one realises that there are occasions when desperate remedies, when kill-or-cure hitting, alone can win a game.' But Lyons did not slog; he 'really played sound cricket, such as many had not dreamt him to be capable of, yet his strokes made the ball travel like a cannon-shot.'

Bannerman, meanwhile, was inching towards his first Test century in a 12-year career. He batted throughout the Monday and scored 67 runs. He stonewalled into Tuesday, the field packed so close that a barracker called out, 'Look out, Alick, or W.G. will have his hand in your pocket!' The cordon reminded one onlooker of Albrecht Schenck's 1878 painting *Anguish* in which crows close in on a dead lamb watched over by its mother. Of the 204 balls he received from Attewell, Bannerman scored from five. *Wisden* said his innings 'would in a match of less interest have thoroughly tired out the spectators'. Shaw, dozing in the pavilion, said: 'I cannot defend such a wearisome display as this. It would empty the most popular cricket ground in the world.'

Bannerman did not make three figures, popping a catch to Grace, but his seven-hour vigil helped extend the lead to 228 and brought Australia into the match. It also opened the cracks in England's morale. During the innings, Lohmann was reported to have shouted at Grace, 'Not for a thousand a week would I join another team captained by you!' Horan said Grace 'was not popular with his team, especially [in] the second test match'.

Mostly this was frustration as the match, and series, slipped out of their grasp. Grace intensified the crowd's barracking by refusing to let Moses bat, then denying a substitute for McLeod, whose brother

Norman had died overnight. McLeod batted on the Tuesday, making a valuable 18, but wanted to leave on the night express for Melbourne. The teams wore black armbands, but Grace bickered with Blackham over the substitute. Australia nominated Eric Hutton, a university student. Grace asked Blackham, 'Is he a better field than McLeod?' Blackham said he was. Grace said, 'Then get someone else.' Harry Donnan fielded.

Perhaps seeing the chance for redemption, when Australia were finally out late on the Tuesday, with a few overs to play in dark drizzle, Grace decided to open the innings. 'If there's any trouble out there, who's more likely to deal with it than me?' But what was 'almost certainly the worst day of W.G.'s cricketing career', in Rae's view, ended when he was one of three wickets to fall, along with Abel and Bean. The wicket rolled out easily the next day, and Stoddart made 69, showing what might have been possible if Grace had held himself back. The old man couldn't take a trick. Turner and Giffen ran through the visitors, achieving a 72-run victory by mid-afternoon.

The celebration, said *Wisden*, was one 'of almost indescribable enthusiasm', comparable with Australia's 'Ashes' Test at the Oval in 1882 and 'the great but unsuccessful fight on the same ground in 1880'. The *Argus* reported that 'the ladies who crowded the reserve smashed their parasols on the seats and battered umbrellas were kicked about the lawn'.

An elated Horan rated it 'the greatest cricket win on record, and I make this statement, not on the spur of the moment, but after careful reflection and due deliberation'.

Grace later wrote that losing the series 'was the best thing that could have happened for the game in Australia', although he could not erase an undertone of condescension. The tour's aim was not to 'show how immensely superior English form was to Australian, but to give an impetus to the game, which according to all accounts, was very badly wanted'. Had England won, 'I believe the rising generation and the enthusiasts would have lost heart and the game out there received a blow that would have taken years to recover from. Instead of that, interest was quickened considerably, and before we left there was nothing talked about but making sure of a thoroughly representative team to come to England in 1893.'

It was at this time that the ideas of 'Test' cricket, and the 'Ashes', took a step towards formalisation. Shaw said 'the ashes of Australian cricket were redeemed'. It was apt, given the course of events since 1882, that the 'ashes' were no longer those of English cricket but Australian. Horan said, 'The issue is eminently pleasing and consolatory to Australians, all of whom hoped that the "ashes" may long remain with the men who so splendidly won them back from the fine team brought out by Lord Sheffield.'

An element of the Sydney crowd, however, continued to rub the English the wrong way. Shaw deplored 'too many betting men favour[ing] the pastime with their presence and support.' Bookies were offering win odds through the Sydney Test and 'punters were not content to operate upon the game itself, for after it was over the wish was expressed that Giffen, Turner, and Lohmann should play a single wicket match, though it must have been known that such a proceeding would be most distasteful to those interested in the good ordering of Australian cricket. Wild rumours were also afloat as to bookmakers having paid £50 each to certain players on the winning side, in recognition of their victory, but the Englishmen declined to treat the statements seriously.'

Speculators would also offer big money – £500 – for short 'wager-matches' after the third Test in Adelaide. Shaw said 'such wagering contests were never even considered by any member of the English team, nor do I think the proposals were otherwise than distasteful to the members of the Australian team, whose perfervid admirers, I make bold to say, showed the possession of more money than discretion.'

The series was settled, but Grace was not. Some up-country games failed to soothe him, and when the English were back in Sydney 16 days after the Test match, Grace was embroiled in another fight.

When NSW were batting, umpire Teddy Briscoe gave Percie Charlton not out to a catch behind off Lohmann. Grace claimed he said, 'I wish you would pay attention to the game; we all heard the catch.' But Briscoe said Grace's words were, 'You will give no one out. It is unpardonable. You must be blind. We might as well go home tomorrow.'

Briscoe quit in protest. There was a 45-minute break between innings while Charles Bannerman was found to substitute.

'Not one word had been said at the time of the incident to lead us to believe that Mr Briscoe had such a thought in his head,' Grace declared. He blamed critics who 'kept harp[ing] unnecessarily upon the point, and caused Mr Briscoe to act in a way that he would not have acted if he had been left to his own judgement'.

Briscoe complained to the NSWCA, which asked Grace if he had used offensive language to the umpire. Grace wrote that the issue 'will have to be gone into thoroughly, and some new plan adopted or cricket will not be worth playing as there is not the slightest bit of pleasure in playing under the present system of umpiring in Australia'.

The NSWCA demanded further explanation. Grace wrote: 'I did tell Mr Briscoe that his decision was unpardonable, and that he must pay more attention, as everyone except himself knew Mr Charlton was caught at the wicket. Any other remarks were not addressed to the umpire, but to me by Attewell, and I agreed with him. I did not insult Mr Briscoe, nor do I think him a cheat, but, I am sorry to say, he is not a good umpire.'

The matter rested there. Had another match been scheduled in Sydney, the NSWCA might have sanctioned Grace, but the Englishmen set off on a tour of Tasmania, Victoria and South Australia before returning home. Shaw sounded a conciliatory note in the English camp: 'This feeling as to the umpiring, too common even in these days, is to be deplored. It ought to be charitably remembered that the faultless umpire is unborn.'

Grace enjoyed Tasmania and the up-country games generally, and was happy that since 1873–74 rail had replaced many uncomfortable sea voyages and carriage rides. Shaw lamented the loss of 'romance', but Grace liked the improved efficiency and comfort.

Even in the backblocks, though, there was no relenting on the cricket field. Grace threatened to stop the game against Northern Tasmania when the wicket had been rolled and watered overnight. When it was explained that local laws differed from Marylebone's, he backed down.

By the time of the Adelaide Test, Grace didn't show up for the official pre-match function: he, like Sheffield, wanted nothing to do with Creswell. When the game started on 24 March, Grace wanted 'Dimboola Jim' Phillips to umpire, and objected to the South Australian choice, Tom Flynn (the uncle of Warwick Armstrong). The inexperienced replacements, George Downs and Will Whitridge, would have an error-strewn match.

Grace then complained about the pitch having been covered. Shaw had no objection to 'wicket nursing' of this kind, as it '"steadies" the wicket and diminishes the possibility of cracking as the game develops'. He talked Grace into accepting the pitch. Then there was the field, which Grace said was too long. He wanted the ends roped off. Again he lost. Sensibly, Blackham let Grace win his final point, which was to toss the coin himself. Annoyed at calling wrongly in Melbourne and Sydney, Grace wanted Blackham to call. He did – incorrectly – and England piled up 499, untroubled by either the pitch or the field dimensions.

Rain on the second afternoon left Australia a sticky dog to bat on. The umpires delayed the start of the third day, whereupon another quarrel broke out. The *Australasian* reported that 'Grace and several members of his team were much annoyed and disagreeable insinuations were freely made ... it was apparent that the Englishmen considered the Australians responsible in some way for the decision of the umpires, though Blackham had refused to hold any communication with them, and left them the entire responsibility.' The paper said it was Grace's fault, for rejecting Flynn as umpire. 'In this the members of his own team admitted that he was entirely wrong.' Grace threatened to abandon the match, then tried to bully the umpires into starting. When they eventually did, Briggs took 12 wickets and, assisted by Lohmann and Attewell, dismissed Australia twice in little more than a day.

'Grace was delighted to have won,' explains Rae, 'but he must also have been aware that he had lost something as well – the affection and respect of a large section of the Australian public. While he was on the field he was constantly barracked, while a chorus, made up mainly of boys, greeted his every move with rounds of mock applause ... At forty-three he had behaved just as he had at twenty-five, and rather than learning from his mistakes, he simply repeated them seemingly confident there was nothing to regret and nothing to apologise for.'

It had been a heavy, if not uncharacteristic, fall for the great man since the beginning of the summer. Horan, a balanced and sympathetic observer, summarised:

'Grace seems to have fallen under the ban of the crowd which in November last on the same oval were ready to bow down and worship him as a sort of cricket god.' He concluded that Grace 'is a bad loser, and when he lost two of the test matches in succession he lost his temper too, and kept on losing it right to the finish. Blackham stated that Grace behaved like a thorough sportsman during the second combined match, and the great wicketkeeper's remarks served to successfully combat adverse comment ... But since that match Grace seems to have developed a condition of captiousness, fussiness, and nastiness strongly to be deprecated. His objection to Flynn was nothing short of a gratuitous insult to a first-class umpire, and I regret to be obliged to say this, for I have always endeavoured in my comments to show that Grace was not as bad as he was painted ... [but] the great cricketer has only himself to blame for any strictures passed upon his conduct by those who were inclined to view him in the best light.'

He was no more popular with his own men. Expenses of £16,000 and receipts of £13,300 meant there were no profits for the professionals to share. So the great toilers, Lohmann, Briggs, Attewell, Peel, Abel and company, had nothing but £300 — a tenth of Grace's fee — to show for their labours.

Shaw, who had lost heavily on Australian tours himself, concluded with sly humour: 'Had Lord Sheffield wished to make a profit out of the tour he could have done so. But he determined that no one should have the slightest ground for suggesting that he did make a profit. Everything was done on a princely scale, from the fee of the captain downwards.'

For the great Lohmann's health, that tour was the beginning of a sharp decline. He bowled 5143 balls in all matches, a record. Grace once said, 'George, it's time for a change, isn't it?' Lohmann replied: 'Yes — don't you think I'd better go on at the other end?' (The same story would be told of George Giffen, another bowlaholic.) Batsmen often found Lohmann most dangerous when he looked ready to give up. But *Wisden* later said that his 'exertions … had a prejudicial effect upon him'. Within a few months, he had consumption. Ralph Barker comments that Lohmann 'had crammed too much of his vitality and enthusiasm into a few short years of greatness'. He went to South Africa to recover, but would be out of Test cricket for the next four years.

BLOOD, CHAMPAGNE
AND A BAIL-UP

L ord Sheffield's tour was not the great goodwill exercise that some
historians have made it. The team was farewelled only by 'a number
of cricketers'. The *Sydney Mail* said: 'The reason of the apathy displayed
was that a feeling of dislike to Grace was spreading and it was therefore
felt inadvisable to attempt any demonstration. For this Grace has only
himself to blame.'

Nevertheless, the tour revived interest in Anglo-Australian cricket,
the three Tests attracting nearly 145,000 spectators in total. Blackham's
team had been a worthy match for England's best. It was a long decade
since Australia had won any kind of rubber. Altham notes: 'Before the
matches began the Australians had a very modest opinion of their own
powers; before they were over confidence had returned in measure all the
greater for having been so long in abeyance.'

After the doldrums of the late 1880s, Sheffield's hope was that a
true contest in England could once again be contemplated. On his arrival

home, he said his team's reception had been 'unparalleled in the history of cricket in Australia, and I am quite sure I may also say it is without parallel in the history of cricket in England. I hope, therefore, when the Australians come to England next year – as they are coming – and when they visit this park – as they intend to do – that the people of Sussex will assemble on this ground in their thousands and give them such a ringing welcome as Sussex throats know how to give, and as will show them that you have recognised and appreciated the magnificence of the welcome that they gave your fellow countrymen last winter in far-away Australia.'

It is perhaps for his diplomacy, and convenient amnesia, that Sheffield is remembered as, in Altham's words, 'the Maecenas of cricketers'. When Lord Harris had seen the kind of wild behaviour Australian players and followers were capable of, he didn't want them at Lord's. When Lord Sheffield saw it, he forgot it.

During the Adelaide Test match, delegates from the colonies resolved to set up an Australasian Cricket Council. NSW, Victoria and South Australia would comprise it, with Tasmania, Queensland and possibly Western Australia and New Zealand to join later. The ACC would regulate inbound and outbound tours, appoint umpires, and settle disputes referred by the colonies – or at least that was the idea.

Later in 1892, the council was inaugurated in a meeting at the Oxford Hotel, in Sydney's Darlinghurst. The ACC had 15 delegates, including current players Giffen and Bruce. At its September meeting it named six 'certainties' to pick an 1893 tour to England: Blackham, Bannerman, Turner, Trott, Giffen and Lyons.

It also had to decide what to do with Lord Sheffield's gift of £150 for the furtherance of Australian cricket. Victoria wanted the money split between the colonies and spent as they pleased, but this was overturned, by a one-vote margin, in favour of the purchase of a premiership shield made by the Polish-born Melbourne jeweller Philip Blashki. The Victorian and NSW governments allowed the shield to cross borders without customs duty.

South Australia beat NSW in the first Sheffield Shield game in Adelaide, and, as the original idea was to make it a 'challenge shield', South Australia should have been its first holder. But Victoria urged a change to the format, to award the shield to the overall season winner, which happened to be themselves, ascendant in all four of their matches.

Giffen topped the batting and bowling aggregates and averages — another of his unmatched feats — but other leading players spent a nervous summer waiting for the touring team to be picked. Horan asked Trott about his chances of selection. Trott answered: 'Well, that 196 against East Melbourne got me as far as Albany; the 63 in the first innings [against] New South Wales took me to Colombo; the 70 not out in the second innings carried me to Suez, and being put on to bowl first against South Australia placed me in the Mediterranean; once there nothing can keep me back, you know, and so I am safe in England.'

The selectors were faced with contentious choices. Sammy Jones, who had shown glimpses of greatness in England, played in NSW's first two games but did not turn up for the third. The *Bulletin* wrote that his erratic behaviour 'should be a warning' to other players. Bonnell takes this as a further inference that the illness Jones caught in 1890 was an STD.

Sydney's Syd Callaway and Harry Moses were chosen for the tour, then withdrew. The selectors picked themselves, plus Walter Giffen, Billy Bruce, Gregory, Trumble, Bob McLeod and Affie Jarvis. George Giffen said that the 'strength of Australian cricket had materially improved' and the team had 'tolerable hope of success'.

Walter Giffen's selection was something of a surprise, as he had failed in his Test appearances in 1891–92 and shown only moderate form for South Australia. It was rumoured that George threatened not to tour unless Walter was selected, and his loyalty had made him a figure of fun at times. A verse was written, saying in part:

'Pray what's the use of being great,
An indispensable big brother,
If Walter may not share the gate
And get his whack like any other.'

Jack Lyons was quoted teasing Giffen: 'You'd better take the whole bloomin' family with you, George.' And when a heckler called out to George during a wicketless period in an Adelaide match, 'Put on brother Walter!' George reportedly stopped the game and went after the man.

In his autobiography, Giffen put his own version of the 1893 team's selection: 'The public of Australia, which had taken very little interest in the doings of the 1890 team, manifested considerable enthusiasm in 1893' but 'the selection of the team was subjected to much adverse criticism. A good deal was said about the inclusion of my brother Walter, and it was even alleged that I had declined to join unless he were also chosen. This, however, was absolutely untrue, and those who made the assertion quite over-looked the fact that about the time the Australian Eleven was selected, Walter had been picked, on the strength of really excellent batting in intercolonials, to be one of the eleven which played in the second and third test matches against the Earl of Sheffield's team. Surely a man who was considered to be good enough for an Eleven of Australia at home was not out of place in a touring fourteen, especially when Moses, one of the eleven, declined to make the trip! Walter was not a success in England, and nobody was more surprised than myself, for I had always thought that he would acquit himself well on English grounds.' George, of course, omitted to mention that Walter had scored 22 runs at 7.33 in his Test appearances and had only played in a single first-class match, scoring 21 runs, before his selection.

In February, the selectors met in Sydney to choose the thirteenth and last man. It was down to Harry Graham from Victoria, Frank Iredale from NSW, and Jack Reedman from South Australia. The six selectors split down colonial lines. 'I shall never forget the exciting scene we had in Sydney,' Giffen said. 'The pros and cons were keenly argued, until at last Iredale was knocked out of the running, because it was thought that he had not sufficient stamina to last through an arduous tour. Then came the tug of war. Jack Blackham rose to his feet and became quite enthusiastic over Graham whom he described as the best batsman Australia had produced since Charlie Bannerman's time. Old Jack's eloquence gained the day, and his judgement was thoroughly vindicated.'

Then the ACC stepped in. To foster goodwill among the newer cricket colonies, they wanted a Queenslander. Thirty-year-old journeyman Arthur Coningham was only an occasional Queenslander – he was born in Victoria and was now representing NSW – but he had taken nine wickets in the most recent intercolonial and was the next best thing. The son of a glass finisher, Coningham was a well-performed runner, pigeon shot, billiards player, rugby player and rower, and a cricketer of vivid colour. But he had little support from the senior players. Giffen said 'a cry was raised' for Coningham. 'The members of the Cricket Council took the matter up, with the result that it was practically put to us that we must take Coningham, and we did so against our own judgement.'

Having won that fight, the ACC lost the more important one. It wanted the players to hand over control of tour finances. After seven mostly profitable tours, the players had no such intention. The ACC installed one of its members, Victor Cohen from Sydney, as manager, a decision that would prove divisive and disastrous. The ACC secretary, NSW's John Portus, further riled the players by writing to Lord's to say the council had approved the selections, an imprimatur the players did not think they needed.

Even through the 1892–93 summer, there was no certainty that the tour would take place. Opposition still lingered in England, with old grudges and memories from the 1880s. Lord Hawke had said in December 1891, 'I do not think that there is any chance of a representative team strong enough to meet the leading counties coming in 1893. The matches of the present team in Australia show that they are nothing like powerful enough to send a really good team to England. The whole thing is a money-making business from start to finish.'

The *Sportsman* editorialised that Hawke might have provided 'an unfortunate lever ... which may turn the laugh against us', and so it proved when Blackham's Australians beat Grace's team. But as we have seen, the true obstacle was not cricket. In January 1892, previewing the possibility of a tour, *Blackwood's Magazine* questioned Australians' manners on the field, their mercenary spirit and the influence of betting. It asserted that 'gentlefolk in Australia no longer had anything to do with cricket there'.

Nottinghamshire suggested Australia not tour until 1894, but all objections were overridden by Sheffield's enthusiasm. He was Australia's greatest friend. And so, as Altham notes, 'When in the spring of 1893 the eighth team, under Blackham's captaincy, sailed for England, it was hailed not merely as at last truly representative, but as something like the equal of the best of its predecessors.'

Carrying such expectations quickly proved beyond the Australians. The first morning of the first match, at Sheffield Park, shaped the summer. Grace and Shrewsbury put on a century stand, and the inability to penetrate with the new ball would dog Australia from then on. Giffen took 26 wickets in the first three matches (and scored 180 against Gloucestershire), but an off-spinner taking the new ball did not bode well. Turner had entered his decline, and was ill. The hard, dry wickets were not conducive to his breakbacks, and the appearance of Ferris for Gloucestershire was a sobering reminder of what they had lost. Murdoch playing for Sussex was another, though his double failure might have vindicated the Australian group's refusal of his plea to join them. *Wisden*

lamented his absence, for his steadying influence if nothing else, but the 1890 tour had convinced his old mates that his time had gone.

By the end of May they had won two, lost three and drawn two. Even though they had a better June than the 1890 team, they still lost three matches that month. If Australia enhanced their reputation at all, it was in their uphill efforts. Against the MCC, a swashbuckling 149 from Lyons and five second-innings wickets from McLeod very nearly pulled off a miraculous comeback. Giffen said Lyons's innings 'completely paralysed the bowling' and 'eclipsed even Massie's brilliant performance at Oxford eleven years before, because not only did Lyons score more rapidly, but the bowling was better, the occasion was more important, and the runs were made at a time of desperate need'.

Although they had meritorious wins over the Players at the Oval and the North of England at Old Trafford, the Australians' deficiencies were opening up by the time of the first Test, at Lord's from 17 July.

Giffen told the press, 'We missed a fast bowler badly ... but their fast bowlers did not always miss us.' England had a crop of express bowlers, not all legitimate. Lancashire's Arthur Mold and Essex's Charles Kortright were the fastest, and gave the Australians a battering, but neither had a Test career of any significance due to the illegitimacy of their actions. When Kortright bowled at the Lord's Pavilion end in the Gentlemen–Amateurs match of 1898, with the colourful pavilion behind him, an observer wondered whether he would be charged with murder or manslaughter when he inevitably killed a batsman.

Of more lasting concern to Australia was the Surrey pairing of Bill Lockwood and Tom Richardson. Both were fast, and, like the greatest bowling pairs, contrasting: Lockwood was unpredictable and dangerous, Richardson lionhearted and accurate. If Lockwood was Thomson, Richardson was Lillee. Barker said Lockwood 'had a long, bouncing run, and a perfect rotary action, swinging freely from the shoulder. His arm was high, and the actual delivery seemed effortless ... Only [Ted] McDonald and [Harold] Larwood can be said to have approached the sheer flowing beauty of his action in full motion, and he made the ball flick higher from the pitch than any other bowler. The devil seemed to be in the ball itself whenever Lockwood bowled.'

Lockwood would be one of the most fascinating characters of the Golden Age, a wild erratic genius who swept in and out of the game, back to the Nottingham suburb of Old Radford where he was born, lived and died. Charles Fry called Lockwood 'without qualification the best fast bowler I ever played with or against'. He bowled with a loop, obtaining a disconcerting dip like a slower bowler. 'Ranji once said, and I concur, that one could be 120 not out on a plumb wicket and then be clean bowled by Lockwood and walk away to the pavilion not knowing what one would have done if one had another chance.'

Lockwood had few friends. Home Gordon wrote: 'He was never likeable, and there was in his bowling a viciousness somewhat characteristic of the bad-tempered fellow he always showed himself.'

Perhaps Albert Knight captured Lockwood best — and made him most familiar to our eyes — when he wrote that 'when the mood was his, and good or evil genius prompted, the sting and devil of his knuckle-raising deliveries was incomparable. Richardson would break back and bruise the batsman's thigh, apologising with [a] grave and sincere smile; Lockwood would break back and nip a piece of one's thigh away, looking at one the whole [time] and wondering why the blind gods should waste so superb a delivery on mere flesh.'

The dark-haired Richardson, born in a gypsy caravan at Byfleet in Surrey, was the consummate professional. He had grown up playing on Mitcham Common. Murdoch thought he chucked, and in 1893 Nottinghamshire accused him of throwing his faster ball. That season, he ironed it out. Barker writes: 'Whether Richardson actually changed his action, or whether batsmen were so astonished at his pace that they concluded he must be throwing, is not clear; most of the great fast bowlers of the nineties, Lockwood included, had to live down accusations of throwing.' But for Richardson the suspected throwing was 'easily cured' and didn't arise after 1893.

As if to emphasise Australia's lack of a new-ball weapon, Lohmann returned from South Africa in mid-June, fully recovered and expecting to make a run for the Test series. But within a fortnight he relapsed and was ruled out. Meanwhile, the Demon himself was playing club matches for Hampstead, twice taking all ten wickets in an innings and once scoring 155. During the first Test, *Cricket* wrote: 'There are good judges, and not a few of them, who are of the opinion that the Australian team would not have done a bad stroke if they had been able to secure the services of a fast bowler, even as Spoff now is. At all events, he would have furnished the variety which has been at times so sadly lacking in the Australian bowling.'

Grace missed the first Test match with a split finger, leaving the captaincy to Stoddart. An England rugby representative, the son of a merchant, Stoddart was impulsive, easy-going and popular. He risked batting first on a damp wicket, and Shrewsbury proved Australia's master again, scoring 106, becoming the first man to pass 1000 runs in Test cricket. When the young Yorkshire aristocrat Stanley Jackson came in, his professional partner warned him, 'Back up with your legs, sir, or Charlie Turner will have you out.' Jackson made 91 in just under even time on debut.

In English eyes, nobody better embodied the coming Golden Age than the Hon. Francis Stanley Jackson. Fry would write: 'He was exceptionally good-looking in the Anglo-Saxon Guards-officer way: blue eyes and a neat golden-brown moustache. He was always turned out, flannels, pads, and boots, to perfection.' And he was the only 'great batsman' Fry knew who did not change his game for wet wickets.

Jackson's father, Lord Allerton, had big business concerns in Yorkshire, and cricket was only one part of Stanley's grand plan. He entered politics in 1896, elected to Leeds Council, and became an MP at Westminster in 1915. Later he was an influential administrator at the MCC. As a cricketer, Fry said, Jackson 'always gives an impression of being all there, and having a very definite idea of what ought to be done and how to do it. Nothing excites him much; nothing can put him off his guard. Yet there is much enthusiasm for cricket behind those somewhat cold blue eyes and that unruffled brow.'

As one of the first Golden Age players to arrive in Test cricket, Jackson spanned two eras. In this, his first Test match, Charlie Turner took 6/67. By his last, 12 years later, he would be facing Warwick Armstrong and Tibby Cotter.

England's 334, assisted by four dropped catches, made them safe in the match. Lockwood roared through the Australian top order, but two more youngsters, Graham and Gregory, broke up the field with quick singles and scored 107 and 57 respectively. The 'Little Dasher's century was the first on debut for Australia since Charlie Bannerman's. Rain prevented an intriguing finish, but Blackham's team left Lord's well satisfied that they had matched England from behind.

As the wickets dried further, Australia rebuilt its reputation in batting. Trott and Gregory made hundreds against Middlesex, and against Oxford and Cambridge Past and Present at Portsmouth, Bannerman, Bruce and Trumble all passed three figures and the total of 843 was a world record. The opposition bowling was questionable, but the Australians motored towards the second Test at the Oval with more self-belief than any touring team since 1884.

In three days of 'tropical heat', it all came unstuck. Grace returned, won the toss, and England racked up 5/378 by stumps. The next morning Jackson finished off the century he had missed at Lord's, though not without a tremor. He was 99 when Mold, the worst batsman in England, joined him. Jackson negotiated some tricky balls from Giffen before lifting one onto the roof of the covered seating for a five. Mold vindicated Jackson's hurry by running him out next over.

On a perfect wicket that had given England 483 runs, Australia lasted less than two hours for their 'wretchedly poor' 91. Following on,

Bannerman (passing 1000 Test runs), Trott and Giffen all passed 50, and Giffen said 'Australia should have saved that game', but they were always too far behind to survive Lockwood's pace and Briggs's probing spin.

The innings defeat, which would prove decisive in the series, prised open serious rifts in the Australian team. *Sporting Life* reported that on the way to their 13 July match at Brighton, 'Members of factions within the team lost their tempers on a railway journey into Sussex. When the train reached Brighton, porters saw one of the Australians' compartments spattered with blood.'

The pugilists were never identified, but several names came up in speculations. Blackham and Bruce were rumoured to have physically threatened each other, Bannerman, when deputising as captain, clashed with George Giffen, and Giffen in turn quarrelled with Turner, who ended up not going on the American leg of the tour. Drink was commonly believed to be a source of division. Coningham, a teetotaller, told the *Australasian*: 'Well, when a man is full of champagne overnight, he is not fit for much next day. One morning coming down the stairs we found one of them asleep there with his clothes on, his head on the stair mat.' Harry Graham, who euphemistically 'lived life to the full', would die penned in Seacliff Asylum, near Dunedin, at forty, his promise unfulfilled. *Wisden* said: 'Had he ordered his life more carefully, he might have had a much longer and more successful career.'

While a non-drinker, Coningham proved uncontrollable on the tour, absenting himself without explanation once he realised the selectors saw him as having been foisted upon them by the ACC. Even though he had married Alice Dowling the morning the team had sailed from Sydney, it was rumoured that he was going to see girlfriends, and Blackham was unable to rein him in. Coningham's trip was worthwhile in one respect, however: he received a medal for diving into the Thames and saving a drowning boy.

Another pebble in the team's shoe was the presence of Cohen, whom the senior players viewed as an ACC spy. *Sporting Life* said: 'Fines as penalties for ill-natured behaviour lost effect because they were not enforced. Manager Cohen complained of disrespectful language and said he had to defend himself from assault by "some drunken brute'" in the team. The *Sydney Mail* and *Bulletin* both attacked the Australians' heavy drinking, saying the teetotallers had to work too hard to make up for the drinkers. Other Australian press reports blamed Australia's deterioration on distracting news from Melbourne: the land boom was busting in a market in which many of the players had speculated.

Whatever the causes, after the second Test Blackham failed to hold their morale together. At Old Trafford, Lord Hawke made a statement about the Australians by taking out Jackson and Peel so they could play for Yorkshire. Rain and a doubling of ticket prices made for poor crowds, and Australia did well to remain on terms after Richardson announced his arrival in Test cricket with five wickets on the first day. Gunn scored the first Test century at Old Trafford, before Richardson's five second-innings wickets drove Australia towards defeat until Turner and Blackham, as solid a last-wicket pair as ever played, batted long enough to save a draw. Turner dislocated a finger while batting, and Grace used his medical skills to relocate it. Turner obliged him by getting out almost immediately after.

Grace showed how much happier he was on home turf by constantly standing in Australia's path that summer. He and Stoddart put on three century opening partnerships and several other important ones. As Giffen said, 'It seemed nothing short of marvellous to me, that, nearly twenty years after I first met him at Adelaide, he was still England's greatest batsman, playing oftener against us than any other Englishman.' At 45, the old man was still a long way from finished.

But the Australians were done. Against a sixteen of Blackpool in cold weather, Coningham showed his general contempt for proceedings by gathering kindling to light a fire in the outfield. A spectator offered him hot potatoes to warm his pockets. Coningham would later sue a Catholic priest for allegedly having an affair with his wife, and feature in Cyril Pearl's *Wild Men of Sydney*. He trained as a chemist but also worked as a tobacconist, hairdresser and bookmaker. His bag at Randwick said 'Coningham the Cricketer', a fame he owed in part to a singular achievement, 18 months after the tour, when he finally played his first Test match: against Stoddart's 1894–95 Englishmen, he took a wicket with his first ball. It was a very short Test career, however, and his character showed through in two other incidents that summer. In a game in Brisbane against England, called for no-balling, he threw a ball angrily at Stoddart. The mild-mannered English captain was stirred to demand an apology. In another game, Coningham demanded double the fee Queensland could afford to pay him. Their opponents, NSW, knowing what a drawcard he was, paid up, and he repaid them by scoring 200 runs. That was Coningham — eccentric, gifted, contrary, the type of character Australian cricket was already, in its infancy, deciding it would only accommodate if he could pay his freight in wickets and runs.

While a record seven Australians passed 1000 runs on the 1893 tour, this owed as much to dry wickets as to improved batting. *Wisden*'s new editor Sydney Pardon was reluctant to join Australian critics in terming the tour a 'failure', but admitted it fell far short of 'sanguine expectations'. George Giffen, Bruce, Trott, Gregory, Lyons, Bannerman, Trumble and Graham had good tours, but Coningham, Walter Giffen and Jarvis were 'nothing better than makeshifts'. 'No cricketer is likely to do himself justice when he knows that he is only playing in order that someone else may have a holiday,' Pardon said. Turner and Blackham 'did one or two brilliant things, but were far from keeping up their previous form'. Blackham 'captained the side with any amount of zeal, but we doubt if by temperament he is quite fitted for so anxious and onerous a position.' Fielding, always the barometer of a team's well-being, was 'at times most brilliant, but on some occasions inexcusably faulty'.

On their way home, the Australians lost to the Gentlemen of Philadelphia by an innings and 68 runs. Giffen said the locals 'met us at a disadvantage, inasmuch as after a rough trip across the "Herring Pond" we had to play without any practice, and with all of us feeling the effect of the ocean swell, we gave a poor exhibition of fielding'. But the result caused a sensation, and the Eighth Australians would be best known for their indiscipline. Even their last days were fractious. Just before they arrived home on 20 November, Cohen, who had kept his own financial accounts, declared a dividend of £50–60 per man. Players stormed his cabin and inspected his records, comparing them with their own. After some vigorous discussion, Cohen agreed they should get £190 each, wiping out the ACC's hoped-for profit.

On arriving home, an angry Cohen gave interviews to the press, saying that throughout the tour players had assaulted him, some were drunk and unmanageable most of the time, players had publicly abused him during the Lord's Test, and they had broken into his cabin. He said their behaviour was 'so bad ... that the next team will not be welcomed at all. Another team should not visit England for years to come.'

But it was the ACC, not the militant players, which would fold. The players were, for the moment, on the right side of history. Alfred Shaw, who had been involved with more of the early tours than anyone else, described these historical forces when assessing Lord Sheffield's contribution to international cricket:

'If he were asked what good had resulted from these international contests in England, he would beg his Australian audience to carry their minds back twenty or thirty years, and then say if the first visits of the Australian teams to England had not produced results far beyond mere cricket.' For English people, 'to whom Australia would have otherwise been a sealed book,' nothing awakened them more to the relations between the two countries 'than the advent of the Australian cricketers'. A common joke had it that the discovery of Australia was due to cricket, not Captain Cook. 'The advent of Australian cricketers to England did discover to a vast portion of the English community the real Australia. It led them to open their maps, and, more than that, their eyes and mind. The knowledge so acquired brought Australia nearer to England, and taught Englishmen that Australia, instead of being the land of the convict and bushranger, was a country teeming with the charms and allurements which a bountiful Providence had placed at the disposal of those who would take the trouble to seek her.' Many men who had traded 'the direst privation in England for affluence in Australia' had first had the idea while 'watching, as simple spectators, an international match in the Mother Country'.

Test cricket, having survived its cleansing fires, was again on the advance.

'THE MATCH OF
THE CENTURY'

George Giffen came home refreshed by six months' constant play. Starting the Australian season with 205 at home to NSW, he carried South Australia to its first Sheffield Shield. Not for nothing did Adelaide parents teach their children to say at bedtime, 'God bless Mummy and Daddy and George Giffen.' He was in the midst of a 12-year period in which he scored one-third of SA's runs and took five-eighths of their wickets. He has never been matched, for that state or any other.

Billy Murdoch made a surprise reappearance, playing three times for NSW before he missed the last day's play against Victoria in Sydney 'for business reasons'. He would be ducking an almighty row. After umpire Jack Tooher delayed play on the third morning to allow the wicket to dry – Victoria ended up collapsing on the sticky dog – Blackham accused him of favouring the home team. Tooher threatened never to umpire again wherever Blackham was playing, and the NSW premier and NSWCA president, George Reid, weighed in, saying Victoria were 'blue mouldy for a fight'. The VCA cajoled the Australian captain into apologising, at first without success.

As the winter drew on, Harry Moses, the NSW captain, said he would retire if Blackham did not back down. Only when it looked like the stand-off might affect the plans for the next English tour did Blackham withdraw the insinuation that Tooher was cheating, while maintaining his belief that the umpire was wrong.

The 1893 property bust had hurt cricket. The Melbourne Cricket Club was £2336 in debt after the collapse of the City of Melbourne Bank. Frank Grey Smith took out a personal overdraft from the National Bank, then approached Lord Sheffield to see if he might bring an England team to restore Melbourne's finances. Sheffield declined, but Andrew Stoddart agreed to round up a team. In a rare show of coordination, the ACC helped plan a five-Test series. The SACA's Creswell said three Tests would suffice, whereupon he was threatened with the cancellation of the Adelaide Test.

Adelaide was becoming a force in cricket beyond its Shield win. Aside from the Test men – the Giffens, Lyons and Affie Jarvis – it was producing a rich young crop. Ernie Jones, a wrestling, drinking, footballing former Broken Hill miner, was emerging as the fastest, if not always fairest, Australian bowler. Two teenaged left-handers from Prince Alfred College emerged: Joe Darling, the son of a parliamentarian who didn't care much for cricket, and Clem Hill, whose father had scored the first club century on the Adelaide Oval. Both boys had scored double- and triple-centuries for their school, and were being rushed into the colonial team. Very soon they, and Jones, would be the new heroes of Australian cricket.

In the first week of November 1894, Stoddart's team docked at Port Adelaide in the SS *Ophir*, soon to be the Royal yacht for Edward VII.

They would contest one of the most memorable series ever played. In his biography of Stoddart, David Frith argues, 'The 1894–95 rubber sparked off the frenzied interest which has always since surrounded Test matches between England and Australia; it saw a new dedication and application by the players involved; the Press gave the public what it wanted – detailed coverage, with comments by retired cricketing warriors; the *Pall Mall* gazette gave the word 'test' a capital 'T', and spent large sums telegraphing the action across the world every few minutes. The English, from their Queen down, loved it.'

Stoddart proved an instant favourite, a relief after Grace's hauteur. Large crowds turned out in Adelaide to see the locals, spearheaded by Darling and George Giffen, beat England for the first time, and in Melbourne, where the Lancashire amateur Archie MacLaren, prematurely imperious at 22, scored 228 in his first innings on Australian soil. Ben Wardill said of Yorkshire's beefy, song-loving Jack Brown, 'He won't get ten runs in five months, and had better go home.' Brown was a bit of a character. In an up-country game, he and Johnny Briggs put a couple of spectators in flannels, stationed them in the deep, and repaired to the refreshment tent. Brown scored centuries against South Australia and NSW; later in the summer he would prove Wardill wrong most conclusively.

Cricket in Australia had come alive again. Batting had improved, both technically and with the assistance of more carefully prepared pitches. Charley Checkett was getting the most of his Adelaide Hills soil, while in Sydney Ned Gregory, Dave's brother and Syd's father, switched from Merri Creek to Bulli soil, which produced faster, truer bounce, and designed and built an iconic new scoreboard.

Audiences responded. For the first Test in Sydney, 62,113 turned out over five days to see one of the most remarkable matches ever played.

It certainly contained more switches of fortune than any previous Test. After Richardson dismissed Lyons, Trott and Darling, the last to his first ball in Test cricket, in the opening hour, Australia amassed

586. Giffen, 'determined to vindicate myself' after criticisms that his Test record didn't match his domestic form, had put himself through a rigorous winter training program that paid off with 'the best innings I have ever played'. His 161 was his only Test century. 'The Midget' Gregory bettered him, scoring 201 and adding a record 154 for the ninth wicket with Blackham, who made his Test-highest 74. Nearly 30,000 fans contributed £103 for Gregory after two glory days for Australia.

Giffen said, 'With 586 runs on the slate, we never for one second dreamt of losing the game.' Yet they did. Chasing 177 on the fifth afternoon of the timeless match they cruised to 2/113, with Darling and Giffen in total command, the latter becoming the only player ever to take eight wickets and pass 200 runs in an Anglo-Australian Test match.

At the Baden Baden Hotel in Coogee that night, recounted Giffen, 'the match seemed as good as won. All of us thought so that night save Blackham, who feared rain. I know I turned in to rest with an easy mind on the subject. When I awoke next morning and found the glorious sun streaming into my room, I was in ecstasy. But the first man I met outside was Blackham, with a face as long as a coffee-pot. The explanation of his looks came with the remark, "It has been pouring half the night, George."'

Over in England's quarters, Bobby Peel was also up all night, drinking to dull the pain of five teeth he'd had extracted. When he was still drunk on arrival at the SCG, Stoddart put him under a cold shower. Peel wiped himself down and said, 'Give me the ball, Mr Stoddart, and I'll have the buggers out before lunch.'

He did, with some help from Briggs and a wicket sticky under the hot sun. 'Some one said the rain beat us,' said Giffen, 'but Blackham was nearer the mark when he rejoined, "No, it was the sun that did it."' Australia lost eight wickets for 53 and fell 10 runs short. Throughout the collapse, Blackham paced about the balcony muttering 'Cruel luck', over and over. When he was out for 2, unable to bat through the pain of a split thumb, his 17-year Test cricket career was over. The third of the four pillars of early Australian Test cricket – Murdoch, Spofforth and Giffen being the others – had fallen.

Betting, which had been combated but not eradicated, was heavy during the Test match, and MacLaren won £200 after placing £4 on England at 50/I. The Tattersall's Club bookmakers did so well, nonetheless, that they raised a collection to reward Gregory for his innings.

One footnote to that Sydney Test would have great repercussions. When the Australians were fielding, they came in for lunch and had a wash before eating. 'One can well imagine our surprise on entering the dining-room,' Darling wrote many years later. 'In those days the players dined with [NSWCA] delegates and hosts of their friends, "dead heads" who had been invited to lunch, not at the expense of the delegates, but as part of the expenses of the match – when three of us were unable to obtain seats, and had to wait until such time as these hangers-on had finished ... It was not until the players took a stand and demanded that a room be set aside entirely for the two teams to dine in that these so-called legislators for the benefit of Australian cricket gave way.'

He was only a debutant, but Darling foresaw the biggest conflict in Australian cricket over the next 20 years: the fight for control between the players and the Sydney 'dead heads'. Darling would, in time, be at its centre.

Fourteen thousand Melburnians waited for a new Australian captain to come out and toss with Stoddart on 29 December. Finally it was Giffen who emerged, on his teammates' vote. The two teams combined for 198 runs in their first innings and 808 in the second. The strange match resolved into a duel between the captains. Stoddart stonewalled for 173, the best innings of his career – 'Well,' he said, 'I had to buck up for England, home, and beauty' – while Giffen bowled 78.2 overs and took six wickets. When the Australian players urged Giffen to take himself off, he said, like George Lohmann, 'Yes, I think I'll go on the other end.'

England's 2–0 lead did not disguise their emerging problem, which was Lockwood's utter loss of form. One of many English cricketers who have found Australia 'a tough place to tour', Lockwood was extremely accident-prone off the field. During the NSW match, he dived off a boat in Sydney Harbour for a swim and nearly drowned. Rescued by passing yachtsmen and revived with brandy, he then had a glass splinter embedded in his finger when Peel's soda bottle exploded. 'One feels that he must have been a careless fellow,' Ralph Barker comments with nice understatement. On another occasion, some Englishmen went shooting. 'Lockwood frightened everybody by standing in the wrong places and on one occasion firing his gun by mistake. "He is a most uncomfortable chap to be out with on this sort of expedition", wrote Albert Ward, the Lancashire batsman, who was one of the party.'

The highly strung Lockwood could not pull himself together on the field. While Richardson recovered from a miserable start – he took 5/251 in his first two matches on tour – Lockwood was a non-event. Their contrasting fortunes highlighted their differences: Lockwood a mercurial, brittle genius, Richardson an iron horse. Lockwood had a habit, if he was being no-balled, of trying to trick the umpire by overstepping the line and pretending to bowl but holding onto the ball. 'It was a piece of childishness,' writes Barker, 'quite outside the scope of the less sophisticated Richardson.' To highlight the worthiness of the Surrey Express, Barker says of the shooting expedition: 'An interesting sidelight on character is that Tom Richardson would not take part in the shoot, though he went with the party and acted as game-carrier. He would not spoil the atmosphere by making an issue of it with his teammates, but he hated hurting beast as well as man.'

Australia won the third and fourth Tests by unveiling a brittle genius of its own. Harry Trott's tall, wilful, immensely strong younger brother Albert, who bowled medium-pace breakbacks, had been hammered by Giffen in Adelaide because he bowled too straight. He set up a target on a pitch that he named 'George Giffen', and practised cutting the ball back between the inside edge and the pads. Now he was picked to play England on the same ground, but it wasn't his bowling that made the immediate impact. In heat that reached well above 40°C, the Australians collapsed before Albert Trott and Syd Callaway put on 81 for the last wicket. Richardson the Lionheart took 5/75, reminding Giffen of Spofforth: 'With the broiling sun streaming on the back of his curly black hair, and the intense heat trying him severely, he bowled like a veritable demon ... England has not, to my way of thinking, had so deadly a bowler in my time.'

Giffen and Callaway ran through England for 124. Stoddart had the chance to avoid trying to save the follow-on and make Australia bowl again in the heat, but sportingly said, 'We are going to play the game and get every run we can.'

In Australia's second innings 411, Albert Trott whacked 72 not out off the exhausted visitors. 'While most of us were in our element,' Giffen said, 'the Englishmen were almost prostrated. Some of them took two or three shower-baths during the night, which, of course, was the worst thing they could have done.'

In the final act of the most astonishing all-round debut in Test-cricket history, Albert came on as first change in England's second innings, got his breakback working, and took 8/43.

He did it again in the fourth Test. Coming in at 7/119, he hit 85 not out in 120 minutes. He now had 195 runs in three Test innings and the English still hadn't found a way to get him out. After Giffen and Turner tore through England for the win, becoming the first men to pass 100 Test wickets, the Sydney crowd waited outside the members' gate. England's all-rounder Bill 'Bandbox' Brockwell observed: 'It is a demonstrative, ribald crowd that, especially the boy section of it, has so much to say in a way that is personal that even a big man like [Jack] Lyons won't face it alone.'

The decisive fifth Test in Melbourne was billed as the 'match of the century'. It started with the controversy of the decade, when Giffen and Blackham voted their third selector, Turner, out of the team in favour of Bathurst's Tom McKibbin, who had only played five first-class matches. In light of the ensuing result, and Turner's and McKibbin's respective Test records, history has deemed the move a monumental blunder. When told he was dropped, Turner exclaimed to Lyons: 'I'll never play cricket again!' Lyons replied: 'It's no use talking like that, Charlie. You'll have to go to England if we go next year.'

Giffen said 'there was a great deal of controversy, but on intercolonial form and with a good wicket in prospect I am sure we acted wisely.' It's worth assessing his and Blackham's judgement. The weather in Melbourne was forecast to be hot and dry, the pitch hard and fast — conditions in which Turner was least effective. He had pulled out of the Adelaide Test with a late illness, which did not endear him to his colleagues. And in the month since the fourth Test in Sydney, McKibbin's figures did outshine Turner's: 34 wickets at 12.5 to seven at 23.5. Australia, encouraged by Albert Trott's performances, were also looking for generational renewal. At the end of February 1895, the selection was not as wrongheaded as it seems.

More than 90,000, a record, crowded into the MCG over the five days of the big match. 'Special trains brought human freight in hundreds from Sydney and Adelaide,' Giffen said. The *Argus* reported: 'There appears to be an idea somewhere that there is a Depression here. To the spectator on Saturday (crowd 29,123) at the MCG that word had no meaning.'

Giffen said that at the toss, Stoddart was 'white as a sheet, and I have been told that the pallor of my own countenance matched his. It was a trying moment, for both knew that with two such strong batting sides, much depended on the toss.'

When the coin fell Giffen's way, the *Sydney Morning Herald* reported that he 'ran to the coin and Giffen, with a joyous shout and a dive down on to the coin, exclaimed, "It's tails!"'

Giffen said he 'felt as though a great burden had been lifted from my shoulders. Poor Stoddart gave me a despairing look, which said as plainly as words, "I'm afraid it's all over, George."'

It should have been when Australia compiled 414. But MacLaren's 120 confirmed him as a top-shelf Test batsman and kept England in touch. In England, Grace said, 'news was telegraphed every few minutes, awaited with extraordinary interest'. Queen Victoria was said to be following keenly. Richardson's incredible stamina and a dust storm kept Australia's second innings to 267; Albert Trott's dismissals for 10 and 0 gave him a Test average of 102.50. England lost Brockwell and Stoddart early, and the rubber appeared to be Australia's. But Jack Brown, who Ben Wardill predicted would not score a run, scored fifty in 28 minutes, another fifty in an hour and was finally dismissed for 140 in five minutes under even time. In a whirlwind, he and the watchful Albert Ward (93) stole the match and series, England coasting home by six wickets.

Giffen, as captain, bowled 31 overs and took Brockwell's wicket. Captains who bowl are often criticised for keeping themselves on too long, or not long enough. Giffen explained: 'I have been blamed for keeping myself on too long in that innings. I know I did not bowl well, but throughout I acted in concert with Harry Trott, and more than once, when I wanted to go off, he said, 'No, Giff, you are bowling better than any of us, and had better stay on.'

McKibbin had little effect, which enraged Turner's supporters. After the match, McKibbin kept the ball. Stoddart said he would trade his soul for it, but McKibbin accepted a photograph of the England captain, under Blackham's persuasion.

'The jubilation in English cricket circles was unbounded,' Grace wrote, and the first five-Test series was indeed one of the greatest. The Melbourne Cricket Club made £3599 on the tour, wiping out its debts.

Brown's century was arguably the most exciting innings in a Test, and one of the greatest Ashes innings. Celebrity was reported to turn his head, however. Trying to recover from the ongoing celebrations, he tipped a bottle of beer down his sink and became a teetotaller. But he never gave up smoking, and died of a heart attack 10 years later, aged 35.

Stoddart, Ward and Brown had the series of their lives, Richardson took 32 wickets, and Peel 27. But no individual performance has ever come near Giffen's 475 runs and 34 wickets. And for four of the Tests he was captain. The Australian public presented him with a purse of 400 sovereigns. But for Giffen there was little celebration: he had written a victory speech for the fifth Test, and having lost it, he resolved that Australian cricket would now need a captain from the younger generation.

As Lyons had discussed with Turner, Australia would be touring England in 1896. This time the invitation was issued to the Australasian Cricket Council, which took the opportunity to try to assert control over international touring.

Creswell became secretary of the ACC, which appointed Giffen, Bruce and Garrett as selectors, strangely asking them to choose the team *before* the main intercolonials.

Among the three, Giffen would tour, Bruce would not because of the demands of his legal profession, and Garrett's position was most interesting. At 38, the last survivor of the first Test match in 1867–77 had revived his career as a captain and batsman for NSW. He rarely bowled anymore, but his batting had improved with age and he led NSW to the Sheffield Shield title in 1895–96. He became the public's favourite to lead the 1896 tour – 10 years after his previous tour. The *Daily Telegraph* said: 'Mr Garrett undoubtedly has the necessary qualifications, and no other available player has them to the same extent.'

Even the *Age*, in Melbourne, agreed that 'Garrett would be a captain with brains, experience, and a level head'. But Garrett told the *Referee*'s J.C. Davis, 'There is no probability of my going. If I thought of doing so I would not act on the selection committee.'

The trio sat on the living-room floor of Garrett's home in Strathfield and went through the candidates. 'The interest taken in the selection of the 1893 team,' said Giffen, 'contrasted with the excitement aroused in 1896…as a breeze to a tornado.'

The problem, as he and other players saw it, was the ACC's interference. 'I, in common with many other cricketers, cannot see what the Council really has to do with the matter. If it financed the tours, the position would be entirely different, but it did not take upon its shoulders one iota of financial responsibility; as in former years, the players had to bear the whole of what risk there was. Certainly it is not very great; still, things might go entirely wrong, and a loss ensue. This being the case, it seems to me that the players should be allowed to select the team themselves; that is to say, half a dozen or so men whose claims are indisputable should choose their companions. It is significant, that invariably when this course had been followed in former years there had been very little cavilling, whereas in 1896 the selection caused no end of heartburning.'

Under the sway of the ACC, which insisted on even representation across the colonies, five notables did not tour. The veterans Bannerman and Jarvis were overlooked. Lyons, having taken up a stockbroking career, was considered to have played too little recent first-class cricket. Turner was selected, but declined. In their Sheffield Shield encounter in Sydney, played after the touring team was chosen, Turner took 6/35 off 43.3 overs on a shirtfront pitch, the best figures of the season by anyone and, he said, his best bowling *ever*, while Lyons smote 46 in 25 minutes.

But none of these omissions compared with the firestorm over Albert Trott. In the most recent season, he had only scored 101 runs in eight completed innings and taken 14 wickets at 25.28. But Horan's view that he was the best young all-rounder produced by Australia in a generation was widely shared. He appeared to have fallen victim to a quota system — Victoria had five places, including the plum, the captaincy, which had gone to, of all people, his elder brother. When Albert next saw Harry in Melbourne, he cut him dead. His next move was to emigrate to England and qualify for Middlesex; he would even represent England twice.

J.C. Davis sheeted blame to the ACC, not the selectors. 'The Council should either entirely control these teams, or, while taking no part in the selection, merely reserve the right to see that they are representative of Australian cricket. By taking no share in the responsibilities of organisation and management it cannot in common fairness continue to appoint the selectors and manager without reference to the players. It is unbusinesslike. And, after all, the [players] are the only persons interested in the financial success of a team. Failure in this respect would entail personal loss to them.' A decade later, Davis would be singing a different tune.

Giffen thought that if the team had been 'chosen according to the old method', Lyons and Albert Trott would have been taken. 'Public feeling ran very high, Sydney people crying out for the inclusion of Turner, Melbourne urging the claims of Trott, while we in Adelaide could not realise that Lyons was no longer fit for an Australian Eleven.'

That was not the end of it, but barely the beginning. The ACC had exercised its discretion to appoint the manager, Harry Musgrove. One of the strike-breaking Test players of 1884–85, Musgrove had made a career managing theatre companies. Overcoming the players' early suspicions, he would end up a popular and efficient manager, Giffen saying he was 'undoubtedly the best I have ever travelled with to England', but this judgement only came after Musgrove crossed the lines to take the players' side against the ACC.

At the time of his appointment, the senior players were unhappy. Until 1893, the players had chosen their own manager on every tour except 1886, when, on the Melbourne-sponsored venture, Wardill went. In 1893, the ACC-imposed Cohen had been resented as a spy, the instrument of an ACC attempt to seize the players' profits. Now Musgrove's appointment promised a repeat of that debacle.

As a final trial, the selected Australian team played The Rest in Sydney. Victoria's Jack Harry — an extraordinary former miner who took up bowling at 34, would occasionally switch bowling arms, and had only kept wickets twice in 12 years — had been chosen as 'keeper, but injured his knee and was replaced by NSW's Jim 'Mother' Kelly. Harry protested, but gained no support from the ACC. He claimed compensation and, after rejecting an offer of £50, settled for £160, which was paid by the players, not the barely solvent ACC.

More excitingly, 18-year-old Clem Hill, who had scored 150 not out and 56 against Stoddart's team and 206 not out against NSW in Sydney, claimed a spot by scoring 74 in the trial, which, Giffen said, proved 'how great a mistake had been made in excluding Clem Hill from the originally chosen band'. Hill was one of nine debutants in a talented but very inexperienced side; the others were Harry Donnan, who had hit the first Sheffield Shield century four years earlier, Iredale, McKibbin and Kelly from NSW, Alf Johns from Victoria, Darling and Jones from South Australia, and the bulky all-rounder Charlie Eady from Tasmania, who later sat as a member of the Tasmanian upper house with Joe Darling. The only tourists who had been to England before were Harry Trott, Giffen, Gregory, Graham and Trumble. Graham, whose brief brilliance was fading, was most likely the subject of a piece by the journalist James Edmond before the tour, examining Musgrove's abilities as manager. He would have to control 'one man who has a sturdy theory that he cannot make a score unless he has had six rums, several long beers, and sundry whiskies the night before ... That batsman will go through a window if interfered with in his programme. The great qualities required in a manager are discretion, a colossal thirst, and the power to settle brawls resulting from mixed drinks and jealousy.'

Taking nine debutants was criticised. Iredale, writing in J.C. Davis's *Australian Cricket Annual*, defended the selection: 'For years the older hands had kept the younger ones back, until at last the younger players had literally forced themselves into the team. The one great fact was forgotten that every man in the team had earned his place. Of how many new members of previous teams could the same thing be said?'

At the other end of the career arc, the leader of The Rest in the Sydney trial was Percy McDonnell, the hard-hitting stylist who had taken over Murdoch's mantle as Australia's champion batsman. He lived in Queensland now, having moved to improve his health. Within six months heart disease would claim him at just 35.

'WHATEVER
ARE YE AT?'

The Ninth Australians practised at Mitcham Common before their first game at Sheffield Park, where, as usual, Grace awaited. In his 47th year in 1895, he had enjoyed an Indian summer – 1000 runs in 22 days' batting in May, his hundredth career century, a season total of 2346 runs at 51. In three decades, he had scored more only in 1871 and 1876.

He was taking on a new Australia. In front of 24,930 people, Grace and Jackson squared up to the burly Jones, quite a character. Rather than entering the field through the gate, he liked to jump the fence. He had limitless energy. In a Buckingham Palace reception during the tour, the Prince of Wales asked him if he attended St Peter's School in Adelaide. Jones replied: 'Yes, Sir. I take the dust-cart there each Monday.' (A variant on this story is that when Lord Hawke asked if he had been to Adelaide University, Jones said, 'Yes, My Lord, with a load of bloody sand.')

He showed no more deference to cricketing royalty. Giffen said, 'on the field his mission seems to be to make things hum'. His first three balls hit Grace in the ribs. The fourth, which Rae calls 'the single most famous delivery W.G. ever faced', passed through the Champion's beard and went to the boundary. 'I can see W.G. now,' Jackson wrote. 'He threw his head back, which caused his beard to stick out.'

With his incongruous piping voice, Grace squeaked: 'What – what – what?'

At point, wondering if he was facing the first crisis of his leadership in his first over, Trott said, 'Steady, Jonah'.

Jones looked at Grace and said: 'Sorry, doctor, she slipped.'

Grace and Jackson withstood the new ball, but the Champion's chest ended up black and blue, and Jackson had a rib broken (though Jackson said Jones hurt him even more when he shook his hand afterwards to apologise). Shrewsbury, batting three, took one look at Jones and deliberately hit a catch to slip. According to Charles Fry, Gunn's 'first ball from Jones whizzed past where his head had just been'. Next ball, Gunn backed away and poked what looked like another deliberate catch to slip.

The match was drawn, but a new Australian spearhead had arrived, amid the inevitable mutterings about a bent arm. Trott's team generated more excitement by beating Essex, C.E. de Trafford's Eleven, Yorkshire, Lancashire, Oxford University and Gloucestershire during the next month.

W.G. was not the only Grace they had to contend with. After the Australia–Gloucestershire match, E.M., 'The Coroner', challenged Donnan to a single-wicket match. A.A. Thomson writes: 'As E.M. ran up to bowl, some of the drunks who were seen more frequently at cricket matches then than now began a chorus of jeers. E.M. turned on the ringleader like a charging rhinoceros and the unhappy toper, the fear of death heavily upon him, incontinently fled. Out of the ground and over the Downs the chase proceeded and E.M. was absent for a long time.

When he got back, even his most facetious friends felt diffident about asking him what he had done with the body.

'"He's still running," said E.M. grimly ...'

By early June, all the Australians were enjoying some measure of success, though they had a rude awakening when an old-timer named F.R. Spofforth took 6/49 and 5/51 against them at Wembley Park. The 42-year-old Demon played one other first-class match in the season, taking 9/82 for the South of England against Yorkshire at Scarborough.

After a storm at Lord's, the Australians' bubble burst. Playing the MCC, the first three batsmen, Kelly, Graham and Trott, combined for 18 runs; the next seven made zero. Jack Hearne (4/4), turning it a foot, and Dick Pougher (5/0), shooting low at variable pace, did unspeakable damage. Giffen did not bat, through illness; 'A Country Vicar' wrote that he could have batted, but refused.

An innings defeat was a formality, though Darling showed his growing maturity by remaining not out (0) in the first innings and scoring 76 in the second. None of his teammates doubted his grit. It was already folklore that when Darling had come into the South Australian team, Ernie Jones had challenged him to the standard initiation ritual of a wrestling match. The smaller Darling had beaten Jonah, who had slid on his back 'into the corner where the showers were located'. It didn't end there. On tour, Jones had a habit of surprising teammates, while they were out walking, by smacking them across the legs with a cane. Darling procured a stick of his own, and crept up on Jones to give him a whack. It cured the big fast bowler's habit, much to the relief of his teammates. If only for a Joe Darling in the era of Mervyn Hughes.

With 10 days to go until the first Test, the Australians tried to regroup, but found another wet wicket at Leeds and lost to Midland Counties at Birmingham. A promising tour had, within a week and a half, careered off the rails. Still, even the weakest Elevens had dusted themselves off for Test matches, and the home team had headaches of its own.

Marylebone had picked an extremely strong team for the first Test, with one exception. Three times the Australians had played the new prodigy of English cricket, Kumar Shri Ranjitsinhji. His name meant 'The Lion that Conquers in Battle', though English teammates preferred to call him 'Smith'. Ranji, 24, had been born in the village of Sarodar, now in the Indian state of Gujarat. His father was a Rajput aristocrat, and at seven Ranji became heir to the Jam Sahib of Nawanagar when the previous heir was murdered. Ranji's inheritance was usurped when he was still a teenager, and he was taken to England by Charles Macnaghten, a former Cambridge Blue under whom he had studied. At Trinity College, Ranji played poker, drank, suffered from asthma, and ran out of money, while developing into an unorthodox run-machine. Dismissed from Trinity, he moved to Brighton and qualified for Sussex where, in net practice against the professional bowlers, he laid a sovereign on his bails to tempt them to knock it off. By 1896 he had risen to be among England's best batsmen, beyond dispute after two centuries in a day against Yorkshire. But when it came to Test selection, even though Ranji had been told to 'hold himself in readiness', Lord Harris and the MCC blocked his way.

The Times said: 'Some cricketers were, on principle, against the inclusion of Ranjitsinhji in the English side. The Marylebone Club committee thoroughly weighed the matter, and, while recognising the wonderful ability of that cricketer, thought it scarcely right to play him for England against Australia.'

Their reasons appear to have been complex. Qualification for counties, as we have seen, was a contentious matter, and Harris objected to selecting a 'bird of passage' cricketer. On the other hand, England had previously selected Midwinter, Murdoch and Ferris, all birds of passage, all white men. Ranji's omission could not survive the taint of racism. Harris would defend his record in race relations as a future Governor of Bombay, but this did not mean Ranji's non-selection was not on racial grounds. Cricket journalist and author Sir Home Gordon was, according to Rae, threatened with expulsion from the MCC if he 'had the disgusting degeneracy to praise a dirty black'. Ranji's biographer, Simon Wilde, says Harris might have been acting under pressure from the British government.

When the match began, the pressure shifted back onto the Australians' wobbly batting. Lohmann had returned to his best on a tour of South Africa with Lord Hawke's Eleven, and a rowdy Lord's crowd of 25,414 paying customers (plus 5000 members) spilled onto the field to see him. Those at the back threw sand and other projectiles at those in front, until an arrangement was reached whereby each group would take turns at standing up and sitting down, an over at a time.

Australia were out for 53 in 75 minutes, helpless before Lohmann and Richardson. 'Nothing can be said in extenuation of Australia's miserable batting failure at Lord's,' Giffen said, 'a failure which, considering the excellence of the wicket, is a greater reproach to Australian batting than England's was at the Oval towards the close of the 1882 match.' He said to the team, 'We'd better pack up our traps, boys, and go home.'

But Australia still had Ernie Jones. The miner whistled another one through Grace's beard. Opinions varied on how upset Grace was. Harris thought he uttered a mild 'Whatever are ye at?' while Home Gordon said he was 'conspicuously ruffled'. 'The veteran looked volumes, [and] was so seriously discomfited that he took some time to recover his composure and then only after having made some observations to the wicket-keeper, while the twelve thousand spectators positively hummed, so general were their audible comments.' Grace always called Jones 'the fellow who bowled through my beard'.

In his 66, Grace achieved his thousandth Test run, but it was Abel's 94 that took the game away from Australia. In an interesting sidelight, Albert Trott, now of Middlesex, fielded for Australia when Donnan hurt his hand. The brothers had patched up their differences. Harry, in the second innings, played his career-best knock, scoring 143 and putting on 221 for the fourth wicket, the record Test partnership to that point, with Gregory. Iredale said: 'I shall never forget their great stand, and to me it will remain as the greatest achievement of 1896.' Trott was dropped and almost run out on 99, but his and Gregory's centuries showed that the Ninth Australians would not lie down.

Although less uncouth than some of their predecessors, Trott's men knew how to play hard. On 61, Trott edged an apparent catch to Tom Hayward. Trott stood his ground. The famous English sporting journalist, J.A.H. Catton, approached Hayward during lunch and asked if the catch was fair. Hayward said: 'Do you think I should have tossed the ball up if I had any doubt about it?' Another English player added: 'No-one but a ------ Australian would have stood still.'

Six consecutive wins later, Trott's Eleven ventured to Old Trafford to try to save the series. The unceasing grind was beginning to show on the young Australians, Darling telling the businessman George Bull, 'I'm dead tired out; in fact, all of us are, and if we could only have a few days' complete rest we'd be a different set of men for the next match.' They were having to wear two pairs of socks to cushion their feet from grounds 'the consistency of pig iron'. But there was no let-up. The Lancashire Committee showed some fibre and selected Ranji. He insisted on clearing his selection with Trott and Musgrove, who said they would be delighted to see him play. After Australia compiled 412 (the teetotal Iredale scoring 108, fortified by a lemonade his captain spiked with brandy to settle his nerves), they saw plenty of him. Trott, in what *Wisden* called 'a stroke of genius', opened the bowling with his leg-spinners, at Darling's suggestion, and quickly had both Grace and Stoddart stumped, but Ranji countered handsomely. His first-innings 62 was an appetiser for an unbeaten 154 in a touch over three hours in England's follow-on. Pardon described the innings as 'marvellous', but made the point of referring to Ranji as 'the famous young Indian' and 'the Indian cricketer'. The Australians, more generously, regarded him as an Englishman and praised his batting without reserve. Giffen said it was 'absolutely the finest innings I have seen ... Ranjy [sic] is the batting wonder of the age. His play was a revelation to us, with his marvellous cutting and his extraordinary hitting to leg. I have never seen anything to equal it.' Between the start of play and lunch on the third day, Ranji scored 113, continually hooking Jones's bouncers off his nose. He quipped to Dick Lilley that it was 'very important to get the head well behind the ball in order to get a good sight of it'. He got too close to one, which he missed. Barker wrote that Ranji 'felt nothing, but afterwards was aware of a sticky liquid trickling down his neck. He put his hand up to feel what it was and found that the ball had nicked his ear and split it open.'

Giffen became the first Test cricketer to achieve the double of 1000 runs and 100 wickets, not bad for a supposed underachiever at Test level. After Ranji's century, Australia needed 125 to win. In Lohmann's illness-enforced absence, Richardson bowled unchanged for 42 overs. Altham contends 'no finer example of courage, stamina, accuracy and pace is to be found in all the annals of the game'. Richardson dismissed Iredale, Darling, Giffen, Trott, Donnan and Hill, leaving the Australian captain in such nervous despair that he preferred travelling around Manchester in a cab to watching. In the end, Gregory's 33 and Trumble's unbeaten 17, together with a crucial chance Lilley put down off Kelly, saw Australia to just their third Test win on English soil, their first since 1888. Giffen, who had seen more of the bad days than most, concluded: 'I regard our performance ... as distinctly the most meritorious feat Australian cricketers have accomplished since the 1878 team beat MCC in one day. We now, I think, approach nearer to the all-round standard of English excellence than ever before.'

While following the tour, George Bull praised the young Australians' 'steadiness in living and keenness in the game', but saw how the Tests strained them. 'There is not one of them, I venture to say, who will forget as long as he lives the terrible tension of that last day at Old Trafford. There is a grey spot on the back of my head that will live (unless I dye it) as a souvenir of that memorable afternoon.' He met one 'first-class English amateur who said at the Oval that he'd rather face a battery of guns than go through it again'.

In celebratory mood, Trott, Donnan and Hill passed 100 against Derbyshire. Jones, Trumble, Giffen and McKibbin were among the wickets and they went to the Oval full of confidence that was enhanced when England's top professionals revived the oldest quarrel in cricket.

Since 1878, an English professional's fee to play Australia had remained at £10, nothing short of an insult. For their tours of Australia, the professionals received £300 pounds – again, virtually unchanged in a quarter of a century. Around them, England's amateurs received, in 'expenses', amounts ranging up to Grace's hyperbolic £3000, and the Australians were again doing nicely from gate money. As one 'celebrated cricketer' told the establishment cricket writer, Colonel Phillip Trevor, 'I [wanted] £20 for the Test match as a professional, but I could have afforded to be an Australian amateur at £100.'

In August 1878, the Players had gone on strike after asking for £20 to play Australia. Now, in August 1896, five professionals – Lohmann, Gunn, Richardson, Abel and Hayward – asked for the same to play in the third Test.

The life of the English professional had advanced somewhat since the disputes of the early 1880s. When Dave Gregory took his Eleven to England, professionals earned about £80 a year, compared with £85 for an unskilled labourer. Charles Alcock noted that Surrey pros had one pair of flannels for the whole season, and Ted Pooley, the wicketkeeper famously jailed in New Zealand, ended his playing days in an institution, saying, 'It was the workhouse or the river.' By 1890 the average professional earned £275, including coaching and staff work, compared with £95 for an unskilled labourer. This was an improvement, but pay for Test matches had been stuck at £10 in an age when, as John Major writes, 'England was still a nation for the few, but no longer the very few. For most of the population it was a time of optimism. As the decade began, prices fell and wages rose. Diets improved and leisure activities widened.'

Professional cricketers felt they were missing out. The five expressed their plea in a letter to the Surrey Committee: 'We ... do hereby take the liberty to ask for increased terms viz twenty pounds. The importance of such a fixture entitles us to make this demand.' Surrey refused to negotiate, objecting to both the tone of the letter – that word 'demand' – and the fact that four of the five signatories were from that very club.

After the rebuff, one of the players went public, telling the *Daily Mail*, 'We want £20 apiece and expenses. The Australians will probably take away £1700 or £1800 [from the match] and the Surrey Club will probably benefit to the same extent or more. We professional cricketers in England do not get anything like adequate payment for our services. The enormous crowds which now follow the game benefit the clubs, and, in fact, everybody but those who have done at least their fair share towards bringing the game towards its present state – the professional players.'

Lohmann was believed to be the anonymous speaker, and Trott was quoted saying, 'I am astonished and deeply sorry to hear that Lohmann is the leading spirit of the movement, especially after the handsome treatment he has received at the hands of the Surrey Club and the English public generally.'

The *Weekly Sun* on 9 August jumped on Trott's apparent hypocrisy: 'The charm of this criticism would be more apparent were Trott to tell an excited public the exact terms upon which he, personally, undertook the trip to this country. If I mistake not, the burden of the complaint made by Lohmann and his brethren is that the terms are not equal all round. Given fine weather, the Australians will benefit to an extent undreamt of by the English professionals. Of course, the Australians are amateurs.'

As in the great quarrels of a generation earlier, the fight was three-cornered. The professionals were aggrieved that the Australians earned so much more than them, and also that their own 'amateur' teammates were, as Lohmann said, 'paid more than us professionals'.

The *Weekly Sun*'s columnist 'Orbit' said, 'My sympathies are entirely with the pros, and whether they get what they are asking for or not, they are entitled to our respect for having raised another protest against the shoddy amateurism which waxes fat on "expenses".'

Now everyone was affronted. Grace threatened to boycott the Test unless Surrey defended his honour, which they did, issuing a statement on the morning of the match, saying Grace had never received more than £10 to play at the Oval to cover his expenses 'in coming to and remaining in London during the three days. Beyond this amount Dr Grace has not received, directly or indirectly, one farthing for playing in a match at the Oval.'

Three years later, Grace wrote that it was 'an unseemly controversy, in the course of which many irritating statements of an absolutely false character were made with regard to prominent amateur cricketers'. He might not have been paid more than £10 for games at the Oval, but not even Grace would have the hide to claim he did not gain handsome 'compensation' from cricket. Even if nobody believed his protestations, he was still forgiven. Pardon, in *Wisden*, wrote that 'the work he has done in popularising cricket outweighs a hundredfold every other consideration'.

It was harder for others. Stoddart, another accused of shamateurism, pulled out of the match. Various theories were offered but Frith says 'he withdrew chiefly because of his vilification' by the press.

In the end, friends persuaded Abel, Hayward and Richardson to back down. Nottinghamshire's Gunn was absent, and Lohmann did not feel he could negotiate on Gunn's behalf, so neither played.

Lohmann felt wretched. He, like his Surrey teammates, now wanted to play, but he could not desert Gunn. Surrey had just granted

Lohmann a benefit and had paid for him to go to South Africa. During the Test match, he wrote a letter to the Surrey committee apologising for using the word 'demand', 'which I now see to be so unfortunate, [and] was inserted against my wish and better judgement'. He expressed abject gratitude and contrition to Surrey and its members. Surrey reinstated Lohmann for its remaining matches in a season which yielded him 93 wickets at 15, but he returned to South Africa the next year and didn't play Test cricket again. His health deteriorated and he died of tuberculosis in 1901, aged 36. His Test strike rate of a wicket every 34 balls over his 18 Tests has never been bettered.

The Test, after the 'strike', was an anticlimax. Rain sheeted down on the Oval and wrecked any hope of good cricket. During the wait for play, the *Star* reported: 'The talk round the ropes amongst the spectators is all about the great strike and its probable consequences. The voice of the people in this instance is unmistakably in favour of the professionals.'

Seeing the weather, Spofforth turned up at Kennington and begged Trott to let him play. He guaranteed he would remove England for less than 50, genuinely believing he was a better bowler at 42 than ever. Trott knocked him back.

The match started at 4.30 pm on the first day to appease the patient crowd. Iredale thought the match was only commenced due to the 'big gate'. The Australian bowlers couldn't get their footing on the wicket or grip on the ball, and Darling said he had never fielded in worse conditions. Nonetheless, Trumble, McKibbin and Giffen knocked over England for 145, and when Iredale and Darling put on 75 for the first wicket, an improbable dream beckoned. But their separation brought a swift collapse and a deficit of 26. England fared no better, and at the end of the second day's play, when England were 5 down and 86 ahead, Grace went to the Australian room and said, 'Well, Trott, you are going to beat us, as now the weather is settled there will be a good wicket tomorrow.'

It stayed dry overnight and, Darling said, 'we went down to the Oval very sanguine of winning. One can well imagine our surprise when we found that there had been a "local rain" of about 22 yard long and 6 feet wide, just where the wicket was.' The practice wickets, on a lower part of the ground, were dry, but the centre square was mysteriously sodden.

The Australians did not blame English players or officials for this blatant sabotage, but pointed the finger at the ground staff. Grace, aware of the cheating yet not above taking full advantage of it, ordered his lower order to be all out 'in half an hour … We must have them in by twelve-thirty at latest.'

Ranji, who had been dismissed on the second afternoon, had had a bad night with his asthma, then trod on a carpet nail, and arrived late for the start. As he and Fry pulled up in their cab, they couldn't make sense of the scoreboard: 14 runs for seven wickets. It couldn't be England, who had been 5/60 overnight. They still couldn't believe it when they got into the ground: England were already all out, and Australia nearly so. Trumble had taken his match haul to 12 wickets and Australia had needed just 111 to win, but on the doctored wicket they were never a ghost of a chance against Hearne and Peel. Richardson only bowled one over as the slow men dismantled the tourists. Last man McKibbin's 16 was the top score in Australia's 44. 'It was a great blow to us,' said Iredale, 'and for a time quite took all the heart out of us.'

If the pitch tampering was a shakedown by underpaid ground staff, it worked. Trott started a policy of giving tips to groundsmen.

Such resilience was typical of Trott's wry humour. So was his response to Spofforth, who came to the Oval to commiserate on Australia's loss. 'Terrible, isn't it? Things could hardly be worse,' Trott replied. 'But tell me, Spoff, are there any decent leg shows on at the theatres?'

Despite the loss, the 1896 tour was the most successful in a generation. Trott's Eleven did not lose a match to a county. The day after their disappointment at the Oval, they travelled to Sussex, where

Ranji – on his way to a record season of 2780 runs, never once, in the words of Yorkshire's Ted Wainwright, playing a 'Christian shot' – gave them a fine dinner and entertained them with juggling and magic tricks. Australia won there, and at Cheltenham, where they dismissed Gloucestershire, Grace and all, for 17. By 5 September, when they concluded a draw against a strong South of England, they had won 19, lost 6 and drawn 9. Horan, who hadn't held out great hopes when Lyons, Bannerman, Turner and Albert Trott were left out, now rated them the best Eleven since 1882. Altham admits 'the supremacy we had enjoyed for fourteen unbroken years was now in serious jeopardy'.

A proud Giffen, concluding his last tour, said: 'We were undoubtedly strong in every branch of the game, and, strangely enough, most powerful where every one when we left Australia thought we were weakest. I allude, of course, to the bowling.' He said McKibbin, Jones and Trumble were as good, considering the wickets, as Spofforth, Boyle and Palmer. Their bowling in the Manchester Test 'stands on the very highest pinnacle reached by Australians'. Only three centuries were hit off them, and the highest total by an opposition was 367. 'What more need one say in our praise?' He felt that the reason for Australia's improvement was the wise captaincy of Trott and the rejection of big hitting in favour of careful batsmanship. 'I am not sure that in the long run the more careful and safer methods of our batsmen could have been much improved upon. Certainly for the first time in the history of the Australian Elevens we had great batsmen who all had to be got out; they were not in the habit of throwing their wickets away.' Pardon was a little less forgiving: the batting 'was apt to become monotonous, many of the players carrying caution to excess, and playing with far more steadiness than is necessary on perfect wickets ... The batting on many occasions [was] so uniformly careful in character as to be decidedly wanting in attraction to those looking on.' Pragmatism, as ever, had its price.

Of Trott's captaincy, Pardon wrote that he was 'the absolute antithesis to Blackham' and, Murdoch aside, 'incomparably the best captain the Australians had ever had in this country ... Blessed with a temper that nothing could ruffle, he was always master both of himself and his team whatever the position of the game. More than that his judgement in changing the bowling was rarely or never at fault.' A master of hunches, a good captain and a lucky one, an able man-manager without being the best player in his team, Trott was the Mark Taylor of his day.

Grace said, 'the tour was singularly free from hitches and unpleasantness of any kind', and clapped Australia from the field after their last match against him at Hastings. The 'unpleasantness' of Lord Harris's not picking Ranji and the professionals' strike at the Oval were not, for once, the Australians' direct fault.

Grace was also diplomatically overlooking the latest chucking controversy. Pardon did not hold back when it came to the bowling actions of Jones and McKibbin. He said earlier Australian Elevens would never have brought them. 'Jones's bowling is, to our mind, radically unfair, as we cannot conceive a ball being fairly bowled at the pace of an express train with a bent arm. The faults of our own bowlers with regard to throwing have been so many and grievous that we are extremely glad Jones was allowed to go through the season unchallenged, but now that the tour is a thing of the past it is only a duty to speak plainly on the matter. We do so with the more confidence as we know that our opinion is shared by a great many of the best English players.' McKibbin's throwing was less noticeable than Jones's, he said, 'but there can be little doubt that he continually threw when putting on his off break'.

In 1896, with gate receipts rising again to the levels of the early tours, the contest between players and administrators was resumed. Trott's Eleven took home £679 each, the best dividend since 1884. Musgrove, by the end of the tour, was a players' man. In September, he received a request from the ACC to cancel the planned American and New Zealand legs of the tour. But the players, for pleasure and profit, wanted to do both, and Musgrove, now fully charmed by Trott, switched sides. He did not reply to the ACC's request. After another protest from the ACC, the team issued a statement regretting the ACC's action and reaffirming its touring plans. Musgrove said the 'whole trouble has been caused by the wire pullers in one of the colonies represented in the Council'. A player couldn't have put it better.

Fulfilling their obligations, the team enjoyed the final legs. They lost a first-class match to Philadelphia, Giffen saying 'it was the fact of their bowlers plying us with baseball curves that upset our batsmen'. The Americans' John Barton King, that country's greatest cricketer and one of the best swing bowlers ever born, ripped through Australia in later matches, and their captain, George Patterson, amused the Australians with his enthusiastic field directions: 'Say there, come a little sooner!' and 'Swing round out there!'

To relieve the tedium of long train trips, the Eleven organised mock prize fights between Trumble and Gregory at train stations. Giffen said, 'the townspeople who gathered thought it a great shame that we should have stood quietly by and allowed our Giant to hammer the Midget.'

In New Zealand, Trott's men developed a ritual of performing a mock haka in which the captain did a call and response with his men:

Trott: 'What's the matter with the Mayor of Brooksville?'
Team: 'He's all right!'
Trott: 'Who's all right?'
Team: 'The Mayor of Brooksville!'
Trott: 'That's all right then!'

The performance hit a snag in one town, where the Mayor had just had a serious operation. The Australians' haka was interrupted by someone telling them the Mayor hadn't been too well but was 'getting better now, thanks very much for asking'.

It was all very jolly and a marked contrast to the bitterness of the previous decade's tours. Australia, like England, was entering a Golden Age, each country producing waves of new talent that would resonate through history.

'YOU'RE A CHEAT, AND YOU KNOW IT!'

Trott's tour had reinvigorated the Australian Eleven. Discipline off the field, caution in batting, and the careful management of a new crop of stars promised a true contest with England after many barren years. Giffen heaped praise on his successor: 'As captain of the 1896 Australian Eleven he was a distinct success, his genial nature – I doubt whether any one ever knew him to have a downright quarrel with another player – helping him to gain that ascendency over his men, without which no captain, however skilful, can secure the best play of his team.'

But the disciplining of the Australian Eleven by no means drained the game of contention. A great push against chucking was underway. On 25 January 1897, Spofforth wrote in *Sporting Life*: 'With the last eleven there was one who hardly ever delivered a "fair" ball, and although I am quite aware I may raise a "hornet's nest" about my head by mentioning names I allude to Tom McKibbin who, I shall always maintain, should never be allowed to play under the existing rule.'

He condemned umpires for not calling throwers, and proposed a committee of county captains who could suspend throwers for a first offence, then add fines and longer suspensions. He said Peel threw occasionally, but McKibbin was the worst offender. Conspicuously, he did not name Jones. Giffen defended both Australians: 'Some critics say [Jones] throws, but to my mind his delivery is perfectly fair.' He also thought McKibbin bowled fairly.

Finance and organisation, not throwing, were becoming the major points of contention. Giffen began his final withdrawal from Test cricket, declaring 'popularity will not keep me'. Junior staff were leapfrogging him in the Adelaide postal service, where he was still earning just £3 a week. He would miss the games against Andrew Stoddart's 1897–98 Englishmen. Stoddart said, 'Australia will not be Australia without Giffen.'

The arrangement of England's tour was the usual shambles. The ACC had been set up for precisely this purpose, but had been beaten to the punch by a syndicate of the Melbourne Cricket Club and the Sydney Cricket Ground Trust. A NSW delegate to the ACC, Charles Lloyd, moved that the body be disbanded. He was defeated; but if the Council had no control over inbound or outbound tours, what was it for?

Stoddart did not claim that his team, with 10 first-time tourists, was truly 'all-England'. Over five hot and mostly miserable months, they proved him correct.

Their playing weakness was not entirely his fault, and financial imbalances continued to cause tension. The *Sydney Mail* said, 'Stoddart was not invited to bring out the best possible England eleven. He was asked to engage an attractive team, including as many new men as would pass muster, and as few professionals as was absolutely necessary to ensure respectable bowling results. In the selection of amateurs in the England team preference was given to men who asked for nothing more than bare expenses, and gentlemen like Hylton Philipson, who shouted for his own trip on the 1894–95 tour, are most welcome.'

In London, the *Athletic News* put it in a nutshell: 'For an Australian team to visit England, the Australians select the men and take the oof [money]. For an English team to visit Australia, the Australians also select the team and take the oof.'

Before the captain was brought down by influenza, an attack of insect bites and then the theft of his watch, the Englishmen started their tour well enough. Clem Hill took a four-and-a-half-hour 200 off them in Adelaide, but Ranji replied with 189. Adelaide had never been treated to such style. England beat Victoria and NSW, MacLaren scoring a pair of centuries and Ranji an unbeaten 112; he had only been allowed into NSW when the government waived its 'deterrent tax', a legacy of anti-Chinese sentiment from the gold rushes, under which non-white arrivals had to pay £100.

After an up-country tour, the Englishmen returned to Sydney for the first Test match. On 8 December, three days before the scheduled start, Stoddart received a cable telling him his mother Elizabeth had died. 'He was grief-stricken to the point of collapse', comments Frith, and he spent the tour fighting severe depression.

Ranji was also down with quinsy, an infected cyst in the throat, and if the Test had started as planned on Saturday 11 December he would not have played. But it was raining in Sydney, and although the pitch had been declared playable the SCG Trustees unilaterally delayed the start until the Monday. The first Stoddart knew of this was when he saw a newspaper poster outside a pub.

The delay drew 22,620 on 13 December, and worked out well for the English. MacLaren, in his debut as captain, scored 109, but was overshadowed by the recovered Ranji's sublime 175, made out of 293 in 223 minutes. Those who saw both Ranji and Bradman would not concede that the Australian was a better batsman. A heavier run scorer, yes, but, as Fry wrote, 'I have seen Don Bradman tear the bowling to pieces in astonishing fashion, but I have never seen him make a century on a fiery wicket against good-length bowling that kicked as well as broke. And I have never seen him make 260 not out on a difficult mud wicket when no other batsman on the side that day scored double figures.'

MacLaren, meanwhile, would be a dominant figure of the Golden Age. Neville Cardus called him 'the noblest Roman', but the imperious stance and hauteur at the crease were overcompensations for feelings of inferiority. The son of a Manchester merchant, MacLaren had trained as a prep school teacher. Often short of money, he borrowed from anyone, including professionals. Even Australia's scorer-baggage man from 1905, Bill Ferguson, said MacLaren 'borrowed £5 from me once to pay his champagne account, and I am still waiting for it to be returned'. The MCC threatened MacLaren with expulsion for not paying his subscription, and he said of Lord's, 'I always felt I would get half a dozen if I came in at the wrong door there.' He polarised teammates, being intelligent and single-minded but also petty, intolerant, humourless and prone to depression. Fry called him 'an iron and joyless captain ... Under him you entered every game bowed down with the Herculean labour of a cricket match against Australia; you went as in a trance to your doom.' The more kindly Ranji said, 'Archie without his grumbling would be like curry without chutney.'

His onfield captaincy, always shrewd, was good enough to winkle Australia out twice in Sydney. Though the mighty Richardson was struggling with rheumatism, MacLaren urged him on for 68 overs. In Australia's follow-on, Darling became the first left-hander to score a century in a Test and Hill fell four runs short of being the second. England dominated the match as McKibbin lost form under the constant commentary on his action.

Spofforth had called for umpires to assert themselves, and now the man had arrived. 'Dimboola Jim' Phillips, gifted cricketer, journalist and businessman, would stage a one-man umpiring crusade. He was a stickler all round, as he showed on the second-last day in Sydney. Australia's Charlie McLeod, who was deaf, was bowled a no-ball.

Unaware of the call – thinking it was his partner Darling who had called 'Look out!' – he walked. England's wicketkeeper Bill Storer ran him out, and to general outrage Phillips upheld the appeal. Storer apologised later, gifting McLeod a bat.

McLeod, who also had an injured finger, bounced back to score a maiden Test century in Melbourne. Paddington all-rounder Montague Alfred Noble came into the Australian team, but believed his Test career was over when he shouldered arms to Richardson and was bowled for 17.

In the middle of the Federation Drought that gripped eastern Australia from 1895 to 1903, a heatwave hit Melbourne, which experienced 25 days of 35°C-plus temperatures. Altham writes, 'the stifling nights robbed our men of sleep and left them jaded and dull-eyed in the morning.' Over Christmas, 35 Australian residents died from heat-related causes, and so did England's cricket resolve. Stoddart was in, then out, and his men lost by an innings. Noble needn't have worried too much about losing his place; in the second innings he combined with Trumble to take all 10 wickets and initiate the key Australian bowling combination of the turn of the century. Trumble tied down and tricked batsmen with his dip and turn, while Noble exploited an American baseball-style grip to become one of cricket's first true swing or 'swerve' bowlers.

They were needed in Melbourne, as McKibbin was ineffective and Jones was no-balled for throwing. Phillips had called his 'extra-fast one' in the South Australia–England match in November, and now became the first Test umpire to penalise a bowler for a chuck – once. Trott stopped Jones from bowling in England's second innings, but not for the rest of the series, in which Phillips stood, silent on the issue throughout.

The Adelaide Test, played in a 'brickfielder' dust storm and more extreme heat, brought another innings win. Darling became the first man to score two hundreds in a Test series, and then MacLaren became the second. Ranji, Hayward and Hirst contributed runs, but the English were cornered by a new, vocal mood in Australian cricket grounds.

Emboldened by their team's rise, the surge in national spirit and economic recovery, Australian crowds barracked the English mercilessly. MacLaren was roasted for comments about the wicket in Melbourne, and Ranji, who had remarked critically on the Adelaide Oval and the skills of local players, was greeted at the crease with cries from the outer of 'Get 'im for a duck!', 'Bowl 'im, Jonah!' and, no doubt, much worse. J.C. Davis saw no nationalist mitigation in the barracking, calling it 'the sheer desire to be abusive'. Ranji vowed never to play in Adelaide again.

It continued in the fourth Test in Melbourne, where Hill played one of the greatest of all innings to be unbeaten on 182 at the end of the first day, out of Australia's 7/275. The nuggety, clean-shaven left-hander leaped upon long hops outside his off-stump and defied the textbook by hammering them wide of mid-on. Richardson told him: 'You make me feel I took up fast bowling for your benefit.' Australia were 6/58 when Hill was joined by the quasi-all-rounder Trumble. 'Now cut out all this rubbish,' Trumble said. 'You leave that ball outside the off-stump alone. Do you hear me?' Hill said, 'Hughie Trumble made every run I got that day.'

Superstitious about having his photo taken, Hill dodged the snappers at stumps, but they got him and when play resumed, he added only six.

For the third time running, England had to follow on. Stoddart, a feeble number eight, did not want to bat under the bushfire smoke, and Ranji joked that Australians were the only people who would set fire to their country to win a cricket match. Ranji said MacLaren got out when he had a fly in his eye, which, when reported, triggered a new round of jeering.

The *Referee*'s J.C. Davis came to Ranji's defence, saying of flies, 'The little bugger will always persist in bobbing up just when he is not wanted' and reminding readers that in 1896 the Australians had complained at Lord's about 'the moving bell-toppers behind the bowler's arm'. Davis thought complaint was natural in defeat, 'because we know it is soothing in the moment of defeat or personal failure to have something of the kind to think of'.

The tour's final month degenerated further for the dispirited Englishmen. Stoddart received a poison-pen letter from Tasmania saying his team wasn't welcome after staying in their hotel rather than play during bad weather on the previous tour. Stoddart also turned on his own men, complaining about Briggs's eccentric 'Quaker' hat. 'It's bad enough to be defeated,' he said, 'but by George don't let the fellows be ridiculous.'

Stoddart dropped himself again from the fifth Test in Sydney, where Darling completed a trio of centuries, this time a spectacular 160 in 171 minutes. Sydney's crowds, vocal on the expanding Hill, jeered the Englishmen when their appeals were turned down, hooted Richardson for bowling a head-high full-toss at Darling, and laughed at Hearne when the number ten was hit by Jones. At lunch on the second day, Richardson came into the dressing room 'with tears in his eyes' after the crowd's treatment of him, although he had the last laugh by taking 8/94.

The press were writing stories about the Englishmen drinking too much and fighting among themselves, and finally the players were cracking. When an lbw appeal by Briggs went against England, Storer said to umpire Charlie Bannerman: 'You're a cheat, and you know it!' Throughout the game, Bannerman said, Storer had turned 'to me whilst in the field, not for an appeal, but in a nasty manner. I replied, "You mind your own business and I will mind mine."' Storer refused to apologise. When threatened with being reported to Lord's, he said he would rather be dealt with by Marylebone than by Australians.

Australia sealed a 4–1 win. The two captains had played their last Tests. Stoddart, while sitting out the game, enjoyed his one stroke of luck in a dismal season when he won a £1350 sweepstake on the Newmarket Handicap. He gave £25 to each of the professionals.

During the series, Harry Trott experienced mysterious weight loss and after a serious case of sunstroke sustained in a Shield match just after Christmas, could not see out of one of his eyes. In the following August he suffered two seizures which saw him committed to Kew Asylum in February 1899. While he recovered to live quietly and resume his cricket career, he was finished at the highest level and would die heartbroken after his brother Albert shot himself in the head in 1914. Albert, who suffered from dropsy, was under the misapprehension that he had a terminal illness. He left his clothes to his landlady and an estate valued at £4.

Stoddart would, in 1915, also join cricket's growing number of suicides. As Grace's successor in 1894–95 he had been one of England's most popular captains, but in 1897–98 he was beset by the heat, the barracking and his grief over the death of his mother. He was magnetic with the local ladies, but not even this offered solace. When it was remarked that he was in Australia looking for a wife, one wag asked: 'Whose wife?'

After the fifth Test he gave Davis an interview, saying: 'This system of barracking, if allowed to go on, will inevitably reduce cricket to a low level, for your better class players, with any sense of feeling, cannot keep on playing under such circumstances. The jeering by the crowd has occurred on all the grounds, and in all our big matches …

'I don't mean that those who jeer and hoot should be turned out of the ground. I would suggest that an appeal be made to their better feelings. If some of your influential men were to walk round the ground, speak to the people, and reason with them, quietly and rationally, I am sure a great deal of good in the direction of preventing these scenes would be achieved.' He spoke of an occasion in Brisbane when he had done this himself. 'Every man has a generous spot in him; most of those who jeer and hoot have good points, and, if you appeal to their better nature, I am sure they will give it over.'

Regarding the press, he took exception to attacks on Ranji. 'In Adelaide a prominent pressman cabled home that as Prince Ranjitsinhji had been giving himself airs and was making himself exceedingly unpleasant, there had been dissensions between the amateurs. That message was cabled home to a prominent paper. I asked him to at once send another cable stating that what he had said was an infamous lie.'

At a function in Melbourne, Stoddart repeated his comments about barracking. The reaction from Australians varied. 'Mid-On', in the *Age*, said Stoddart 'will leave a very general impression that he is a better winner than a loser'. Trott, replying to Stoddart's Melbourne speech, said barrackers 'are a perfect nuisance. And yet we can't do without them. I think barracking should be stopped, and they could easily do it by sending a few private detectives among the crowd. They did it in Melbourne once, and three men were taken to gaol. I think they got about a week, and there was no more barracking there for about six months!'

Iredale felt that Stoddart's tone had been misreported. 'I don't think he said it in any carping spirit, but he really thought he was doing good to the game by speaking as he did.' One of Stoddart's teammates, Norman 'Chubby' Druce, put it into perspective: 'As he had only made one mistake in 10 years … it will only be considerate to treat him as a first offender and let him down lightly.'

At a tour-ending dinner in Adelaide, Henry Yorke Sparks, one of the founders of the Adelaide Oval, disagreed with Stoddart and said there would always be barracking. George Giffen interrupted him with a cry: 'Rubbish!'

The hard-to-accept truth was that the barracking was an outward sign of the very nationalism Britain had been encouraging. As Federation approached, Australia was catching up with its cricket team, which had for 22 years been one of the few institutions to gather under a national banner. The *Argus* proclaimed that 'Trott and his ten good men and true have done more for the federation of Australian hearts than all the big delegates put together.' The obnoxious fringe, who took their national pride too far, were nothing but a conspicuous expression of this broader movement.

'AND I THOUGHT
I COULD BAT'

Insolvent in 1894, the Melbourne Cricket Club was now flush again, on a £2388 profit from Stoddart's tour made from receipts of nearly £25,000. It began negotiations with Lord's to sponsor its first tour since 1886, with the support of senior players who wished to stop the ACC's encroachments, weak though they had been.

In July 1898 twelve players, led by Trott and Darling, wrote to Creswell asking that their colonial associations withdraw from the ACC. The others were Hill, Jones, Jack Worrall, Trumble, Bill Howell, Charlie McLeod, Gregory, Noble, Kelly and Iredale. Trott had already tried to get the VCA to pull out, declaring the ACC 'a useless body'. Fearing Melbourne's influence, the NSWCA responded with a plan to pool intercolonial takings in the ACC and make it responsible for inbound tours by English teams. But the players sided with the Melbourne club, which ignored the ACC and appointed Darling, Gregory and Trumble as selectors and Wardill as manager for a tour of England in 1899.

Journalist Harry Hedley, writing as 'Mid On' in the *Leader*, said of the ACC: 'How men can be found in the colonies to keep the farce going is a mystery. It can only be explained by crediting those who do so with possessing a keen appreciation of that which is comical.'

Eleven of the twelve signatories of the anti-ACC letter were chosen. The asylum-bound Trott was replaced by Victoria's reserve wicketkeeper Alf Johns, with young East Melbourne all-rounder Frank Laver also coming in.

The credibility of this early selection survived the Australian season, though one youngster was forcing his way through. Victor Trumper, 21, later thought by prying researchers to possibly be the illegitimate son of a housemaid, born perhaps in Auckland and maybe adopted by his mother's cousin in Paddington, grew up playing back-lane cricket and went to Noble's school, Crown Street Superior Public, where he was banned from games because teams couldn't get him out. He fancied himself a fast bowler for Paddington, but focused on batting from 1897–98, when he averaged 204.2 for the club. As the England tour loomed, he piled up score after score for NSW: 292 against Tasmania, 252 against New Zealand. He made 872 runs at 62.36 for the season, on top of 562 in three innings for his club.

In the final pre-tour trial between Australia and The Rest, six days before the Eleven sailed on the SS *Ormuz*, Trumper stroked 75 off Jones, Noble and Trumble. Darling needed no more persuasion: Trumper was given a place on the tour as 14th man, doubling as Wardill's assistant manager on a stipend of £200.

Darling, Iredale, Trumble and Laver would give some vivid insights into life on the *Ormuz*. Darling wrote that some British army officers and wives on board 'did not think that the Colonial cricketers were their class and arranged a concert and did not invite any of us to attend. To get even we then arranged a concert of our own and asked everyone on board to attend. It was such a great success that we set up an entertainment committee, and made Frank Laver the secretary.

From then on everybody became friendly and for the rest of the voyage complete harmony reigned on board.'

The Australian propensity for nicknames was flourishing. McLeod, always last onto the field, was 'Lightning'. Darling and Hill were nicknamed for their similarities to boxer Paddy Slavin and South African leader Paul Kruger. Laver was called 'Vesuvius' because he'd been called 'Mr Lava'. The high-spirited lot devised a song:

> 'We're Australian cricketers all
> "The Major" is our father
> And off the cricket field
> We love the ladies, rather.
> (Chorus) Pour Bacchus et les amours ...'

Disciplined, yes, but straitlaced they were not.

Their 4–1 victory over a team containing Stoddart, MacLaren, Ranji, Richardson, Hirst, Hearne and Briggs entitled Australia to, if not favouritism, then warm enthusiasm. Yet Australian Elevens no longer had the novelty or great celebrity of the Gregory and Murdoch teams, as Iredale observed:

'There is more than a shade of difference between the welcome of an Australian cricket team in the cities and towns of England and the welcome accorded an English team in Australia. Out here we rouse up the Lord Mayor, or the county Mayor, the civic fathers gather, champagne is uncorked, and there is much eloquence concerning "golden bonds of kinship", and other things that will not win a Test Match. When the Australians get to Tilbury and right up to London itself – after a railway trip through acres of chimney pots that suggest tenement problems and pinched, wan people – they go to their hotel, but somehow London's mighty pulsation does not seem in the least affected. Official welcomes on the various towns are unheard of. The manager is interviewed by railway agents, who make competitive offers for the whole tour, the Australian flag is run up at the hotel in London, a few theatre invitations arrive, several cricketing notables look in, but the general feeling in the vastness of London is that one has been swallowed up.'

Lord Sheffield was no longer promoting the tour opener, and this time the Australians started against the South at Crystal Palace Park, where Grace had set up his London County Club, modelled on the MCC. He led a very strong team to 246. The Australians lost early wickets, and, wary of the ambush, Trumble had a warning for Noble: 'Take care W.G. doesn't talk you out.' Noble recalled: 'Sure enough, after the first over, "W.G." came up and said: "Good day, young fellow." "Good day," I replied and walked away. At the end of the next over he again tried, but I ignored him. For several overs this went on without my taking any notice of him. I had a very uncomfortable feeling about my apparent rudeness, and wondered just what he was thinking of me. After a while, however, I convinced myself that I was well enough set not to be talked out of the game, so, next time he approached me, I replied, and from then on we conversed freely.' Noble, who made a century, began to think Grace was genuinely friendly and Trumble had been pulling his leg.

The Australians drew with the South and lost badly to Essex, Trumper opening his representative career with 0 and 3. Laver said, 'the ground became covered with a surging mass of howling humanity. People threw their hats in the air, cheered and yelled and cheered again, until the enclosure fairly resembled Bedlam.'

Even though the 1880s and 1890s had worn the sheen off the great Australian adventure, touring life was still an enchantment to young men. Iredale wrote: 'I had heard so much of the green fields, the glorious summers, and the richness of food, that my heart fairly hungered for a sight of the promised land. A good many of our team were similarly situated. I saw enough of England to love it thoroughly, and each afternoon that we travelled through the different counties I posed myself at the windows of the train, kept my wits alert, and watched very earnestly the kaleidoscope views as they passed me.'

Darling's team returned to London, where for the first time the colours of sage green and gold were flown above the Inns of Court Hotel in Holborn. They got on track with an innings defeat of Surrey, Bill Howell making history by taking 10/28 in the first innings. Wins over a professional selection at Eastbourne (including Albert Trott) and Lancashire rounded out their preparation for a Test series starting earlier than usual, due to the programming of five matches. The Tests were, however, limited to three days, a risky pursuit in English weather, and Marylebone was later criticised for not scheduling matches that could be played to a conclusion.

While Australia's cricket administration had fragmented in the players' favour, England now had a central board of control with a single selection committee, comprising Grace, Lord Hawke and Warwickshire's captain Herbert Bainbridge, to overcome the inconsistencies that had proved so embarrassing in 1896. Yorkshire's Jackson and Sussex's Fry were also invited to the selection meetings. Fry was surprised at his inclusion, as he had not yet played a Test and his county record was thin, but he came with Ranji's recommendation and was a favourite of Grace after his fluent 80 for London County against the Australians. Fry believed, realistically, that he was only invited to selection meetings because Grace was on the panel, wishing to stop Hawke, who did not rate Fry highly, from taking 'undisturbed control'.

Fry was far from daunted. He was an Oxford classics scholar, a world-record holder in the long jump, a representative soccer player, the founder of *C.B. Fry's Magazine* and author of several books. He would stand for Parliament as a Liberal and work alongside Ranji on the formation of the League of Nations. He commanded the training ship *Mercury* on the River Hamble near Southampton for nearly 40 years, worked as a barrister, and still found time to score nearly 31,000 runs with 94 centuries, six of them in successive innings in 1901. And that is the short version.

Fry knew the single selection committee was a response to the embarrassment over the Ranji affair in 1896. But a single committee created as many problems as it solved. 'We used to meet on Sunday at the Sports Club, either for lunch, in which case we separated barely in time for dinner, or for dinner, in which case we separated barely in time for bed ... The discussions were interminable.'

The opening Test would be the inaugural one at Trent Bridge, and it was expected that Nottingham's 43-year-old champion, Shrewsbury, would be chosen. Had the club controlled selections, he would have been a certainty. But the MCC committee felt that Shrewsbury and Grace were too immobile to field anywhere but point, so there was only room for one veteran. Shrewsbury was also being punished, Fry later revealed, for his apparent cowardice against Jones's speed in the notorious Sheffield Park match of 1896. So Shrewsbury watched the game glumly from under George Parr's tree, sitting with Fry's mother. When Fry joined them, Shrewsbury told him he was hurt: 'I think you might have played me on my own ground.' Fry said he felt 'half ashamed that Arthur was there by George Parr's tree instead of in the middle'.

Shrewsbury was not long for cricket, or for this world. The man who, as a batsman, carried such confidence that if he was not out at lunch would ask the Trent Bridge attendant to have a cup of tea ready to bring out at four o'clock, could be a nervous wreck off the field. Phobic about his privacy and his bald patch, he was as successful in his sportsgoods business as he was at cricket, but some chasm remained. By 1903 he was so nervous that he could not bear to be in the same room as a person laughing. Haunted by the fear that he was suffering a terminal illness, while staying with his sister, he solved his crisis by shooting himself in the chest, then the head. He was 47.

At Trent Bridge in 1899, Grace, aged 50 years and 317 days, led England out. Only one older Test cricketer has played: Yorkshire's Wilfred Rhodes, who, poetically, was that week chosen for his debut.

England had a shortage of fast bowlers, as Richardson, Lockwood, Mold and Kortright were unavailable through injury or poor form. MacLaren had a teaching commitment, but otherwise the team, boasting a top seven of Grace, Fry, Jackson, Gunn, Ranjitsinhji (who that year would become the first man to top 3000 runs in a season), Hayward and Johnny Tyldesley, was as strong as any Golden Age line-up.

Darling had problems putting a fit Eleven on the field. Iredale had measles for a fortnight, Hill had a growth on his nose that would soon require an operation putting him *hors de combat*, and Worrall had an injured knee. But such was the bowling form of Trumble, Noble, Howell and Jones, and the emergence of assistant manager Trumper, that they went out full of hope.

While Australia opened with 252, all eyes were on the lumbering England captain. Sections of the crowd, sympathetic to Shrewsbury, jeered Grace. Jones's first ball was 'sensational', said *Cricket*. 'If Grace had not been to some extent prepared by previous experience … there might have been a bad accident; as it was he ducked in time.' Umpire Valentine Titchmarsh called it a no-ball — for overstepping, not chucking — but Grace resembled a dinosaur. He put on 75 with Fry, but many singles were lost due to Grace's slowness and they took no twos. Grace was eventually caught behind for an unedifying 28.

Jones's five wickets and Hill's 80 set up a declaration 289 runs ahead. Grace was again heckled for dropping Hill early, but later picked him up with a crisp one-hander. The Australians' batting, building on the defensive foundations that had revived their fortunes since 1891, drew criticism, *The Times* saying there was 'never anything very attractive' about them, *Wisden* bemoaning their 'extreme slowness'.

But they were effective, and when Grace, Fry, Jackson and Gunn were out for 19 an Australian win seemed inevitable. Ranji, however, recently returned from India where he was reinstalled as the heir to the throne of Nawanagar, was brilliant and lucky. He was dropped on 29, and his running between wickets gave Sydney Pardon palpitations: 'What should have possessed him to attempt short runs when there was nothing to gain and everything to lose one cannot pretend to explain.' When Ranji was 30, Laver appeared to run him out, and the Jam Sahib was walking off when Dick Barlow, veteran of the great early contests with Murdoch's Eleven, called him back. Laver shouted, 'Barlow, you are a cheat!'

Earlier in the match, Barlow had given Hill run out. Darling said: 'Possibly Hill could have been out, but what we took exception to was Barlow's attitude in giving Hill out. The wicket was hit in the throw-in and Barlow, before anyone had time to appeal, jumped up in the air just as an excited player does in a close match with his arms stretched out and yelled for all he was worth, "OUT!"'

Darling complained to Lord Harris, who withdrew Barlow from future Tests, saying he had 'misplaced loyalties to his old team'. But Barlow's intervention had done enough to save the match. Ranji scored 93 not out, the one obstacle to an Australian win.

On the train back to London, Grace said to Jackson: 'It's all over, Jacker, I shan't play again.' The ground, he said, was getting too far away from him. He met Hawke and Bainbridge at the Sports Club and, while waiting for Fry, said he was standing down. They argued against him, and he wavered. When Fry arrived, Grace said, 'Here's Charles. Now, Charles, before you sit down, we want you to answer this question, yes or no. Do you think that Archie MacLaren ought to play in the next Test match?'

MacLaren had not played a first-class match that season, due to his teaching commitments, but Fry said yes.

Grace said: 'That settles it.'

Fry had no idea he was voting the Champion out. 'Then, and not till then, did I discover that the question W.G. had asked me meant, "Shall I, W.G. Grace, resign from the England eleven?" This had never occurred to me. I had thought it was merely a question of Archie coming in instead of one of the other batsmen, perhaps myself. I explained this and tried to hedge, but the others had made up their minds that I was to be confronted with a sudden casting-vote. So there it was.'

Grace was determined to retire anyway. 'There is no doubt,' Fry said, 'that it was best for W.G. to retire. But I still think that some other instrument of his fate might have been chosen.'

In one of the stranger selection meetings, they brought in Gloucestershire's big-hitting Gilbert 'The Croucher' Jessop as a fast bowler, spinning all-rounder Charles Townsend for batsman Billy Gunn, and Walter Mead for his only Test, to replace the far better-credentialled Jack Hearne. They also chose the 21-year-old Rhodes, whose Test career would last until 1930. Shrewsbury was again overlooked. Jackson, the senior amateur, was the logical choice to succeed Grace as captain, but his Yorkshire patron Hawke allowed MacLaren to be picked instead, in what Hawke's biographer James Coldham called 'an act of betrayal'. Fry said the reason was that Jackson played under Hawke at Yorkshire and did not 'figure in the public mind as an established captain'.

Grace was done in Test cricket. He hadn't played his first Test match until he was 32, and suffered through a decade of the worst wickets in Test history. His Test record doesn't do justice to his might as the greatest player before Bradman. But his Test figures are strong nonetheless: 1098 runs at 32.29, nine wickets at 26.22, and 39 catches in 22 appearances.

In the second Test at Lord's, notes Altham, the 'Australians finally and decisively broke the spell of failure which has persistently dogged them on that ground'. The match was a watershed in what it truly meant to be an Australian Test cricketer.

Before the match, Jones came to the England dressing room and borrowed a shirt that Fry had invented, 'which gave freedom to the arms and did not pull out at the waist … So I lent him a shirt,' said Fry, 'and I never saw it again. And no wonder; it served him well.'

Bowling fast and with a straight arm, Jones rumbled England, his 7/88 a showcase of big-hearted fast bowling. Pardon wrote in *Wisden* that he 'bowled with a fairer action' and 'strove to keep within the law'.

Jones was, Fry thought, the difference between the teams: 'It was an era of fast bowling, when the critical phase for the professed batsman was to escape an accident early in his innings', and Jones was the best. Ranji told Fry, 'the man we have to fear is that chucker'. Somewhat indulgently, Fry took this as 'not that Ranji thought that Jones's action was unfair, but that his pace was dangerous'. It was Noble, now, who had his action questioned: when the Australians practised at Lord's, three different observers in 10 minutes told Pardon he was throwing.

England had plenty of fast bowlers but couldn't settle on whom to pick. 'We had more batsmen and bowlers than we knew what to do with,' said Fry.

The rampant Jones, meanwhile, held onto Fry's shirt. In the Old Trafford Test, when Iredale took a miracle catch off 'the best straight drive I ever made in my life', Fry heard Jones call out teasingly, 'That's the shirt, Charlie!'

Jones continued to menace batsmen throughout England. In one match, Darling recalled, Jessop was 'deliberately bowling at the Australian batsmen and hit several of us on a fiery wicket. Jones retaliated … Jones had only two men on the onside and goodness knows what would have happened if he had been told to bowl the same as Larwood did to a packed leg field'.

Jones did have a soft side. In the match against Gloucestershire, Jones told Darling he did not want to bowl at the pipe-thin Townsend. 'I am frightened that if I hit him the ball will go right through him,' he said. But when Darling wanted to fire Jones up, he told Jim Kelly to stand up to the wickets. 'Jones always used to boast that there was not a wicketkeeper who would dare stand up close to his bowling.' He said,

'All right, Jim, I will soon shift you.' Another motivational trick was to tell Jones the batsmen only thought he was medium-fast. Darling did just this in one of the Test matches. After removing the batsman with a thunderbolt, Jones said to Darling, 'That will show him whether I can bowl fast or not.'

Darling was learning the full responsibilities of the Australian captaincy – cricket leader, psychologist, mentor, shop steward, figurehead, speechmaker, diplomat. He felt the pressures keenly. 'First of all you have all the eyes of the cricketing world following you very closely and when winning everything in the garden is lovely, but when the side is not doing well that is the time when the poor old captain comes in for adverse criticism. Just imagine a man captaining a side of athletes, and that is what it amounts to in captaining a side in England. Many of these athletes are pretty good with their fists and a captain is called upon very often to assert his authority without fear or favouritism. His actions are watched very closely by the members of the side and freely commented upon by the players afterwards. Let a captain display fear or favouritism, then he forfeits the respect of every member of the side.'

Disciplining his members was a major challenge – the inability of Blackham, Scott and Murdoch to exercise control had been a feature of the three poorest tours. Darling had one unnamed player who, in New Zealand, 'had slipped into [captain Trott], and if it had not been for the assistance he received from the other members of the team he would have got a really good hiding. Later, when touring England with the same player, I had little or no trouble. Whenever he played up, I would wait my chance and get him by himself and tell him what I thought of his behaviour, quietly pointing out where he was wrong. After that I had only to shake my head at him on the field when he was going off pop and that was the end of it.'

Jones was often hard to handle. Named as 12th man for one county game, he went absent. When Darling held a disciplinary meeting Jones told his teammates to go to hell. Three players moved that he be sent home. 'Before a vote was taken,' Darling said, 'I got the player by himself and told him that unless he apologised to the whole team at once, nothing would save him and although I had not moved or seconded the motion, I would do everything in my power to see that the resolution, if carried, was given effect to. The player, seeing that he was beaten, apologised and that was the end of the matter, but he was taught his lesson and he gave no further trouble.'

Darling didn't single out individuals. During a break in the match against Nottinghamshire, some of the team were visiting the Player's cigarette factory when news came that the game had restarted. Darling was on the field with five substitutes and five Australians when the latecomers arrived to jeering from the crowd. Darling fined them £5 each.

Yet Darling led a jolly team. While waiting for new batsmen on the field, the Australians sang music-hall songs. Jim Phillips wrote in *Cricket* that the Australians 'play more in unison, they exchange views in the dressing room, and their captain is thereby materially assisted in many of his plans'. Phillips's criticism went to England's amateur–professional divide: team tactics, he said, were decided by the amateurs, without consulting the professionals, who were afraid to speak out. 'Surely, if a man is good enough to play on the same side he is good enough to dress in the same dressing-room.' The old Australian deference to English ways was dead.

Darling abjured the class division: 'it was a very common thing for an amateur and professional to open the innings. The professional had to be waiting at his gate, but dare not go on the playing ground before the "supposed" amateur came out of the members' pavilion and entered the playing ground first. The amateur and professional then walked to the wickets from different gates, about fifty yards apart, and did not actually meet until they got near the wickets. Australia has never made any difference between the amateur and professional, and that is one of the main reasons why Australian teams pull so well together ... the sooner England follows the good example set by Australia the better it will be for English cricket … I have heard some English captains speak to their professionals like dogs, and if they had been playing for Australia their cricketing career would soon have ended, as no Australian would stand it for one moment.'

The Australian captain had come a long way from Murdoch's time. Among Englishmen, however, belief in the caste system still had its adherents. In his *The Complete Cricketer* (1906), Albert Knight, a professional himself, waxed lyrical about the amateur's 'joyful delight of one doing that task because he loves to do it'. The professional 'may do his work outwardly well, and yet be deficient in the sentiment whence great action springs, and so bar the perfect realisation of great sport … he plays the game as he does his work, well and soundly, but lacking the artist's eye and spirit, which works emotionally, from an inner heart which feels.'

It is no wonder that writer and broadcaster Benny Green later called Knight 'the only professional with an amateur's pen.' As long as these attitudes persisted, the Australians felt they had a competitive edge.

On the second night of the Lord's Test, Trumper was walking around Piccadilly Circus contemplating his innings the next day when he saw a young music-sheet seller shivering in a doorway. Trumper bought his entire stock 'so he could return home, get dry and go to sleep'.

Hill scored 135 the next day, a great Test innings. Hill's counter-punching, crouched left-handed style, in tough conditions when the match was up for grabs and the bowlers were ascendant, fulfilled English expectations of Australians' batting rusticity. Yet it was Trumper whose 135 laid itself over Hill's as precisely as a solar eclipse. Iredale wrote: 'When [Trumper] came forth into the cricket firmament, and played his game, no one knew what to think.'

Plenty were willing to have a try at describing him. From behind the stumps, Dick Lilley decided Trumper was 'undoubtedly the greatest

Australian batsman I have ever seen'. Altham, two decades later, wrote: 'Before Trumper had been batting even for half an hour it was obvious that a new star of unsurpassed brilliance had joined the cluster of the Southern Cross.' Even Fry's wife pitched in, embarrassing the Australian with a magazine article extolling his 'healthy pink skin, long muscular neck, small, keen, bright eyes' and comparing his use of the bat to Paganini's of the violin. Johnny Moyes, the Australian cricketer-writer who played against Trumper, said, 'he opened the windows of the mind to a new vision of what batting could be'.

Between the plain and the purple, perhaps the best summation came from what Darling said when Trumper returned to the pavilion unbeaten:

'And I thought I could bat.'

Like Bradman three decades later, Trumper had an ineffable gift for piercing a well-set field. Asked how to place the field for him, Yorkshire's left-armer George Hirst said, 'It doesn't matter much where we place them for Victor; he does pretty well all the placing.' Recounting the story, Tommy Horan was reminded of what Jem Shaw, the gun Nottinghamshire round-armer, said about Grace: 'Oi poots 'em where oi loikes, and 'e poots 'em where 'e loikes.'

Sometimes it seemed only Trumper's own superstitions could unsettle him. His kitbag was easily identifiable — nobody could be so messy. But Trumper had his reasons, believing his gear brought him luck when it was dirty from success. Aside from laundries, he was also put off by clergymen, who he thought cruelled his luck, and he went to extreme lengths to avoid them.

The passing of the baton from Grace to Trumper was poignant. Later in the tour, Grace paid a tribute of his own, coming into the Australian rooms asking for a bat signed by Trumper. He swapped it for one of his own, saying, 'From today's champion to the champion of tomorrow.'

Trumper played no more important innings that summer than the 135 that set up a 10-wicket win at Lord's. Six weeks later, he played another that went into folklore. Since 1882, Murdoch's record of 286 had stood unchallenged as the record for an Australian in England. On the same ground at Brighton, Trumper put it in the shade with an even 300 not out. Pardon said it was 'from first to last ... of the most perfect character'. The bowlers could not find a safe length; Trumper made their balls 'Trumper-length'.

Darling became Trumper's protector and admirer. Long before the onset of the illness that brought Trumper down at 37, Darling was concerned for his health. 'Unfortunately owing to the fact that he did not enjoy the best of health Trumper had many bad days, but when fit and well there was only one cricketer in it as champion of the world, and that was Trumper.'

Iredale was another tourist who showed concern about Trumper, a young innocent abroad among older heads: 'Notwithstanding the fact that he loved his trip and the experience he was going through, I felt somehow or other that his mind and thoughts were of his home; he loved his home and the ties that surrounded it, and though he came with us on many occasions to theatres and elsewhere, one felt that whatever may have been in the place where we were, it was certainly not the real man.'

After the triple century, Darling upped Trumper's payment from the £200 assistant manager's fee to a share of the tour's profits. Not one teammate begrudged him a penny.

On the question of payments, the friction between English professionals and amateurs and the Australians underwent something of a renewal as the Australians' popularity returned. The 1893 tour had lost money, but the 1896 tour generated £680 per player and the 1899 tourists netted £800. Trumble said: 'We have some good days in England but the best of all is when we finish up.' Laver, who was independently wealthy, celebrated payday by buying one of the first motor cars and having it sent back to Australia.

Darling's Australians were enjoying the prerogatives of gentlemen. While the team was playing Hampshire, Trumper, Johns and Laver crossed to the Isle of Wight to attend the Cowes Regatta and were presented to Prince Edward. The Australians hobnobbing with such company had always aggrieved the English professionals, and now their resentment was again about to spill, with cataclysmic consequences, all the way back to Australia.

After Lord's, Tests at Headingley and Old Trafford were drawn. Headingley was the most exciting match of the season. England called up Briggs to capitalise on the rain-drenched wicket, and Australia lost Kelly, Noble and Gregory for ducks, but their fears were allayed by Jack Worrall's best Test innings of 76. Then Briggs, watching a show at the Empire Theatre that night, suffered an epileptic fit and was sent to Cheadle Asylum. By 1902, after being hospitalised for two years, he was dead. In his ward, he hallucinated that he was bowling and told the nurses his figures.

In Australia's second innings, the unobtrusive length-bowler, Jack Hearne, the only English bowler to have distinguished himself on Stoddart's tour, took a hat-trick – England's first (and best) in Test cricket – of Hill, Gregory and Noble, but the Test, which was poised 50/50 before the last day, was unfinished and the cavils about three-day matches grew louder. England had the better of the Manchester draw, Australia surviving thanks largely to Noble, who batted just over three hours for an unbeaten 60 in the first innings before keeping his pads on in Australia's follow-on and enduring just over five hours for 89. *Wisden* called his batting 'a miracle of patience and self-restraint'. Upon such feats was Australia's reputation for defence founded; it gave another spur to the raptures over Trumper.

On the last day at Old Trafford, an incident occurred which underlined Darling's hardness as a captain and led to a change in the laws. When Hayward had to leave the field with sunstroke, MacLaren sent out Tyldesley, a greyhound, instead of the nominated 12th man, Rhodes. Darling walked out to protest and, said Worrall, 'was the recipient of much hooting, which he bore stoically'. MacLaren gave way, but Darling was booed when he batted, and upon his dismissal 'the joy of the multitude knew no bounds'. The episode precipitated the requirement that captains exchange team lists before matches.

For a young captain, Darling was emerging as a legal reformer. An episode later in the tour brought about another change to the laws.

During a rain break in the Australia–Surrey match in May, Tom Richardson filled his footholes with sawdust. Not only did one of the umpires permit it, but held his umbrella over the bowler. Darling was surprised, but did not protest. Later in the tour, in the Scarborough match against C.I. Thornton's Eleven, Darling ordered sawdust for the bowlers' footmarks. According to Worrall, the local captain, Jackson, 'came round to our tent in high dudgeon, and waited for our captain's return. When he came back, wet, grubby, and happy, after his exertions, Jackson objected strongly to Darling's action, remarking that such a procedure was not done in England. That was a chance for Joe, who said that as far as he was concerned it was purely an English custom and related the Surrey incident. Jackson was astounded.' Darling had not only won his point, but the MCC agreed to change the law to allow sawdust.

In the fifth Test at the Oval, England again had the better of a draw, their 576 being their highest home score until 1930. Centurions Jackson and Hayward, leading England to 435 runs on the first day, lifted the clouds. Australia were again at their best digging in for a draw; *Wisden* said that 'as match-savers [they] have never been equalled'. First it was Syd Gregory with a hundred and Darling with 71. Then, following on, it was Charlie McLeod, whose 77 showed why Fry called him 'an accomplished strokeless player who, according to Ranji, had the widest edge to his bat of any class batsman', Worrall, 75, and Noble, 69 not out, resisted the local hero Bill Lockwood, who burst back into Test cricket with seven wickets. When Richardson had broken down under the workload of a decade, Lockwood re-emerged for Surrey after an absence during which he had suffered the death of his wife and one of his children, become an alcoholic, and been dropped by the country. But after turning teetotal he was again the most dangerous fast bowler of his time. His effort at the Oval was, according to Barker, 'perhaps the finest piece of bowling of his career', but was not enough to draw the series.

As a dry summer drew to a close, the Australians played out more draws than wins. Draws might have been only good for swimming in, but Darling was content. Much praise was given to his captaincy; as Australian teams were becoming less 'colourful', they were increasingly successful. Darling's firm discipline, his intolerance of drunkenness or theatrical behaviour, and the premium he placed on team unity and fitness earned him his players' complete trust.

Darling's Eleven was a hard-nosed group and, with only three losses in a 35-match tour, was widely rated the best since 1882. Pardon thought so, and *The Times* went further, saying, 'Mr Darling's eleven of 1899 is the best that has ever come from the Antipodes.'

Alfred Shaw, however, held out for a more historic appraisal. 'The 1882–84 elevens,' he said, 'were pre-eminently spectators' teams. Their play was invariably bright and pleasing, and withal highly scientific. It cannot truthfully be said that this was characteristic of the Australian team that visited England in 1899. Possibly some readers ... may think I have a bigoted opinion of the merits of the older school of Australian cricketers. I wish to earnestly assure them that is not the case. I have looked the facts fairly and squarely in the face, with a perfectly open mind, and I have come deliberately to the conclusion that the Australian teams we have recently seen in England can in no sense compare with the brilliant sides that Mr W.L. Murdoch had the honour of leading in 1882 and 1884.'

It was always interesting to know the views of those whose experience spanned generations, especially when technological progress meant that the Golden Age players would be the first to be recorded by moving pictures. Shrewsbury, when asked by Fry, was measured in his comparison, saying, 'Their batting is stronger than in Murdoch's time, but their bowling is not as good.'

Historians such as Altham record how the 1899 Australians 'came in for a certain amount of criticism for lack of enterprise, and certainly they played sixteen drawn games, but the great majority of these were in the latter half of their tour, when the effects of their arduous and practically uninterrupted programme were beginning to make themselves felt'. Darling, such a dasher at home in 1897–98, had changed his style to accommodate more pragmatic needs. In the Middlesex match at Lord's, he stonewalled so long the crowd hooted and whistled 'Old Black Joe', 'We Won't Get Home Till Morning' and 'Dead March in Saul'. In a county match, a man sat behind the bowler and shone a mirror in Darling's face. Darling stopped the game until the man desisted.

The freshest Australian in England appeared to be Albert Trott, who did the double with 1175 runs and 239 wickets. He launched a straight drive over the Lord's pavilion, a blow still unmatched, playing for the MCC against the Australians. The *Sydney Morning Herald* described Trott's hit as 'the fulfilment of his heart's desire'. He had already hit two into the upper level, then, off Noble, hit it so far that the 'ball struck one of the posts of the chimney appearing above the top-most outline of the pavilion, and rebounding, disappeared behind. It was a tremendous hit and, to adopt theatrical parlance, "fairly brought down the house".' The only other hit thought to compare to it was one by 'Buns' Thornton at Hove in 1876, which was alleged to have carried 150 yards, but in practice, not a game.

Uniting the eras of Murdoch and Darling, the *Review of Reviews* hearkened back to the old songs about 'bearding the lion in his den' by returning to the theme of Australian pride in coming to England and winning 'at home': 'The passion for cricket burns like a flame in Australian blood and ... the passion is intensified by an unfilial yearning on the part of young Australia to triumphantly thrash the mother country.'

The 1899 team did not, in fact, 'triumphantly thrash' England. Three-day limits saved them from losing a Test or two. And three years later many of the same players, returning under Darling with some new weapons and a good deal more experience, won an even higher place in the pantheon. But in 1899, an Australian series victory in England was a rare thing. Only once had it happened before, in a one-off Test with an extraordinary twist. The 1899 team's victory in England was celebrated loudly because few believed it would happen again soon.

'NOW WE CAN GET ON WITH THE GAME LIKE GENTLEMEN'

B ack in Australia after such a dizzying northern summer, the turn of the century was anything but golden.

Darling's team had cancelled their tour of South Africa, due to hostilities between the British Empire and the Boers. The cricketers played a fundraiser not for themselves but for the Australian Bushmen's Contingent and NSW Patriotic Fund, raising £640 for the Boer War.

The lame-duck Australian Cricket Council dissolved itself on 2 January 1900 with assets of £10/10/-. Frank Iredale said it 'failed because it was not given plenary powers and all its members were against it. In matters that dealt purely with cricket, they made a hideous mess of it. Passing measures that none of the members believed in, and which none of the associations adopted, was the beginning of the end. Towards the end of its existence, its meetings degenerated into huge outings or picnics for the delegates.' He could have been talking about today's International Cricket Council.

No governing body was yet able to succeed without the game's most powerful participants: the Elevens who toured England. Darling said any future council should include active players, but others said the downfall of the ACC had been precisely because four of its seven delegates – Darling, Hill, Worrall and Trumble – were players who wanted to block it from organising international cricket. Behind them stood the Melbourne Cricket Club, which, in the wake of the ACC's failure, held unparalleled influence. As well as cricket, it had a presence in Australian Rules football, baseball, croquet, lacrosse, lawn bowls, lawn tennis, rifle shooting, skittles, musical concerts, cinema, ballooning and the Austral Wheel Race. But its power attracted an enmity amounting to hatred from the NSWCA and the VCA.

At a meeting in Sydney on 15 May 1899, the ACC president, NSW's John Gibson, had said: 'The Council has become a farce. Its history resembles a game of shuttlecock and the NSWCA has been the shuttlecock ... The Melbourne Cricket Club has to understand that it is not going to be allowed to govern cricket in Australia.'

To administrators from the state associations, player power and the Melbourne Cricket Club were a juggernaut that had to be stopped. A Sydney solicitor who had joined the NSWCA board and the ACC, Billy McElhone, wrote to Lord's saying the NSWCA was withdrawing from the ACC for the 'sole reason' of 'the matter of the players' representation'. The fight did not finish with the death of the ACC, but was reserved for another day.

On the field, improved pitches and timeless matches saw mammoth feats of patience which were not shared by those in the paid seating. Monumental scores became common: in 1900–01, Hill scored 365 for South Australia against NSW, who, in the return match, racked up 918. During the previous season, South Melbourne's Warwick Windridge Armstrong scored 270 in a club match against Melbourne.

Crowds ebbed away from cricket, and the remnants perfected the art of barracking slow play.

Darling, pressured by his father, sent a telegram to the *South Australian Register*: 'Have purchased property; intend residing in Tasmania.' He had better things to do, in his father's judgement, than chase interminable leather. The property in Tasmania's Midlands was called Stonehenge, and his mission was to eradicate rabbits. He was not leaving cricket, but he would henceforth pick his battles.

English cricket was having its own troubles. In 1900, Phillips no-balled Fry and Mold for throwing. Mold was notorious, but Fry was perplexed. No-balling him, he said, 'was all right if he disliked my slightly bent arm action, but it was no reason why he should have no-balled me for my other nine balls of the over when I delivered slow round-arms and slow over-arms with an absolutely rigid elbow'. For the second innings, Fry bandaged and splinted his arm, but 'old Billy Murdoch, our captain, who had ostentatiously put me on to bowl in the first innings at Jim Phillips's end, because he knew that Jim had come down to Brighton to no-ball me, twisted his black moustache, showed his white teeth, and refused to put me on. I was both astonished and annoyed, but he refused further particulars.' In Fry's view, there was something conspiratorial about Murdoch helping the Australian crusade of Phillips, who 'was ambitious to achieve the reputation of a "strong umpire"'. But Phillips had the support of *Wisden*'s Pardon: 'The no-balling of Mr Fry was only a case of long-delayed justice. As a matter of fact he ought never, after his caricature of bowling in the MCC and Oxford match at Lord's in 1892, to have been allowed to bowl at all.'

That December, at a county captains' meeting at Lord's, Phillips's actions were endorsed by all except Mold's Lancashire captain, MacLaren. The next summer, Phillips went to Old Trafford and no-balled Mold 16 times in 10 overs. This stopped counties from picking chuckers and effectively ended the careers of Mold and Kortright. His work done, Phillips went off to be a mining engineer, initially in Africa's Gold Coast and later in Canada.

In Australia, umpire Bob Crockett took up the same challenge, no-balling NSW's Aboriginal fast bowler Jack Marsh twice in Melbourne and 17 times in Sydney. Marsh was fast, but more than that he confused umpires with his unorthodox action. It is possible that, like Sri Lanka's Lasith Malinga, he might have looked doubtful but been actually legal. In one match, to defend himself, Marsh splinted his arm and bore a medical certificate saying he couldn't bend it. Umpire Billy Curran, who threatened to no-ball him, walked out of the match, saying he'd been humiliated. Marsh's career did not survive when Noble – himself an accused thrower – refused to pick him for NSW and, a year later, MacLaren refused to take his England team onto the field at Bathurst unless Marsh was withdrawn from the local team.

The Melbourne Cricket Club invited Marylebone to organise a tour in 1901–02, as a 'centralised' solution to the haphazard history of unrepresentative England teams cobbled together by private promoters, but Lord's showed little resolve and on 13 May 1901 announced it could not recruit a representative England team. MacLaren took up the challenge. Ranjitsinhji and Fry reneged on promises that they would tour, Lord Hawke refused to make Rhodes and Hirst available, Jackson had too much business and politics, while several counties wouldn't release prospective players.

Only MacLaren, whose fond memories of the 1897–98 tour included plenty of runs and a marriage to Kathleen Maude Power, a young Toorak woman whose father, Robert, had played for Victoria, and Tom Hayward had been to Australia before. But MacLaren was renowned for his 'spots' – players he discovered outside the county system – and this time he was bringing the greatest of all.

Sydney Francis Barnes, a gaunt, cussed Midlander-turned-Lancastrian, was 28 when MacLaren offered him £300 plus expenses to tour Australia. Barnes was not a county cricketer. He had played four times for Warwickshire between 1894 and 1896 but snubbed their offer to join the staff and joined Rishton in the Lancashire League.

During five seasons for Rishton, Barnes rebuffed approach after approach from Lancashire, only representing the county twice in 1899 and instead moving to another league team, Burnley. In August 1901, MacLaren had one place left to fill on his Australian tour when he persuaded Barnes to play for Lancashire against Leicestershire.

As a bowler, Barnes seems to have resembled Anil Kumble – a fast leg-break bowler, tall with a high action and looping flight, and subtle, disguised variations. He used the off-break at times but mastered the deadliest ball in cricket, then as now – the one that swung into and broke away from the right-hander. But wickets did not buy him friendships, and nor did he seek them. Barker profiled him: 'Fate had played a strange trick on him; he was a character, but not a personality. He lacked the charm for which his eccentricities might have been forgiven.'

Against Leicestershire he took 6/70 in 29 overs and 12 days later accepted MacLaren's invitation. The Lancashire committee told MacLaren he was mad, as Barnes had only taken 13 first-class wickets at 35.30; but in the nets MacLaren could barely lay bat on Barnes, good enough reason to suppose that the Australians wouldn't have much idea either.

The tour's fate ran in parallel with Barnes's fitness. While he was playing, England beat South Australia, Victoria and Australia, and lost to NSW and Australia in the second Test match (where Trumble took a hat-trick of Arthur Jones, Billy Gunn and Barnes). Barnes took 41 wickets at 16.48, erasing any question over whether he could penetrate on marble Australian wickets. In the first Test he took 5/65 and 1/74, in the second, where rain fell, 6/42 and 7/121.

The series was 1–1 and England had scored 388 at Adelaide when Barnes, in his seventh over, caught his spikes in the turf and wrenched his knee badly. Without endorsing it, *Wisden* repeated a widespread slur that he could have bowled more, voicing a prejudice against him that would dog his career and limit his chances in Test cricket.

MacLaren was at his imperious best with 929 tour runs at 58.06. When Darling stacked the leg-side field MacLaren said, 'How can I play my famous hook stroke with all these men about?' Darling said he had the right to put his men wherever he wanted. MacLaren duly stepped around the ball and hit four fours to the off-side boundary. Darling was forced to concede. 'Thank you, Joe,' said MacLaren, 'now we can get on with the game like gentlemen.'

But runs could not allay the disappointments of a losing tour. MacLaren was in running battles over umpiring appointments: in successive matches against NSW, he vetoed the NSWCA's choice in favour of Bob Crockett, but then had Crockett sacked for Charlie Bannerman. He was outmarshalled by Darling, who virtually reversed his batting order on the Melbourne sticky in the first Test, ensuring that a match-winning 186 runs were added by a unique Australian bottom three of Hill, Reg Duff and Armstrong. The season was a triumph for Hill, except for his statistically unique run of 99, 98 (caught by Johnny Tyldesley on the Adelaide bike track) and 97 in successive Test innings. Trumble took over the captaincy when Darling, after establishing a 2–I lead, went back to Tasmania to put in some time with family and farm before taking a team to England.

Australian crowds showed how much they enjoyed a winner, with more than 300,000 flocking back to the Tests. Their numbers meant money, however, and money meant dissent. Three of the bons vivants English amateurs – Arthur Jones, Jessop and Charlie McGahey – put in last-minute claims for £50 on top of the expenses they had already received from the Melbourne Cricket Club. They also left an unpaid £4I wine bill at Scott's Hotel, which Melbourne quietly paid, and finished the summer in a routine squabble over tour revenues with the NSWCA.

'THE REST WILL SHIVER WITH FRIGHT'

By early 1902, the Australian Test team was as strong as it had ever been. Trumble, Noble and Hill had an easy job of selecting fourteen players. Five debutants – Duff, Armstrong, all-rounder Bert Hopkins, wicketkeeper and undertaker Hanson Carter and left-armer Jack Saunders, who could vary his pace according to the conditions – reinforced the stars of 1899. There was unprecedented respect and harmony among the senior players. Trumble said they chose Duff, for instance, 'because Alf Noble says he is a champion'.

The main dissent came from the overlooked Worrall, who wrote in London's *Sportsman*: 'No recognised body or institution in the whole of Australia appointed or asked [Trumble, Noble and Hill] to pick the members of the Australian team to visit England. It is an extraordinary position and not one that could take place out of Australia.'

His statement was absolutely inaccurate – MacLaren had chosen the 1901–02 English team, and other English tours had also been chosen by ad hoc committees of promoters and captains – but was a reminder that the ACC's failure left tours to England, as always, in the hands of the Australian players.

The Melbourne Cricket Club again underwrote the tour, but the players ran it. The club's investment was £900, which the players repaid by 4 July. From then on, the profits were theirs. As Wardill outlined in a speech in Adelaide on 18 March 1902, the financial basis of the tours hadn't really changed since Dave Gregory's time, except for the upfront investment. 'There was no-one else willing and able to undertake to manage the visits of English teams to Australia, and therefore [we] thought the club worthy of their best esteem. In taking teams overseas, all [Melbourne] had done was lend their name to the teams going home, and provided financial assistance to set them on their feet in England. It was simply a matter of grace, so that the teams would not go home in any other way than they should go. That was the only bond between Australian cricketers and the Melbourne Club.'

He further expanded in an article for the *Evening News* in England: 'We have no great leisure class in the colonies as you have here, and in order that the best men might come to England, it is necessary to conduct each tour strictly on business lines. The players take all the risk and, if the tour should break down from any cause, the loss is theirs. Should profits accrue after defraying all expenses they are divided equally among the members of the tour to recoup them for loss of time and salary during their eight months absence.

'... if you call the Australians professionals, then the English amateurs who come to the colonies are even more so. Take the last team, for instance. The Melbourne Cricket Club paid everything: steamer passages, rail and hotel expenses, tips etc. In addition each man received a sum running into three figures of pin money and, indeed, in the case of one of the amateurs, the Melbourne Cricket Club were debited with the cost of the outfit he bought before embarking.'

This is a concise summary of England's shamateurism, and the ambiguity of the Australians' status amid what David Kynaston calls England's 'class-based apartheid'.

There were still defenders of England's system at Lord's and in the committee rooms of every county. As recently as 1895, a brand-new pavilion was built at Old Trafford with three bathrooms for the amateurs and one for the professionals. In 1898 *The Times* sniffed that 'the old professional box tacked on to the Pavilion at Lord's is always an eyesore to many of the Marylebone Club members'.

Support for the status quo also came from less-predictable quarters. Ranjitsinhji, who had presumably been unhappy with the racial snub imposed on him in 1896, extolled the virtues of teams that combined amateurs and players, because 'if the high standard of what may be called "sportsmanship" is to be maintained, amateurs must continue to form a fair proportion of the entire body of first-class cricketers'.

There was no separation between the Australian and English 'amateurs' when they left Adelaide on 19 March: they were together on the SS *Omrah*. The English professionals travelled third-class. The English were recovering from an arduous and unsatisfying tour, while Darling put his men on a long rein. When the *Omrah* arrived at Marseilles, some got on a train to Paris, others went to Monte Carlo, and a third group continued to Plymouth. Trumble, the vice-captain, came later on the *Oceana* with his new bride, Florence Christian.

Fred Spofforth, who had spent the summer in Australia, sailed on the *Omrah* as well. He had recently written provocatively that Rhodes was the only England bowler he rated highly, and that there were at least fifteen throwers in county cricket. When it came to ex-players having a go at chuckers, however, nothing Spofforth said could compare to the incendiary article awaiting the Australians in the *Sportsman* of 15 April.

The article claimed, bluntly, that Noble was a chucker. The anonymous author said he had written to Phillips urging him to no-ball not only Noble but Saunders, who had taken nine wickets on Test debut in Sydney. The accuser, it transpired, was Worrall. One of Darling's first acts on arrival was to lead a deputation to the *Sportsman*'s office, where the editor was persuaded to stop publishing Worrall. Phillips did not no-ball either Noble or Saunders.

Darling, after two months in Tasmania and a leisurely voyage, left no doubt about his disciplinary intent. The tour had a committee that could expel any member who 'by wilfully and repeatedly making himself objectionable ... in any way jeopardis[ed] the success of the team on the field'. A fine of £100 applied to anyone writing for the press, and the players agreed to several other restraints.

This venture was more like a modern tour. Wearing, for the first time, the green and gold colours of Federation, with the coat of arms of emu and kangaroo, the Eleventh Australians commenced operations on 5 May with a cold, rainy draw against Grace's London County. Less notable than the cricket was the double-act of elder statesmen, Grace and, still wearing the gold sovereign he had won at the Oval in 1880, Murdoch.

Grace and Murdoch were letting their inner schoolboys run wild at the club. Grace was known as 'Father', Murdoch 'Muvver'. Coupling at a dance, they barrelled Sammy Woods and former England player Arthur Hill into a fireplace. Once they leapt into a cab together, their combined bulk causing the floor to fall out. In a match in Wiltshire, Grace bet Murdoch he could catch more fish than Murdoch scored runs. Grace got up in the dark and landed 100 fish. Murdoch scored 103. For the MCC that season, they put on 120 for the first wicket, beating their combined age by 20.

Little distinguished their play against Australia, though Grace did have Darling caught for 92. Leslie Poidevin, the Australian cricketer and medical student who was playing for London County, said he was 'at a loss to see the use of the man stationed behind himself, but, curiously enough, that is where W.G. snared the Australian captain'. Three weeks later the 53-year-old W.G. took 5/29 – Duff, Hopkins, Kelly, Jones and Howell – for the MCC. As Arthur Conan Doyle wrote of his bowling, 'There was nothing more childlike and bland than that slow, tossed-up bowling of Doctor Grace, and nothing more subtle and dangerous.'

Darling's team got through their first month with four wins and three draws, but the opposition was not troubling them as much as the elements. The weather was so cold that Samuel J. Looker taunted them in the *Evening News* with a three-stanza poem that started:

> *'Does your circulation fail, Kangaroo?*
> *Got a frost-bite in your tail, Kangaroo?*
> *Do you find it hard to play*
> *When it's hailing half the day,*
> *And it's even cold for May, Kangaroo?*
>
> *Are your Noble, Duff and Hill, Kangaroo?*
> *And your Trumper feeling ill, Kangaroo?'*

The first hitch came before the London County game, when Trumble, fielding a drive from Hill in the nets, broke his thumb. He would not reappear until 9 June – good news for his honeymoon, perhaps, but potentially catastrophic for the Eleventh Australians.

Amid the wettest spring in recent memory, influenza hit Noble, Howell and Darling severely. Saunders contracted an eye infection, then tonsillitis, and Carter looked like he'd been punched by a prize fighter after a ball hit him in the eye.

Edgbaston hosted its first Test, replacing Trent Bridge in the roster, and England fielded a team that was, in Fry's words, 'generally agreed to have been the strongest that ever at any time represented us'. The assessment may still stand 110 years later: MacLaren, Fry, Ranji,

Jackson, Tyldesley, Lilley, Hirst, Jessop, Len Braund, Lockwood and Rhodes. Batting first, they made 9/376, spearheaded by 138 from Tyldesley, whom MacLaren rated as highly as Trumper, while Fry had him on par with Jack Hobbs.

Heavy rain on the first night gave Australia a quagmire, and they were lucky to make their innings total of 36. Only Trumper, who scored half their runs, achieved double figures. Rhodes – who got his chance in big cricket for Yorkshire when Lord Hawke threw Bobby Peel out of the team for playing while drunk and watering the Bramall Lane wicket in unorthodox fashion – took 7/17 with his left-arm spin, but Fry thought the other left-armer, Hirst, gave the batsmen more trouble. They 'hurried to the other end and tried to hit Rhodes, without success. Well as Rhodes bowled, it was Hirst who was responsible for the debacle.'

Due to more rain, Australia's follow-on did not commence until 5.15 pm on the last day. Keen to see another rout, crowds broke through the barriers, but too little time remained.

The bubble around Darling's team seemed to have burst. A cocky English poet was writing them off:

'Our Cornstalk cousins like us well,
Our country, our abodes,
And yet the truth they fain must tell –
They cannot face our Rhodes.'

The weather showed the Australians no mercy two days later at Bradford, where, in front of a heaving crowd of 33,705, they achieved a slim first-innings lead only to be bundled out for 23 in their second. Rhodes was not even needed: Hirst, 5/9, and Jackson, 5/12, did not relinquish the ball.

A batting recovery against Lancashire came to nothing when rain washed out two of three days, and the vaunted best-ever Australian

Eleven was looking like one of the worst. The lowest Test score, followed by the second-lowest first-class score; talk was turning to the bunnies of the late 1880s and early 1890s. *Wisden* reported that 'one or two of the men new to England were so thoroughly downhearted that, had such a thing been possible, they would have been quite willing to pack up their bags and return home.' A week before the second Test at Lord's, Australia could not put an Eleven on the field against Cambridge University. Noble, Darling, Saunders and Howell were sick, Trumble reappeared but fell ill with influenza, and the 38-year-old camp follower Roley Pope found himself called up once again.

Pope's last cricket match had been for the MCC in 1891. Since then, he had set up a successful ophthalmic practice in Sydney, and was giving himself a nine-month sabbatical to follow medical developments, opera and cricket around Britain and Europe. He had sailed with the team on the *Omrah* and would be following them through most of their 1902 games, Test and county, and even to South Africa.

Pope's match against Cambridge was less eventful than his 1890 match when Murdoch laughed him off as a bowling fraud. He scored 2 not out and, fielding as a substitute for Cambridge, caught Bert Hopkins, who said, 'You beggar, I did feel like making runs today.'

England chose their same glossy Eleven for Lord's. There was talk of postponing the Test because of the Australians' health problems, but Darling declared them ready. On 12 June rain chased the players back to their hotel until they were summoned to start within the hour. Fry opened the batting with Ranji and said that Darling, 'for some reason which he could never explain', gave Hopkins the new ball. Hopkins dismissed both before MacLaren and Jackson put on an unbeaten 102 in what would be the only action before rain caused an abandonment.

Lucky to have survived the month, Darling's men regrouped. The pitches dried out and the Australians celebrated the belated arrival of summer with five straight wins.

On 3 July Bramall Lane hosted its first and only Test match. The Grinders of Sheffield came out in force, but the factories poured out a brown haze that lay like a twilight over the game. England had to omit Ranji, who strained his leg while scoring 230 for Sussex against Essex, and Lockwood, recalling Fry and introducing, for his first Test on home soil, S.F. Barnes. Australia brought in Trumble for Jones: the pitch was soft, the paceman unwanted.

MacLaren was only given permission to send a telegram for Barnes a few hours before the match. Barnes was booed by the Grinders, who thought they were going to see their own Schofield Haigh; his reply was to take 6/49. Noble (5/51) and Saunders (5/50) ensured that Australia's 195 was good for a 49-run advantage. Fry, shifted to number five, said: 'When I was stumped in the first innings I literally saw no ball at all to play at.' Jessop said that even when the sun was shining and the factories were idle, 'the light is still only moderate' and batting was 'more a matter of luck than judgement'. In later years, the routine cry in Sheffield would go out, 'Stoke the furnaces, boys, the Australians are batting.'

In the second innings came the turning point. Trumper and Hill, who had carried much responsibility while their teammates were sick or injured, blossomed in the gloom. In 50 minutes Trumper struck 62, redolent of Massie's innings in the famous Oval Test. An admiring Noble said – overturning all the cricket wisdom of more pragmatic times – 'It is not how many runs a man makes but how he makes them that counts.'

Whereas Massie's 55 had stood alone, Trumper was followed by the greatest left-hander yet seen. Hill's 119 in 145 minutes ranked alongside his Melbourne 188. It was a stirring response to the accusations of safety-first batting. Australia's 289 altered the entire summer; not even an illegal rolling of the pitch for England's second innings could rob them of a stunning win. The only resistance came from MacLaren, 63, and Jessop, who clouted 55 before being lbw to Trumble with, Fry said, 'a ball which hit him in the middle of his chest on the lower shirt button; he was trying to hit a straight ball to square leg from the position of a doormat'.

It was much to Darling's credit that he chose not to complain about the pitch rolling, but privately he said, 'we were so incensed with the action of the groundsman ... that when he came into our dressing-room to receive his usual 2/2 the only tip he got was when one member of our team got him by the back of the neck and tipped him out through the door'.

While the Australians went on an unbeaten five-match streak, the English selectors, Hawke, Gregor MacGregor and Herbert Bainbridge, went into panic mode. Barnes, who had the best average and strike rate of any English bowler, was dropped. Nobody doubted the reason. Barker suggests 'it looked very much as though his face didn't fit. He didn't play for England again for more than five years.'

At the height of the Golden Age, England selected a team with a distinctly bronze hue. The fall guy for the poor selections became Hawke, who, his adversary Fry wrote, turned up at every meeting with pockets stuffed with newspaper clippings about the candidates. 'The events of this match in combination with others are the origin of the caustic saying that Lord Hawke lost more Test Matches than anyone who never played for England. This is rather severe. Lord Hawke was chairman of the selectors from 1899 to 1909, and again in 1933. He was not a good chairman. He was too much concerned with the fortunes of Yorkshire; he regarded the Test Matches as spoiling the county championship, and he was much too observant of what he thought was public opinion. He has been much misrepresented as a strong man of cricket.'

Three Yorkshiremen were in the team – Jackson, Rhodes and Hirst – but Hawke refused to release a fourth, the wet-wicket specialist Schofield Haigh. Apparently annoyed with Fry, Hawke proposed selecting Sussex's Fred Tate. Fry said Tate was a dry-wicket bowler who couldn't field or catch. But 'Lord Hawke was huffy, and we gave way to him, me protesting. So the truth is that this remarkable match ought to be called Lord Hawke's match.'

When MacLaren was shown the team list for Old Trafford, he cried: 'Look what they've given me! Do they think we're playing the blind asylum?' To spite Fry, Hawke had dropped the Sussex opener for Abel, even though Fry had scored 3147 runs at nearly 79 the previous season. In his book on England's captains, Alan Gibson writes, 'It seems fairly clear, as one looks back over all the different accounts of this affair, that the selectors chose Tate as a reserve because they thought MacLaren could not possibly pick him, and so their original 11 would stand.' But to defy Hawke, MacLaren made Hirst 12th man, so the chairman could suffer the painful sight of one of his precious Yorkshire bowlers not playing at all.

Darling won the toss; thus began one of the most fabled days of Test cricket history. A 14-year-old Neville Cardus, in the crowd, prayed to God for Trumper to score a century and Australia to be out for 137.

MacLaren told Darling after the toss that because the wet pitch would be slow and unresponsive, his strategy was simple: 'Keep Victor quiet.' The English captain went to his bowlers and said, 'If the Australians are only 80 or so at the lunch interval, we've won the match; the pitch will be sticky after lunch. So keep Victor quiet. Then we'll bowl them out as quick as they come in.'

Darling only had one plan when he boarded the team coach each morning. He would ask the coachman, 'Is Vic aboard?'

MacLaren set his field deep and waited for the pitch, the thick atmosphere, and Lockwood, Rhodes, Braund, Jackson, and, if necessary, Tate, to do their work.

By lunch, Trumper was 103.

Years later, MacLaren said: 'Good God, I knew my man. Victor had half a dozen strokes for the same kind of ball. I exploited the inner and outer ring — a man there, a man there and another man covering him. I told my bowlers to pitch on the short side on the off. I set my heart and brain on every detail of our policy. Well, in the third over of the morning, Victor hit two balls straight into the practice ground, high above the screen behind the bowler. I couldn't very well have had a man fielding in the bloody practice ground now, could I?'

Braund expressed a bowler's helplessness: 'I bowl up a ball, he comes out to it, I know that I have beaten him in the flight, and then, at the last moment, he will lay back and cut me for four. The very same ball next time he hits to square leg. Now what is a fellow to do?'

Trumper said: 'Spoil a bowler's length and you've got him.' He had them all, except for Lockwood. Duff (whom Fry memorably described as having 'a face like a good-looking brown trout, and full of Australian sunshine') contributed 54 to an opening stand of 135 in 78 minutes, while Hill and Darling added half-centuries, but Lockwood overpowered the lower order and Australia's 299 was a fair result for England. In reply, their shining light was Jackson's 128.

Australia led by 37, no lead at all when Lockwood was at his mercurial best. He had fallen off the wagon again since 1899, and his benefit had been rained out. But Surrey looked after him by arranging an additional benefit match and investing the £1000 it raised in Mexican Railways debenture stock, giving him an income over time. In what Fry called 'one of the finest bowling performances in the history of Test Matches', Lockwood destroyed Australia. They were 3/16 when Darling was batting in left-right combination with Gregory. Darling came on strike for the last ball of an over. Braund, the bowler, asked MacLaren, 'Can I have Mr Palairet across to square leg?' MacLaren replied, 'What, do you want me to ask Lionel Palairet to run right across Old Trafford for one ball? Send Fred Tate out there.' Palairet was an amateur, Tate and Braund professionals.

Only one ball, but it changed the match. Darling skied Braund with the spin to backward square, where Tate, in one of the many positions that were out of position for him, dropped the ball. Australia added another 48 runs while Darling was in, and Tate had made the first of the mistakes that would attach his name, cruelly, to that match.

Lockwood returned a match analysis of 11/76. Among cricketers, Fry said, Lockwood 'would be at the top of the poll for the best genuine fast bowler in the history of the game'.

After heavy rain, England needed 124 to win. Abel and Palairet got them to 0/44 by lunch when MacLaren said to Darling, 'I think we've got you this time.' Darling replied: 'Oh, have you? Why, we've only to get two or three of you out and the rest will shiver with fright.'

Ranji failed again. His Test scores in 1902 were 13, 0, 2 and 4. A little-known cause of his failure was some gamesmanship from Darling that pushed the boundaries of fair play and recalled the extremes of Dave Gregory's time. Darling wanted to feed Ranji's leg-side shots and frustrate him with a stacked field. He moved Syd Gregory and himself, his best fieldsmen, to leg. 'Ranji always used to have a look where we were both fielding before the bowler started to deliver the ball and as soon as he had his last look and the bowler was actually on the point of delivering the ball, we generally shifted our positions by a few yards, sometimes one way and sometimes the other and occasionally one only would move or we would not move at all. Ranji never knew where we were actually fielding when he was about to make his stroke and this eventually put him clean off his game.' At Old Trafford, Ranji played a nice shot into what he thought was a gap and Gregory caught him. 'From that day Ranji was never again the same batsman,' Darling said. 'The reason was that we got on his nerves, as he never knew where we were actually fielding.'

After the Old Trafford Test, MacLaren told Darling that Ranji was in such a 'blue funk' he'd nearly sent him in last.

Meanwhile MacLaren was still there at 5/100, just 24 short. Rain drove the players off twice, and then Trumble and Saunders got to work. After Duff, running flat-out in the outfield, caught MacLaren to give Trumble his hundredth Test scalp, the England captain threw his bat across the dressing room and said he had 'thrown away the match and the bloody rubber'. Hill took an equally spectacular running boundary catch to remove Lilley – who told him it was 'a bally fluke' – and in the final act Tate joined Rhodes with eight to win.

Grace liked to say, 'There is no crisis, only the next ball.' When Tate walked out the rain came again and the poor man had to sit for 40 minutes fantasising about, or dreading, that next ball.

When the match resumed, Wardill's wife was so tense she ran her knitting needle through her hand. Tate slashed a streaky four, the Australians urging it over the boundary so he could not run three and get Rhodes on strike. Then Tate swung again at Saunders, missed, and Australia had won by three runs.

And so ended Fred Tate's match, though Fry said it was really Lord Hawke's match, and Australians thought of it as Trumper's match. Hugh Trumble took 10 wickets; it was his match, too. And Darling's match: he was now the first Australian captain to win two series in England. An inconsolable Tate was reported to be weeping in the dressing room, muttering that he had a 'boy who will set it right'. That might be apocryphal, but he did: his boy Maurice would set it right. Fred never got another chance. Maurice, who was at the match, later recalled that Fred wept all the way home.

The pressure off, Darling's batsmen enjoyed the next fortnight. Trumper took twin centuries off Essex, Noble hit 284 and Armstrong 172 not out against Sussex (Tate 41–9–136–0) in putting on 428 for the sixth wicket, and Darling and Noble scored centuries in Hampshire. They won a reputation for attractive batting. Darling was prepared to discipline his players for this object: in one match, the *Australasian Star* later reported, 'Armstrong so palpably played for a not out that Darling threatened to send him in first so that he would have to get out.' Armstrong was accused of being an 'average monger', but in 1902 Darling still had him more or less under control.

With a hectic social life surrounding Edward VII's coronation and the ongoing celebrations for the end of the Boer War, Darling's men might have been forgiven for easing off for the Fifth Test at the Oval, but a first-innings lead of 141 (Trumble 8/65, following his 64 not out at number nine) showed they were on their mettle.

England only avoided the follow-on by nine runs before Lockwood took another five wickets to tear apart Australia's second innings. Still, an Australian win seemed a formality when Palairet, MacLaren, Tyldesley, Hayward and Braund were in their respective dressing rooms and England still needed 214.

Then Jessop, who had been threatening this kind of thing for a while, in Fry's words, 'let himself loose like a catapult at the bowling and scattered it to smithereens. If ever an innings ought to have been filmed, that was the one.'

The Croucher's lightning century (his other nicknames were the Electric Battery, the Human Dynamo and the Human Catapult) from 76 balls in 75 minutes was why he had been picked, and why hitters were favoured: they could turn a match on its head. Hirst, 58 not out, was the necessary ally. Rhodes, last man in, was famously reported to say, 'We'll get 'em in singles', and he more or less did, with one boundary added in. (He claimed the runs, but not the comment, which, he maintained, was 'a pressman's invention'.) After losing a Test by three runs, England won one by a wicket. *The Times* pronounced: 'As long as cricket lasts Mr Jessop's great performance will be remembered.'

Fry said: 'I have seen the spectators at Test Matches strained and excited, but this is the only Test match in which I have seen a spectator burst into tears when the winning run was scored.'

The Oval Test was the second, and last, loss for the Eleventh Australians. Far from being worn out by the long series, their slow start meant they were still fresh by August. After the Oval, they defeated MCC, Gloucestershire, Kent, Middlesex, Lancashire, the Players and the South of England, and drew with C.I. Thornton's Eleven, the South and the Players. All these opponents contained English representatives, but Darling's team was supreme once the weather fined up. Trumble took 15/68 against the South in his last game on English soil, completing his fourth 100-wicket tour, something not even Spofforth or Turner had achieved. In that match W.G. scored 17 not out and Fred Tate found a little balm for the wounds of Old Trafford by taking 6/48 in Australia's second innings, making sure that it was all his own labour by clean-bowling Trumper, Duff, Gregory, Armstrong and Hopkins, and holding a return catch from Kelly.

Trumper's 120 at Hastings was his eleventh century of the summer, and in his final innings he fell a boundary short of his twelfth. His aggregate, 2570 runs, and his average, 48.49, so far exceeded that of any previous Australian in England (the record was Darling's 1941 runs in 1899, the next-best Murdoch's 1711 in 1882) that he seemed of a different genus altogether. The tributes poured forth. Fry said Trumper 'had no single style but every style'. Hill, who made 1614 runs at 31.64, and four centuries including the series-changing 119 in the Sheffield murk, said, 'I wasn't fit to lick his boots as a batsman.' A despairing MacLaren concluded: 'You couldn't set a field for him. He was the most fascinating batsman I have ever seen. He had grace, ease, style and power.' And Ranji, whose place as the world's pre-eminent batsman had been taken, said: 'Every stroke he made so fascinated me that I couldn't take my eyes off him.'

Cricketers of different eras cannot be compared. They can only be measured against their own. In 1902, one of the wettest summers, Trumper was as far ahead of his contemporaries as Bradman was ahead of his. Pardon praised his modesty and integrity: 'I may express my extreme satisfaction that the efforts to secure him for an English county failed. It would have been a paltry and unworthy thing to deprive Australia, by means of a money bribe, of her best batsman.' And Test cricket of its biggest drawcard. Darling's Australians had restored the international game to its pedestal above domestic cricket, and there it would remain.

'It will always be a matter of dispute,' comments Altham, 'whether the team brought over by Darling in 1902 was, or was not, the best that has yet represented Australia in this country.' The teams of 1882 and 1899 had their fans, but in a five-Test series the Eleventh Australians beat an exceptionally strong England team in conditions to suit England. Of 39 first-class matches, they won 23, drew 14 and lost two. One of those losses was Jessop's miracle at the Oval, and the other was on an absolute bog in early June at Headingley. It is fair to say that the 1902 team was clearly better than any that had come before, and still arguable, considering the strength of their opposition, that they have never been bettered since. Armstrong, after leading the 1921 Australians to a 3–0 Test win and just one tour loss, said, 'The 1902 side could play 22 of my chaps and give them a beating.'

On the field they 'completely subordinated all personal considerations to the prime object of winning matches,' Pardon wrote in *Wisden*. Considering the broader history of behaviour in the previous quarter-century, he was equally impressed by their off-field discipline:

'The team would not, with all their ability, have been able to show such consistently fine form week after week throughout a long tour, if the men had not taken scrupulous care of themselves when off the field. I make no apology for insisting rather strongly upon this point. Everyone who is at all behind the scenes in cricket knows perfectly well that in the case, both of English elevens in Australia and Australian elevens in England, the brightest hopes have sometimes been wrecked through want of self-control on the part of players on whom the utmost dependence was placed. In this connection it is, of course, impossible to mention names, but the famous cricketers who have captained elevens in this country and the Colonies will know perfectly well the cases I have in mind.'

Darling could still be mocked by his teammates; he wasn't all that frightening. Hill would tell a story about the return journey in 1902. Darling had 'a pair of tweed trousers which he had had for about six years, and we thought it time he got rid of them'. Some players threw the tweeds overboard and drew up a document marked 'Secret' – signed by all the team – making a pact of silence. When Darling came to pack his bag, he said to Bill Howell: 'That's strange. I suppose one of those natives at Trinidad took a fancy to them.' Howell agreed that he had 'seen a dark chap about the deck'.

Beyond their achievements, the 1902 Australians glow romantically like no other Eleven. They took on a nonpareil England team and beat them. If a team is only as good as that which it beat, the 1902 Australians were the best of the best. This was the greatest of all the early series for, as Fry said, 'Almost every man on both sides contributed something to the history of the game.'

COUNTER-
REVOLUTION

With the Boer War over, Darling's Australians had agreed on a goodwill tour of South Africa on their way home to make up for the cancelled visit in 1899. They weren't going just for the diplomacy. A South African mining magnate, Abe Bailey, guaranteed £2000 to cover the 18-day tour. The Australians won the three-Test series 2–0, with Armstrong, Hill, Saunders and Howell picking up the slack as some of the stars of the Ashes series, such as Darling and Noble, lost form. South African player Louis Tancred wrote of them, 'nothing counted so much for success as strenuousness and intensity'. They arrived home on the *Sophocles* on 11 December, after nearly nine months away, with profits of £830 per man, including a bonus for the South African leg. Trumper also received a purse of 100 guineas raised by subscribers in Sydney.

The Australian season was already underway. A 'homecoming' match against a Rest of Australia Eleven had been planned for the MCG, but Jack Worrall had been selected for the Rest. Horan wrote that the match 'was abandoned because the Rest includes a player whose contributions to a certain London paper were strongly objected to by members of the Australian Eleven'.

Within a fortnight, the Test men were again using their muscle against the Victorian. Armstrong, Trumble and Saunders refused to play alongside him, and Trumper, Noble, Duff, Hopkins, Kelly and Howell would not play against him in the Boxing Day Sheffield Shield match – the biggest game of a non-Test summer. By forcing a choice between themselves and Worrall, the heroes of 1902 were challenging the VCA's authority to select a team. The Melbourne Cricket Club's delegates to the VCA – James McLaughlin, former Test player Billy Bruce and twice-tourist Alf Johns – supported the stars' demand.

Worrall tried, at first, to mollify the angry players. He said his candid criticisms of Noble's and Saunders's actions to his friend Phillips were not meant to become public. When the players ignored his olive branch, he gave up, saying, 'The whole thing is a deliberate attempt to ruin me', motivated by 'personal spite' and 'a spirit of pure vindictiveness'. MacLaughlin called him a liar and soon the Melbourne club and VCA were at war again. In the hope that his withdrawal might settle matters, Worrall did not play first-class cricket again.

Beyond the throwing issue, Worrall's criticisms of the selection of the 1902 team highlighted a belief that the Australian Eleven was a closed shop. The boycott threat further confirmed the bitter opinions of those who felt the Eleven, and the Melbourne Cricket Club, were too powerful for the greater good of Australian cricket. When Worrall stood down from the VCA, to which he had been Carlton's delegate, he said: 'What is urgently needed in Australia is a Board of Control comprised of representatives of three associations of Victoria, New South Wales and South Australia. Something must be done to stop the encroachment of an oligarchic institution like the Melbourne Cricket Club.'

Only a year after the Australian Cricket Council had folded, some ambitious would-be administrators were watching the brawl, hearing Worrall's complaint and making plans.

New South Wales, under Noble's captaincy, won the Sheffield Shield, and an English team managed by Lord Hawke and led by Middlesex's Pelham Warner dropped by for three matches after a tour of New Zealand, but the most talked-about individual performance of the summer came from a 43-year-old postal worker in Adelaide.

Giffen was still tormenting the Victorians. On a good pitch benefiting from Creswell's initiative to lay a tarpaulin before the start of matches, Giffen bowled 37.5 overs on the first two days and took 7/75. Coming in to bat when Hill failed, he scored 81. Victoria's second innings was then choked by his 38.2 overs and another eight wickets. Chasing 257, Hill and the recognised batsmen failed again but South Australia very nearly won, thanks to a last-wicket stand of 101 between Joe Travers and the eternal Giffen, who scored an unbeaten 97. Never has the word 'unbeaten' been more apt. This was the ninth and last time he took 10 wickets and scored 100 runs in a match, and the sixth time he took 15 wickets or more. He has never been remotely challenged in first-class cricket.

Back in August 1902, in one of the last first-class games of Darling's tour, the Australians had come up against a Middlesex leg-spin bowler named Bernard Bosanquet. He had told teammates he was privately practising a ball that came over the top of the wrist, like an orthodox leg-spinner, but, due to a repositioning of his hand, would turn *in* from the off. Formerly a medium-pacer, he had discovered the ball while playing 'twisty-grab' at the billiard table with Oxford University mates in 1898. He had tried it at Lord's in 1900; the ball bounced four times but bowled the batsman. The wrong 'un, also travelling under the aliases googly and bosey, was born. R.C. Robertson-Glasgow captured its strangeness when he called it 'the ball that squints'.

Reports differ on whether Bosanquet tried the ball on Jim Kelly, opening the batting for Australia at Lord's in 1902. Bosanquet dismissed Kelly lbw for a duck. Some reports had Kelly coming into the dressing room and swearing, to general disbelief, that Bosanquet's leg-break had turned in, not away. Other witnesses said Kelly was trapped by a normal leg-break.

Bosanquet toured New Zealand and Australia with Lord Hawke's team in 1902–03, but again it is unrecorded whether he tried the one that came in. By 1903/04, he was a clear choice as wrist-spinner on what Warner would call a venture 'to recover those Ashes'.

Warner was neither first- nor second-choice England captain. Initially, MacLaren had planned another tour along the lines of 1901–02. When he couldn't recruit Barnes and Lockwood, he asked the Melbourne Cricket Club for a one-year postponement. Melbourne, rather uncharitably, invited Marylebone to revive its previously postponed plan. Lord's also had some trouble with recruitment – MacLaren was now in a huff, Stanley Jackson was too busy with commerce and politics, and Charles Fry was also engaged with 'outside pursuits' – but it still rounded up a strong, fairly representative team under the leadership of Warner, whose considerate man-management had impressed Hawke in 1902–03.

Marylebone would not send a team to Australia without strings attached. It told Wardill it wanted a 'joint' invitation from the three major cricket states, half the gross gate, matches to be played under its own laws rather than Australian variants, and Phillips as its travelling umpire. Wardill consented to the first three conditions. He wrote to the NSWCA and SACA on 27 June 1903 saying Melbourne would control matches at the MCG but the rest were theirs. The SACA was eager to stage another Test match, and the NSWCA had a new surety over matches at the SCG. Back in 1883, the NSW government had broken the tight link between the NSWCA and the SCG, appointing as Trustees to the latter representatives from other sports. Phil Sheridan, a member of both the NSWCA and the SCG Trust, cast his lot with the Trust. Ever since his decision, the NSWCA had had to pay the Trust for the use of a ground it had originally regarded as its own. The NSWCA had been paranoid for years over the Trust's motives. As far back as 1894, Victor Cohen, the notorious ACC-appointed manager of the 1893 tour, accused Sheridan of setting up the Sydney Cricket Club in imitation of Melbourne, to seize the usage of the ground just as Melbourne had seized the MCG from the VCA. The renaming of the Association Ground as the Sydney Cricket Ground in 1894 only sharpened the NSWCA's fears.

In 1903, the Supreme Court resolved the brawl in the NSWCA's favour after a case run by the association's legal adviser William Percy McElhone, the ambitious Roman Catholic son of a wealthy and litigious state parliamentarian and Sydney Municipal Councillor who was owner of a cab and bus company, and whose methods included outwitting his adversaries with legal logic or, if that failed, punching them in the nose. Billy was to follow his father into local government politics, becoming Lord Mayor of Sydney in 1922. A member of the NSWCA for 35 years, he had no substantial cricket-playing pedigree, though his nephew Eric would play seven matches for NSW, with some success, before the First World War. Much of what was said of McElhone, as will be seen, was negative. But he did have supporters such as fellow NSWCA committeeman George Barbour, a classically trained teacher at Sydney Grammar, who averred: 'It has never been my fate to be associated with a straighter or more fearless protagonist, always astute, but when the position called for straight speaking he never shrank and he could call to his aid an expressive and forceful vocabulary. A master of men and a master of situation.'

That mastery would be set against the Melbourne Cricket Club, still the default Marylebone of Australia. It now had more than 4000 members and a cluster of the best cricketers in the country, led by Armstrong, who combined his cricket with a staff job on £228 a year at the Melbourne club.

Of the Maryebone demands, the one that Wardill and the senior Australian players could not accept was Phillips as umpire. Phillips had written to the VCA saying Saunders threw all of his faster balls, which the players saw as evidence of prejudice. Wardill wrote to Lord's, 'It would be a very unpopular thing to bring him, as the public are well aware through the press of what has taken place.' Lord's gave way, Phillips never umpired in Australia again, and the 42-year-old practice of a visiting team bringing its own umpire was abandoned.

Lord's was treating the tour seriously. Altham later wrote, 'It was felt that the honour of English cricket was now seriously at stake, and very properly the MCC set out to vindicate it by undertaking, for the first time in history, to send out a team under their direct auspices.'

Four straight series wins by Australia had not only challenged the English to make international cricket their highest priority, but revived the buried idea of the 'Ashes'. Warner, who wrote a book about the tour, was credited with this revival. A neat right-hander, he had only played two Test matches, against South Africa, and was never in the same rank as Ranji, Jackson, MacLaren, Tyldesley and Hayward. But as a touring skipper he had a democratic bent, insisting on professionals and amateurs staying in the same hotels and getting the best out of both. Even-tempered and pragmatic, he would found *Cricket* magazine, stand on the MCC committee for 60 years, manage the Bodyline tour, and carve out an administrative career that consolidated the prestige of international cricket.

But he could not get Sydney Barnes on the tour. Since being dropped after the Sheffield Test in 1902, Barnes had been on the outer. In his debut Players–Gentlemen match, in 1903, he bowled one over before claiming an injury. Newspapers attacked him for receiving his fee and suggested he was feigning the injury. Lord's didn't like him, and soon Old Trafford had had enough of him too.

As a MacLaren 'spot', Barnes was considered loyal to his captain, but they clashed in the last match of the 1903 season, against Nottinghamshire. Barnes was unhappy with his new Lancashire contract, figuring he could earn a greater personal reward by returning to the League. The Old Trafford committee said if he didn't sign, he couldn't play in the match. Barnes refused to sign but walked onto the field anyway. Committee members called to MacLaren, who had to order Barnes back to the pavilion. *Wisden* said 'temperament is a great thing but in it Barnes has always been deficient'.

Barnes went back to league cricket for the Church club, sometimes representing minor county Staffordshire. His brief, late, perplexing, astonishingly potent Test career was considered over. He was 30, and *Wisden* wrote him off, saying if he'd had Briggs's or Barlow's enthusiasm for cricket 'he might have made a great name for himself', but he had blown his chance.

Warner's voyage on the SS *Orontes* was eventful enough, according to Bishop James Welldon of Calcutta, known as 'The Porker' when he was on the staff at London's Dulwich College. The Bishop had to avert his eyes from 'the wrong lady who always wanted to sleep in some other cabin than her own; and the other young lady who in a moment of abstraction mysteriously disappeared down an air chute'. When Warner asked Welldon if it was Christian to pray to beat Australia, the bishop replied: 'Anything that tends to the prestige of England is worth praying for.'

The MCC team walked into a typically tempestuous Australian scene. Before their opening match, George Giffen asked the SACA for £10 for expenses. Creswell offered £5 for 'loss of time', which Giffen rejected. Two days before the game, Giffen consented to play as long as his expenses were donated to the Children's Hospital. Creswell said they would be paid directly to Giffen. Finally, Giffen, who wanted to play, consented 'merely out of courtesy to the English team', donating his money to the Children's Hospital himself.

The confusion over Australian and Marylebone rules took all of two days to break out into conflict. Warner declared at 8/483, which the South Australians regarded as illegal under local laws. They were told to play on. Thus did the colonials learn who was running the game.

Warner's team went undefeated into the first Test at Sydney. On match morning the Australian players voted for Noble as captain in the absence of Darling, who was farming in Tasmania. Noble had started his working life as a banker, but when he saw that he might not obtain sufficient leave to play cricket he trained for more flexible self-employment in dentistry. A born leader, he would take NSW to six Sheffield Shields in eight seasons and hold strong, Darling-influenced views about the Australian captaincy as 'the embodiment of all the hopes, virtue, courage, and ability possessed by the ten men under his command'. He believed every player should aspire to be an Australian captain and conduct himself accordingly. This was the first generation who had grown up with international cricket as a known, prestigious goal.

Noble came to the wicket at 2/9 and scored 133, his only Test century, before crowds of 17,351 on the first day and a record 35,499 on the second. The middle of the match was played under the shadow of Tip Foster's 287 in his first innings in Test cricket, a matchwinning effort due to his addition of 245 runs with Lilley and Rhodes, the last two batsmen. Foster's SCG record stood for 108 years, before Michael Clarke's 329 not out against India surpassed it.

After Foster's innings, another ugly controversy erupted. Australia batted again 292 runs behind, and Duff and Hill were making a good fist of it at 2/191 when Hill was given run out by Bob Crockett. An outraged chant of 'Crock! Crock! Crock!' went up, and missiles began landing on the field. Warner believed the uproar had started from the Members' Stand, but in actuality it started in the middle, where Hill refused to leave and told Crockett, who he thought was grandstanding, that he 'ought to stand for the Senate'. A cartoon the next day showed the fieldsmen hiding under manholes and the umpire in a protective cage. Warner threatened to take his team off, before Hill finally left and Noble quelled the unrest. Trumper went on to score 185 not out, the first hundred runs in 94 minutes. Although in a losing cause, Dick Lilley rated Trumper's innings higher than Foster's.

Trumper was again resplendent in Melbourne, scoring 74 of Australia's 122 on a treacherous gluepot, but his teammates were bewildered by the teasing slow left-armers of Rhodes. Few had expected the wet-wicket specialist to succeed in Australia, but his 15/124, with eight catches dropped, settled the argument.

In those two Test losses, Armstrong bowled leg-theory: skidding leg-spinners aimed outside the batsmen's pads with seven or eight men on the on-side. He did so against Noble's wishes, a direct challenge to the new captain. After retirement, Noble wrote: 'I deprecate most strongly the use of leg-theory as a means of saving runs; it is a method usually introduced only to save your face. There is nothing clever about it ... [and] its use is not good for the game.'

Gaining confidence in his captaincy, by the third Test Noble stopped Armstrong. Another gem from Trumper, a three-hour 113, and a second-innings 112 from Gregory launched Australia to a fightback victory. Armstrong, who had lost the battle of wills with both Noble and the Englishmen, failed with bat and ball and would be dropped for the only time in his 20-year Test career.

In Armstrong's next match, for Victoria against the MCC, with Harry Trott out of the asylum and back in charge, the Victorians were all out for 15 in their second innings. It took 45 minutes, of which a quarter was taken up by batsmen walking off and on. Rain, of course, played a part, Rhodes taking 5/6 in 37 balls. Trott, who must have thought he was in his hospital bed having a bad dream, scored 9 of the 15, and Armstrong was caught behind for a duck.

To this point Bosanquet had not landed his googly accurately enough to cause havoc, though he would have had more stumpings if Lilley wasn't so often deceived. A week after the Victorian match Bosanquet's second-innings 6/45 sank NSW with all Test hands; for good measure, he also hit 54 and 114. He liked the SCG, and in the fourth Test he ran through the Australians' second innings with 6/51 in a single spell. On the second day, the Sydney crowd rioted again – not against the wrong 'un but against rain delays. Warner now had 'those Ashes', and not even Trumble's poetic sign-off in Melbourne – a hat-trick with his last three balls in Test cricket – could dampen Marylebone's satisfaction.

Arguments over money were always worst in times of prosperity. The bigger the cake, the bigger the fight. In 1903–04, the combined Test match audience of 313,284, paying a gate of £12,441, exceeded all precedents (if not squaring Marylebone's ledger – the club lost £1500 on the tour, in accordance with a business plan drawn up by rank amateurs).

For the fifth Test in Melbourne, an administrative mix-up between the VCA and MCC caused Gregory and Armstrong both to be named 12th man. Wardill apologised to Gregory and sent him a cheque of £8/18/- to cover his expenses. Gregory returned the cheque and said he was entitled to the full £25 fee for playing.

The Australian players didn't care whether they were designated amateur or professional. They just wanted their money. Armstrong claimed £18 from the VCA for expenses in 1902–03. It offered him £12, so he turned 'professional', earning £5 per game in 1903–04 and 1904–05. Bill Howell, a farmer, played for nothing for NSW but asked for £15 to travel to Adelaide. The NSWCA said it could only pay if he called himself a professional. Howell, according to Darling, 'did not care what they called him, but he expected to receive the money, so they paid him the £15 and called him a "professional"'.

What the players didn't know was that this designation would be turned, legalistically, into a stick to beat them with.

A new breed of administrators was laying the ground for another assault on player power. McElhone now ruled the NSWCA, along with A.W. Green, the treasurer and no fan of player power. 'There were some players who felt that they should rule,' he later wrote, 'and that men who gave up night after night should take a back seat.' Their man in the VCA was Ernie Bean, a workaholic public servant whose great strength, similar to McElhone's, was an unstinting ambition to organise his association into a force that would govern cricket and break the players' and the Melbourne Cricket Club's hold over the cash cow, the tours to England.

At a conference in July 1904 Bean and the VCA formed a new club cricket structure: from now, players would have to play for the district in which they lived. This seems an innocent enough reform, and had been achieved in Sydney and Adelaide in the 1890s. But the real motive was to break up Melbourne's powerful clique of stars drawn from outside its area. Emasculating Melbourne, indeed, was the rule's target.

McElhone was also at the conference. He was involved in a fight with the SCG Trustees, who had bypassed the NSWCA in 1903–04 and shared their gate receipts with Marylebone. Seeing a new post-Federation wave of national sporting bodies – in cycling, athletics, tennis and the Olympic sports – McElhone figured that the future belonged to whichever group could first organise itself into a representative national coalition. Melbourne was still a private club with no ambitions beyond helping the players run their own tours and controlling big cricket and other entertainments at the MCG. McElhone tried to outflank Melbourne by joining the VCA's Bean in approaching Queensland and Tasmania to form a successor body to the ACC.

McElhone and Bean did not trust Creswell, who went a long way back with the key players. Although Creswell clashed with Giffen from time to time, he was close to the Adelaide players' clique led by Darling and Hill.

Only in November 1904 did Creswell hear about the NSWCA-VCA-Queensland-Tasmania discussions. The SACA was outside the loop, which suited McElhone and Bean. Yet if they were hiding things from the SACA, how could they claim to truly represent Australia?

The other business of the July 1904 conference was a circular from Marylebone, promising a 'warm welcome' for an Australian Eleven in 1905. McElhone and Bean knew that Wardill was on two months' sick leave when the letter arrived. McElhone pounced on the circular, construing it as an 'invitation'. He figured that if he could raise £1500, he could organise and own the tour. He replied to Lord's, presumptuously 'accepting' the 'invitation'.

When Wardill returned from leave, he assumed the Melbourne Cricket Club and the players would organise the tour as usual, and got to work with Darling and Frank Laver, whose business skills would make him an ideal player-manager. To Wardill's great surprise, the VCA asked for help in raising £500 for the tour McElhone and Bean were trying to arrange. Wardill refused, of course, and after Darling spoke to Creswell the SACA decided not to raise the £500 McElhone had asked for.

Now that the SACA was not involved, the McElhone-Bean plan was exposed in London for what it was — an act of pre-emption and presumption, what Darling called 'a grab for power'. The tour was 'a matter for the players and I don't see that it concerns the associations at all. The England trip is a financial speculation on the part of the players ... If they lose money on the trip, the associations will not recoup them. The players have as much right to appoint their own manager as I have to appoint a manager of my business.'

Darling and the players did not want the money McElhone was raising. They were quite happy with what they could get as an advance from Wardill, which they would, on past form, repay very quickly.

Harry Hedley, the influential columnist 'Mid On' in the *Leader*, attacked McElhone and Bean: 'Why the associations should construe [the Marylebone letter] as a special invitation to themselves is hard to understand. In fact, it was not an invitation to anybody, and to put it forward as an excuse for attempting to upset arrangements under which Australian cricket has become world famous during a period extending over twenty-six years is paltry and absurd ... The two associations may continue to say that they will "finance" the team, but they cannot force upon its members an advance of money which they have not asked for, which they do not require and which they decline to accept.'

In England, MacLaren offered support in the *Daily Chronicle*: 'It is a pity that the NSWCA frequently opposed the Melbourne Cricket Club, which has always managed affairs satisfactorily. It is possible that a thoroughly representative board can be formed, but doubtful if its control would be any improvement on what players have already done, their mistakes being few and far between.'

The senior players were happy with the status quo. As in Murdoch's time, going to England was their only hope of making any kind of reward from a game that took up most of their lives and deprived them of preferment in their jobs.

But the opposition was better organised. On 13 December, Bob McLeod, a former Test player and sole dissident on the Melbourne Cricket Club committee, told a meeting: 'Cricket should not be in the hand of two or three players. The money was required for the game, not the players. The trouble did not come from the players but from those wanting to make mischief. The association controlled cricket all the year round and now it was told it had nothing to do with it.'

Darling had his doubts about whether the administrators had the 'game' at heart. He saw the formation of a Board of Control as a grab for the profits Melbourne had made on the Stoddart, MacLaren and Warner tours of Australia as well as the outbound tours. The NSWCA and VCA, he said, 'wanted the plums ... by a lot of underhand scheming ...'

The *Bulletin* – the workers' friend in everything but cricket – rejoined the fray on the same side as 20 years earlier, ridiculing Hill as 'beefy and bingy' and better 'for the task of roller, instead of player'. The Melbourne *Herald*'s columnist 'Old Cricketer' added his (pseudonymous) voice: 'Three potent, grave and dignified tribunals set at nought by half a dozen wilful cricketers. What is to be done?'

What was to be done, immediately, was that the Melbourne Cricket Club and the players organised their tour to England. The selectors were Darling, Noble and, in a nod to the anti-Melbourne forces, Bob McLeod. They picked a team of established stars and three first-timers: two South Australians, reserve wicketkeeper Phil Newland, whose work at best was ordinary, and batsman Algy Gehrs, and Sydney's Tibby Cotter, who had promised in his debut against Warner's MCC to replace Ernie Jones as a genuine spearhead. Laver would go as manager and treasurer as well as player, and Bill Ferguson would pay his own way as scorer and baggage man. A 24-year-old clerk, Ferguson worked in 'one of the most monotonous occupations known to man'. He longed to travel, and heard that the Australian team of 1905 was looking for a baggage master and scorer. A formal application 'could so easily be lost amongst the piles of correspondence', and he had no qualifications, so he thought of an approach that was 'more subtle, even though it might be, and in fact was, more painful'. He went to see Noble as a patient – there were no extractions but 'I bought enough gold fillings to last me a lifetime'. Through Noble he met Trumper and Laver and asked for the job. From New Zealand, Laver sent a letter on 3 February inviting Ferguson to join them at a wage of £2 a week plus train fares. 'We hold to ourselves the right to dispense with your services at any time upon giving you a week's notice.' Fergie bought his fare for £17 on the SS *Suevic* and met the team in England. He would remain in the role for Australian teams – also moonlighting for England and South Africa – until the 1950s, and, for good measure, his sister, Elizabeth, became Noble's wife in 1914.

The well-performed Saunders was omitted from the tour, probably because the selectors feared English umpires would call him for throwing. 'Mid On' in the *Age* condemned this: 'In paying deference to these threats, the Australians are showing a lack of backbone which is humiliating to themselves and extremely unfair to Saunders.' Armstrong, meanwhile, was one of the last chosen. Though he had a good 1904–05 summer with the bat, his cynicism with the ball disturbed Noble, a captain who took a stronger stand against leg-theory than Darling. In the Sheffield Shield game in Melbourne, Armstrong had reverted to leg-theory to contain Reg Duff. Armstrong's former Victorian teammate Elliott Monfries said, 'My word, Armstrong, you've got a hide bowling stuff like that to Reg with only two men on the off.'

Armstrong snapped: 'Well, did he hit me?'

He won the argument, but Noble was not amused.

'A THOUSAND PITIES'

H aving lost their gambit to steal the tour from the players and Melbourne, McElhone and Bean were far from discouraged. McElhone reprimanded Noble, who was the NSWCA nominee on the selection panel, for snubbing its efforts to organise the tour. It was the beginning of a sustained personal attack.

While the Australian Eleven were travelling to England via New Zealand, Fiji, Canada and the USA, McElhone tried to ambush them. Unable to seize the tour *to* England, he turned to tours *from* England. In January, at the NSWCA offices in Sydney, delegates drafted a constitution for an 'Australian Board of Control for International Cricket'. On 21 February, the NSWCA wrote to Marylebone saying the new Board of Control (BOC) would manage England's tours to Australia. A confused MCC secretary, Francis Lacey, notified Wardill, saying he didn't understand the Board's letter. Wasn't the Melbourne Cricket Club the body that represented Australian cricket, and hadn't it done so successfully, in harness with the state associations, in 1903–04? A furious Wardill wired Lacey: 'Does your Club propose sending next team Australia if not this Club will do so & wish your assistance Board Control not endorsed by this Club or South Australian Association.'

But Lord's was beginning to get cold feet about becoming involved in murky antipodean politics. Sitting on the fence, Lacey replied: 'Don't understand, please write fully.'

Wardill and McElhone both wrote to Lord's contesting each other's claim to invite an MCC team. Wardill suggested Lacey ignore representations from the Board, which, as it did not include the SACA, had no legitimacy as a national body. Wardill deputed a Melbourne committeeman, Major Thomas Morkham, to smooth things over with Lord's, while the Board used Lord Jersey, an MCC committeeman, as its lobbyist. The Australian players made statements that they would stick together and with Melbourne. From Auckland, Hill wired Wardill: 'Australian players will stick to the Melbourne club if they bring out a team. Each one said certainly they would. Have spoken to all the fellows and every one is very much against the associations.' Three days later the Melbourne committee voted to secede from the VCA.

On 26 April the team arrived at Liverpool, where Darling, who had skipped the Pacific tour, joined them. They voted him captain, with Noble as deputy and Hill the third selector. This would be the last time they could freely exercise their most cherished democratic power.

Ten days later, while the Australians were distracted by their first match – against the Grace-led Gentlemen at Crystal Palace – McElhone staged another backroom coup. In the Board's first conference, at Wesley College, Melbourne, he hardened its constitution. The January document had said the Board aimed to 'control, regulate and if necessary finance' tours to and from England. Now McElhone took out the words 'if necessary'. The Board now designated itself not an optional but a mandatory controller of the tours. The earlier constitution also allowed for player representation on the Board. This was interesting; some thought the ACC had failed because it did not consult the players enough, while others thought it failed because it consulted them too

348

much. McElhone was of the latter persuasion, and now he forced through the explicit exclusion of players from the Board. Finally, in case his intent wasn't clear, he changed the constitution so that the players could not appoint their tour manager without the Board's approval.

The Melbourne Cricket Club and the SACA withdrew from the conference. In England, Darling referred to McElhone's clique as the 'freeloaders who appear at New South Wales matches'. Ever since he had seen their snouts in the trough in 1894–95, he had never liked the 'so-called legislators'. In the Sydney Test of 1901–02, he had banned them from the dressing room. 'McElhone and some leading notoriety seekers were present with some other "dead head" friends, who had rushed the afternoon tea provided for the players. The waiters were very busy with this crowd when we arrived, so much so that we could not get a look in even sideways.' Darling had to commandeer the tea urn. 'I made it very clear that the tea was for the players, and as the public expected the players to return to the field promptly they had to be served first and the rest could wait, as they had all the afternoon in which to enjoy their tea.'

The committeemen also took the players' seats in the pavilion; 'what we objected to was the lack of decency and courtesy shown by these "dead heads" in not getting up and leaving our enclosure so that the players who were tired could have a much earned rest and watch the game in comfort.'

Darling had refused to toss in the Test match until a man was put on the dressing room door keeping the committeemen out.

'This was like a bombshell to the New South Wales Cricket Association "dead heads" who were debarred from even entering our room let alone bringing their friends in and usurping our seats,' Darling said. 'At first, they tried to defy us, but when I told them that we players insisted on having control of our dressing room and players' reserve, and that, if our demands were not agreed to, the Test match would not start, and I would not even toss with MacLaren until we got what every reasonable thinking man must admit was our rights, they grudgingly put a man on the door.'

McElhone's hope, in 1905, was that Darling would be too occupied leading the tour to contest the Board's grab for power. The Australians won all seven of their matches before the first Test, the highlights being Laver's 12 wickets against Oxford and Armstrong's belligerent 248 against the Gentlemen at Lord's, the morning after the team had accepted Nellie Melba's invitation to see her in *La Traviata* at Covent Garden, where they gave her a signed bat and a bouquet in the shape of cricket stumps.

Darling was more tolerant of bigwigs coming into the dressing room at Lord's. Laver told of the future prime minister Arthur Balfour coming in 'and while shaking hands with some of our team, the wearing apparel was very scanty. One gave his right hand to Mr Balfour whilst he held his trousers up with his left. Another had one leg in his trousers and the other out. Others were drying themselves after a bath without even that much covering.'

The Australians were again becoming as famous as the teams of the early 1880s, with all the complications that celebrity entailed. Laver wrote that Duff 'received hotel accounts and letters from landlords who had been imposed upon by a person passing himself off as Duff. Prior to our arrival in Bath, one man pretended he was Gehrs.' Trumper, meanwhile, received a letter from a woman asking why he hadn't met her when the team left for New Zealand. A newspaper said: 'It is very possible that this was not a joke played upon Trumper by his friends, but it is quite on the cards that the epistle really came from a heart-broken girl, who had met some young man who had told her he was Victor Trumper.'

Female attention was not unusual. At Canterbury Week, Laver said, 'Ladies of title, and their daughters and friends, spoke to one of our side whenever he went near enough to them in the outfield. Some made eyes; others smiled. Two beautiful daughters of one of the Peers of England waited, after the game was over, to have a few words with two of the

Eleven ... From one of the most prominent young ladies at the match, one of us received a characteristic letter enclosing her photo; and this was not the only letter of the kind that reached us. Taking it all in all it was a unique and pleasing experience.'

There were limits, however, to how far Darling's Australians would go to parlay their celebrity into profit. For instance, their contract levied a fine of £100 on players who corresponded for any newspaper. 'The proprietors of one newspaper were so anxious to get articles on the game by one of our members that they offered to pay this amount if one fine would cover a series of articles by that member,' said Laver, but none broke the rule. When English players wrote for papers, he said, 'it struck us as being questionable'. Such differences are a reminder that the Australian Elevens were not necessarily more avaricious than their opponents, and were unwilling to compromise their unity for the sake of lucre.

Ferguson, meanwhile, was finding plenty to do. During the match at Worcester, he had to rush back to the hotel to rouse the middle-order after an early collapse. He also had to contend with Hill's wife Florrie, who kept scorebooks which disagreed with his own. Ferguson was keenly aware of the politics of the team's entourage. He was very fond of Trumper's wife, less so of Mesdames Hill and Newlands, as he felt that they ostracised Annie Trumper. 'Maybe they thought Vic's wife did not measure up to their class socially, yet she was worth the pair of them, as far as I was concerned.'

Without intending it, the English team would weaken the Australians' industrial bargaining power.

Redressing the error they had made in 1899, the English selectors made Jackson captain. MacLaren felt rejected, but on the morning of the first Test Jackson took him out to the Trent Bridge marl for a pitch inspection and consulted him throughout the season. The leadership change brought out the best in both men.

Barnes was again rejected, though Fry said he remained 'the best bowler in England'. But with Bosanquet spinning confusion and Jackson at his peak, England had enough bowling.

Australia kept on terms in the first phase, thanks to Laver's probing and persistent 7/64. But when MacLaren and Hayward took control in the second innings, Armstrong, with Darling's consent if not orders, bowled ball after ball down the leg-side with only one man on the off. The audience of 19,000 booed Armstrong so noisily that he often stopped to wait for silence, which only stirred them more. He bowled 52 overs and took 1/67. MacLaren, according to Laver, showed his displeasure, 'kicking at the balls [when on strike] and sitting on his bat when Hayward was receiving Armstrong at the other end'.

While *The Times* offered a bland 'the policy is much to be regretted in the interests of the game', *Cricket* lamented a retreat from what was thought to be the essential Australian spirit: 'It has always been counted as one of the greatest points in favour of the Australians that they never despair, no matter how much the game may seem to be going against them. It would be a thousand pities if they were to lose the reputation which they have so deservedly gained as a team of fighters.'

But Philip Trevor in the *Daily Mail* supported Armstrong, instead blaming the English batsmen's lack of initiative and rounding on 'those people ill-mannered enough' to boo Armstrong.

Trumper ricked his back in Australia's first innings and in the second, according to Altham, he 'left the dressing-room supported by two of his colleagues, in an heroic effort to reach the crease, but he could get no farther than the pavilion gate'.

Australia, thoroughly outplayed, grumbled about the fairness of Bosanquet's googlies and the playability of the light. Darling, stung by the reaction to his condonement of Armstrong's leg-theory, decided not to appeal against the light and save the game. When a wicket fell on the last afternoon, the not-out batsman Charlie McLeod 'ran to the pavilion and signalled,' observed Fry from under George Parr's tree. 'The big brown moustache of Joe Darling emerged. There was a consultation at the gate. Joe Darling surveyed the quarters of the sky as a farmer would, then shook his head, slowly indeed, but not without emphasis, turned his broad back, and went in.'

Fry considered 'it certain that the umpires would have stopped play, and Australia would have drawn the match. Joe Darling was a sportsman of the best. We had by that time morally won the game, and Joe Darling was not the man to slide out on a side-issue. And, mark you, McLeod need not have discussed the question; he could have appealed himself, but he, too felt disinclined to escape on an appeal when his side was beaten on the play. Would that happen nowadays?'

England won – 'We all admired and liked the Australians of those days,' Fry said, 'but, by Jove! we did like beating them,' – yet Australia regained some prestige by taking their defeat fairly and not squirming out with a light appeal.

Darling might have had other things on his mind. He went to Lord's with Noble, Hill and Laver to lobby Harris, Warner and Jackson against McElhone's Board. Darling did not object to a board per se. He favoured a central authority if the players had board seats and could 'appoint their own manager and … arrange and control everything in connection with [the tours], same as they are now doing'. The current Board was, of course, hostile to those ideas, and Darling was able to persuade Lord's to have nothing to do with it. Laver wrote: 'It was agreed that the Australian Board of Control as then constituted was unsatisfactory, and did not represent the true interests of all parties concerned, and until it did the Marylebone Cricket Club felt they could not recognise it.' Marylebone would welcome any Australian visitors 'under the same conditions as have existed in the past, if the teams were representative of Australian cricket'.

In Sydney, the editor of the *Referee*, John Corbett Davis, had previously supported the players in their disputes with administrators.

Now he switched sides. Armstrong's biographer Gideon Haigh suggests Davis was influenced by McElhone, a former schoolmate at St Aloysius College in Sydney, and certainly Davis's arguments had a legalistic, McElhone-like ring. He wrote that Lord's should not deal with Darling and the players because Lord's was run on the principle that professionals could have no 'legislative rights'. It is curious to think that an Australian should appeal to the anachronistic snobbery against professionals that Australian teams had done so much to alleviate. The legalism of the argument hints at why McElhone had been so eager to designate Bill Howell a 'professional', even though Howell was a full-time farmer and had no regular cricket position or income.

Meanwhile, rain saved Australia at Lord's, though Darling would contend that poor umpiring stopped Australia winning both there and at Headingley. The truth was that Darling, Noble, Hill and Trumper were out of form, and the bowling had not compensated for the loss of Trumble, Saunders and Jones. Cotter tried to scare the batsmen, Jones-style, but in Sydney J.C. Davis found another excuse to berate the players: 'I hope we shall see no more of the monstrous style of bowling adopted by Cotter. Deliberately to pitch halfway down the wicket, with no other object than to frighten the batsmen by making the ball go over their heads, is emphatically not cricket.'

Davis was not quite accurate: Cotter's offence had been to lose control and bowl beamers, not bouncers. At Crystal Palace, an attempted yorker had hit Grace above the heart. Darling said Grace was furious, calling the ball 'unfair and unsportsmanlike'. In the final Test at the Oval, Cotter beamed a spluttering Jackson.

More reprehensible was Armstrong's regular reversion to leg-theory at Lord's and Headingley. Fry, who at Repton had been taught, 'If one hit the ball in an unexpected direction on the on side, intentionally or otherwise, one apologised to the bowler', said Armstrong's bowling was 'bound to make cricket dull for the spectators'. Armstrong was 'rather angry' with Fry, but soon the worst fears were being realised, as county sides were copying it. Darling and Armstrong contended that England's Len Braund had started it in Australia in 1901–02. Darling wrote that English crowds 'jeered Armstrong every ball he bowled for over half an hour. Yet, when Braund bowled the same theory in England, they cheered him.'

Headingley saw Armstrong's worst excess, 51 overs of unchanged leg-theory. Altham said Tyldesley ran 'away to leg and forc[ed] the leg-ball through the gaps on the off-side'. Jackson also adapted, scoring 144 not out. But nobody was happy with it. Leslie Poidevin wrote in the *Referee* that Armstrong's methods 'have aroused the ire and indignation of many crowds, have inspired the phlegmatic members of the press box to endless sarcastic sallies and condemnatory passages. The player-critics have branded them as uncricketlike.' The MCC began discussing prohibiting leg-theory, but the tactic faded after 1905, only to be revived 27 years later in a new and violent mutation. Darling distinguished his tactic from Douglas Jardine's, saying that in order to make Cotter bowl at the off-stump and not at the batsmen's bodies, Darling never gave him more than two men on the leg-side. If he'd given him a leg-theory field, 'my 1905 Australian Eleven would have been hooted out of England and deservedly so'.

Perhaps most poignant was leg-theory's effect on young watchers. A.A. Thomson was taken to the Headingley Test as a boy. He remembered Armstrong 'bowling practically at the square-leg umpire' while McLeod 'discharged the ball more or less in the direction of point'. The crowd, 'a large number of angry Leeds "loiners" [a term for Leeds locals], wanted to know the reason why.'

It was obvious why: Australia were being battered, and a draw was the best they could hope for.

The Golden Age was meant to be a highpoint of sportsmanship, but the truth was more complicated, and more modern. Darling, while condoning leg-theory, would not brook intimidation of umpires by excessive appealing. Laver spoke of meeting an American baseball captain who claimed a fair hit when he knew the ball was a foul. 'Baseball is my business,' the American said, 'and if I can get any points in my favour, I will do so even if I have to tell lies or cheat for it; the umpire is there to look after his part of the transaction.' Laver commented: 'At first glance it might seem there is truth in his remarks — that the umpire is there to look after his part of the transaction; but that does not justify anyone trying to mislead the umpire by making untrue statements. Liars are a scourge to sport and society, and should not be tolerated. Silent deceivers are almost as bad, if not quite as bad, and to be the willing instrument by which others deceive is the same.' In 100 years, nothing, apparently, has changed.

Injury and illness did no favours to a weakening Australian side. Kelly broke a hand, Laver had to play bandaged-up and Gregory became a virtual passenger after injuring himself in Scotland. Hopkins had to be stitched up after cutting himself in a bathroom, and, said Laver, 'both teams suffered through eating pigeon pie'.

The Australians' fielding was unprecedentedly poor. Gregory had lost his pre-eminence as a cover fielder and Armstrong was a disaster in slips, dropping catch after catch, particularly off Noble. It got to the point where Darling moved him out of the position but Armstrong kept trying to sneak back. In one game, Cotter was bowling, and as the left-right batting combination caused a change in the field, Armstrong crept back into the cordon. Cotter began running in, but Hill, noticing Armstrong from mid-off, waved his arms and shouted, 'Hey!'

Cotter stopped. Hill pointed at Armstrong and called to Darling, 'He's there again, Joe!'

Darling said, 'Come out of that,' and a sheepish Armstrong left the cordon.

One reason cricketers are superstitious is that the game has always carried a pre-industrial flavour. The refusal to cover pitches, giving the weather gods a decisive hand, cohered with an agrarian mindset: what will be, will be. In 1902 the weather had consistently favoured Darling's team. In 1905 it decided against them. Jackson won every toss and it only seemed to rain before Australia batted. At Old Trafford, England and the weather beat Australia, just as Australia and the weather had beaten England three years earlier.

In the fourth Test, Darling's 73 was his last significant innings; he was weeks from retirement. So too was Jackson, whose second century was propelling him to an all-round tally – 492 runs and 13 wickets – almost in the Giffen–Grace league. Darling and Jackson were born on the same day, 21 November 1870. They were quintessential Golden Age cricketers, bound for big things in life outside the sport.

There was an elegiac feel to the final matches. At Bournemouth and Hastings, Grace played Australia for the last time. Aged 57, he scored 2, 22 and 2.

Although beaten 2–0 in the Tests, Darling's Eleven was not going gently into the night. Fed up with losing toss after toss to Jackson, in the Scarborough Festival match Darling appeared stripped to the waist, offering a wrestle for first innings. Jackson accepted – as long as the rugged George Hirst could stand in for him. Jackson ended up tossing a coin, and didn't even look at it landing. He knew he'd win, and he did. During the game, though, Darling was still playing for keeps. Jackson got a favourable decision on a run-out appeal, and Darling said: 'This was bad enough, but what disgusted all of us was the fact that Jackson turned to the umpire who was standing at square leg and told him it was a good decision.' So much for festivities.

The 1905 Australians would never shake the stigma of leg-theory. Sydney Pardon wrote: 'The motive was clear enough, Darling's object being to avoid at all costs the risk of losing the rubber while there remained a chance of winning it. It was, however, contrary to all the traditions of Australian bowling to play simply for safety, and the prestige of the team unquestionably suffered.'

One interesting footnote to the discussion about negative cricket came from Laver, who presented a visionary solution:

'It must be acknowledged that the length of time cricket takes in this age of progress and bustle is far too great. The pruning knife should be applied to curtail it as much as possible without affecting the main interest and sportsmanship of the game. I shall not be surprised if, one day, a rule is brought into force abolishing the second innings altogether. Football, baseball, lacrosse, and nearly all national games are decided on two or three hours' play. These games have a great advantage over cricket for that very reason. Life is too short for long contests.'

Laver was evidently a man who saw into the future. He was about to find himself under assault by those who wanted to consign him to the past.

'DEAD HEADS' RULE

Financially, the 1905 tour was a return to clover for the players. Laver had been a popular, hard-working manager, and the team had repaid its float from the Melbourne Cricket Club as early as 21 June. A happy day arrived at the tour's conclusion, when, on gross takings of £15,000, Laver announced a distribution of £900 per man.

But the 2–0 Test defeat and Darling's retirement harmed the players' prestige. Wardill had hoped to invite an English team to follow the Australians in 1905–06, but by August he abandoned the plan, 'although had our fellows done better in the Tests, there might have been a chance'.

Many in Australia were cheering Darling's team down. The *Town & Country Journal*'s 'Stumps' columnist wrote that their defeat was good for cricket. 'Had the 1905 team been successful, it was quite on the cards that future elevens would again be selected on the same "mutual admiration society" lines.'

The closed shop of the Australian Eleven, as its critics saw it, was under full-frontal attack. The VCA's end-of-year report condemned 'the irresponsible system which has hitherto obtained in the control, management and selection of Australian teams visiting England', and called for central control. McElhone accepted Queensland's application to join the Board, and promised it a Test match on the next England tour. He would keep winning Queensland's vote by stringing it along with this promise. Queensland eventually got its Test match – in 1928.

Wardill was playing a double game. While tentatively seeking peace with the Board and considering its offer of a seat at the directors' table, Melbourne was covertly signing up Australian players for a Test series against England in 1906–07.

Darling heard about this plan while playing for South Australia against Victoria in Adelaide. 'I called a meeting of the leading South Australian and Victorian players and it was decided that if the leading players in New South Wales were also willing to sign a letter asking the Melbourne Cricket Club to bring out an English team, we would all bind ourselves to play for Australia, if we were selected.'

That match was played from 11–15 November 1905. The ship was leaky; a week later McElhone heard that NSW's Test players might be signing contracts with Melbourne. The NSWCA warned Melbourne that if it brought out an England team, it would not be welcome in NSW, and NSW players would not be permitted to play. Melbourne eventually drew up a schedule that cut NSW out of an England tour. The proposed Test matches would be played in Perth, Adelaide, Melbourne, and, in cooperation with the New Zealand Cricket Association, where Melbourne was sending a team in 1905–06, Christchurch.

Even if no games would be played in Sydney, 11 NSW stars were prepared to play for Australia – the Test players Noble, Trumper, Duff, Carter, Cotter and Hopkins, and emerging talent 'Sunny Jim' Mackay, Austin Diamond, George Garnsey, Jack O'Connor and the Reverend Ernest Waddy. Mackay was making his name as the heir to Trumper and Hill, scoring 902 runs at 112.75, his five centuries highlighted by a 203 against Queensland and a 194, in a partnership of 268 with Noble (who scored 281), against Victoria. The NSW group represented Australian cricket's past, present and future.

McElhone went to war, suspending the NSW signatories immediately. The NSWCA's secretary Percy Bowden, described by Jack Pollard as 'a corpulent, companionable man who played the tambourine at a Sydney bicycle club on minstrel nights, and an administrator who never acted without his committee's instructions', was McElhone's hatchet man. Bowden said the players 'entered into the agreement with their eyes open with the express intention of defying the government body in this state'. Once the contracts became public knowledge, the *Sydney Mail* said 'there will be a hard fight and the Board of Control will stand or fall by the result'.

Darling said the Board was targeting individuals, including himself. Bean and McElhone, he said, 'openly boasted that they would not be satisfied until they drove out of the game all the players who had signed that letter'. In a speech to the SACA, Darling said the players 'have pledged to stand or fall together. If New South Wales disqualify their players, the players in other states will stand by their colleagues. If an English team comes out to the present Board of Control, the Australian players will not play against it. The Marylebone Cricket Club knows that.'

Even non-signatories would stand by the banned stars, as one anonymous player confirmed to the *Australasian Star*: 'Do you think I would play to the detriment of those who have been suspended? I would be the worst sort of black leg.'

The subsequent strife is a fascinating and seldom-told story. Haigh says that what happened in 1906 'is rivalled in importance perhaps only by the World Series Cricket breakaway of 1977, which in a sense was merely an outcome of the board hegemony established seventy-one years earlier', and that the infamous fistfight and boycott of 1912 were only 'aftershocks' from 1906.

In the autumn of 1906, events moved quickly. The Board had everything at stake: if the players and Melbourne organised an England tour to Australia, the Board would be as irrelevant as the defunct ACC.

The SACA's Creswell, looking for a compromise, wrote to McElhone on 19 April asking the Board to reinstate the words 'if necessary' to its constitution. It must never be overlooked that control of the finances of a tour to England was the great prize. If the Board came in as an underwriter of that tour, as the Melbourne Cricket Club had been, rather than its promoter and controller, only providing finance 'if necessary', the players would recognise its authority. But McElhone rejected Creswell's request. He wanted one almighty battle.

On 1 May, Wardill told the Board that the Melbourne Cricket Club was withdrawing from the VCA and therefore rejecting its proposed Board seat. South Melbourne and Richmond also pulled out of the VCA, and Wardill proposed an alternative club competition, the Victorian League of Cricket.

Lord's had been watching closely. Three days later, Francis Lacey declined the Board's invitation to tour 'until the Board is truly representative of Australian cricket'. Wardill immediately announced that a joint 'representative' authority of the Melbourne Cricket Club, the SACA, the WACA and the players was inviting England to send a team, and wrote to the SCG Trust asking to reserve dates for Test matches in 1906–07.

McElhone summoned the NSW players one by one to demand they repudiate their contracts with Melbourne. Bowden said simply: 'It's either the association or eleven players who are going to run this show.'

An interesting footnote to the meetings is that Trumper, Cotter and Hopkins could not attend, as they were conducting a tour of regional Queensland with the theatre entrepreneur J.C. Williamson. This tour angered both the NSWCA and QCA, but pleased country Queensland associations who felt they had been snubbed by Brisbane. The tour's success unnerved McElhone, who thought he had Queensland in his pocket.

With the exception of Waddy, the summoned NSW players stuck to their contracts. An anonymous player told the *Australasian Star* he was happy 'the climax has come at last ... They simply run us for all they are worth. It is the first-class men who put the association in the position they are today. Through the efficiency of the players, we hold a position in the front rank of the world's cricket, yet we find the association ready to turn and rend us limb from limb at the slightest provocation.'

The press took the Board's side. The *Sydney Morning Herald* opined: 'Professionalism may kill cricket unless the public firmly impresses upon our players that the game is not played for their sake, and that, as important as the players of today may be, there are more important matters still in the future of our great national game.'

McElhone's friend, J.C. Davis, agreed. 'It is ridiculous that Australian cricket can be controlled by one club and that club the Melbourne club.'

The argument was virtually the same as in 1884–85, only now the stakes were higher, the game was more developed, and the administrators were considerably more determined and organised. When Darling spoke, he could have been channelling Murdoch. He agreed that a central board was desirable 'provided the Board does not interfere in the financing of Australian teams to England. The cricketers have initiated these trips and taken all the risks. They have done all the work in connection with them, and hard work it is, too ... Many ruin their prospects of business advancement and when their days are done they have no situations to fall back on. Trips to England to a certain extent tend to unsettle a man, and no employer can put in a responsible position a man who is always wanting to get away to play cricket.'

Right up to the present day, the Board has claimed to stand for the broader interests of the game, whereas the players have been portrayed as only standing for themselves. But in 1906, the board and associations were more or less broke, and had no record of tending to the welfare of the grassroots. They were seeking authority based on trust. But they were hard men to trust. In 1905 Darling described how the players saw them: 'To some of these notoriety seekers, being a delegate to the Board of Control is one of the finest advertisements any young lawyer or business man could get. First of all he gets a big cheap advertisement out of it. He is brought in touch with the highest and wealthiest men in the land ... he and his friends revel in all the cigars and drinks they want, not at their own expense, but out of the general expenses of the match. If anyone had seen half as much as I have seen they would be thunderstruck at the amount of money that is expended on entertaining ... Yet the players now in England are compelled to pay their own motor or cab hire to the ground.'

McElhone decided to take his argument to the public, and to London. He gave the *Sydney Morning Herald* an interview in which he said Lord's didn't understand that the Melbourne Cricket Club was not an Australian counterpart of Marylebone. Melbourne didn't govern Australian cricket, he said. The Board of Control did. Moreover, the Board 'have not the slightest intention of interfering with the profits of an Australian Eleven in England, but they insist on the whole of the monies going through the hands of the board and being divided by that body among all the players entitled to share in its distribution.'

This was a big statement: the Board didn't want the players' money, but it didn't trust the players to manage it. McElhone repeated the undertaking in a letter to Creswell. As later arrangements made clear, this was an outright lie – McElhone's Board did want the money as well as a hand in managing it – but in 1906 he was trying to win a public relations battle. He touched on a sensitive nerve when he went on to imply that cronyism guided tour selections: 'matters other than the cricketing capabilities and the personal stability of players are taken into consideration'.

McElhone's was a voice for those who felt they had been closed out of the Australian Eleven's little club; a voice for the embittered. McElhone's key informant in this was the Victorian opening batsman

Peter McAlister, who carried a deep grudge for his non-selection on the 1905 tour. Only rarely did McAlister's form warrant his consideration for an Australian team, and it certainly hadn't in 1904–05, when he had scored 150 first-class runs at 18.75. He had spread one story that his East Melbourne clubmate and friend Laver had betrayed him by voting against his inclusion, and another that Noble offered him a place on the 1905 tour provided that he would only accept a half-share in the profits. This fed the conspiracy theories harboured by every player who thought he'd been unfairly left out of one of the lucrative tours, and McElhone pounced. Not only were the Australian Elevens greedy and mercenary, he said, but nepotistic. McElhone's views were encapsulated by *The Times* in London, which turned on the Australian players, saying 'money has governed the arrangements of every trip. Men have been chosen on condition they accept half instead of full shares in the prospective profits. Last trip, one man went for little more than his steamer fare and there is strong suspicion that another purchased his place as a certainty by agreeing to forgo £200 of his prospective share. It is time that the extreme politeness of English sportsmen should come to an end, and that Australian professionalism should be taken for what it is.'

Laver denied voting against McAlister in 1905; indeed, after that tour he wrote that a batsman of McAlister's steadiness would have been an asset. Noble denied he had ever offered McAlister a place, half- or full-pay. Darling was quick to respond to the *Times* article, writing: 'Not only is it wrong about the 1905 Eleven, but it is also wrong for previous tours I have made.' Laver also wrote to *The Times* saying 'all shared alike' on the 1905 tour.

No support came forward for McElhone's and McAlister's insinuations. No players from forty years of touring said they had bought their way into a tour or been ripped off by an unequal share. The only players known to have received any less than an equal profit share in 12 tours were Alick Bannerman, who had taken flat fees as a professional cricketer, and the wicketkeepers Jim Kelly and Alf Johns, who in 1896 had agreed to divide their portion as an alternative to one of them not going.

But McElhone was fully on the attack. On 10 May 1906 he wrote to the SCG Trust, citing the Supreme Court case he had conducted, demanding the use of the SCG on every Saturday from October 1906 to April 1907, plus several midweek dates.

On 14 May he called a special meeting of the NSWCA. Noble, who attended as a delegate of the Paddington club, spoke against McElhone, drawing attention to the real issue.

'In the past, the teams that went to England had an absolutely free hand in the making of their arrangements. Now the New South Wales Association came along with all its forces and said to the players: "We no longer want you to manage your own affairs. You have to clear out. We are going to do it for you."'

McElhone replied, to the applause of club administrators, 'The players should realise that the game is not being played for their benefit.'

The motion to ban the 10 NSW players was carried. Cotter, Trumper and Hopkins were banned when they returned from Queensland. The bans were applied by grade clubs too, except for Paddington, which said the NSWCA's actions were motivated by 'a personal hatred shown to Mr Noble'. But when the NSWCA said it would expel Paddington, Noble and Trumper stepped down voluntarily from their club.

Noble, Trumper, Duff and Cotter, greats of the Golden Age, were banned from cricket. J.C. Davis affected melancholy, writing, 'This is the saddest business one has ever known in Australian cricket.' But the Board would not win through appeals to sentiment. It had a strategy.

Part of that plan was to denigrate the players. The *Australasian Star* reported a 'prominent Australian batsman' denying 'that cricket and drink were in any way associated. "We have heard very frequently," he said, "that certain prominent cricketers are addicted to drink. It is unfortunate that some members of the public will persist in making these statements about men who get into prominence in any game or any walk of life.'" It was true that Duff died of alcoholism at 33, Armstrong carried whiskey in his bag, Noble carried lumps of sugar in the belief that they absorbed alcohol if dissolved in a drink, and just about every prominent cricketer except the teetotal Trumper enjoyed at least a tipple. It was also true, as the 'prominent Australian batsman' responded, that in those times you could say the same about men in any walk of life.

More materially, the Board had an ace up its sleeve.

Melbourne's point of weakness was its stewardship of the Melbourne Cricket Ground. It did not own or legally control the ground, but it ploughed hundreds of thousands of pounds into its renovation and maintenance, managed the venue, and governed it through appointments to the MCG Trust. But in 1906, the Victorian Premier, the eponymous Thomas Bent, appointed six new Metropolitan Cricket Ground Trustees to outnumber the MCC's three. The Prime Minister, Alfred Deakin, called Bent 'the most brazen, untrustworthy intriguer who the Victorian assembly had ever known'. The Victorian government might not have been directly in league with McElhone and Bean, but it played into their hands when the new chairman of the MCG Trust, James Mackey, granted the VCA's request for dates for two Test matches in 1906–07.

Even though the request and its grant were absurd – the VCA was not part of any body bringing an England team to Australia – the Melbourne Cricket Club's soft spot had been found. If it lost control of the ground, it was done as a club, financially and in every other way.

Faced with expulsion from cricket, Noble was also weakening. On 23 June he cabled Wardill saying release from the contracts might 'pave way settlement'.

Creswell, meanwhile, cut to the chase. Having read McElhone's promise 'not to interfere' with finances on the overseas tours, Creswell asked Bean if the Board could clarify what it meant in its constitution by 'financing'.

Bean and McElhone drafted a clarification to placate the SACA and the players: 'The Board shall see that all profits from the tour be distributed equally between the members of the team. The Board has no intention of interfering in any way with the profits earned by the players on the tour.'

This was the clincher. It was also a lie. But Creswell – wanting, like all involved, an end to the brawl – took the bait. His reward was three Board seats for South Australia, creating an imbalance that would hamper the governance of Australian cricket for the next century. Wardill was upset, but the Board offered directorships to Melbourne, McElhone lifted the NSW suspensions, and Bean withdrew the VCA's request for the MCG. Effectively, all McElhone was doing was withdrawing the threats and punishments he had made in the previous month, in return for which he wanted Wardill and Creswell to take back their invitation to Lord's to tour in 1906–07.

They did. Melbourne also disbanded the Victorian Cricketers' League. 'The Board had won,' Haigh concludes. 'Indeed, it had won overwhelmingly; the extent of its victory was not yet clear.' The agreement 'ended at a stroke forty years of cricket tours to Australia backed by private interests ... The position of the players was likewise never the same – the board, once it eclipsed the Melbourne Cricket Club, dictated from a position of strength.'

On 28 July 1906, the SACA joined the Board, albeit provocatively naming Darling as one of its three delegates.

In victory, McElhone and Bean showed no graciousness, a quality beyond their ken. An anonymous Board delegate told the *Australasian Star*: 'We have been flouted, our authority has been ignored. Now when we look like coming out on top, why should we turn to them the other cheek? The players will have to pay the price of their actions.'

The rebel NSW players had to wait another two months before the bans were lifted. Even then, the 10 were precluded from holding any office before July 1909. Noble said that after the players' concessions, 'it is disappointing that the association did not see fit to meet us half way.' He applied for a position as a NSW selector for the next four seasons, and was, each time, the only nominee who did not get a vote from the committee.

The VCA, meanwhile, fined its three recalcitrant clubs and pressed ahead with district cricket. Melbourne, which had no electoral district, would participate as an 'extra club' playing whoever had a bye. Wardill seemed to lose heart for his job, and would retire in 1911. Over the remaining six years of his life, he could well have toyed with some Board names on which he might have practised the marksmanship which had once made him part of the Australian rifle team.

For the moment, the Board's victory was comprehensive but Pyrrhic. It sent a letter to Lord's, inviting England to tour under the Board's auspices in 1906–07. Marylebone replied that it was now too late, and would wait another year.

'CASH HUNTING
IS OBNOXIOUS'

W hile Australian tours to England had always been the golden fleece of cricket, English tours to Australia had struggled to make money. The sheer mass of cricket that could be played over an English summer, and the consistent inability of England to send its best team to Australia, meant that Test series in Australia remained the poor relation. After all the brawling in Australia, Lord's was in no mood for charity. For the 1907–08 tour, it asked for a £10,000 guarantee.

On 5 April 1907, McElhone wrote to the Board's member associations requesting the funds. The SACA and QCA delegations, arriving at Young and Jacksons Hotel in Melbourne on 19 April, were surprised to find that McElhone and Bean had already cabled Lord's agreeing to the massive guarantee. Melbourne's representative on the Board, Edward Mitchell KC, challenged the legality of an agent, the Board, binding its principals, the associations. He said, 'Bean then got very angry' and betrayed a 'childlike ignorance of business and legal affairs' before backing down.

The MCC was coming, but would the Board have a team to set against it? Trumper played only twice during 1906–07, possibly bruised by the brawling. During the winter he would become founding treasurer of the New South Wales Rugby League, a body establishing professionalism with more success than the cricketers. Of the NSWCA, he said, 'I won't crawl to them, especially as their object seems to be to heap every indignity on us.'

The brightest new talent in Australian cricket had walked out in disillusionment. Sunny Jim Mackay accepted an offer to play in South Africa, and the young man most likened to Trumper was lost. In the Transvaal he worked in a diamond mine and suffered an eye injury when hit by a motorcylist. He returned to coach in Melbourne in 1908 but never repeated his *annus mirabilis* of 1905–06.

Armstrong spent the 1906/07 summer fighting Bean and the VCA. The flashpoint was when he told them he could not get time off from his job at the Department of Home Affairs for a match against South Australia, only for the VCA to go to the Department to check whether Armstrong was telling the truth. In a disciplinary hearing with the VCA, he said, 'The players nowadays seem to be treated like a bunch of schoolboys, and they are getting full up with it. If it goes on, there is no knowing what will happen'. At the end of the season he left the public service to follow a new business career as a stock and station agent. It was reported that he would retire from cricket. Bean, Armstrong's sworn enemy, said: 'Once upon a time, players put the game first and money afterwards. Now it is just the opposite.' It is hard to imagine what 'once upon a time' he had in mind.

Noble, meanwhile, tried to make the best of the situation and obtain a seat on the Board. The NSWCA lifted its ban on the rebels holding office, but his nomination for a board position was voted down in humiliating fashion. Charles Lloyd, the vice-president of the NSWCA, said Noble's very nomination was 'a question of taste' and 'a menace to the good government of cricket'. Noble saw that the past wasn't going to be buried, and that vendettas would be pursued.

The Board and NSWCA weren't above acts of generosity when it suited them, however. Syd Gregory, who had been bankrupted when a partner in his sportsgoods store embezzled funds, was given a benefit, as were Jim Kelly and, in early 1909, Noble. But as would soon become clear, these gifts came with strings attached.

By 9 August 1907, the Board was busy doing what it thought a board should do. It set out the Sheffield Shield timetable, nominated a panel of umpires, and set up a fund for the distribution of profits, if any, from England's tour. It discussed a visit from a Fijian team, but McElhone and Bean objected, as they thought it would violate the White Australia Policy.

Eleven days later, McElhone wrote to the associations saying the Fiji tour was now on. He wouldn't explain what had changed his mind, but when Melbourne had found out about his objections, it offered to arrange the tour.

When the Board next met, Darling asked for the 9 August minutes to be read. McElhone objected but was voted down. When McElhone read them, the minutes indicated that he had always supported the Fiji tour. Darling said: 'The minutes were faked as the Board had definitely turned down the application. McElhone, the secretary, had voiced his opinion against a team of black fellows visiting White Australia, and yet contrary to the Board's decision, he recorded the Board's approval in its minutes.'

Compared with the tectonic changes taking place from 1905 to 1912, the on-field action seems almost incidental.

The MCC team of 1907–08, under Arthur Jones, played a record 18 first-class fixtures as the Board scrambled to recoup its £10,000.

The English team was far from its strongest. Jackson, Warner and Fry were unavailable, and MacLaren, Hayward, Hirst, Tyldesley and Lilley pulled out after selection. As usual, Lord's did all it could to avoid choosing Sydney Barnes, but after Hirst's withdrawal a deficit in bowlers was noticed and he was issued an invitation. Since quitting Lancashire, Barnes had guided Staffordshire to two good seasons, including their first minor counties championship in 1906, when he took 99 wickets in 10 matches at 8.41 and averaged better than 23 with the bat. Noble said Barnes was 'the best bowler in the world at the present day' after he took 6/24 against NSW.

The Englishmen had a rocky start, from the day their steamer pulled into Fremantle and a rough-looking fellow rowed out to them taunting them with 'Five to one on Australia! Any odds you like, England for the Tests!' Thus did they reacquaint themselves with Ernie Jones. Going into the first Test match, in Sydney, Arthur Jones caught pneumonia and was hospitalised. The captaincy went to Irish-born opening batsman Fred Fane, and a batting place went to George Gunn, Billy's nephew, who had come to Australia to rehabilitate his health following a haemorrhage of the lungs and also to check on sales of the family's Gunn & Moore bats.

The Australian stars were back in the fold, with one telling addition. Victoria's 38-year-old opening batsman McAlister, faithful servant of the VCA and the main rival to Armstrong for the state's captaincy, had been appointed by the Board as one of the three Test selectors, alongside Clem Hill and Frank Iredale, who had retired from playing but was carving out a career as a bureaucrat in McElhone's NSWCA. Presumably with Iredale's help, McAlister talked his way into the Test team. The Noble-Armstrong-Trumper-Hill clique thought he was a Board spy, and he did nothing to justify his self-selection, scoring 155 runs in eight innings.

McElhone was able to stage a Test series, but such was his appetite for a fight, it was a close-run thing. Under financial pressure due to the excessive guarantee he had promised Marylebone, McElhone refused to give the SCG Trustees the standard 18 per cent of gate receipts they asked for a Sydney Test match. He said that he would move the Test to the Sydney University ground, but his bluff was called when the University Senate said the applause would upset the professors. He had to back down and pay the SCG Trustees their asking rate.

Most Australian players shared Darling's contempt for the NSWCA 'dead heads', and on the first day of the series Trumper pinned to the dressing-room door a list of those permitted to enter. McElhone, whose name was not on the list, tore it down. Trumper refused to go onto the field after lunch, and the game was held up for 15 minutes until the sign was restored.

The following day, *The Age* reported the incident, but McElhone disputed its account. Trumper wrote to *The Age*: 'The players' room has always, so far as we can remember, been reserved for them and their immediate friends. Otherwise the position would be intolerable, because, if not, men could not even dress or speak with necessary privacy. The list in question was posted on the players' door by the decision of the team, and it was restored at the instigation of Mr McElhone only when he saw that the team was determined to insist upon it. Therefore, your report is correct.'

During the match, the press reported that Trumper and Noble appeared worn down and distracted by the squabbles. Neither champion was at his best, but the game provided one of Test cricket's closest finishes. Gunn made a wonderful 119 and 74 in his first Test, his delight in a military band playing selections from Gilbert and Sullivan while he was batting causing Jim Kelly to remark from behind the stumps, 'Hey, George, you seem to be taking more notice of the band than of our bowling.' Australia stumbled to 5/95 in search of 275 in the fourth innings. As McAlister – his 41 being his best innings for Australia – Hanson Carter, 61, and Tibby Cotter staged a quixotic recovery, Fane only gave Wilfred Rhodes seven overs on a drying wicket. When Hill later asked Rhodes why he was playing at all, Rhodes said, 'I'm in, I suppose, for my singing, Clem.'

Australia were still 56 runs short when Cotter was joined by fellow bunny Gerry Hazlitt. They swished and slashed, keeping out 'Pip' Fielder and the great Barnes, getting Australia home with two wickets to spare before an unduly pessimistic crowd of 3364.

Trumper and Noble scored centuries in the Boxing Day match with Victoria, but peace was elusive. This time Armstrong was on the outer, having stood down from the Victorian team because the VCA did not accept his expenses claim. The VCA attacked him in print for his 'greed', and the Melbourne *Herald* labelled him a shamateur. The *Argus* stated the obvious: cricketers 'are not quite sure whether they are professional purveyors of amusement, or sportsmen who love athletic victory for its own sake.' Bean, backed by McAlister, moved that Armstrong be suspended from state and therefore Test cricket, but other VCA members, recognising Armstrong's service and fearing the inevitable public backlash if he was sacked from a Test match, accepted his apology when he said he had not known his claim was exceeding the maximum expenses allowance.

England had omitted Surrey's Jack Hobbs from the first Test, and the young professional, on his first tour, was devastated. A fine 77 against Victoria won him his Test debut, and his 83 set him off on a career that no Englishman has ever matched. The Test was another cliff-hanger. Noble bounced back to form with twin 60s, Kent's Kenneth Hutchings scored 126, Barnes, Jack Crawford and Cotter got among the wickets, and this time it was England's fourth-innings pursuit that achieved an unlikely win. Chasing 282, they were given no hope at 8/209. Barnes and keeper Joe Humphrey got them to 243, and then Barnes and Fielder edged them closer. The former could hold a bat in a manner suggesting he knew what to do with it, and Fielder would score a first-class hundred for Kent, batting number 11 and adding a record 235 for the last wicket with Frank Woolley against Worcestershire. The burly Kent fast man probably considered himself on a lucky streak: a few days earlier, he, Joe

Hardstaff and Rhodes had avoided prison time, being fined £1 each in the Melbourne Magistrates Court for behaving unlawfully at the Old White Hart Hotel.

With one run to win, and Armstrong bowling leg-theory, Barnes got his body on the leg-side of the ball and pushed what should have been an easy single to cover. Fielder, however, was daydreaming at the other end. Hazlitt had the ball before Fielder had started running. Barnes said that had Hazlitt 'kept his head and just lobbed it to the wicketkeeper, Fielder would have been out by yards. Instead, however, he had a wild shy at the sticks, missed and the match was over ... Pip kept on running flat out and my last view was of him disappearing into the crowd around the pavilion. Had not the pavilion been in the way I think he would have finished up in England and been the first to bear the good news.'

Adelaide's heat debilitated both teams the next week, the temperature reaching 40°C-plus on the last three days. Australia appeared destined to lose when they conceded a first-innings lead and Hill came down with influenza. The game had a rustic feel: Creswell had just been fined in the magistrates' court for allowing his sheep to graze on the pitch next to the Adelaide Oval, and Queensland woolbroker Roger Hartigan was playing his first Test with only four days' leave from his employer. On the fourth day he requested an extension 'as I am still batting'. His employer cabled back, 'Stay as long as you are making runs.'

Hartigan would make 116 in a 243-run stand for the eighth wicket, in even time, with the ailing Hill. The papers called him 'Clement 'Ill'' and he had to pull away from the crease repeatedly to throw up. But the partnership broke England's hearts, and Australia would win the match by 245 runs.

The Englishmen went to Tasmania for two games and some cooler weather, and maybe a bit extra — a Launceston newspaper reported that the dashing local wicketkeeper Norman 'Joker' Dodds had a 'peccadillo' with a 'boon companion' in the English team. The veiled comment has often wrongly been concluded to hint at a sexual encounter; the most reliable evidence suggests the two players bent the elbow too freely. Meanwhile, the Victorians continued quarrelling, with Armstrong and Laver rebelling against McAlister's captaincy in the Shield match in Sydney. Incensed at the punishment Armstrong had been levied at Christmas, the players decided to depose McAlister by staging a vote for Armstrong. The clash, according to VCA official Mat Ellis, almost 'led to blows over the captaincy'. Armstrong, with a full head of steam, scored a century in the match and another in the fourth Test at Melbourne, his first in a Test against England, as Australia won by 308 runs. England's resolve had been broken by the Hill-Hartigan stand in the Adelaide furnace, and although Gunn, Hobbs, Barnes and Crawford were outstanding, the normally dependable slow bowlers Rhodes (seven wickets at 60 apiece) and Braund (five at 92) could not match the general strength of the Australian bowling, led by Saunders.

Altham notes that the series was closer than the 4–I result suggests. In three Tests England 'played up to a point so well as to have much the better of the argument, [but] each time they allowed the game to slip from their fingers in face of the indomitable fight put up by Australia'. The icing on the cake, for the fighting Australians, was Trumper's overdue return to form with a sublime 166 in the fifth Test in Sydney.

McElhone's battle to win control of the tour had many costs, the most tangible being a deficit of £2598. He complained about player payments to the Australians, which, at £25 a Test plus expenses, came to £2387. 'It is very evident that in all future Tours these and others expenses must be considerably reduced, otherwise serious financial difficulties will have to be contended to the detriment of the Game,' he said ominously. The Queensland, Tasmanian and West Australian associations were annoyed at receiving none of the promised 'profits'; the NSW, Victorian and

South Australian delegates were uneasy about how they would balance their books after they paid, pro rata, the shortfall to Lord's. If one of McElhone's claims to power was financial responsibility, it had just been blown.

The showdown was coming, as the 1909 tour of England would be the first since the Board's establishment. McElhone saw his chance to raise the funds he needed. In the lead-up to 1908–09, he began his press campaign, briefing his mouthpieces at the *Bulletin*. On 17 September, the magazine reported:

'"The Players", those indefinite wraiths that have haunted Australian cricket like a nightmare for the past two years, are making their last effort to keep Australian tours on a boodle basis. Hitherto the Australian XI has gone to England practically on its own, and whatever money was made was divided among the players according to their own sweet will. That the men did not share equally is well known, and that they shared according to the value of their play is doubtful. Weird stories are told of young players going "on terms", which meant they were squeezed, and only got a show on the team on the understanding that they took a sum below what was due them on a fair and equal division of profits. Certain individuals who considered themselves the salt of the expedition demanded special rates, and got them ... Cash hunting is obnoxious. The Board was created to control international campaigns ... the Board of Control must take charge of the coming expeditions ... The players are all allegedly amateurs.'

Darling, a Board member but brave enough to stick to his principles, took up the fight, making a speech extolling the SACA on 28 September: 'If other Associations had treated the players so well we would not be seeing the problems that are now existing in NSW.'

The *Bulletin* returned fire, saying the NSWCA had 'treated the crowd Darling represents with lavish generosity' and the players 'ought to get down on their marrowbones and worship it'.

A month later, McElhone gave the first firm indication that he was reneging on his promise not to interfere in tour finances. He told London's *Cricket* magazine: 'To adequately control the game, the Board must control the players, and unless it takes charge of the finances it cannot succeed in that direction. The claims made by the players for expenses etc are such that international cricket is, to all intents and purposes, practically run, not for the benefit of the game, but for the financial benefit of the players.'

Everyone knew this was the crux of the matter, but in 1906 McElhone had only been able to make peace with the players, Melbourne and the SACA by promising not to 'take charge of the finances' on overseas tours. Creswell, seeing what was happening, went to the Board's meeting in December 1908 with a motion confirming that the 1909 tour would be conducted 'under the usual arrangements'. There was a long silence before McElhone announced that the Board wanted 10 per cent of profits from the tour.

He was out in the open now. Having paid too much for the 1907–08 England tour, and lost his battle with the SCG Trust to get more revenue out of matches there, he had to reach into cricket's big honeypot, laying bare his duplicity to everyone involved with the game.

Creswell did not have the numbers to defeat McElhone at the Board table, with Bean's Victorians and the ever-gullible Queenslanders forming a solid majority with NSW. After some discussion, however, the Board said it would collect all revenue from the 1909 tour, retain 5 per cent of the first £6000 and 12.5 per cent of the remainder, and distribute the rest equally among the players. The players would be offered an alternative: an upfront flat fee of £400 plus expenses.

After the announcement, the *Argus* interviewed Noble and Hill. They said they would not accept the offer. Noble said: 'The terms are not good enough. The calculations are based altogether too high for the takings of a tour, and by the time all expenses and the Board's percentages are paid, there will be nothing like a fair recompense to a man who has to take the risk of leaving his business for several months.'

In most cricket disputes, the employer could appeal to some higher principle of justice and split the players into factions. Normally, this takes the form of pointing out to the rank and file that their militant leaders have been ripping them off. If the 'weird stories' of players being treated unequally were true, the Board might have split the cricketers. But they were not true, and the players remained united. On Boxing Day, Noble invited the leading Victorian and NSW players to a meeting at the Port Phillip Club Hotel. Afterwards, Noble said: 'We all believe that a Board of Control is necessary in Australia. I have voiced this sentiment in Sydney many, many a time, and they didn't believe me when I said that the Melbourne Cricket Club should not control cricket in Australia.' But, he said, the present Board 'is going beyond its powers when it now interferes to such an unjustifiable extent in the earnings of the cricketers in England.' He said the Board's demanded cut was tantamount to taking three extra players who did nothing. A grim Cotter said, 'If there is a wet season, we may have to work our passage back.'

The meeting at the Port Phillip Club Hotel was held during the visit of the New South Wales side for the Sheffield Shield match. The home captain, McAlister, was not invited. He had again been spreading the story that Noble had offered him a place on the 1905 team for a half-share. Noble said: 'Every cricketer knows, or should know, that I am strongly opposed to anything of the kind.'

Another reason for McAlister's and McElhone's resentment, which now amounted almost to a hatred, of the Australian Eleven was the 1905 publication of Laver's book, *An Australian Cricketer on Tour*. Detailing the 1899 and 1905 excursions, Laver told lively stories about the exotic and exciting places the team visited and the great times they had. McAlister boiled over his exclusion from these adventures. McElhone seethed over Laver's descriptions of the cordial relations between the team and the King's sons, Princes Edward and Albert. Laver's happy birthday message to Edward in 1905 'threw the little Prince into absolute ecstasies of delight', said the *Daily Express*, and the Prince of Wales asked his father to stage a private game with the Australians. It looked to McElhone as if these cricketers were acquiring airs beyond their station.

If the players were not already annoyed by the Board's demand to dip into their finances, they were incensed by its appointment of McAlister as tour 'treasurer'. The players would still be able to appoint their 'manager', as per the Board's constitution, but he would be weakened by being made accountable to McAlister, and therefore to the Board. It was a transparent move to circumvent the players' insistence on having their own manager. Noble said it 'seems very much like appointing a Grand Inquisitor, seeing we are allowed to appoint a manager whose duties are to look after the finance'.

So naked were McElhone's manoeuvres that he might have been trying to provoke the leading players into a boycott. The Board was ready for that contingency, one member complacently telling the *Australasian*: 'We have them beaten. We would like very much to get the best men as players, but if we cannot get them we will get the best we can. The Board of Control is no longer going to exist in name only.'

Yet nobody knew what the Board was going to do with the money it planned to seize from the players. Creswell couldn't get McElhone to answer that question at its December 1908 meeting. Armstrong, 'disgusted' that the Board was backtracking on the 1906 settlement, said: 'We should have a little idea where the money is going.' The truth was that the money was going to backfill McElhone's inept financing in the previous 12 months.

Tommy Horan – who had been on the other side of the argument in 1884 – was now with the players.

'Australian players in the last thirty years have done immense service to advertising Australia ... If the Board could advance any sound argument in favour of taking away from the Australian team a large share of the proceeds of the tour, the Board might get the support of reasonable men. So far not a solitary sound reason has been put forward for levying this extortionate, and therefore the sympathy of the public is entirely with the players.'

On New Year's Day 1909, at the end of the Shield game, the national selectors met. The Board had appointed two friendlies, McAlister and Iredale. The third was Hill, who had replaced Darling as the SACA's representative when the former captain had retired to Tasmania with no little dismay at the way things had gone.

The selectors' first meeting sorted out the 'certainties' – Hill, Noble, Armstrong, Trumper, Vernon Ransford and, in a sop to the QCA, Hartigan.

Noble and the leading players asked for a meeting with McElhone. He took a week to respond, then said no. Finally a summit was arranged in Sydney on 14 January 1909. McElhone reasserted that the tour manager had to be accountable to the Board. He made a provocative claim that past managers had made 'defalcations', against which the Board now had to protect itself to look after its legal liability. The players couldn't believe what they were hearing. Evidently, when he talked about what past managers 'may have got away with', he was alluding to Laver.

His tactical coup was to ask the players to prove that the Board's terms were less fair than on previous tours. The players could not produce documentary records to support their case. The tour was, after all, a speculative venture. Compared with the 1893 tour's dividend, the Board was offering a good deal. Compared with 1905, it was not. The players did not know what they would earn from the tour, but they wanted control. The meeting heated up, McElhone accusing Noble of untrustworthiness, a gross affront to the Australian captain who, perhaps more than any cricketer of the era, embodied the principles of honour and discipline.

McElhone was skilled, however, at PR. Having attacked the Australian captain, banning him from NSW and now saying he couldn't trust him, McElhone drew attention to the benefit match the NSWCA had put on for Noble in March 1908. Was the Australian captain so ungrateful as to bite the hand that had fed him?

McElhone was aiming to decapitate the head, and while he could not yet take out Noble he had a victory on 23 January when Hill said he would not tour under the terms dictated. Hill, the biggest-scoring and arguably best Australian batsman of the Golden Age, would never tour under the Board's control.

On 5 February the remaining 'certainties' chose Laver as manager/player. Noble considered him still good enough to perform a useful onfield role when needed, and he had the players' trust. But the appointment was a provocation to McAlister. The Board left Laver out of the two tour trials, considering him a 'past' player. The falling-out between the two East Melburnians had turned toxic.

The final selections, made on 15 February, were contentious. An easy one was the textbook Sydney left-hander Warren Bardsley, whose 264 in the Melbourne trial was unanswerable. But Hill was stunned when Iredale and McAlister proposed Syd Gregory, well past his best, Bert Hopkins, whose £200 fee was paid by the Board, plus the Board-friendly Victorian wicketkeeper William Carkeek, known universally as 'Barlow' for his stonewalling ... and *McAlister*.

Hill could not believe it. McAlister, who would turn 40 during the tour, was a proven failure at the top level. He was to be tolerated as treasurer only because the players had been outflanked. Now they had to stand him as a player. Hill said Tasmania's Dodds and South Australia's Gehrs had better records and, obviously, greater potential. But Iredale and McAlister let him blow himself out and would not be swayed. Hill said he was 'washing his hands of the entire affair' and 'did not consider that the best men had been chosen'.

McAlister went from the meeting to a dinner thrown by his friends. In his grateful speech he said, 'It has been my ambition to get into the

Australian team. I have been fighting for years to get this trip and no-one has had to fight harder than I have.'

He wasn't wrong there. Once the team was submitted, the Board arrogated to itself a right to appoint Noble as captain and McAlister, by a 6–5 vote, as vice-captain. As tour selectors it appointed Noble, McAlister and Gregory – constantly in dire financial straits and now owing his place to the Board's intervention.

'NOT A HAPPY FAMILY'

This most controversial team left Sydney on the SS *Orontes* on 17 March. Laver offered McAlister a make-up handshake before leaving, which McAlister repudiated. 'Mid On' in the *Leader* saw through the farewell banquets and pious speeches: 'Little bands of small-minded sycophants may prattle their nonsense in bar parlours and send-offs and spout sentimental drivel ad nauseam, but for the first time an Australian team is about to leave for England with no public confidence.'

Because there was no trust between players and Board, Laver was immediately obstructed. Tickets and contracts were not ready, a 'bridging loan' still had to be organised to float the team over its first weeks in England, and there were even quarrels over the letterhead on the stationery he would use. Nothing was too petty for the Board, which decided to pair players randomly in their cabins and hotel rooms, obviously to stop anti-Board cliques, and refused the customary cash advances for players to buy their kit.

Contracts were finally produced, but Armstrong and Trumper were among those who refused to sign. Haigh, in his biography of Armstrong, writes that the bickering came down to one transcendent question: 'For whom were the players playing? McAlister would have said for the board; its secretary had negotiated the tour, its selectors had picked the party, its members had appointed him treasurer. Laver would have said for themselves: they were playing the cricket, they were sharing the profits, they had elected him manager.'

Of perhaps greater political significance was that on 24 March John Creswell collapsed and died, aged 50. His broad range of interests and positions throughout the community had gained him the title 'Adelaide's busiest man'. He was the senior and best Australian cricket administrator; and having been through the wars of the 1880s, he was also the most experienced. He was a crucial counterweight to McElhone and Bean, and now he was gone.

When Creswell died, the team was at sea squabbling with McAlister over the bridging loan. Laver, having decided he did not want to be beholden to the Board, borrowed £300 pounds on his own account. But McElhone didn't want to be disadvantaged, so he advanced his own money to the team's London agent, Leslie Poidevin, who foisted it upon Laver when the *Orontes* arrived.

Noble had made his own plans to regain control of the tour. Once the team arrived in London, he called for a player vote on the leadership. McAlister objected, saying the Board had already appointed the captain and vice-captain. But Noble said legitimacy rested with the players' will, not the Board's. He was voted captain unanimously.

Unsurprisingly, the cricket started in poor fashion. Australia lost to Surrey and the MCC, albeit by narrow margins, in the lead-up to the first Test at Edgbaston. Altham summarises the English mood: 'Though Australia had beaten us by four games to one [in 1907–08], it was felt that the margin of difference between the sides was not such as to suggest that they were likely to hold our full strength at home, especially on rain-affected wickets. By the end of May 1909 this estimate seemed justified.'

McAlister was overlooked for the first three matches, and Iredale, in Australia, opposed Noble's plans to draft Laver into the playing roster. After six matches, Noble picked Laver anyway. It would turn out to be the sweetest of masterstrokes.

To the Australians' surprise, England's selection panel of Lord Hawke, H.D.G Leveson-Gower and Charles Fry could find no place – or appetite – for Barnes, who, the week of the first Test, took 21 wickets for 65 runs in three Staffordshire League matches. Hawke was holidaying in Aix-les-Bains, leaving the selection to the two current players. The logical choice as captain, Jackson, stood aside due to what Fry called 'diplomatic difficulties', and MacLaren, now 37, was drafted in, despite having been ill and out of cricket. 'I have not much good to say of our meetings,' Fry wrote. 'To begin with, Archie MacLaren was not playing cricket regularly, and he was not his true self.' When it came to picking an opening batsman, for instance, MacLaren opposed Hobbs, as he had never seen him play.

Edgbaston provided a poor wicket, on which Hirst and the exquisite left-arm spin of Colin Blythe dismissed Australia for 74. Armstrong's 5/27 – Noble had convinced him to give up leg-theory – kept Australia in the match until Hirst and Blythe again shared all the wickets, leaving the home side 105 to win. For England's second innings, Fry persuaded MacLaren to let him and Hobbs open. Both had made ducks in the first innings and Fry wanted to 'bustle for our pairs of spectacles. After sucking his pencil Archie agreed.'

Bat dominated ball for the only time in the match. Fry called himself 'a spectator at the other crease' watching Hobbs play 'as great an innings as I ever saw played by any batsman in any Test match, or any other match'. It was the only time he saw the equal of Ranji. 'Hobbs, on the difficult wicket, took complete charge of the good Australian bowling, carted it to every point of the compass, and never made the shred of a mistake.'

Australia, noticeably weaker than in 1905, divided and unhappy, seemed ripe for disaster. Instead, they would not lose another match in three months. For this, some rate Noble's 1909 tourists as the best Eleven of all.

In a move characteristic of Hawke's selection panels, England made five changes to their winning team. Fry was out, having to attend to a legal case as a barrister, but Jessop, Rhodes, Thompson and Blythe were omitted for John King (who was to make 60 in his only Test), Hayward, Albert Relf and Schofield Haigh. Home Gordon wrote that the selection prompted 'universal and profound disgust'. In the Australian camp, Noble agreed with Armstrong 'that if we could not beat the team we had better sell our kits'.

Even MacLaren himself, in an astonishing interview with the *Daily Dispatch*, capitulated: 'We have a bad batting side; in fact it is the worst batting team that England has had for many years. I foresaw the trouble. I did not want to be the captain. My cricket career is coming to a close and I realised that these Tests would not do my reputation as a leader any good. However, I have had to play in spite of my personal wishes. We must make the best of the situation, but it is not wise to make sweeping alterations unless we have better young men. Where are they?'

One possibility was Surrey's dashing all-rounder Jack Crawford. But Leveson-Gower, his county captain, quarrelled with him after refusing to select a full-strength county team to play Australia, and would not choose him for England. Crawford would move, for his cricket, to the saner climes of South Australia.

At Lord's Noble sent England in, and Australia gained the advantage with a maiden 143 not out from Vernon Ransford. Armstrong's 6/35 to cripple England's second innings was a revelation, not because he could renounce negativity but because he might have been the first Australian to bowl wrong' uns in England. *The Times* said he 'at times got the off-spin with the leg-break action'. Others said it was more like a topspinner. In *Wisden*, Sydney Pardon wrote: 'Again and again he made the ball do enough to beat the bat, and once or twice, unless I am mistaken, he varied his leg breaks by turning a little the reverse way.' The English weren't expecting it and Australia won by nine wickets.

MacLaren, who had scored 36 runs in three innings, offered to resign but Lord's kept him on, perhaps as a fall-guy. For the third Test at Headingley, Fry was back from court, Rhodes and Jessop were recalled, and the Lancastrians Walter Brearley and John Sharp came in; out went King, Gunn (after 1 and 0 in what was to be his only home Test), Jones, Relf and Haigh. At the very last moment, under some pressure, Hawke consented to choosing Barnes for his first home Test match since 1902.

In a low-scoring match the master took seven wickets, but it was an unhappy affair for England. Jessop tore muscles in his back while throwing. Hobbs was given not out when he trod on his wicket while setting off on a run, and the Australians, particularly Armstrong, got nasty. Two balls later Hobbs, very upset, let one go and it bowled him. 'I still bear this incident in mind against Armstrong,' he said three decades later.

As England settled in, Noble said to Macartney: 'You go on and get them out and I'll bowl at the other end to keep the runs down.' Noble bowled 13 inexpensive overs and Macartney took 7/58 with his slow left-armers. England capitulated again to Macartney, and also Cotter, in the second innings, giving Australia a 126-run win. Macartney's match figures of 11/85 prompted Fry to say, 'This redoubtable little cricketer was afterwards so prodigiously successful a batsman that we are liable to forget his bowling, which made him one of the finest all-rounders ever.'

McAlister played at Lord's and Headingley, scoring 49 runs at 16.33, fulfilling all his promise as a Test opener. He had little to do as treasurer. The players would not deal with him, and it must have been a lonely tour. He was not a strong enough character to do the dirty work the Board had given him. Colonel Justin Foxton, McElhone's Queensland patsy on the Board, travelled with the team as an 'observer' and was treated with disdain, as befitted a man whose military title referred to his rank among Queensland's reservists, and who was nicknamed 'Chinese' because of his hiring preferences on his tobacco farm. McElhone was a clever man, but he had sent two of his weakest links on the tour. McAlister never bought a ledger, and in his financial capacity he did little more than 'check the turnstiles regularly'. When he deputised for Noble in tour matches, Armstrong refused to play under him. There is a photo of the 1909 team, from Laver's collection, showing the players and others in a wide-bodied rowing boat in Scotland. At the bow of the boat, on his own, half-turned to the camera, is McAlister. All the others are together towards the stern. They are a portrait of what Gilbert Jessop called them: 'Not a happy family.' McAlister is with them, but not of them. This McAlister is the man who, when the team travelled to Nottingham, was left in London without knowing they had gone. Six decades later, Board secretary Sydney Smith told David Frith that during the 1909 tour McAlister had been punched by 'an anti-Board man' in the team. A viewer of that photograph can only wonder if the palace intriguer who had worked so hard to get on a tour really believed, in the end, that it was worth it.

He had something to do after the third Test, when he and Poidevin attended the inaugural Imperial Cricket Conference at Lord's. There was discussion of a triangular series involving England, Australia and South Africa, though McElhone was not as keen on this as a South African tour of Australia, a safer way of raising money. He commenced secret negotiations with South Africa about a tour in 1910–11. He was happy with McAlister's work in England, so far, whatever that work was. Bean wrote to McAlister, saying 'you were subjected to so many unsportsmanlike attacks from sections of the Melbourne press' but 'your judgement has been subsequently vindicated by success'.

On a wet wicket at Old Trafford, Barnes and Blythe took five Australian wickets each and gave England a sniff of those Ashes, but Laver's 8/31 swung the match Australia's way. The best figures by an Australian in England for almost a century, Laver's performance was rich reward for Noble and the players, and an embarrassment to McAlister and his bosses. For the series, Laver topped the bowling averages with 14 wickets at 13.50.

Having had the better of the draw at Manchester, Australia also had a moral victory in a high-scoring stalemate at the Oval, where Bardsley became the first player to hit two centuries in a Test. Before the game he said to Ferguson, 'Bill, I am going to score two centuries in this match.' After the first innings, Ferguson asked if he would get the second, and Bardsley said, 'Certainly.' The only halter on Bardsley's run-scoring was consideration of his teammates, as Trumper reminded him when he ran him out for 219 against Essex. 'How many more did you want, Curly? Remember there are others in the side who'd like an innings.'

England was now matching Australia for zaniness, their selections, said *Wisden*, touching 'the confines of lunacy'. They chose Essex's Claude Buckenham as their fast bowler on the hard white Oval track, but MacLaren made him 12th man and opened the bowling with 37-year-old debutant googly bowler Douglas Carr. MacLaren kept Carr on for 69 overs in the match, a third more than Barnes and double anyone else, and was booed off the field in his last Test.

Having retained the Ashes, Australia were not letting up. One of England's debutants – they went through 25 players in the Tests – was the slim Kent left-hander Frank Woolley. At that time, bowlers were permitted 'trial balls' at the beginning of a spell, but the laws didn't codify how many trial balls could be bowled or how long they took. Common sense usually prevailed. But Woolley had to wait an outlandish 19 minutes for his first Test ball, as Armstrong bowled one trial ball after another. No fieldsman bothered to take them, so they had to be fetched by boys from the crowd. E.D. Sewell wrote sardonically that Armstrong was trying to learn 'how slowly he could make a bowled ball reach the screen'. More seriously, Sewell said that for the Australian player in 1909, 'cricket is nothing but a hard business proposition, and he plays it mercilessly, with not an atom to give in his demeanour, but "take all" as his motto. Which should be on the pocket of his blazer. Joe Darling's teams of 1902 and 1905 were the least saturated with this warlike spirit of playing cricket of any that I have seen, but with at least two of the others the marching orders were, quite simply: "Win – at any price!"'

That they did. They only lost four matches for the tour – three in the first month and one at the Scarborough Festival. They won 13, but drew 22. Altham said they had a fine record but 'there seemed rather a lack of distinction about the team'. Trumper's form was middling, and the best-performed batsman by a long way, with 2180 runs at 46.38, was the correct but uncharismatic Bardsley. Fry and Pardon thought England underestimated what was actually a very good Australian team; certainly the Australian newspapers thought this, spending the summer decrying the English press for 'one-sided' coverage. Pardon could not find praise high enough for Bardsley and Ransford: 'Nothing in recent cricket has been more remarkable than the fact of Australia losing two champion left handers [Darling and Hill] and at once finding two others to take their places.' Armstrong, Laver and Macartney gave great service as all-rounders. Laver's biggest contribution to the players' success was yet to come.

He skipped the last two matches and went to Germany and Italy. After two weeks' holiday in Scotland, the Australians went home in separate groups. Both of them stopped in Colombo. Noble, Hopkins, Armstrong and Cotter played in an invitation eleven on 30 October, but raised eyebrows by insisting on a fee of £10 per man. The *Times of Ceylon* reported 'we are better off without these matches altogether if they are to be regarded entirely as money making affairs'. But a week later, it was McAlister's second group of himself, Bardsley, Ransford, Carter, Carkeek and Whitty who behaved so badly – in some unexplained way – that the Board received an official complaint from the Ceylonese.

The reason the thirteenth Australians came home in two factions became clear later. Laver would report: 'It was not till towards the end of the tour that [McAlister] asked me, when by a chance remark he appeared to realise, for the first time, that he had been neglecting his duties ... something about the balance sheet, as if he took it for granted I was going to prepare it, but to his unconcealed astonishment, I informed him I wasn't going to prepare a balance sheet for the Board, as that was his duty.'

McAlister was not only perfidious and ridiculously ambitious, but weak. He had not done what he was asked, and now hoped that his old friend, now bitter enemy, would help him out of his spot. Laver showed him cheque books and bank books, but no accounts.

Both were summoned by the Board. Trumper had caused a stir, arriving home earlier than his teammates, by announcing that the tour's receipts were £13,500, minus expenses of £6000, leaving profits of £7500. Laver was asked to show his books, but he told the Board the books he had prepared were 'personal mementoes', and as McAlister was treasurer they should ask him. McAlister said Laver had refused him information, and he wasn't able to keep an adequate balance sheet. The Board finally announced that the tour grossed £13,228. It retained £1003, and the players got a total of £7359 divided equally, or £460 per man. The summer had been wet, and the Australians were treating county games with decreasing interest, reserving their strength for the Tests. Financially it was the worst result in more than a decade for the players, but it was worse for McElhone, who had forecast a gross of £18,000. He had miscalculated again; and again he would find someone else to carry the can.

THE FINAL
CONFLICT

In sports industrial disputes, administrators usually hold one unbeatable advantage. As the Chinese proverb says, 'Wait by the river long enough and you will see the corpses of your enemies float by.' No matter how popular or prestigious players are, administrators can usually afford to wait them out. The Australian stars of the Golden Age were right when they said they were the reason for cricket's popularity and wealth. But this was also their weakness. Stars fade. McElhone and Bean could simply dig in and wait for Noble and Hill and Armstrong and Trumper and the rest to retire — or better still, provoke them to quit. They saw themselves as the game's permanent government, keepers of the sacred flame of Victorian amateurism, men who would give decades of their lives to administration, by comparison with whom the players were merely a passing parade.

Taking the long view, McElhone and Bean were continuing the work of the ACC, which was continuing the NSWCA-VCA struggle against the players dating back to the 1880s. Now, as then, they were in a way proxies for England, which never liked the way Australian cricketers could come 'home' and enrich themselves, creating rifts in the settled order of amateurs and professionals.

If we follow the money, the decisive moment in the death of Australian player power was Marylebone's decision to take over England tours of Australia in 1903–04. Up to then, private promoters such as Lillywhite, Shaw and Shrewsbury and Lord Sheffield had led cricket tours of greater or lesser success, and come home lighter in the pocket. When Lord's found itself a thousand pounds poorer as a result of Warner's tour in 1903–04, they would have no more of it. After the Melbourne Cricket Club and the Australian Board slugged out local control in 1906, Marylebone determined not to lose money again. So it demanded a guarantee from McElhone in 1907–08 that was so ruinous for the Board that he had little alternative but to grab for the players' cash in 1909 and beyond. Perhaps, as the Australian players gleaned these riches from English crowds, the transfer can be seen as a repatriation of funds to the mother country. In any case, it served McElhone's ambitions, because the prize he was eyeing was not money but control.

The first of McElhone's enemies' corpses floated by on 13 January 1910, when Noble wrote to the Board that 'with the greatest regret' he was retiring from cricket. At 37, after four tours of England, he might have been ready for retirement, but he soon made it clear that he had left the game prematurely as a result of the Board's chicanery.

Harry Hedley described Noble's treatment by the Board as 'a crime and a calamity'. A sad Horan commented: 'The pity of it is that such a splendid cricketer should be lost to big cricket solely through the lack of tact and judgement on the part of those who control the game in New

South Wales. When bitter prejudice gets the better of sound judgement, we can never have fair play.'

The next enemy McElhone was able to see off was Phil Sheridan. The last of the original SCG Trustees, Sheridan, 77, died suddenly on 15 January. The previous day, McElhone's NSWCA had finally cornered the Trust into an agreement that gave the association a virtual monopoly. The VCA also sealed a long-term deal with the MCG Trust.

Laver faced constant pressure to give the Board his records from the 1909 tour. McAlister, humiliatingly, had cobbled together some financial information based on what he termed a pile of receipts 'thrown at him' by Laver. But Laver argued that his only books were private mementoes, containing photographs, notes and details of personal transactions, which he gave the players. McAlister refused to accept his own book – a cynical refusal considering the Board was willing to harass Laver out of the game for not providing documentation.

In early 1910, the Board's secretary, Colin Sinclair, accepted Laver's explanation that the books were private property. Soon after, Sinclair was replaced by a beaver-like and more biddable public servant, Sydney Smith.

The next year was relatively quiet. Charlie Turner's benefit deepened the players' dislike of the SCG's 'dead heads' – the public contributed £426 for the Terror at a shilling a head, whereas the members donated just £53, or sixpence each.

McElhone's secret talks had succeeded in luring a South African team to Australia. He couldn't afford to wait for the next England tour, and figured the South Africans would draw Ashes-sized crowds at a cheaper rate. The South Africans, however, had not come down in the last shower, and asked for a £5000 guarantee plus half of the gate. McElhone haggled them down on the guarantee and offered half the 'ground takings' – the gate receipts minus the substantial amounts collected in the grandstands – but there was some acrimony in the dealings, which were not finalised until the South African team was on the Indian Ocean.

On 3 October 1910, the VCA replaced McAlister as sole selector with the much more popular Hugh Trumble. Victoria's Board delegates Bean and Harry Rush were not happy with this, and the Board reappointed McAlister as the Victorian member of the national panel. It was unprecedented that a state's delegates to the Board voted against that state's own wishes. But it wasn't the last time; a year later, McElhone would do the same in favour of Iredale, retaining him as a national selector when he had been dumped by NSW.

At the same meeting, the Board appointed Hill as Noble's successor to the Australian captaincy. What appeared a tribute was in reality an insult. Australia's captain had always been voted for by the team, not appointed by the Board. Noble maintained this with his 'player revolt' in London in 1909. Now Hill was being made Australian captain by the Board, in the same meeting at which it rejected Noble's second application to become a selector.

The season would be a good one for the Australian stars. The googly craze had taken over cricket, and South Africa brought no fewer than four exponents. One, Aubrey Faulkner, proved a world-class star with bat and ball, but Australia won the series 4—I thanks to an Indian summer from Trumper and Hill, torrents of runs from Bardsley and Armstrong, and good back-up from the fast bowlers Cotter and Bill Whitty. In the fourth Test Australia introduced its own googly specialist, Herbert Hordern, who had learnt his cricket at North Sydney but perfected it while a dental student in North America. Hordern, nicknamed 'Ranji' for his dark complexion, had toured England in 1907 and 1908 with Pennsylvania and Philadelphia University teams. Once, in Jamaica, he took 16/86 and woke the next morning to find small boys examining his bowling hand. His 1910—11 season brought him 58 wickets at 14.84, and 14 wickets in his two Test appearances.

The saddest note was the death of Billy Murdoch. The settlement of the estate of his father-in-law, John Boyd Watson, had taken 22 years, and Murdoch was visiting Australia to complete that task and see some cricket. He was watching the fourth Test at the MCG when he predicted a South African collapse. To his surprise, they lost five wickets. Saying, 'I'll never make another prophecy again. I've brought bad luck on those boys,' he complained of a 'bad feeling' that turned into 'neuralgia'; in fact he was suffering a stroke. He lost consciousness at the ground and died at hospital. Flags flew at half-mast and his body was taken to Sussex. Few missed the symbolism in Australia's great player-leader passing away at a time like this, never fully reconciled with his homeland after the events of 1884–85.

McElhone, while a tireless strategic thinker, was a proven quantity as a bad economic manager. The South African tour was not quite the black hole that the 1907–08 England tour had been, but the receipts of £8861 went nowhere near covering the guarantee and costs, so again he had to levy his associations to make up the difference. He resolved not to let the profits from another tour to England slip through his fingers.

In the winter of 1911, McElhone positioned himself for a final assault on the players. His nemesis, Ben Wardill, retired. Melbourne reapplied to join the district competition, and the VCA again rejected them. It was even considering barring non-district players – that is, Melbourne's Armstrong and Ransford – from state eligibility.

Even after Wardill's retirement, McElhone remained paranoid about the club. Horan wrote that Melbourne had no ambition to control Australian cricket, but when trying to convinced Bean and McElhone of this, 'you might as well talk to the wall.'

McElhone became chairman of the Board, and ordered Smith to renew its demand that Laver hand over his 'accounts'. Laver thought he had already resolved this. Patiently, he offered to come to their office and answer queries. McElhone refused. At the next Board meeting, Hill suggested bringing in an independent auditor to check Laver's books.

McElhone said: 'It is not a question of books. It is a question of Mr Laver having been disloyal to the Board.'

Preparing for the season ahead, McElhone and Bean again flouted convention and their own associations' wishes. The VCA had reappointed Trumble as a selector, and the NSWCA chose Trumper. Instead of accepting these two titans, or Harry Trott and Monty Noble, who also applied, the Board reinstalled McAlister and Iredale. The well-informed Reginald Wilmot, writing as 'Old Boy' in the *Argus*, said: 'It seems extraordinary that the best two captains in Australian cricket, Messrs Noble and Trott, should have been rejected by their associations, and that the delegates on the Board appointed by their associations should vote in opposition to the wishes of those associations as voiced in the choice for state selectors.'

It is obvious, a century later, that the process was rigged. But at the time there was still an expectation of fairness and a hope that McElhone would honour the 1906 peace agreement, enshrined in the Board's own constitution. Few could believe that a prominent solicitor would act as he did. It took Darling, an outsider to Sydney and Melbourne, yet experienced in Board affairs, to provide clarity. 'Everything on the agenda for meetings was discussed privately at a prior meeting of five delegates from Victoria and New South Wales and two from Queensland, who in that period sold their votes for a secret promise of a Test match,' he said. 'Western Australia was denied even one delegate, as the ruling clique were afraid he might vote against them.' McElhone dismissed Darling's views as those of an embittered ex-director.

On the boat from England, meanwhile, was what Altham calls a team 'better balanced and better equipped at all points than any which had left our shores'. Fry, the chosen captain, couldn't leave the inns of court, but Warner stepped in with hopes of repeating his 1903–04

triumph. Australia was evidently weaker, and Warner had a full deck of champions: Hobbs, Woolley, himself and 'Young Jack' Hearne in the batting, and the bustling all-rounder Johnny Douglas, who, in case any arguments needed settling, had won the Olympic middleweight boxing gold medal in 1908 by defeating Australia's multi-skilled Snowy Baker. There was also the best new-ball attack since Richardson and Lockwood: Sydney Barnes and Frank Foster, a zippy left-armer, whose bounce and swing harried even the best batsmen.

The tour's only setback came at the beginning. Warner scored 151 against South Australia, but then, on the train trip to Melbourne, suffered a ruptured duodenal ulcer. He gave the captaincy to Douglas, who benefited from advice sessions at Warner's sickbed.

Still adjusting from losing their captain, England were unsettled in the first Test in Sydney. Trumper made a chanceless 113, young Manly doctor Roy Minnett scored 90, Hordern bamboozled the English and took 12 wickets, and Australia carried on from the previous summer. Douglas put Barnes into a funk by taking the new ball himself, and Ralph Barker describes how the master bowled at half-strength, 'scowling and sulky at what he regarded as a personal insult'.

As well as Australia performed in Sydney, though, the English spotted cracks. Foster cabled Fry that this was the only Test match England would lose.

A drizzly Melbourne on 30 December brought more predictions. Barnes was ill with a fever, and Hobbs, after a look at the flat wicket, said to fast bowler Bill Hitch, 'The side that wins the toss will win the game.' Australia won the toss.

Barnes, still furious with Douglas, was angry enough to get out of bed and accept the new ball, Barker noting that 'his whole demeanour suggest[ed] a chilling certainty that he could get the batsman out, and that he would grudge every run until he did so'.

With the first ball of the match, he bowled Bardsley. In his next four overs he removed Charles Kelleway, Hill and Armstrong. Considering the slippery ball and perfect batting wicket, it was considered the greatest spell in a Test since Spofforth. Australia were 4/11. Hitch said to Hobbs, 'Jack, we've won the match.'

What exactly was it about Barnes? Fry, the great pen-portraitist of the Golden Age, gave a great image: 'He is tall, loose-limbed, and a deliberate sort of mover, with easy hips after the manner of the African races. He takes a long loping run and swings his arm over with disengaged carelessness and consummate control. He could swerve the ball in and out, but did not much use this device. He relied on disguised changes of pace and of break, which he never overdid. His best ball was one, very nearly fast, which pitched on the leg-stump to hit the top of the off, sometimes even on a good wicket. He had the knack of making the ball rise high from the pitch. I never batted against a bowler more interesting to play.'

Dizzy from his fever, Barnes took a break. After lunch, he re-entered the attack. He had an inimitable capacity to annoy. 'His meticulous, fussy field placing irritated the crowd,' said Barker, 'and they shouted at him to get on with it, so he threw the ball down, folded his arms, and refused to bowl until the noise had subsided.'

He removed Minnett for 2, and left the rest for Foster, something of Wasim Akram with a short, accelerating run-up and rapid delivery. 'The peculiar quickness of his arm-swing,' said Fry, 'made the ball come from the pitch like lightning.'

By stumps, the momentum had swung, on the field and off. The following day, the rest day in the Test match, McElhone staged his coup. His lapdog Foxton – the Queensland Board delegate expecting a Test match in Brisbane any day now – moved that the Board appoint one of its members as a 'secretary' for the 1912 tour, for a fee of £400 paid out of the tour income.

Hill and three other directors said the appointment contravened Regulation 9 of the Board's constitution, which empowered the players to name their own manager and control their affairs. McElhone organised that the Board was appointing a 'secretary', and the players could still nominate their own 'manager', even though, as Rush chimed in helpfully, there would be no point, as the secretary's duties left nothing for a manager to do. Foxton, very possibly too slow to understand what he had done, asked if the appointment of a 'secretary' contravened Regulation 9. Rush said: 'Oh, we swept Regulation 9 away last night.'

For all its legalistic subtlety, this was the final declaration of war. McElhone was not only going to reach into the till, but he would make the till his own. Gone were his promises from 1906 that the Board had no intention of interfering with the players' finances. Laver said: 'The Board breaks its bond by doing in an underhand manner what it could not do openly. It agreed that the players should appoint the manager yet it practically ignores that agreement, for the secretary is nothing more than the manager.'

The *Sydney Morning Herald*, up to now supportive of McElhone, was appalled. The Board, it said, 'has gone about its work not quite as the impartial body it ought to be ... What is quite clear is that the representative players really have some rights left. They are not entitled, perhaps, to all the rights they once had, but as the men who call the game they cannot be wholly ignored. The public is mainly concerned with the game after all. It is only faintly concerned with the financial share of the players on tour. It does not begrudge them their due share.'

From the players' point of view, the most distressing aspect of the dispute was that they weren't out to impoverish Australian cricket. They were in favour of a central authority. What they objected to was the dishonest, underhand measures McElhone and Bean took.

McElhone's mouthpiece, the *Bulletin*, put the matter in terms that a Roman Catholic schoolboy such as he would understand: 'The Board of Control has made itself respected by proving that it holds the right end of the waddy, and intends to use it with all its might and soul if it comes to a real row.'

Meanwhile, the players were involved in the turning point of the Ashes summer. The 20-year-old 'Young' Jack Hearne scored 114, and

Hobbs, with 126 not out, steered the visitors to an eight-wicket win. Between them, Barnes and Foster dismissed 15 distracted, demoralised Australians.

The teams travelled to Adelaide, the dispute about the 'secretary' boiling. While practising for NSW's Shield match with South Australia at the Adelaide Oval, Macartney was hit on the head by a net pole. Hill cabled McAlister and Iredale, in Melbourne and Sydney, saying he would monitor Macartney's fitness until the day before the Test. He suggested that as Armstrong and Trumper were on the scene, they might help him choose the final Eleven. McAlister replied in the negative: he and Iredale retained their rights as selectors.

The day before the Test, Macartney said he was better. Hill pressed for Macartney and leg-spinner Jimmy Matthews in place of Whitty and Minnett. McAlister replied: 'My team forwarded yesterday. Still oppose Macartney's inclusion … if Iredale agrees with you favour yourself standing down not Minnett.'

Such was the uproar that followed the telegram – a former player of McAlister's credentials suggesting Hill step aside, in an Adelaide Test match no less – it is worth stepping back and seeing what McAlister might have meant. Hill was the world record holder, the only man to have exceeded 3000 Test runs. That summer his Test scores had been 46, 65, 4 and 0. Minnett, a novice, had scored 90, 17, 2 and 34. McAlister's suggestion is so far beyond stupidity that it cannot be taken as serious. The *South Australian Register* reported drily: 'The older men scorned the suggestion of Mr McAlister and the younger generation were no less indignant.' Instead, it seems, he was angling to provoke Hill. That he did.

Before the Test match, Hill and the players met to discuss the 'secretary' proposal. They were all against it (except Bardsley, who, seen as too close to the NSWCA, wasn't invited). But the 1912 tour squad hadn't been picked yet, and it was agreed that if the younger players stood up against the Board they would jeopardise their chances of selection. So the six 'certainties' stepped forward: Hill, Armstrong, Trumper, Carter, Cotter and Ransford. On 17 January they wrote to the Board saying they would not tour England unless the Board obeyed its own constitution. Thus were the 'Big Six' born.

Macartney later wrote that 'persistent ill-feeling seriously affected the morale of the side' in Adelaide, and Barnes, Hobbs and company were not merciful types. Barnes and Foster rumbled Australia for 133, to which England – Hobbs 187, Foster 71 – responded with 501. Hill's brave 98, and 72 from Carter, showed the staunchness of the Big Six, but England's seven-wicket win was comprehensive.

After the Test, the Big Six requested a meeting with the Board. Their letter said a 'representative clothed with the powers of a manager' was against Regulation 9, but they would accept it if the Board paid his salary and they could select their own manager. Or what? 'Failing compliance with our requests, we have to inform you with much regret that none of us will be available for selection or to play if selected.'

The Board did not even wait for the letter. Sixty-eight applicants, including McAlister, Jack Worrall and future Australian captain Herbie Collins, had applied for the tour secretary's position. Foxton learned from McAlister that the players had distributed £400 in tips in 1909, so clearly, he said, they had the secretary's salary to spare. The *Argus* replied that the Board members must have been lucky to be brought up free 'from all contact with the wicked world of hotels, steamers, wharves, railway stations and other places where tips are given and received'.

Once the Big Six threatened their boycott, the Board reacted as if this was what it had wanted all along. It is more evidence that McAlister's telegram to Hill was a deliberate provocation. On 22 January, Smith wrote to the players: 'the team which is being sent to England by the Board as the governing body of cricket in Australia … has nothing whatever to do with the arrangements, the Board taking the whole of the responsibility.' He added that the 'secretary' did not violate Regulation 9 and a 'manager' did not seem necessary, but the players could elect one if they wanted. As to the threat of a boycott, he said, 'While the Board is anxious at all times to send the best team possible, still, at the same time, I am sure it will not permit any number of cricketers to dictate.'

While the Englishmen took their Tasmanian sojourn and NSW played Victoria in Sydney, a 'special Board meeting' was held at Bull's Chambers in Martin Place, Sydney, on 2 February. The *Bulletin* welcomed the Big Six's boycott, describing them as 'gentlemen of somewhat avaricious nature who on recent Test form have fallen from the ranks of players to that of has-beens'. In the meeting, the Board read the players' letter onto the record and endorsed Smith's response. McElhone's majority stood firm: they would appoint their secretary. McAlister applied for the job and was expected to get it, but McElhone, remembering McAlister's incompetence in 1909, backed Ernest Hume from NSW. Bean, who had intended to vote for McAlister, switched his support to George Crouch, a partner in a Queensland butter brokerage, who got the job from a factionalised Board. Hill and two others abstained.

What happened next is a notorious Australian cricket story but also, it should be clear, the boiling point of a dispute that had been building for more than three decades. Could it have come to blows in, say, England? Alan Gibson reveals that he was debating this point with Jack Fingleton in 1977, when the World Series row was occurring. Fingleton argued that the publicness of Australian rows 'is really a point to Australia, because once they have had a public, healthy blow-up they all feel better about it, and are soon friends again; whereas in English feuds the suppressed venom poisons the system. There may be something in this, but I doubt if it applied to Australian cricket [in 1912].'

The night after the board meeting, 3 February, Hill and McAlister found themselves in the same room for the first time since the infamous telegram. With them at Bull's Chambers were Iredale, Smith, and J.C. Davis. Smith later wrote what, in his recollection, happened.

Before the meeting started, Hill and McAlister traded barbs: Hill criticising McAlister's non-selection of Laver in the Victorian team, McAlister retorting about Hill's under-bowling of Kellaway and Minnett in the Tests. Davis added a derogatory view of Laver's play, to which Hill said he thought Davis was no judge of cricket. Soon after, Davis left.

Once the meeting was underway, Hill and McAlister began attacking each other's captaincy. Hill reminded McAlister that Armstrong had refused to play under him in 1909 and asked McAlister to list any matches he had won as a captain. When McAlister did so, Hill dismissed them as second-rate matches. McAlister said he'd done well in the Gloucestershire match in 1909 when Trumper 'almost made a hash of things', to which Hill said: 'Fancy you comparing yourself to men like Trumper and Armstrong.'

The exchange, in other words, was petty. Both men had steam to let off – remembering that McAlister must have been severely disappointed not to have won the Board's vote to go to England again – and reverted to trivial insults. Hill twice made to leave, once saying that if McAlister liked Minnett so much, he might as well give him the captaincy, and later said McAlister might want to lead Australia himself. Finally, McAlister said Hill was the worst captain he'd ever seen.

Summing up player-administrator relations over the previous four decades, Hill said: 'You have been asking for a punch on the jaw all night, and I'll give you one.'

He leaned across the table and hit McAlister, either 'a violent blow to the side of the face' (Smith) or 'a gentle slap' (Hill). Iredale said first it was a 'back-handed clip', later changing his description to 'a severe blow to the nose and side of the face'.

Iredale continued, 'Very few blows were struck; it was more like a wrestling match.' They wrestled for some time – Smith estimated 20 minutes, though that would seem highly unlikely, for reasons of physical fitness as much as anything else – before Smith pulled Hill away by the coat-tails before he could shove McAlister out of the third-floor window. Furniture was knocked over and pictures were smashed. Hill would accuse McAlister of being drunk, though Smith contested this. When Smith shepherded Hill outside, McAlister shouted: 'You coward!'

In the corridor, Smith told Hill to go back to his hotel. Hill said he was quitting the committee. Smith, ever the bureaucrat, asked him to put his resignation in writing.

Bizarrely, McAlister and Iredale then picked the fourth Test team and the first 10 members of the 1912 tour. They included the Big Six.

Two days later, the three selectors arrived at Spencer Street station on the same train, presumably not in adjoining seats, and were mobbed by reporters. McAlister's 'nose was cut and there was a bruise under the left eye and numerous scratches disfigured his face', said the *Argus*.

Hill told reporters: 'When a man is insulted and insulted, well, it must reach a limit.'

McAlister said: 'It was no open-handed slap. Look at my nose!'

Neither made any detailed public statements thereafter. The punch-up was not the cause of the dispute, only its final act. The Big Six were not motivated by the fight, but by what McElhone and Bean had been doing over the previous six years.

England already had their best-ever batsman and best-ever bowler. They didn't need help to defeat Australia in the next two Tests. Hobbs and Rhodes added 323 in Melbourne, giving reformed tail-ender Rhodes the distinction of world-record partnerships for both the last and first wickets. Hill received a standing ovation and batted with tears in his eyes.

For the fifth Test in Sydney, the Board had six reserves ready. The Big Six played, though they had not responded to the Board's invitations to join the tour of England. Woolley scored 133 not out, while Barnes took seven wickets to raise his series total to 34 at 22.88, equalling Giffen's record; Foster finished with 32 at 21.62. The other five England bowlers took 29 wickets between them. When Trumper received a stirring ovation, he turned to England wicketkeeper Tiger Smith and said, 'Tiger, they think I'm finished.'

Horan, now firmly a players' man, wrote that the Board was 'making an awful hash of Australian cricket. The game has been sacrificed for the sake of making players understand that the will of McElhone, Bean, Foxton and Co is law ... All thoughts of the best interests of Australian cricket have been subordinated in order that the dignity of this majority of the Board may be upheld ... The cheering for Hill proved that the Sydney papers who support Mr McElhone have not been reflecting public opinion ... Iredale and McAlister would never be chosen as selectors if merit were the principal consideration ... It would be well for Australia's reputation if even at this late hour the English engagements were cancelled, and international cricket dropped until things right themselves.'

England rounded off their tour with a 70-run win in Sydney. Fry praised Douglas: 'everybody found fault with his captaincy, the result of which was a triumph for England over Australia by 4 to I.' In true English style, Lord's was soon to dump Douglas as captain – for none other than Fry.

In Australia, the cricket was firmly in the background. There was even controversy in Sydney over the choice of Jack 'Ginger' McLaren, the first native-born Queenslander to play Test cricket. McLaren, a diabetic, had allegedly worked as a special constable breaking a wharf labourers' strike in Brisbane. A union boycott of the Sydney Test was only averted when McLaren's denials were accepted.

During the Sydney Test, Noble had a letter published in the *Sydney Morning Herald*:

'I say that the Board of Control has acted unjustly and has violated its own constitution. I am a strong supporter of the Board as a Board, and I believe in the principle of Board control, but I am strongly against its present personnel. They have had six years now to bring everybody into line, and to legislate for Australian cricket, and they have absolutely failed. In these six years they have not been credited with one single act of conciliation or forbearance. They have held the pistol of coercion at the heads of the players the whole time, and gradually taken from them all their privileges. Where a happy issue and solution of the present crisis might easily have resulted, we now have the spectacle of a non-representative team going to England.'

The pistol-at-the-head negotiation, which boards would adopt for decades to come, was an image shared by the Big Six. During the Test, *The Age* interviewed Hill and Trumper at the Hotel Australia. Hill said: 'The Board did not think it worthwhile to give any statement of the reasons why it did not want Frank Laver. It simply put a pistol to our heads. It was a case of take it or leave it.'

As supporters of *a* Board but not *this* Board, Hill and Noble blamed McElhone's vindictiveness. Noble called the Board 'a democratic body being ruled and governed by a despot'. Hill wrote in similar vein in the *Sydney Morning Herald*: 'If it is considered desirable that the control of Australian cricket should be placed in the hands of one man, by all means do it openly, but do not pretend to invest the Board with control, when you know an individual controls the Board.'

The Board readied to announce its touring team, minus the Big Six. Warner pressed for a delay while he tried to broker a compromise. He visited Hill at home in Adelaide but found the captain adamant. Laver urged the Big Six to forget about supporting him and go to England. They instead presented him with a five-drawer document cabinet, inscribed 'To Laver from "The Six"'. Warner frantically organised meetings with the Six and McElhone. Seeing the intransigence of both sides, even when he 'begged', he recruited Lord Chelmsford, the NSW Governor, who told Trumper, Carter and Cotter that their boycott would be 'quixotic'. The players met McElhone, but nothing was solved. Jim McGowen, NSW's first Labor premier, invited the players to Parliament House, but found them resolute. Trumper, who would have been vice-captain on the tour and therefore captain if he broke ranks with Hill, voiced the players' despair in an interview with the *Leader*: 'What are we to do? Go down on our knees and ask the Board to let us go to England on any terms they like? No, they have got the thing down to bedrock, and it can stay there as far as I'm concerned.'

The English sailed home happy with their visit – even though it had lost £830 – but uneasy about the coming six-Test Triangular Tournament with South Africa and the depleted Australians.

Warner, who had viewed the Australian tour from the sidelines, wrote: 'Australian cricket is honeycombed with an amount of personal feeling and bitterness that is incredible and this must, to some extent, have militated against our opponents showing their true form.'

On 12 February, Smith wrote to Hill saying the Board would meet on 16 February to discuss the selection-room melee. Iredale also wrote to Hill, casting aspersions on Cotter, blaming him for not getting the English batsmen out early and insinuating he was staying up late drinking. Iredale said that recalling Laver as manager/player would have been 'a direct insult to every young player in Australia'. The 16 February meeting, bureaucratically, took Smith's report of the fight 'as read'.

Hill took some consolation from a letter from Carter in Sydney, who had been speaking to J.C. Davis. Davis, he wrote, had told him McAlister had provoked the fight with comments that were 'unfair' and 'in bad taste'. 'No man would take calmly such insults as you were receiving at the hands of McAlister.' Davis was 'quite satisfied that [McAlister] was totally unsuited to hold such a responsible position' and 'the game generally would be the gainer if McAlister were asked to resign'.

The deadline for the Six to accept their tour invitations was extended, but finally lapsed on 22 February. The boycott was now a reality. No Hill, no Trumper, no Armstrong, no Cotter, no Carter, no Ransford.

The selectors — McAlister, Iredale and Hill's replacement, Edgar Mayne — drafted in the perpetually hard-up Syd Gregory, aged 42, as captain, Hazlitt, and McLaren. Mayne, like McAlister three years earlier, voted himself onto the tour.

There were still hopes that the Big Six might be sent to England. A public meeting in Melbourne heard telegrams of support from Noble, Darling and Giffen. Harry Trott spoke, saying 'he was disgusted with the Board of Control to put it mildly. He would like to shake hands with the six men who had stood out against the Board. They had stuck out for the honour of cricket in Australia.' Darling said Bean had told him often that 'the Board of Control was formed with the main object of knocking out the Melbourne Cricket Club ... This is the reason why it was formed, not to improve Australian cricket.'

A 'Citizens' Cricket Committee' was formed in Melbourne, including the wool baron Edmund Jowett, financier William Baillieu, Sir Norman Brookes, members of parliament and other notables. They condemned the Board's 'dictatorial stance' and offered to fund a second tour to England, including the Big Six plus up-and-comers including Arthur Mailey, Jack Massie and Johnny Moyes.

On 2 March, an adoring crowd mobbed Hill, Armstrong and Ransford at Spencer Street station. Hill said the Six would only consider an alternative tour if Marylebone approved.

It did not. Lord's had no desire to interfere in Australian affairs any more than it had. Lord Desborough, the MCC chairman, cabled that all the counties were disappointed and urged compromise. The Australian Board ruled his message 'out of order', shocking Warner, who wrote, 'I really don't know what to say about it. It seems so extraordinary.'

Why would McElhone compromise, even for Lord's, when he had won? He was prepared to throw out the baby of the 1912 tour with the bathwater of the Big Six. They were the cost of business. The *Melbourne Punch* struck an accurate note: 'He has found that all his enemies possess one neck and he has severed it at one blow. He has been more fortunate than most tyrants. The coming year's cricket may bring defeat and failure but the new cricketers who will come on will owe all their opportunities, all their rise to distinction, to the Board, or to W.P. McElhone, which is the same thing. They will be his henchmen, who will obey him and work for him.'

While those henchmen sailed, a pamphlet war erupted in Australia. The Citizens' Cricket Committee, the VCA, Laver, McAlister, Melbourne, and finally Bean and Rush threw claim and counter-claim at each other. Seeking to divide the players, the VCA's pamphlet alleged that Laver took £2000 as his manager/player's share from the 1905 tour. It said one unnamed young player had been offered £179, less than a quarter of the rest of the team. It said another player as well as Trumper had gone to England in 1899 for £200, and that one player had only got £12 on an earlier tour. Laver refuted the allegations about himself, and praised the Big Six: 'Their nobleness and sense of justice was so great that they sacrificed a splendid trip to England in order to stand by a comrade who had been maliciously maligned. This they did, notwithstanding I begged them to accept the invitation of the Board, and to ignore me as manager.'

But the pamphlet war was ultimately irrelevant; in the committee rooms, McElhone had the numbers. On 23 March, some NSWCA club delegates staged a no-confidence motion in the NSWCA's three members on the Board. Trumper, as a representative of the Gordon club, to which he had moved from Paddington, voted for it. The motion was defeated 23–8.

In England, the Australian team was dubbed the 'McElhone XI'. Not the first or last to be called 'the worst Australian team ever', it was the most deserving.

Warner's *Cricket* magazine tried to see the bright side: 'The team now nearing our shores is said to be incensed at the slighting comments passed upon it by the press, and resolutely determined to prove that it is no second-rate combination. Should it come out well at the end of the tour, the Board will hold something very like an ace of trumps.'

Landing 12 days after the *Titanic* went down, the team of 10 debutants and only four Test-quality regulars – Bardsley, Macartney, Matthews and Whitty – would need a strong leader, but Gregory, equalling Blackham's record of eight tours, was not up to it. His best tour of England had been in 1896; he had been a somewhat overrated batsman since, though his contemporaries always rated him highly and he deserved credit for his comeback season, in 1911–12, when he had averaged more than 50. Ironically, if any Australian cricketer had benefited from favouritism in the years of player-selected tours, it was Gregory. But financial ruin had bent him to the Board's will. It had been Gregory who had clashed with the NSWCA in 1895–96 when he asked for £15 expenses. The association said it would pay him if he deemed himself a professional. Gregory declined and withdrew from the team. The NSWCA's then president, John Gibson, said the association must 'put a stop to this absurd practice of amateurs claiming more than professionals'. Gregory had a history he and his bosses would both prefer to forget.

The Big Six's absence 'detracted from public interest' in Gregory's team, argues Altham. English audiences were aware that 'the cricket atmosphere in Australia was at this time vitiated by vindictiveness, jealousy, and mutual distrust'. It soon showed on the field. Australia lost to Nottinghamshire, Lancashire and Surrey, and a Bardsley-Macartney partnership of 362 against Essex was a blip, not a revival.

A rainy summer masked some of the Australians' inadequacies, as the South African batsmen were even less-equipped for wet wickets. Matthews took a unique two hat-tricks on one day, in South Africa's first and second innings, at Old Trafford, where Australia won in two days before meagre crowds. Sewell wrote that there was 'not a soul to meet and greet the Australians. Where in the old days, and from all one hears and reads of English tours in Australia, there would have been an interested crowd, eyes all agog and mouths agape, there was on this occasion scarcely a porter.'

England were clearly the ascendant team. Lord's invited Fry to be captain for the first Test against Australia, but he said he would only accept if appointed for the entire series. 'The idea of appointing an England captain on appro., especially in the case of a senior man like myself, was ridiculous,' he said. He knew Lord's didn't like him, thinking him 'a rebel' after his clashes with Lord Hawke, but Lord Harris liked Fry's spirit and gave him the job.

Australia's blushes were saved, in the first two Tests against England, by rain. When Frank Woolley's left-arm tweak might have caused trouble at Lord's, Fry decided that as there was no prospect of a result he might keep Woolley under wraps. 'This to the unintelligent no doubt appeared preposterous management,' he said, and Pardon was among his critics. Fry's vindication came in what turned out to be the decisive final Test match at the Oval. England had beaten South Africa three times, and Australia had beaten them twice.

So desperate were the hosts to redeem the sodden summer and ensure a result that they asked Gregory if he would consent to another Test match if rain shortened the Oval match. He said he would prefer not, so the Oval Test was deemed timeless, to be played until there was a result.

On a wet first day at Kennington, Fry said, 'The preliminary atmosphere was tense. The Press was on one of its pessimistic and critical wavelengths. A rival evening paper explained my incompetence in two columns.'

A crowd of 30,000 grew restless in the sunshine, 'looking at a wicket they did not know was a quagmire'. Gregory proposed a start 'for the sake of the crowd'. Fry saw it as 'a good gamble on the part of little Syd', as Gregory hoped to win the toss, bat when the wicket was wet and easy, then bowl when it was drying and sticky. A sticky-wicket lottery was Australia's best hope. Fry wouldn't have it. 'So with the rubber depending on the one match I refused to start until the turf was genuinely fit.'

The crowd soon learnt that Fry was delaying a start, and let him know their feelings when he batted in England's 245. Australia imploded from 2/90 to 111 all out. Then Fry, who was bowled three times in the nets while warming up, trod on his stumps on 20, enjoyed a reprieve as he was considered to have completed his shot, and went on to make a satisfying 79 before Australia were all out for 65, bamboozled by Woolley, who took 10/49 in the match. After the game, Sewell wrote, 'A large portion of the crowd gathered before the pavilion and cheered the players in time honoured fashion. It must have pleased Gregory not a little that the loudest, the warmest, cheer was reserved for him.'

They also called for Fry, but the English captain said he 'would not go on to the balcony, because I felt that the time for them to cheer was when I was walking out to bat as captain of my side to try to win the match on a foul wicket'.

Ranji, who was by his side, said: 'Now, Charles, be your noble self.'

Fry replied: 'This is not one of my noble days.'

And that was the end of Anglo-Australian cricket before the Great War. In 1913–14 England took a tour of South Africa, who must have been dreading the sight of Sydney Barnes, who was now, in his late thirties, getting a belated chance to bring his international record into line with his feats in minor cricket. He took 49 wickets in the four Tests at 10.93, taking his haul in seven matches against South Africa to 83. In 1911–12, he had passed 100 Test wickets with the lowest-ever average. Without the prejudice of Marylebone and the outbreak of war, he would surely have put an end to any debate about who was England's greatest-ever bowler.

The 1912 Australians' off-field behaviour kept pace with their performances in whites. An anonymous teammate described Gregory as 'one of the finest fellows', but the team 'got beyond all control, and have completely defied his authority'; Gregory was 'deeply hurt about the matter'. Ferguson, the scorer, thought Gregory had himself to blame: 'Not a good skipper, allowing his team to do just as they pleased ... and they were an unruly bunch. Perhaps there would have been less trouble in the party if Mr Gregory had not himself been keen, at times, to imbibe rather recklessly!'

The Australians' uncouth and drunken antics had them socially ostracised in England. They smirked and snorted at English customs and mocked the cryptic scoreboards. One of them was reported to the Board for 'disgusting language'. On a ferry crossing to Ireland, stewards refused them alcohol when some couldn't find their feet on deck. They came home via America, where they were defeated by John Barton King and the Philadelphians. The *Sun* reported that on the SS *Marama* they 'became continually intoxicated during the homeward voyage, and on several occasions made public exhibitions of themselves'. Edgar Mayne was reprimanded by the Board for refusing to share his cabin with one of his drunken teammates. The Eleven had fallen a long way indeed from the social heights of the Darling-Noble tours. In one disgraceful trip they undid all the ambassadorial good work of the previous 34 years.

McElhone's strategic aims were suited by the Big Six's boycott, but he might have been careful of what he wished for. In diminishing the prestige of Australian cricket, the 1912 tourists went too far even for the anti-player Board chairman. In August, he telegrammed Crouch suggesting the tour be called off early due to the players' behaviour. Crouch did nothing. After the players' return, the Board summoned Matthews, Carkeek and the batsman Dave Smith. Smith didn't show, due to ill health, and none of the three would represent Australia again. The Board decreed it would tighten its tour contracts to include a character test.

The tour returned a deficit of £1286. Once again McElhone had let his hunger for power get in the way of economic wisdom. Macartney,

Whitty, Mayne and Hazlitt came out ahead, having accepted the bird in the hand in the form of the £400 set fee. Embarrassed, the Board waived its cut of tour income, giving the loyal players small ex gratia payments, and turned once again to the associations to make up the shortfall. In a final irony, more bitter than sweet, among the expenses was a contract for Trumper's sportswear company to provide caps and blazers at a cost of £65.

Nevertheless, McElhone had won. And perhaps the winner should have the last word, as McElhone did have many supporters. Iredale wrote of him: 'He was the strong man of the Board, and one who did his duty nobly and well. It was said of him that he was vindictive and never fair, but what I know of him is that this was wrong. No fairer man ever took the reins of government into his hand ... Though "Billy" McElhone is a fighter to the backbone, he is nevertheless one of the kindest men in the world to those who care to study him. Had the dissatisfied cricketers approached him in a conciliatory spirit, they would have found in him a friend, and one more likely to help them than to oppose them. Knowing him as I do, I can truthfully say that, far from being an enemy of the players, he is, and always has been, one of their firmest friends.'

Of the Board, Iredale said, 'there was a unanimous desire to help the grand old game ... They differed from the players because they believed they were doing what was right in benefiting the game.'

McElhone was lauded at a banquet at the Sydney Town Hall, where soon he would swap his Board chairman's post for the Mayoral robes. In his speech, he admitted to 'heartburnings' over what had happened but it was 'inevitable in any movement of reform'. He hoped 'that no private bodies of any nature would ever try again to regain control of cricket'. It was a line that the Board would maintain, through the stringent control and underpayment of its cricketers, for as long as it could.

CONCLUSION

I n December 1890, Billy Midwinter had been the first Test cricketer to pass away, while being 'treated for lunacy' in an asylum. He was 39.

Compared with what happened in Europe in 1914–18, Test cricketers' early deaths are insignificant. But there were a great many who died young, and when this honour roll is read, it is clear that it wasn't just the war that signalled the end of the epoch.

George Lohmann died of tuberculosis in 1901 and Arthur Shrewsbury committed suicide in 1903. While the aristocrats such as Harris, Bligh, Hawke, Ranjitsinhiji and Jackson lived well into the twentieth century, the professionals' lives were mostly short. England's pair of wild Billies, Barnes and Bates, did not live to see the turn of the century. Nor did the three alleged gambling conspirators of 1881, George Ulyett, John Selby and William Scotton. All died as young men in the 1890s. Jack Brown had heart failure at 35, and Tom Richardson died at 42 while walking in France.

An exception – taking exception? – to the rule of short professional lives was, of course, Sydney Francis Barnes, who would still be wheeling away for Staffordshire at the age of 62, when he took 86 wickets at 11. George Duckworth, the England inter-war wicketkeeper, said when he played against Barnes it was the only game when he saw seven batsmen all padded up at the same time. Duckworth's captain wouldn't let him take a walk around the boundary without padding up first. The Bradman of bowlers died in 1967, aged 94.

The round-armer who delivered the first ball in Test cricket and managed so many tours, Alfred Shaw, died in 1907 at the ripe age of 65. The man who had faced him, Charlie Bannerman, lived long enough to see Don Bradman bat for Australia. Many of the pillars of early Australian cricket also managed long lives: Fred Spofforth, Alick Bannerman, Jack Blackham, George Giffen, Tom Garrett, Charles Turner, Hugh Trumble, Joe Darling, Ernie Jones, Monty Noble and Clem Hill would become wise old gentlemen. But the approach of the war would also see a wave of losses. Percy McDonnell, as noted, succumbed to heart disease in 1896 and Jack Ferris to typhoid in 1900. Harry Boyle died in 1907, 'Tup' Scott and Joey Palmer in 1910, Murdoch in 1911, George Bonnor in 1912. The man who started it all, John Conway, had been long alienated from his cricket friends when he died in 1909. Albert Trott shot himself in 1914 and Harry, heartbroken, survived him by three years. Tommy Horan, the great 'Felix', kept working until his death in 1916. Tibby Cotter stopped a bullet at Beersheba in 1917. Dave Gregory, after a glittering career in the NSW Treasury, died as a 74-year-old grandfather in 1919.

The real end of the era, in many Australian hearts, was Victor Trumper's passing in 1915, from chronic nephritis. His doctor was Herbert Bullmore, the grandfather of Kerry Packer. Trumper was 37 and cricket would not be the same. Sixty-one days earlier, Andrew Stoddart put a bullet through his head. Reg 'Tip' Foster, whose 287 on debut made him one of the luminous figures of the Golden Age, died of diabetes-related complications, aged 36, in 1914. One hundred and seventeen days after Stoddart's suicide, the Champion was sick and irritated by Zeppelin raids on England. After taming Spofforth, Lockwood, Richardson, Kortright and Freeman, surely W.G. Grace wasn't scared of a few blimps? 'I could see those beggars,' he said. 'I can't see these.' He went into shock after falling out of bed and died of a heart attack. When, in 1923, Lord's dedicated its new Grace Gates to him, Jackson came up with the three-word inscription: simply, 'The Great Cricketer'.

The great entrepreneurial adventure for Australian Test cricketers had survived the assault of 1909 before perishing under the second Board offensive in 1912. Players would no longer own or manage their tours. McElhone had won.

If the war had not intervened, he would still have won. The Big Six's resistance had been exhausted, so that they won neither the battle nor the war. When planning was underway for tours in 1914, the Board appointed Armstrong captain. McElhone and Bean were still boasting that they wanted to drive the Big Six out of the game, but McElhone left the Board for municipal politics and Bean failed, by the Tasmanian delegate's vote, to prevent Armstrong from becoming Australian captain in 1920–21 and leading the Ashes tour of 1921.

Armstrong and Bean would continue to plot each other's downfall, but the bottom line was that, as Australia's captain in the glory years of 1920 and 1921, Armstrong had become a servant of the Board. He did not like the fact, but the will, unity and financial organisation of players to promote their own tours of England had been broken in 1912. War put an end to any hopes of reviving it.

The great Australian adventure had challenged the social and economic basis of big cricket in England. English cricket's financial foundation was built on the cheap labour of working-class professionals and was strained by gentlemen who demanded a ruinous payment for their entertainment value. The Australian model was built on Grace's lines: amateur players who had other jobs and did not survive on cricket alone, rewarded in accordance with the revenue they raised from crowds.

The Australian adventure embodied a modern idea: that entertainers could enjoy the profits of the spectacle they put on. They were neither professionals nor amateurs, nor quite shamateurs; they didn't fit any English class definition. Their tours to England between 1878 and 1909 shook up the class system within cricket and were a driving force in its eventual eradication.

But another modern counter-idea was also rising: that a central government was needed to control players and see that they did not drain all the income out of the game. They might have been a troupe of travelling entertainers, but they were representatives of a nation. For all his aggression and clumsiness, McElhone was on the right side of history. Cricket enjoyed a national prestige and an economic heft that demanded coherent government. The players ultimately fell victim to their own success.

The extent of their victimhood would only become clear over several generations. After 1920, through the time of Armstrong and Herbie Collins, Bill Woodfull and Don Bradman, Lindsay Hassett and Richie Benaud, Bob Simpson and Bill Lawry to the Chappell brothers, Australian cricketers would not earn as much *in nominal terms* as the teams of Murdoch and Darling. In real terms, they still haven't. Today, in purchasing power, Australian cricketers do not take home as much as the tourists of 1884 and 1905. Nor, certainly, would they be prepared to take the risks. But that was what made those days romantic: the element of danger that cricketers were prepared to take on, to leave their jobs and families for months and years and steam away into the unknown, gambling with their lives, playing by day and travelling by night and enduring the most gruelling privations, in the hope of making their names, and that of their country.

SOURCES

To have footnoted every reference in this book might have given the reader a task akin to batting on the Sydney Cricket Ground wicket in the late 1880s: tough to get going, even tougher to stay in there. Sources are listed below, alphabetically by author. I want to thank three cricket bibliophiles in particular for their kind assistance: Ronald Cardwell, whose knowledge and library of this period is unparalleled; Mike Coward, as generous as ever; and Neil Robinson and the staff of the MCC Library at Lord's.

Books:

Altham HS and Swanton EW, *A History of Cricket* (George Allen & Unwin, London, 1938)

Barker R, *Ten Great Bowlers* (Chatto & Windus, London, 1967)

Beeston RD, *St Ivo & The Ashes: A Correct, True & Particular History of the Hon. Ivo Bligh's Crusade in Australia* (Australian Press Agency, Melbourne, 1883)

Beldam G and Fry C, *Great Batsmen: Their Methods at a Glance* (Macmillan & Co, London, 1905)

Beldam G and Fry C, *Great Bowlers and Fielders: Their Methods at a Glance* (Macmillan & Co, London, 1906)

Berry S and Peploe R, *Cricket's Burning Passion: Ivo Bligh and the Story of the Ashes* (Methuen, London, 2006)

Bonnell M, *Currency Lads: The Life and Cricket of T.W. Garrett, R.C. Allen, S.P. Jones & R.J. Pope* (The Cricket Publishing Company, Cherrybrook, 2001)

Bowen R, *Cricket: A History of its Growth and Development Throughout the World,* (Eyre & Spottiswoode, London, 1970)

Brookes C, *English Cricket: The Game and its Players Throughout the Ages* (Weidenfeld & Nicolson, London, 1978)

Brown L, *Victor Trumper and the 1902 Australians* (Secker & Warburg, London, 1981)

Cardwell R, *James Lillywhite's XI in Goulburn 1876* (The Cricket Publishing Company, Cherrybrook, 2007)

Carlaw D, *W.L. Murdoch* (ACS Famous Cricketers Series No 77, Nottingham, 2003)

Cashman R, *The 'Demon' Spofforth* (New South Wales University Press, Sydney, 1990)

Cashman R et al (eds), *The Oxford Companion to Australian Cricket,* (Oxford University Press, Melbourne, 1996)

Cotter G, *The Ashes Captains* (The Crowood Press, Marlborough, 1989)

Darling DK, *Test Tussles On and Off the Field* (Self-published, Hobart, 1970)

de Moore G, *Tom Wills: His Spectacular Rise and Tragic Fall* (Allen & Unwin, Sydney, 2008)

Ferguson WH, *Mr Cricket: The Autobiography of W.H. Ferguson, BEM* (Nicholas Kaye, London, 1957)

Ford J, *Cricket: A Social History 1700–1835* (David & Charles, Newton Abbot, 1972)

Frith D, *Frith on Cricket: Half a Century of Writing by David Frith* (Allen & Unwin, Sydney, 2010)

Frith D, *The Golden Age of Cricket: 1890–1914* (Omega Books, Hertfordshire, 1983)

Frith D, *'My Dear Victorious Stod': A Biography of A.E. Stoddart* (Self-published limited edition, 1970)

Frith D, *The Trailblazers: The First English Cricket Tour of Australia 1861–62* (Boundary Books, Cheshire, 1999)

Fry CB, *Life Worth Living: Some Phases of an Englishman* (Eyre & Spottiswoode, London, 1939)

Gibson A, *The Cricket Captains of England* (Cassell, London, 1979)

Giffen G, *With Bat & Ball: Twenty-five Years' Reminiscences of Australian and Anglo-Australian Cricket* (Ward, Lock & Co, London, 1898)

Guha R (ed), *The Picador Book of Cricket* (Picador, London, 2001)

Haigh G, *The Big Ship: Warwick Armstrong and the Making of Modern Cricket* (Text Publishing, Melbourne, 2001)

Haigh G and Frith D, *Inside Story: Unlocking Australian Cricket's Archives* (News Custom Publishing, Melbourne, 2007)

Haigh G (ed), *Endless Summer: 140 Years of Australian Cricket in Wisden* (Hardie Grant Books, Melbourne, 2002)

Harris L, *A Few Short Runs* (John Murray, London, 1921)

Harte C, *A History of Australian Cricket* (Andre Deutsch, London, 1993)

Haygarth, Lillywhite, Ashley-Cooper, *Scores and Biographies of Celebrated Cricketers* (London, 1862–)

Horan T, *Cradle Days of Australian Cricket: An Anthology of the Writings of 'Felix' (T.P. Horan), compiled and edited by Brian Mathew Crowley and Pat Mullins* (Macmillan, Melbourne, 1989)

Horan T, *Horan's Diary: The Australian Touring Team 1877–1879* (ACS Publications, Nottingham, 2001)

Knox M, *The Captains: The Story Behind Australia's Second Most Important Job* (Hardie Grant Books, Melbourne, 2010)

Kynaston D, *W.G.'s Birthday Party* (Bloomsbury, London, 1990)

Laver F, *An Australian Cricketer on Tour: Reminiscences, Impressions, and Experiences of Two Trips* (Chapman and Hall, London, 1905)

Lillywhite J, *John Lillywhite's Cricketers' Annual* (London, 1876–)

Lillywhite J, *John Lillywhite's Cricketers' Companion* (London, 1870–)

Major J, *More than a Game: The Story of Cricket's Early Years* (HarperPress, London, 2007)

Mahoney P, *Mary Ann's Australians: The Australian Tour of England 1909* (Cricket Lore, London, 1992)

Marshall M, *Gentlemen and Players: Conversations with Cricketers* (Grafton Books, London, 1987)

Martin-Jenkins C, *The Complete Who's Who of Test Cricketers* (Orbis Publishing, London, 1980)

Martineau GD, *They Made Cricket* (Museum Press, London, 1956)

Montefiore D, *Cricket in the Doldrums: The Struggle Between Private and Public Control of Australian Cricket in the 1880s* (Australian Society for Sports History, University of Western Sydney, 1992)

Noble MA, *The Game's the Thing* (Cassell & Co, London, 1926)

'Old Ebor' (AW Pullin), *Chats on the Cricket Field* (Bettesworth, London, 1910)

'Old Ebor' (AW Pullin), *Talks with Old Yorkshire Cricketers* (The Yorkshire Post, Leeds, 1898)

Pollard J, *The Turbulent Years of Australian Cricket 1893–1917* (Angus & Robertson, Sydney, 1987)

Pollard J, *Australian Cricket: The Game and the Players* (Hodder & Stoughton, Sydney, 1982)

Rae S, *It's Not Cricket Skullduggery, Sharp Practice and Downright Cheating in the Noble Game* (Faber & Faber, London, 2002)

Rae S, *W.G. Grace: A Life* (Faber & Faber, London, 1998)

Sandiford K, *Cricket and the Victorians* (Scolar Press, Aldershot, 1994)

Sewell EHD, *Triangular Cricket: Being a Record of the Greatest Contest in the History of the Game* (J.M. Dent & Sons Ltd, London, 1912)

Sharpham P, *Trumper: The Definitive Biography* (Hodder & Stoughton, Sydney, 1985)

Shaw A, *Alfred Shaw, Cricketer: His Career and Reminiscences* (Cassell and Company, London, 1902)

Shaw A and Shrewsbury A, *Shaw and Shrewsbury's Team in Australia 1884–85* (Shaw & Shrewsbury, Nottingham, 1885)

Smith R, *Australian Test Cricketers* (ABC Books, Sydney, 2000)

Smith R and Williams R, *W.G. Down Under: Grace in Australia 1873–74 and 1891–92* (Apple Books, Tasmania, 1994)

Thomson AA, *Odd Men In: A Gallery of Cricket Eccentrics* (The Pavilion Library, London, 1958)

Trumble R, *The Golden Age of Cricket: A Memorial Book of Hugh Trumble* (Self-published limited edition, Melbourne, 1968)

Tyson F, *The Century-Makers: The Men Behind the Ashes 1877–1977* (Hutchinson, Melbourne, 1980)

Warner P, *How We Recovered the Ashes* (Chapman and Hall, London, 1904)

Warner P (ed), *Imperial Cricket* (The London & Counties Press Association, London, 1912)

Webster R and Miller A, *First-class Cricket in Australia, Vol 1, 1850–51 to 1941–42* (Self-published, Melbourne, 1991)

West, G. Derek, *The Elevens of England* (Darf Publishers Limited, London, 1988)

Whitington RS, *Australians Abroad: Australia's Overseas Test Tours* (The Five Mile Press, Canterbury, 1983)

Whitington RS, *The Courage Book of Australian Test Cricket 1877–1974* (Wren Publishing, Melbourne, 1974)

Wisden Cricketer, *Story of the Ashes: Cricket's Greatest Rivalry as Told by the Writers Who Were There* (Wisden Cricketer Publishing, London, 2009)

Wisden Cricketers' Almanack, (John Wisden & Co, London, 1864–)

200 Seasons of Australian Cricket (Ironbark Press, Sydney, 1997)

Tour records:

Tour of Australian Cricketers through Australia, New Zealand, and Great Britain, Compiled from Authentic Press Reports (Argus, Melbourne, 1878)

The 2nd Australian XI's Tour of Australia, Britain and New Zealand in 1880/81 with Appendices (including Scorecards of Supplementary Matches and the Canadian Tour of Britain in 1880), by Alfred

James (A. James, Sydney, 1881)

The Australians in England: A Complete Record of the Tour of 1882, by Charles Pardon (Bell's Life, London, 1882)

The Third Australian Team in England: A Complete Record (Cricket, London, 1882)

The Fourth Australian Team in England (Boyle & Scott, Melbourne, 1884)

The Australians in England 1896 (Athletic News, London, 1896)

The 1899 Australians in England, by Peter Sharpham (J.W. McKenzie, Epsom, 1997)

The Eleventh Australian Tour, 1902 (Cricket, London, 1902)

Annuals and Guides:

Australian Cricket Annual (George Robertson & Co, Sydney, 1895–)

Australian Cricket & Cricketers (R.A. Thompson & Co, Melbourne, 1856–)

Australian Cricket Record (Gordon & Gotch, Sydney, 1894–)

Boyle & Scott's Australian Cricketers' Guide (Boyle & Scott, Melbourne, 1880–)

The Cricketers' Guide for Australasia (W. Fairfax & Co, Melbourne, 1858–)

The Cricketers' Register (Sands & McDougall, Melbourne, 1863–)

Conway's Australian Cricketers' Annual (F.F. Bailliere, Melbourne, 1876–)

Ironside's Australasian Cricketers' Handbook (W. Bullard, Sydney, 1880–)

Ironside's World of Cricket (W. Dymock, Sydney, 1894)

NSW Cricket Annual (NSW Bookstall Company, Sydney, 1907–)

South Australian Cricketers' Guide (E.S. Wigg & Son, Adelaide, 1876–)

Wills's Australian Cricketers' Guide (J. & A. McKinley, Melbourne, 1870–)

Collections:

Davis Sporting Collection, State Library of New South Wales

E.S. Marks Sporting Collection, State Library of New South Wales

TESTS

Tours	Location	Tests	England	Australia	Draw
1876–1877	Australia	2	1	1	0
1878–1879	Australia	1	0	1	0
1880	England	1	1	0	0
1881–1882	Australia	4	0	2	2
1882	England	1	0	1	0
1882–1883	Australia	4	2	2	0
1884	England	3	1	0	2
1884 1885	Australia	5	3	2	0
1886	England	3	3	0	0
1886–1887	Australia	2	2	0	0
1887–1888	Australia	1	1	0	0
1888	England	3	2	1	0
1890	England	2	2	0	0
1891–1892	Australia	3	1	2	0
1893	England	3	1	0	2
1894–1895	Australia	5	3	2	0
1896	England	3	2	1	0
1897–1898	Australia	5	1	4	0
1899	England	5	0	1	4
1901–1902	Australia	5	1	4	0
1902	England	5	1	2	2
1903–1904	Australia	5	3	2	0
1905	England	5	2	0	3
1907–1908	Australia	5	1	4	0
1909	England	5	1	2	2
1911–1912	Australia	5	4	1	0
1912	England	3	1	0	2

INDEX

433